The Transcendental Philosophy of Franklin Merrell-Wolff

SUNY series in Western Esoteric Traditions
David Appelbaum, editor

The Transcendental Philosophy of Franklin Merrell-Wolff

Ron Leonard

STATE UNIVERSITY OF NEW YORK PRESS

Published by
State University of New York Press, Albany

Printed in the United States of America

For information, address State University of New York Press,
State University Plaza, Albany, N.Y., 12246

Production by Marilyn P. Semerad
Marketing by Fran Keneston

Library of Congress Cataloging-in-Publication Data

Leonard, Ron, 1945–
The transcendental philosophy of Franklin Merrell-Wolff / Ron Leonard.
p. cm. — (SUNY series in Western esoteric traditions)
Includes bibliographical references and index.
ISBN 0–7914–4215–2 (alk. paper). — ISBN 0–7914–4216–0 (pbk. : alk. paper)
1. Merrell-Wolff, Franklin. 2. Mysticism. 3. Philosophy.
I. Title. II. Series.
BF1997.M47L46 1999
191—dc21 98–53600
CIP

10 9 8 7 6 5 4 3 2 1

To the memory of Franklin Merrell-Wolff,
whose love of wisdom and service to
humanity inspired this work.

CONTENTS

PREFACE

The spirit of philosophy arises from the depths of our very nature as seekers of knowledge and understanding concerning the totality of our experience. Philosophy is the most comprehensive and fundamental inquiry into human existence because not only does it attempt to determine whatever is real, but also the grounds for such knowledge.

Perhaps the most intriguing domain for investigation is mysticism—not simply as subject matter, but as a mode of apprehending reality—for mystical experience reveals extraordinary human potential. Enlightened mystics often manifest great illumination, wisdom, and compassion, as well as paranormal powers. More to the point, many claim an immediate grasp of reality—a way of knowing that transcends the senses and the intellect. Mysticism thus challenges the dominant world view of rational materialism—in all of its various forms—but must not be dismissed merely because of its apparent incompatibility. It also opposes dogmatic religion, so our first step in its authentic understanding is to consider what mystics themselves say about their experiences.

A widespread difficulty in the philosophical study of mysticism is that few mystics are philosophers, and of those who are, few are contemporary Westerners. This places a great burden on the interpretative skills of the nonmystical researcher. I was fortunate to discover Franklin Merrell-Wolff, a twentieth-century mystic and philosopher, who provides a clear and penetrating account of the nature and value of mystical experience—to a degree that I have yet to find elsewhere. Moreover, he is deeply concerned to show its relevance to crucial philosophical issues—in particular, the possibility of metaphysical knowledge through mystical insight. While completing my doctoral studies at the University of Waterloo, these considerations led me to choose to write a critical exposition of his philosophy for my thesis. Its purpose was not only to integrate Wolff's systematic thought within the history of Western philosophy, but also to show how mystical realization advances the development of a truly comprehensive world view. This book will be of particular interest to anyone studying metaphysics or epistemology, as well as philosophies of mind (or consciousness studies), language, and religion. Desiring to make this contribution more accessible to the nonacademic reader, while still retaining its substance and intellectual integrity, I have revised it extensively into its present form.

The project began in earnest when I located Wolff living in retirement in the high desert of the eastern slope of the Sierra Nevada mountains, near Lone Pine, California. He was delighted that I was interested in writing about his work, and he invited me to stay with him while I researched his unpublished papers and tapes. Even at the age of ninety-five he was a powerful presence, with a keen mind, a warm heart, and a wonderful sense of humor.

It was clear from the outset that my task could be neither simply to describe and explicate Wolff's work nor to adopt the point of view of any contemporary school for the purpose of understanding and appraising it. What was called for was dynamic, dialectical engagement between these approaches in an open-ended inquiry into ultimate questions—a process in which I too was necessarily a participant. The vastness and diversity of Wolff's material required a narrowing of focus to those central propositions that capture the essence of his philosophy (especially dealing with Primordial Consciousness and a third function of cognition) and treatment of his mystical experiences that ground them. On the other side, it was important to make the overall context as broad as possible, within which to select the most fruitful representatives of relevant traditions—primarily, analytic, phenomenological, and esoteric, in the West; Vedanta and Buddhism, in the East. Because the scope of this sort of enterprise exceeds any established conceptual framework, nothing may be presupposed without question. Furthermore, interrelationships between its elements may not be entirely or explicitly determined, so intuition must balance reason. I have presented much of Wolff's thought in its original formulation so as to preserve the subtle significance that overflows its literal meaning. In the absence of an acceptable neuter pronoun, I have used masculine and feminine pronouns interchangeably in neutral contexts. Also, for the sake of consistency, I have used a single method for translating Sanskrit terms in both text and quotations. My intent is to employ an approach that is most effective in showing how Wolff's transcendental philosophy deals with the perennial problems and issues of humanity. This will make better known the enduring contribution of one of the most fascinating figures of our time, one who exemplifies the love of wisdom that is the true spirit of philosophy.

ACKNOWLEDGMENTS

The process has been lengthy, but not solitary. First and foremost I wish to acknowledge my deepest appreciation to Franklin Wolff, whose gracious hospitality and support of my research afforded the opportunity and privilege of a deeply rewarding personal relationship with him during his final years. I am also exceedingly grateful to his granddaughter Doroethy Leonard for her time, energy, and unwavering support for my work as well as for permission to use Wolff's archival material. James Horne, who supervised my thesis with patient optimism, merits special praise for his style of "intellectual midwifery." The comments and suggestions of Russel Legge and the late Paul Seligman also have been invaluable. In addition, Walter Hodges and Ron Yates (chairpersons of the English Department at Mesa Community College, in Mesa, Arizona) kindly provided access to their computing facilities. Special thanks is due to Carl Nelson for writing a conversion program and general troubleshooting, as well as Bill DeHaan and the Computer Lab staff for much-needed technical assistance. My external examiner, Donald Evans, not only encouraged me to publish, but provided extensive notes and guidance on the process of converting the thesis into a book. William Eastman, former director of the State University of New York Press, greatly facilitated the project. Vesna Wallace, professor of Sanskrit at the University of California Santa Barbara, deserves the credit for rectifying the Sanskrit terms.

In addition I wish to thank these publishers for granting permission to reprint passages from the following works: *Experience and Philosophy: A Personal Record of Transformation and a Discussion of Transcendental Consciousness* (Albany: State University of New York Press, 1994), by Franklin Merrell-Wolff; *Transformations in Consciousness: The Metaphysics and Epistemology* (Albany: State University of New York Press, 1995), by Franklin Merrell-Wolff;

"Philosophy of Religion and the Redefinition of Philosophy," *Man and World* 3 (Copyright © Kluwer Academic Publishers, May 1970): 54–82, by Kenneth Schmitz, and "Self-Consciousness Without an Ego," *Man and World* 4 (Copyright © Kluwer Academic Publishers, 1971): 193–95, by Charles Scott, with kind permission from Kluwer Academic Publishers and professors Schmitz and Scott; "The Phenomenology of Mysticism," *Monist* 59 (October 1976):519–31, by William Earle (Copyright © 1976, THE MONIST, La Salle, Illinois 61301. Reprinted by permission); "Mysticism as Preontology: A Note on the Heideggerian Connection," *Philosophy and Phenomenological Research* 39 (September 1978):57–73, by Leon Rosenstein; "Mystical Experience and Ontological Claims," *Philosophy and Phenomenological Research* 37 (June 1977):445–63, by Norman Melchart; "The Priority of Being or Consciousness for Phenomenology: Heidegger and Husserl," *Metaphilosophy* 17 (April/July 1986):153–61, by Marion Tapper (with permission by Blackwell Publishers); "Panpsychism: Mind as Sole Reality," *Ultimate Reality and Meaning* 1 (1978):115–29, by Charles Hartshorne; "What Is It Like to Be a Bat?" *Philosophical Review* 83 (1974):435–50, by Thomas Nagel; "A Phenomenological View of the Beetle in the Box," *New Scholasticism* 48 (Summer 1974):277–304, by Alan Paskow (reprinted with permission by the American Catholic Philosophical Association; "The Status of the Propositions in the *Tractatus*," *Dialogue* 13 (December 1974):763–72, by Jerome Bickenbach; "First Philosophy: Metaphysics or Epistemology?" *Dialogue* 11 (March 1972):1–22, by Kenneth Dorter; "The Concept of the Self in Husserl and Beyond," *Philosophy Today* 24 (Spring 1980):44–45, by William Fowkes (reprinted with permission by Messenger Press); "An Advaitic Emendation of Kant: A Study in Comparative Metaphysics," *Indian Philosophical Quarterly* 6 (October 1978):175–83, by Ramlal Singh; "On the Status of 'Things-in-Themselves' in Kant," *Revue Internationale de Philosophie* 35 (January/February 1981):346–57, by Nicholas Rescher; "The Use of Paradox in Uroboric Philosophies," *Philosophy East and West* 28 (October 1978):455–67, by John Visvader (reprinted with kind permission by Professor Visvader).

CHAPTER 1

A Unique Philosopher

WOLFF'S PHILOSOPHICAL SIGNIFICANCE

Franklin Merrell-Wolff[1] was a philosopher, mathematician, mystic, and sage. As a young student he became convinced that Immanuel Kant had demonstrated the impossibility of metaphysical knowledge, if our resources are limited to sense perception and conceptual cognition. However, he found in mystical literature unmistakable evidence for the existence of a third function of cognition and felt compelled to verify it personally. He successfully consummated his twenty-four-year quest in 1936, when two Fundamental Realizations*[2] transformed his life and formed the base for his original philosophical formulation.

Several features make clear why Wolff's philosophy deserves serious attention. First, it is grounded explicitly in his mystical experiences, culminating in the High Indifference—the profound penetration of the terminal phase of his fifth and final Realization. His intimate autobiographical accounts of these episodes are invaluable because mystics rarely include personal psychological

---

*To emphasize the importance of mystical experiences that are fully transcendent, the term *realization* will be capitalized when it refers to Fundamental Realization or when it specifies Wolff's fourth or fifth Realizations. It will not be capitalized for references only to mental realization (intuitive insight), partially transcendent mystical experiences, or to the entire set of Wolff's realizations.

material of this sort in their writings. These reports are the essential link between firsthand mystical experiences and their subsequent interpretation and conceptual development. His personal narrative of these realizations and the philosophy that he derives from them substantially advance our knowledge of mysticism, as well as its significance for a comprehensive world view.

Wolff's fascinating life and experiences are sufficient to attract our interest. Moreover, the brilliant intuitive and intellectual reflections of his illumined mind on the nature and philosophical implications of his realizations constitute an unparalleled practical and theoretical legacy. For spiritual seekers, his wisdom, insight, and instruction provide effective guidance along the path of personal attainment. For those whose central concern is to comprehend reality, his articulated thought deepens our understanding of the nature of mystical experience and its relevance for philosophy, psychology, and religion.[3] He characterizes the investigation of the overlap among these three domains of fundamental human inquiry as metapsychological, inasmuch as it is essentially inaccessible to ordinary methods. However, this region is available to direct awareness through a noetic function of consciousness that transcends the empirical realm, and it may be studied by means of continued operation of relative consciousness alongside the nonrelative. Wolff's introduction and treatment of coincident modes of consciousness contribute notably to our exploration and comprehension of mystical states, which, according to mystics' reports, intrinsically transcend the reach of empirical investigation.

What is more important, as he points out, the discovery of a third means of cognition, apart from perception and conception, would have dramatic philosophical implications. Theoretically, it opens the door to metaphysical knowledge. Wolff considers three metaphysical questions fundamental to his work:

1. Is metaphysical knowledge possible?
2. If so, how may it be known?
3. If known, how may it be communicated, and to what extent?[4]

Insofar as mystical experience gives nonsensuous, nonconceptual content directly to consciousness, this would satisfy the central necessary condition stipulated by Kant.[5]

To briefly sketch the problem, Kant introduces the concept of the 'noumenon'—what a thing is like in itself apart from the phenomenon, which is the sensible appearance of a thing. This distinction is implicit in the very concept of 'appearance'. Knowledge of phenomena is formed by the synthesis of the sensible intuition of an object and a corresponding concept provided by the faculty of understanding. For example, the phenomenon of seeing a tree is a synthesis of the specific sensuous impressions with the concept 'tree'. A second well-established cognitive faculty involves knowing the characteristics of concepts and their relations in abstraction from sensible content, such as we find within the domain of pure mathematics. In pondering the possibility of positive knowledge of the noumenon, Kant concludes that it is necessary that an object be presented through a form of intuition entirely apart from sensibility. However, he is unable either to prove or to exclude the existence of such an intuition. Furthermore, even if it were to exist, he contends that noumenal knowledge would still be problematic. The intuitively given content must be enrobed conceptually to be understood, but no concept from the field of sensible knowledge can possibly apply to a domain of a completely different nature.

Wolff believes that he has resolved successfully the Kantian problem, but whereas he has found an experiential ground for metaphysics, this falls short of establishing an exclusive systematic formulation. Although Kant has shown that noumenal reality cannot be intelligibly described, Wolff contends that language may be used symbolically to indicate a transcendent referent. Because diverse symbols may be employed effectively, various metaphysical schemes are possible—in fact, they are desirable as necessarily complementary ways of representing this Transcendent Reality. This overt metaphysical relativism is a subtle, but extremely significant, feature of his philosophy. It allows him (and those who would wish to follow him) to avoid the unnecessary limitations imposed by the traditional system-building approach to metaphysics. Nevertheless, he is obliged to show how the noetic aspect of realization constitutes knowledge, even in the most liberal sense of the term.

Notwithstanding the difficulty engendered by metaphysical indeterminacy, Wolff's metaphysics does exhibit an identifiable character. It favors an approach that is oriented to the primacy of consciousness, which is understood in a special way, as unconditioned either by the immediate subjective experience or by any objective content. Consciousness ordinarily exhibits a subject-object polarity, wherein the subject, in its purity, transcends the object within a given relative structure. He regards his shift of focus from the subject-to-consciousness to Consciousness Itself[6] as a Copernican revolution completing that of Kant, who established epistemological primacy in the subject, rather than in the object. Wolff believes that his approach shows how mystical experience might be made not only comprehensible, but indispensable for a truly satisfactory world view.[7]

His training in mathematics, as well as philosophy, results in an emphasis that is compatible with the distinctive character of the Western mind. Wolff's knowledge and application of Eastern wisdom, methods, and terminology should not obscure his explicit aim to serve as a bridge between East and West. He views this material through the lens of his realizations and recasts it in terms of Western philosophy. In particular, he is deeply concerned that his contribution be understood, at least partially, as an attempt to resolve the central epistemological and metaphysical problems of the post-Kantian world. For this reason he deliberately prefers a primarily philosophical mode of expression.

In addition, because he regards mathematics as the discipline lying at the foundation of the West's theoretical orientation, Wolff desires to reflect this strength by using it to catalyze and apprehend Transcendent Consciousness. He employs the resources of higher mathematics to symbolize nonrelative states of consciousness and indicate distinctions within a zone of awareness that is only partially determinate. His orientation to conceptuality, appreciation for the critical aspect of philosophy, and symbolic and analogical use of mathematics initiates a method of attainment accessible to the West. By so doing, he has largely fulfilled his intention to pioneer a distinctively Western mystical path.

Wolff's Realizations

Wolff regards philosophy as a Way of Life whose central concern is realization.[8] Without this grounding, his work would lack its compelling sense of authenticity and profundity. Even so, because of his intellectual integrity and the value he places on critical intelligence, he insists that these realizations "do not carry this force for other individuals unless they have similar Realizations. So this philosophic statement is not dogmatically affirmed as something that other people must accept. It is put forth as a suggestion for others to consider, not as an authoritative presentation."[9] Thus the challenge to the reader is to verify what she can for herself by her own personal Awakening. A presumption of truth may be built through discursive reasoning, but ultimately only Introception[10] can yield this kind of knowledge.

He defines *realization* as "the Awakening to the Transcendent or Cosmic Consciousness. . . . Realization is not a development of consciousness in the subject-object sense. It implies a radical event involving the shifting of the level of consciousness."[11] He distinguishes realization from experience in terms of the following features: It is a state of consciousness

1. where time is not relevant, in contrast to temporal process
2. based on a function of consciousness other than perception
3. wherein the subject transcends the object.[12]

Realization may be either mental or Fundamental. Mental realization differs from Fundamental Realization inasmuch as only the former permits adequate conceptualization of its essential insight.

Wolff's two Fundamental Realizations followed a series of three preliminary mental realizations. His first premonitory recognition, "I am *Ātman*," was the flash of awareness that the 'I', the pure subject-to-consciousness, is identical to the *Ātman* or Pure Self, not the ego, so it can never be an object before consciousness. The second realization, "I am *Nirvāṇa*," corrected his misconception concerning the nature of *Nirvāṇa* as a subtle external world or space within the objective, relative manifold. Rather, it is identical to the inmost sense of 'I' as pure subject. One may only Awaken to this eternal condition. Third, "Substantiality is inversely proportional to ponderability," was the insight that the substantial ground of Reality, as the Primordial Plenum, lies in inverse relationship to the degree that what appears to consciousness is sensuously ponderable. Although he illustrates this insight by using the language of physical objects, there is no doubt that Wolff intends the principle to extend to all domains of awareness, including both inner and outer perception.

In contrast, Fundamental Realization intrinsically transcends language and concepts, so its essential nature cannot be captured in any discursive formulation. Wolff's first of two, "I Am THAT,"[13] fulfilled the insight of "I am *Ātman.*" However, it was Transcendent and personally transformative. It went beyond the mere idea that the 'I' is identical to the Pure Self, but Realized this existentially through the intentional isolation of the subjective moment of consciousness. The essential nature of his second Fundamental Realization, "The High Indifference," was the transcendence of a state that he describes as utter Satisfaction by a more exalted state of Equilibrium and Equanimity that was neutral between all pairs of opposites, including *Nirvāṇa* and *saṃsāra.* It was a state of utter Fullness and infinite potential, but completely aloof concerning which possibilities would become actual. Despite this affective neutrality, the state was superior to anything Wolff had ever encountered—its supernal value unmistakably self-evident. Just as Fundamental Realization transcends mental realization as the infinite transcends the finite, the High Indifference transcended Wolff's first Fundamental Realization as a higher order of Infinity transcends a lower order of infinity. Ultimately, it is utter Mystery. Practically, its transformative effect was both personal and philosophical, as it resulted in a permanent shift in his base of consciousness and made necessary a fundamental revision of his systematic philosophy.

A positive and pervasive feature of Wolff's work is his overriding concern for penetrating to the truth of substantive issues by using his personal resources (mystical and intellectual) instead of relying upon secondary sources. Reporting his realizations was necessary, he believes, for otherwise there would be no way to establish the epistemological base for his philosophy.[14] When he speaks from the authority of his own mystical experiences,[15] he subordinates all other material to them.

> These five Realizations stand as authority before me just insofar as the field they cover is concerned, and this means that they transcend in that field the authority of any scripture, sutra or shastra that already exists. . . . neither empiric science nor normative science has the power to overrule or lead to the rejection of any of the five Realizations. The Realizations have primacy over all other forms of knowledge, scriptural, scientific or mathematical, which exist so far as I am concerned.[16]

His position on their relative validity is therefore clear and uncompromising. Nonetheless, it is clearly undogmatic, insofar as he contends that it is only for those who have had similar realizations that such pronouncements may be accepted as authoritative.

Although Wolff adapts concepts and doctrines from other systems where it is useful to do so, his philosophy is original, grounded in his firsthand mystical awareness. He also expresses it in whatever terminology—whether created, borrowed, or modified—he finds most effectively communicates it to contemporary Western culture.

> I am not simply making a transformation of Oriental philosophy into Western language. Even less am I producing a statement based upon the Ben Israel religiosity, nor even of Greek philosophical mysticism. What I am doing is producing a statement in terms that are indigenous to the West that will reflect the meaning and the way of Realization.[17]

Wolff's descriptive and explanatory focus is his realizations, so he is greatly concerned with how well the words and concepts he employs portray and communicate this immediate content. Consequently, he subordinates their absolute fidelity of meaning within any traditional context to his practical end.

Finally, Wolff's overall intention is twofold, philosophical and personal, dealing with fact and value, respectively:

1. to design his philosophical formulation to be critically sound to convince any rational, open-minded person, and
2. to convey to the reader the nature and value of Fundamental Realization.

He wishes not only to provide sufficient justification to establish its existence, but also to encourage a personal quest. He contends that motivation for seeking this goal is both philosophical and religious. Clearly, an essential criterion for a wholly adequate evaluation of his philosophy is firsthand awareness of its base, and the only way to verify the existence of this purported cognitive function is to make it active for oneself. Furthermore, he reports that Realization is of supernal value, worth achieving for its own sake, for therein lies the resolution of the sensed problems of the human condition.

These articulate reports detailing his personal transformational process are an unparalleled source of guidance for the seeker. Along with his extensive accounts of the realizations themselves, he includes a wealth of autobiographical material concerning the mystical path, whereas most mystical texts omit this kind of firsthand evidence. He also introduces several unique practical aspects, for example, securing a self-conscious link to relative consciousness during the episodes that he characterizes as Fundamental Realizations. These provide a valuable aid to the reader's individual attainment.

Scholarship

Although Wolff read extensively, his research was mainly limited to English texts and translations. Furthermore, following his departure from the academic world in 1915, he lost contact with most of the ensuing developments in Western philosophy. His withdrawal resulted in a number of gaps in his background, displayed principally in his nineteenth-century orientation to the history of philosophy. On the one hand, this is regrettable, for the combination of his keen mind and profound mystical aptitude would have enabled him to critique insightfully developments in twentieth-century philosophy from a profound point of view. On the other hand, he found it necessary to concentrate his efforts on the greater goal of individual Enlightenment, which he believed an academic focus would likely have prevented.

Despite Wolff's appreciation for the value of scholarship, he consistently subordinates it to that of facilitating the process of attaining Fundamental Realization. His reflective analysis of their interrelationship clarifies his rationale.

> Scholarship is important and is a great aid, but it can also be a barrier, because one may be taken up by the consideration of ideas to an exclusion of other features that are essential. There is such a thing as being overloaded with scholarship so that the ideational process is all the time too active. Incisive ideas are more helpful in the actual *sādhana* than carefully modulated ideation, which takes in a multitude of exceptions. The ideas are tools so far as the *sādhana* is concerned, and a sharply defined tool is a more effective tool than one with the blunted edge of too much modification or consideration of exceptions. The amount of scholarship that is good for the individual would vary from in-

> dividual to individual. But scholarship becomes too great and is a barrier when one is everlastingly hung up with the process of ideation. Remember that scholarship is only a tool. It is not the end; it is not the goal. The goal is another way of knowing; it is another way of cognizing, of being aware, and in principle it should be possible for one to attain this without scholarship. But scholarship can be a very great aid if one is not attached to it, not bound by it, not inclined to view it as an end in itself, and thus make it a substitute for the real *sādhana*.[18]

He considers the personal attainment of Fundamental Realization by each individual far more important than mere intellectual acceptance of mystics' findings.[19] If the philosopher is to Realize this function personally, he must broaden his approach. Wolff contends that the Western scholar places himself at a disadvantage by remaining aloof from this subject matter. Usually it is a virtue to maintain such an attitude, but where direct acquaintance requiring psychical transformation is involved, it presents a barrier. He contends that what is needed is an attitude of self-giving, which is sacred rather than secular.[20] It will be insufficient to provide scholarly commentary at arm's length, so to speak, for one must Awaken to know directly and immediately That to which the mystic refers.

In the scholarship of mysticism, there has always been a division between those who commit themselves to the experience and those who remain reserved. The latter must avoid unwarranted skepticism; the former, excessive credulity. A central philosophical issue concerns authority: Is the mystic in a better position to discuss and evaluate mystical experiences than the nonmystic? If we consider the analogous situation of dreaming, then, other things being equal, the dreamer has an advantage over the nondreamer in a philosophical discussion concerning their nature and significance. Direct awareness is exceedingly helpful, if not strictly necessary, for an adequately qualified appraisal of Wolff's philosophy, mysticism, ultimate reality, or any transempirical subject matter. An attitude that remains *exclusively* oriented to scholarship is incompatible with attaining such awareness—it forcibly preempts it. We might also wonder if such an attitude is not a central factor in the apparent opacity of most accounts of, as well as the philosophy based on, mystical experience. Thus it is reasonable to suggest that for critical commentary (which too is an important part of the enterprise) to be effective, one must first apprehend the content in a more direct manner. This process requires a complementary approach that seeks an optimum balance.

In grounding his essential philosophy Wolff speaks from personal mystical experience, rather than deriving his conclusions from other sources. To be sure, he contends that his major theses cannot be established solely by rational argument from some other base. That is, pure reason, neither by itself, nor in combination with ordinary experience, can demonstrate (or refute) a transcendental reality.[21] Nevertheless, though much can be said from the base of realization, he believes that employing a strictly scholarly style would inhibit its effective communication. For this reason he generally prefers to advance it in modes more appropriate to expression from exalted states of consciousness, the subject matter, and the audience. We see, then, that his treatment of other systems of thought is primarily a means to an end, more than an end in itself, and is best evaluated in that light.

SYNOPSIS

General Approach

Wolff compares his position with the major schools of his day,[22] but we shall further consider how it is related to later developments—in particular, phenomenological and analytic traditions. It will be helpful to determine the extent to which Wolff's insights, analysis, and conclusions may be corroborated by other methods. Whereas every school, system, movement, approach, and so on, is acknowledged to have something worthwhile that must be integrated within a comprehensive philosophical synthesis, none of them has exclusive or invincible authority. Determining the contribution of such a figure to this grand project is a dynamic creative process, for it cannot merely be subsumed within the preexisting world view.

The overarching domain of inquiry is the totality of human awareness. Our guiding telos is philosophy itself, which involves the ongoing quest to resolve the central issues and problems of human existence. Due to the nature and scope of the subject matter, it is necessary that our methodology be eclectic and open-ended.

The explication and critique of the central features of his philosophy require methods of greater diversity, including phenomenology and conceptual clarification. Our overall approach, however, must rely on intuition for insight into the subtleties of the experiences reported, their philosophical significance, and our resulting world view.

Structure and Development

This critical exposition of Wolff's philosophy has the minimal purpose of presenting the contribution of a unique philosopher who yet remains relatively unknown. Our most concrete concern is to provide an accurate factual description of germane biographical material on his life, those who influenced his thought, and especially the accounts of his realizations. The main task in the following two chapters involves the establishment of a three-dimensional context for understanding Wolff's articulated philosophy[23]—biographical, ideational, and experiential. Chapter 2 begins with a brief biographical sketch to show how, to an unusual degree, Wolff is inseparable from his philosophy. We then identify and discuss the central figures who significantly influenced Wolff's orientation within the mystical tradition and the character of his philosophical statement. Chapter 3 elaborates his five realizations—the reports of the mystical experiences that transformed his life and ground his philosophy.

Chapters 4 and 5 deal with special problems that arise regarding mystical experience, namely,

1. the essential nature of mysticism, and
2. the meaningfulness of mystical language.

To establish a context for understanding and integrating Wolff's accounts of his realizations and the philosophy he derives from them, chapter 4 considers the subject of mysticism, the attempt to define it, and its relation to philosophy. Chapter 5 attempts to resolve the semantic problem of expressing and communicating the unique nature of mystical experience, which mystics generally report to be ineffable—that is, beyond both words and concepts. Consistent with Wolff's position, we shall find that the most advantageous interpretation of mystical experience is the view that mystics are aware of a Transcendent, nonphenomenal 'core' that is essentially impervious to strictly descriptive formulation. We are able to escape the semantic paradox—trying to describe the indescribable—because symbols, linguistic and otherwise, may be used meaningfully to 'point' to it indirectly. Hence we are entitled to conclude that the ineffability of mystical experience does not entail that the mystic must adopt a strategy of strict silence. Furthermore, to treat mystical subject matter authentically requires that *we* also employ language symbolically when necessary by using concepts, notions, and linguistic and nonlinguistic forms that overflow standard usage.

The preponderance of this work deals directly with the essence of Wolff's formal philosophy, emphasizing the metaphysical and epistemological issues that he addresses. The key to his approach lies in the nature of consciousness and its role in the determination of reality. Chapter 6 investigates relative consciousness and the subject-object relationship that structures it. The discussion in chapter 7 shifts to the transcendent sense of Consciousness (the ultimate referent of what he symbolizes by Consciousness-without-an-object), and the issue of ontological primacy. Here we shall consider the relationship between consciousness and the self, comparing and contrasting Wolff's position with selected representatives of analytic, phenomenological, and Eastern schools of thought. What is more important, we shall investigate the metaphysical significance of the Primordial Consciousness that Wolff Realized.

The emphasis shifts from metaphysics to epistemology in chapter 8 to consider the noetic thesis that mystical experience is a source of cognition that is derived neither from conception nor sense experience. Wolff regards this discovery as his major contribution to philosophy. Within the context that Kant proposes for establishing the possibility of metaphysical knowledge, we explore the existence, operation, and significance of this third cognitive function.

Finally, chapter 9 summarizes Wolff's philosophy of Introceptualism[24] and its contribution to Western philosophy. It presents a serious challenge to traditional philosophical approaches based solely on relative consciousness—one that cannot be ignored. However, if we accept it in the spirit of philosophy, as love of wisdom, it will lead to a source of enduring value.

CHAPTER 2

Franklin Wolff: Life and Influences

OVERVIEW

Wolff's realizations—the most profound of which is the High Indifference—ground his philosophy. We must not forget this cardinal point, but neither should we ignore the role of noteworthy philosophical influences in providing conceptual and methodological resources. Because Wolff takes pains to acknowledge the significance of such figures to his inspiration, development, understanding, and expression, an explicit treatment is warranted.

Let us first examine the major influences of other philosophers on his mystical and philosophical development, especially his conceptual account of the nature of realization. Our understanding of their impact upon his philosophical formulation will complement the account of his realizations, which are themselves the crucial episodes in his biography. The discussion of these individuals, and the relevant aspects of their thought, establishes an ideational context for his philosophical and mystical orientation. That is, we shall understand Wolff better by studying those extraordinary individuals for whom he feels great affinity and who he believes share the same essential experiential ground for their philosophies.

Both a movement and several philosophers and religious figures affected him profoundly. He considers his primary influences—

Śaṃkara, from the East, as well as Pythagoras and Kant, from the West—to have demonstrated superior intellect and moral character. More to the point, their philosophies include themes that he plausibly interprets as manifestations, at least to some degree, of the noetic activity of Introception (or mystical insight). Certain features of these positions have inspired him, and, suitably interpreted, he has made them his own. Thus a closer look at how each of them expresses this awareness will help us to understand Introceptualism, which he contends shares the same essential ground.

Simply stated, he adopts from Pythagoras the application of mathematical thought to facilitate spiritual ends, as well as to articulate his resulting experiences. Pythagoreanism serves as a model for harmonizing the theoretical and religious dimensions of human aspiration. Kant supplies the epistemological focus (the knowing subject, rather than the object known) and the general context within which Wolff understands the philosophical significance and value of his own quest. This effort is an attempt to confirm the existence of a nonordinary cognitive function that would open the way to metaphysical knowledge. His discovery of Śaṃkara provides an exemplar—one whom he credits with the attainment of this goal. In addition, this spiritual teacher details the methodology (the discrimination of self from all that is not-self) that most aided Wolff's success.

Our study shall briefly characterize each influence and explicate the aspect(s) that Wolff has integrated. At times, when he finds that no concept that presently exists conveys his exact meaning, he often adapts selected ideas from appropriate religious and/or philosophical systems to serve his purpose. Accordingly, whether his presentation of these sources achieves complete accuracy in conformity with historical or scholarly criteria is a secondary issue that should not unduly concern us. We shall allow that when Wolff uses terminology taken from other systems of thought, he retains the same general meaning. However, there may be varying degrees of difference of detail because certain features of his experiences (which he usually discusses) will color his usage. When he asserts a claim central to his philosophy, he ultimately justifies it on the basis of his realizations, not because it conforms to the doctrines of some respected authority.[1]

His philosophy is a unique, authentic expression springing directly from mystical realization and refined in reflection by his critical intellect. He distinguishes his accounts of the experiences themselves, which he attempts to describe in as neutral a manner as possible, from his expression and discussion of their philosophical significance. Although his formulation exhibits certain similarities with several established traditions, it cannot be subsumed by any of them. Furthermore, grounding in immediate awareness, even Fundamental Realization, does not confer immunity to error upon any statement derived from it. Some discursive treatment of the adequacy of particular formulation is always possible. Moreover, Wolff advances an overriding metainterpretation to the effect that the essential nature of mystical experience does not permit the claim of exclusive validity for any particular interpretation. Consequently, he would claim privilege for his articulated philosophy only insofar as it is grounded in his direct awareness of a profound nonphenomenal content, rather than mere intellectual constructs based exclusively upon our ordinary range of experience.

BIOGRAPHY

A succinct preliminary biographical sketch[2] will exhibit the personal context within which these influences operate. Even though Wolff wishes to be appreciated for his philosophy, rather than his personality, the human dimension that attends his formal work is also quite fascinating.

Franklin Fowler Wolff was born in 1887, in Pasadena, California, the son of a Methodist minister. His upbringing instilled within him a deeply religious and ethical orientation that became a permanent feature of his character. Upon entering adolescence he discovered and immersed himself in his own independent, self-directed thought, which quickly led to his rejection of orthodox Christianity. "I had been through the orthodox church and found it utterly barren, so far as cognitive values were concerned, and puny in what it offered for feeling."[3] Mathematics soon became his premier intellectual love, but fulfillment of adequate religious value remained his greatest aspiration.

At Stanford Wolff originally intended to pursue a career in law. He majored in pure mathematics, with minors in philosophy and psychology—refusing to compartmentalize his various interests. In mathematics, he discovered not only intellectual value, but mystical and numinous value as well. He notes that "the feeling persisted that at the root of mathematics there lay a mystery, reaching far deeper than anything attained through the senses."[4] Through his mathematical involvement with the infinite, he sensed a profound harmony, proportion, beauty, and value. He experienced a delight similar in quality to, and superseded in his awareness only by, that of Realization.[5]

Eventually his need for clarity of understanding required a shift of emphasis to philosophy (in a joint major with mathematics) as he pursued graduate studies at both Stanford and Harvard, abandoning his plans for law.[6] After winning a special scholarship conferred by the Harvard Club of Stanford, he attended Harvard during the 1912 through 1913 school year. He found that "philosophy added reflecting and focusing power to the pure light of mathematics."[7] By "the pure light" Wolff almost certainly means intellectual illumination, with mystical overtones, induced by the contemplation of a priori relationships—but not yet is it Illumination in the full sense, as Realized or Awakened Consciousness.[8] In addition, his study of analytic psychology impressed him with the value of, and developed his skill to perform, the clear introspection and articulation of experience. Ultimately, this resulted in his comprehensive account of the process of personal transformation that is so characteristic of mysticism.

At Harvard Wolff became convinced that the existence of a transcendent way of consciousness, not yet comprehended by Western epistemology or psychology, was not only possible, but probable.[9] Upon returning to Stanford in 1914, he accepted a temporary position as professor of mathematics, but after only a year he found himself compelled to make a difficult choice. He felt it necessary to abandon a promising academic career (in either mathematics or philosophy) to facilitate his search for a third function or faculty of cognition apart from sense perception and conceptual cognition. He recollects, "I found myself in sight of the limits to which our present egoistic consciousness has reached, and also had found adumbrations of another kind of Consciousness where alone, it seemed, solution of the antinomies of the subject-object consciousness could be found."[10] He was confident that this new mode of consciousness contained the key to metaphysical knowledge, which Kant had shown to be impossible if cognition is limited to the two familiar forms—namely, perception and conception.

Forgoing outer recognition, success, and security, Wolff displayed single-minded dedication to the project. Repeatedly, he abandoned efforts in a particular direction once he had exhausted its essential value. The twenty-four long years that ensued before his breakthrough were characterized by a vast broadening of experience and activity in the world while he gradually strengthened his commitment. Although he was a conscientious objector to violent conflict, he served as a sergeant in World War I, producing lumber for the war effort. He built a house in San Fernando, where he tended orchards and kept bees—skills he had learned from his father. Later, while prospecting during the Great Depression, he found the solitude and archetypal settings of cave and desert powerful catalysts for his final two preliminary mental realizations.

In 1920 he married Sarah Merrell Briggs, a union that was to prove exceedingly fruitful. She was given the title *Sherifa* by Pir Mursid Inayat Khan, a great Sufi leader who had come to lecture in America, and was thenceforth known by that name. To symbolize their complementary and equal status in their work, they joined their original surnames as *Merrell-Wolff*. The Assembly of Man, which Franklin and Sherifa founded in 1928, had an esoteric philosophical orientation, generally Theosophical in nature, having a basis in the Vedānta and Buddhism.

The following year, the group members obtained permission to build an *āśrama*[11] where they held yearly conventions while completing its construction—a project that continued every summer for over twenty years. They erected it at the eight thousand-foot-level in Tuttle Creek Canyon, nestled in the eastern slope of the Sierra Nevada mountains, between what was to become Wolff's home, two thousand feet below, and Mt. Whitney (the tallest peak in the contiguous forty-eight states). They purposely chose this location because they felt that the highest point within a country is also its spiritual center. In addition, they designed the structure in the shape of a balanced cross to symbolize the principle of equilibrium.[12]

During this phase, Wolff sometimes experienced periods of self-doubt in which he questioned the wisdom of renouncing the security and status of the academic world for the prospect of greater attainment. However, all uncertainty vanished upon his discovery of Śaṃkara, with whom he immediately felt a profound rapport. Precisely, it was *The System of the Vedānta*[13] that held the key to Wolff's breakthrough—the Fundamental Realization of 7 August 1936.

Henceforth, he began writing, not merely *about* Transcendental Consciousness, but *from* it. Because he intends *Pathways* to be primarily an autobiographical report on the process itself, including spontaneous reflection on a variety of subjects, he presents the philosophical dimension informally, rather than systematically. It is a sharing of the journey, which may provide personal inspiration for the reader's spiritual path. In contrast, "Concept, Percept and Reality" and his original manuscript, *The Philosophy of Consciousness Without an Object*, are more systematically organized and designed to satisfy the academic philosopher as well as the learned nonprofessional.

Wolff's group work and public lectures during the second half of his life had significantly increased effect. Those who knew him well found that as a result of Enlightenment his presence carried a force that could induce exalted states of consciousness, as well as psycho-physical heat, in his audience. What is of central importance is that he now could speak with authority concerning the nature and effects of Fundamental Realization.

Sherifa continued as a partner in his work until her death in 1959. The following year, at the age of seventy-two, Wolff married Gertrude Adams and undertook the construction of a house in the mountains near Lone Pine. After she died in 1978, he continued to live there (with the assistance of a series of students and family members) until his death, on 4 October 1985, at the age of ninety-eight.

To the residents of the town he was a mysterious figure who became somewhat legendary, but for those of his group he was an Enlightened spiritual teacher and guide. Moreover, a great number of his visitors, coming from as far as Australia and Nepal, were drawn by his books. Annual conventions, begun in 1929, continued to attract many people, representing a wide range of ages, occupations, and religious backgrounds—including many outstanding professionals from various fields. The remarkably eclectic nature of those who are interested in his work is explained by his philosophy's profound synthetic power, for it recognizes the value of diverse, unique expressions of the spiritual dimension of humankind. Even though it is rooted in mystical realization, Wolff emphatically insists that Introceptualism is not, nor must it ever become, a religion.

THEOSOPHY

Before considering the historical figures whose influence was most meaningful for Wolff, let us first briefly discuss the original movement that affected him. Theosophy[14] is the most pervasive and extensive personal influence in Wolff's life, particularly through his long association with Sherifa. This effect notwithstanding, it is the least germane of his philosophical references, meriting only a single specific footnote in his later books.[15] Several reasons may be suggested for his reluctance to rely overtly upon Theosophical material to a greater extent:

1. He desires to base his philosophy as far as possible on his own immediate awareness.
2. He wishes to employ an original form of expression derived from that base that is familiar to Western philosophy.
3. The preponderance of Theosophical claims cannot be justified in the mode of critical philosophy, which he is committed to respect in his formal work.

This is correct, since Wolff's philosophy owes nothing essential to any external authority. So we may best accomplish our purpose of discriminating his original thought from secondary sources by further sharpening this distinction.

Madame Helena Petrovna Blavatsky (HPB), who, along with Colonel Alcott, founded the Theosophical Society in New York in 1875, was a scholar and occultist, rather than a mystic or sage. She claims neither revelation nor originality, but instead contends that her work is a synthesis of truth from diverse ancient scriptures, much of it obscure or lost, set forth nondogmatically as a "working hypothesis."[16] She maintains that the resulting esoteric doctrine embodies the essence of all the great religions from antiquity to the modern era. Wolff shares her belief that it is "a partial statement emanating from pure Bodha or the Eternal Wisdom of which every authentic religious movement or philosophy is, in its origin, a partial manifestation."[17]

Even so, its presentation as an explanatory system may be criticized for often imposing in advance the structures that it claims to discover. For example, we find a predominant sevenfold framework of categorization,[18] such that each domain of esoteric phenomena is presumed to fall naturally into seven separate divisions. Three-fold and ten-fold groupings also are preferred. We also may detect a tendency to interpret myth literally to explain the course of human evolution, the origin of rational thought, and other phenomena. There appears to be little attempt to distinguish between mythical constructs, intuitive insights, paranormal phenomena, and historical facts. Although Wolff seems to view these shortcomings as innocuous, he acknowledges that the way of thinking and valuing that he encountered in the movement is totally foreign to the standards of scientific soundness. He remarks that its almost total reliance upon highly developed intuition, combined with a devaluation of logic, is both a strength and a weakness. When accurate, it may attain possibilities that are otherwise unavailable; when misguided, it will often leap to ridiculous, untenable conclusions. Hence it calls for clear discrimination.[19] Unfortunately, much of it is unverifiable, and no universally established criterion presently exists for determining truth in such esoteric matters. The agreement of adepts as the sole standard is suspiciously circular, for an established orthodoxy may require that a person accept certain occult "truths" as a condition to legitimize his status as an adept.

Despite such problems, Wolff was powerfully attracted by the high spiritual and ethical ideals of this line of thought and was rewarded by his ensuing study of Śaṃkara, to which it led him. For the most part, his strong logical bent provides an adequate antidote to the excesses of esotericism. He says, for instance, that when doing mathematics he would not rest content until he had solved every problem. He strives to avoid reliance upon extraneous sources in his formal philosophy because he intends it to be convincing to anyone who is open-minded and reasonable. However, here the pregnant subject matter requires that intuition supersede logical thought. He grounds his position experientially in mystical realization and develops it through reflective reasoning, so it owes nothing of any consequence to any other authority whatsoever.[20] In informal discourse he accepts some Theosophical material as presumptive truth but always subordinates it to that derived from his realizations. Therefore, we shall reflect the weight that Wolff has given it in his most serious philosophical writings by suspending concern for the Theosophical influence and concentrating on his original contribution.

PYTHAGORAS

Pythagoreanism

Pythagoras (570–500 B.C.E.), an ancient Greek mystic-mathematician, is difficult to evaluate because the earliest available Pythagorean writings are estimated to date from close to a century later. Furthermore, due to their need for secrecy, he and his followers recorded very little. Then, too, Pythagoras himself quickly became a legendary figure to whom his followers tended to attribute personally all teachings and discoveries of the school. Also, his genius for integrating science and religion formulated a world view that is difficult to comprehend for those less capable.[21] Tradition maintains that he sought and received instruction in Egypt and Babylonia[22] and was taught by Zaratas the Chaldean, Zoroaster, and other Persian magi.[23] In light of these limitations, we should take the term *Pythagoras* as a symbol, rather than the name of the person, for it refers to the founding impetus that he represents of the whole development of abstract scientific thought in the West.

Wolff prefers to minimize the historical uncertainty of Pythagoras's actual exploits, accepting popular accounts as factually true in the absence of evidence to the contrary. He believes that adopting the philosophically precise attitude of suspending judgment would avoid error at the cost of personal inspiration. Our primary interest clearly lies in the nature of the legendary attributes for which he feels affinity, as opposed to the historical correctness of these claims. In any case, an objective presentation of

Pythagoreanism will form a useful context from which to consider how Wolff understands the application of mathematics to mysticism.

He regards Pythagoras's importance to the West as vastly underestimated. With respect to the value of his philosophical and scientific contributions, Robert Brumbaugh would agree,[24] crediting this pre-Socratic philosopher with the

1. discovery of pure mathematics,
2. sharpening of the notion of mathematical proof,
3. awareness that form and structure give things their identities,
4. scientific search for quantitative laws, and,
5. philosophical tradition of formalism.[25]

In Guthrie's opinion, the advancement deserving most emphasis is Pythagoras's "dim idea that things must be defined in terms of their essence, their form or structure and not the material in which they were embodied."[26] He holds the formal element to be real and permanent, the physical and individual aspects merely accidental.[27] Pythagoreans consider that the integers from 1 to 10 possess a real potency, believing the number 10 to be perfect, and that it "contained in itself the whole nature of number" . . . [the] source and root of everlasting nature."[28] According to this view, number not only has a mystical significance as the key to the cosmos, but also has an independent reality to which phenomena are subordinate.[29] Despite the Pythagorean emphasis on form, numbers are not conceived as dimensionless, but are "regarded simultaneously as units, geometrical points and physical atoms."[30] Thus things could be composed of numbers and abstractions given numerical value as well (for example, 4 is the number attributed to justice). This led to the first comprehensive attempt to give a mathematical account of the world.

Pythagoras adopts the notion of the indeterminate boundless (unlimited) from Anaximander, adding the essential idea of limit.[31] Limit (good) and the unlimited (bad) constitute complementary ultimate principles,[32] where the ordering principle of number bounds the unlimited by giving it form. Here we find the rudimentary introduction of the formal element in Western philosophy. Because the Pythagoreans only dimly grasp the distinction between form and matter, their metaphysics exhibits a concrete understanding of number intertwined with mystical and associational elements. Consequently, it would be unwise to interpret their doctrines too literally.

Wolff claims that the Western world is fundamentally Pythagorean, for it is mathematical.[33] He contends that Pythagoras's introduction of the class of irrational numbers justifies his place as the forerunner of modern mathematics. We must acknowledge that the break with the Ancient Greek insistence upon universal determinate rationality led to highly significant developments in mathematics. The most outstanding of these is the extension of the number system to include transcendental, transfinite, and imaginary numbers. This allows us, at least partially, to conceive of domains that are not wholly determinate. Pythagoras also introduced the principle of conceptual proof,[34] the central feature of Western mathematics. Wolff considers his own orientation to concepts as comprising the primary sense in which he is Pythagorean. Of lesser importance is his great attraction to the metaphysical significance of number and the employment of mathematical discipline to produce and symbolize higher states of consciousness.

The Pythagorean emphasis on the theoretical, rather than the empirical (or the conceptual, rather than the perceptual), does not by itself account for Wolff's esteem for Pythagoras. Purely scientific concerns neglect the mystical dimension, which is the overriding factor for both philosophers. Brumbaugh claims that the Pythagoreans believe that freeing mathematics from empirical method has the effect of freeing the soul from the body and from reliance on the senses. "In mathematics, therefore, the soul lives as it were a life of its own, and participates, as far as possible for it while in the body, in the divine nature. It was a view that, through the influence of Plato, would profoundly affect the whole development of Western thought."[35] They studied mathematics in a cosmic context, as proper objects of contemplation, to harmonize the soul and actualize its divine nature. According to Robinson, Pythagoras developed a person's mental and spiritual faculties to attain the goal of Liberation, understood as escaping a continuous cycle of transmigration of the soul.[36]

Mathematics and Religion

Their goal, as Wolff understands it, involves individual transformation. He regards their number concept as well suited to that end, since they believe that the universe is composed of numbers in essentially harmonious relationships, whose contemplation would harmonize the soul. In effect, the Pythagorean preoccupation with applied mathematics serves primarily spiritual rather than material or technical ends.[37] Their study of mathematics involves a religious enthusiasm because their vision of number as ultimate has the impact of a mystical revelation.[38]

Wolff considers himself to be following in the spirit of Pythagoras. Superficially, both studied mathematics and taught esoteric groups to facilitate the development of Transcendent states of consciousness. Pythagoras sought to share his scientific wisdom, but due to the danger of persecution by a Greek society intolerant of their discoveries, such as the irrational nature of $\sqrt{2}$ (the square root of 2), he taught only an esoteric school whose members were sworn to secrecy. More to the point, Wolff appreciates the mystery of number, having experienced profoundly mystical-numinous value through his engrossment with mathematics. That is, even though his study of this subject matter did not result in typical mystical or numinous experience, it produced states of consciousness that had a similar sense of extraordinary value. He finds in the supercosmic view, which involves the infinite, "a sense of profound harmony . . . proportion . . . beauty and value."[39] Mere sensuous loveliness seems crude by comparison. Such exquisite experience brought a delight far exceeding anything he had previously known, approaching that of Realization. This would seem to validate experientially the efficacy of the Pythagorean use of mathematics for religious purposes.

Corroboration also is available from contemporary research. Philosopher-mathematician Charles Musès, who has recently explored certain noetic applications of mathematics, concludes that "the art of mathematics can be used as a technique for altering states of consciousness."[40] He contends that *yantra yoga,* which uses noetic diagrams for contemplation, is based on this principle.[41] Insofar as mathematics can both alter and map conscious states, he claims that it accounts for

> the comparatively easy production of peak experiences—i.e. very intensely exhilarated states of consciousness depending on no external object—by means of mathematical ideas. . . . The mind is thus lifted to a peak point and becomes highly self-stimulating when it attains a state of such self-reflective comprehension in which logic and imagination are perfectly wed. This ecstatic state is very durable because it is voluntarily evocable. . . . The mind evidently finds this state of dynamic fusion of clear logic and profound insight most exhilarating.[42]

Musès has developed practical techniques and materials for this purpose, the results of which he says are demonstrable.[43] This lends support to Wolff's claim that mathematics, if approached in a certain manner, could serve as a distinct form of *yoga*, or spiritual discipline. Still, although Wolff's actual use of mathematical concepts and symbols is intuitively plausible, the theoretical or empirical justification for this practice remains to be developed. Musès's work may be the more adequately grounded in this regard and in any case is a helpful resource for comprehending the use of mathematics for this purpose.

Wolff notes that the Pythagorean concept of number, central to Greek science, is profoundly different from that of Galileo, who stands as the forerunner of modern Western science.[44] Pythagoras gave a certain primacy to numbers as "the building blocks of the universe."[45] Wolff is intrigued by the sense of mystery here, and not at all repelled by the strangeness of this number mysticism,[46] for he contends that there is a profound truth in this notion. He was struck by certain discoveries of a priori relationships within the number realm, for instance,

$$e^{\pi i} = -1$$

where e and π are transcendental numbers, and i is the hypernumber $\sqrt{-1}$. Furthermore, he believes that the widespread occurrence of such numbers in formulas related to natural phenomena—such as growth, physical structures, probability, and so on—holds special significance.

Musès would agree that "there remains something intrinsically mysterious about the number concept."[47] Hypernumbers, especially the nonreal forms of $\sqrt{+1}$, are essential to quantum physics,[48] but he avers that their application is not restricted to that domain. "In our investigation of hypernumbers we have found in general that the further we go beyond i, or $\sqrt{-1}$, the more the mathematics has significance in terms of the nature of consciousness rather than in terms of the properties of mass and energy, to which the lower hypernumbers and the so-called real numbers principally refer."[49] His favorable references to certain of his predecessors suggests that he accepts the possibility that mathematical applications may be extended beyond the range of empirical science to include metaphysics as well.[50]

We have discovered the frequent occurrence of the transcendental numbers π and e in our mathematical formulas for natural phenomena. Regrettably, Wolff does not elaborate on whatever significance these relationships may have beyond this. He hints that the "supercosmic view" involves the notion that mathematical elements and relationships are substantial and in some occult manner determine—not merely map—the form of the cosmos. Inasmuch as he does not attempt to advance this thesis as a strict metaphysical doctrine, it is more reasonable to interpret it mainly as an expression of the exalted state of consciousness attained in pure contemplation of the mathematical realm.

Pythagoras merged the religious impulse with the Apollonian[51] spirit—the search for knowledge for its own sake, the fundamental component of Western civilization already native to Greece. It is this synthesis with which Wolff identifies. However, as Guthrie has indicated already, Pythagoras may owe much to Chaldean and Zoroastrian influences, neither of which is purely Western. Wolff sometimes defines his own role as a bridge between East and West and his task as that of developing a way of Realization harmonious to the West. This path is appropriately oriented to the concept, and mathematics is the outstanding conceptual discipline. From this point of view he characterizes his approach as a mathematical yoga—a fusion between mathematics and religion.

IMMANUEL KANT

Synthesis and Revolution

Wolff regards Immanuel Kant (1724–1804 C.E.) as the most profound Western philosopher,[52] possibly "the greatest synthesizing force in the whole history of thought,"[53] and "*The Critique of Pure*

Reason the most important work in the whole western philosophical literature."[54] Kant's contribution is, as he says himself, no less than a Copernican revolution in philosophy. It shifts our primary philosophical concern away from the object known and toward the knowing subject, thereby conferring primacy upon epistemology instead of metaphysics.

He accepts Kant's critical inquiry into metaphysics as a central theme in his own program, which, like Kant's, exemplifies the quest for certainty and foundations. Wolff considers him to be "the chief representative of the critical spirit in philosophy . . . the recognition that before a valid construction in terms of knowledge is possible it is necessary to study critically the nature and limits of knowledge as such."[55] However, the critical domain within Wolff's philosophy is not restricted to setting the initial conditions for the search for metaphysical knowledge. It also involves the formulation, meaning, and significance of his Realizations, which he considers to constitute the attainment of this knowledge. Because the way of consciousness Wolff experienced is noetic, albeit nonphenomenal, he naturally interprets it as knowledge of the noumenon. However, as Kant has argued, he is aware that it is problematic to attempt to *describe* what a thing is like in itself, wholly apart from its sensuous presentation.

He also manifests the synthetic orientation so notable in Kant, attempting to unify diverse points of view within a more comprehensive framework. His interpretation of Kant exhibits both standard and nonstandard features. Wolff contends that, besides introducing an epistemological bridge between rationalism and empiricism,[56] Kant's idealism might be understood further as having unacknowledged mystical roots. This would depend on the accuracy of Wolff's view that the third function of cognition not only exists, but in some cases may operate autonomously without a person recognizing its true nature. Even so, it would be impossible to prove (or disprove) that it was a factor here.

According to Wolff's exoteric understanding of Kant's contribution, the synthesis of empiricism and rationalism resolves the impasse between the two central opposing, though complementary, developments in the history of Western philosophy. These are based upon an orientation to fact and principle, respectively. Each embodies a valid insight, and both are necessary for science,[57] but their competing claims to primacy lead to two fatal forms of one-sidedness.

> On one side, we find a dogmatism where there is an abundant emphasis on a principle of organization and order, yet no relationship to actual experience. On the other, there is a scepticism that, while closely bound to sensuous immediacy, and thus fully recognizing the force of brute fact, affords no security or certainty with respect to those values most vital in human consciousness. These include uniformity and measurability of nature, the reality and persistence of the Self, and the actuality of the Divine.[58]

Against rationalism, and the whole morass of speculative metaphysics, Kant concludes that unaided pure reason is impotent to solve ontological problems or produce metaphysical knowledge.[59] However, empiricism cannot account for the certainty we have in the domain of pure mathematics and must allow for an active role by consciousness in determining knowledge occasioned by, but not derived from, experience.[60] "The basic structure of human thought is an a priori determinant of the world that we think."[61] Because consciousness functions to integrate experience within a unified whole, according to a priori forms, we may "have confidence in the orderliness of experience."[62] In sum, Wolff's account of the main outline of Kant's contribution appears to be unexceptionable.

Primordial Reason

Even though Kant ostensibly restricts his philosophy to the domain of sense perception and conceptual cognition, Wolff detects evidence of at least partial realization: "In the instance of Immanuel Kant we have a genuine, if not complete, Realization."[63] Wolff contends that he "attained something of Recognition through Manas,"[64] and that "Kant knew the Self, else he could never have conceived of pure apperceptive Consciousness."[65] Anyone who penetrates and grasps the essential meaning of the phrase "the synthetic, transcendental unity of pure apperception" has attained Recognition.[66] It may seem odd to associate Kant with the mystics, even if his familiarity with apperception strongly hints at an adumbration of mystical consciousness. Nevertheless, even though Wolff characterizes his mind as scientific rather than mystical,[67] he contends that "buried deep in Kant's thought lies the Recognition."[68] It would be akin in nature to Wolff's first realization, which was mental rather than Fundamental, but without the necessity for similar interpretation or terminology. Whether his nonstandard interpretation of Kant is correct is of secondary importance, for nothing crucial hinges on it. What is relevant is the effect of this view on Wolff.

Kant stands at the foundation of German idealism, which is the Western philosophical school most consonant with East Indian philosophy.

> The high valuation that Kant has generally been assigned by the philosophers who succeeded him is no more than just, if for no other reason than that it was he who found the way out of the impasse that philosophy had reached. . . . Furthermore, Kant is significant in a considerably larger sense than that of synthesizing the Western philosophic stream, for it was he who opened the way to the bridging of understanding between the Western and Oriental minds. This latter service was not so much contributed directly by Kant, who was not, and never claimed to be, a metaphysician, as by the main stream of philosophy that was founded upon and received impetus from his most fundamental conceptions, namely, German Idealism, or rather, spiritualism.[69]

Wolff contends that an adequate understanding of idealism requires a feeling for the religious problem as fundamental,[70] as well as an essential grasp of Introception.[71] This is because the true goal of freedom of consciousness is not mere liberty from external constraint, but Liberation. In the religious sense, Liberation involves a transformation of consciousness, whose noetic aspect is Introception. More specifically, Wolff regards the insight of the great idealists as evidence for the activity of the Introceptive function. He claims that it is this transcendental immediacy that they knew personally from which their authority is derived. When united with the conceptual function, it yields the basis of their movement.[72]

He contrasts the notion of primordial Reason, as an ontological principle of Law teleologically and structurally ordering the cosmos, to the epistemological ratiocinative process (the activity of reasoning).[73] He characterizes the former as objective, the latter as subjective—apprehension as opposed to comprehension; "knowledge through acquaintance," rather than definitive "knowledge-about"; simple, and thus known all at once as a whole, not as a sequential process. Primordial Reason must be conceived to preexist experience and the relative consciousness, whereas the manifestation of ratiocination depends on experience. Accordingly, both primordial Reason and perceptual experience may serve as a source for concepts, thus making possible a transempirical dimension to knowledge.

Wolff accounts for the problem of its cognition by establishing the necessity for the minimal assumption that there exist ways of cognition beyond the common range. "For the purposes of formal discourse, once we assume or postulate the appropriate cognitive means, then we can accept, in principle, the possibility of direct apperception of a pure Reason, or of a Reason that is preexistent with respect to experience."[74] The further vital inquiry, from mere possibility to immediate actuality, requires firsthand experience, insofar as there can be neither discursive proof nor disproof.

> No attempt will be made here to *prove* the actuality of means of cognition that are not generally active, for such proof is quite unnecessary with respect to those who possess these powers, and it is impossible in the case of those who lack them. It is merely pointed out that the existence of such powers must be assumed if a primary understanding of idealism is ever to be attained.[75]

Wolff does not mention that there are related cases of nonordinary cognition that are subject to empirical investigation and demonstration. Zen archery, for example, in which an archer hits a target in a completely darkened room, would seem to establish the actuality of some form of extrasensory perception or other sort of parapsychological cognition. However, the evidence in the case of primordial Reason would be restricted to immediate awareness.

Idealism has been criticized as empty abstractionism devoid of content. However, if Wolff is correct, lack of empiric content does not imply lack of content in every sense, and if Introception does supply a transempiric content—even though not explicitly stated by the idealists—then idealism would avoid this charge.[76] Of course, the detection of mystical insight when veiled within philosophical discourse is quite difficult, even for a mystic. However, this interpretation is highly plausible and would provide a basis for making idealism a formidable alternative to realism or pragmatism. Wolff believes that idealism is rooted in Introception, a function of consciousness other than sensation, feeling, thinking, or intuition (the four primary functions detailed by analytic psychology). He further suggests that idealists generally have failed to appreciate the nature of their experiential source.[77] Thus understood, Kantian and subsequent NeoKantian developments conceal the mystical as their true ground. Still, whereas idealistic systems stand in need of this sort of grounding, Wolff would admit that any coercive attempt to demonstrate this foundation as a fact must fall short.

Personally, he acknowledges a great debt to Kant as the Western writer "who did most to prepare the Way."[78] "Without him I might have *experienced*, but I could not have understood nearly so well the Meaning unfolded through the Transition."[79] Furthermore, Kant's Copernican shift from the object to the subject, which was of such great moment in the history of Western philosophy, prepared the way for Wolff's Copernican revolution. Specifically, it is the fundamental reorientation from the subject-to-consciousness to consciousness itself. Wolff takes pains to differentiate Introceptualism, his systematic philosophy, from idealism understood as spiritualism—the orientation to that (spirit, subject, or other sort of entity) which is conscious. For Wolff, consciousness is not an attribute of something else, but has ontological primacy—that is, it is self-existent and underived.[80]

Upon accepting Kant's challenge to demonstrate how metaphysical knowledge might be possible, Wolff sought both a theoretical solution and a practical, experiential confirmation. The key to success he found in the inspiration of Śaṃkara.

ŚAṂKARA

Advaita Vedānta

Śrī Śaṃkarācārya (c. 788–820 C.E.), called "a savior of the Hindu world" by Nikhilānanda,[81] propounds a nondualistic interpretation of the *Upaniṣads*, the *Brahmasūtras*, and the *Bhagavadgīta*, the fundamental scriptures of the Vedānta. Eliot Deutsch considers the Advaita Vedānta to be the most widely accepted philosophical system in India, as well as "one of the greatest philosophical achievements to be found in the East or the West."[82] Nikhilānanda claims that it "is the supreme Hindu contribution to the philosophical wisdom of the world."[83]

As Wolff observes, the strict meaning of *advaita* is *nondual.* This is a more precise characterization of Śaṃkara's position than is monism (as it is popularly regarded), for "in the strict sense, the inner core of this philosophy is neither monistic nor non-monistic."[84] Deutsch notes that this terminological refinement is designed to distinguish Śaṃkara's system "from any position that views reality as a single order of *objective* being. Advaita Vedānta is concerned to show the ultimate nonreality of all distinctions."[85]

This subtle point is difficult to comprehend, but exceedingly important for an accurate appraisal of Śaṃkara's philosophy. The usual interpretation of his position as monistic invites criticism that nondualism avoids. This distinction is even more crucial in understanding Wolff, for his philosophy, ultimately derived from his second Fundamental Realization, must be characterized as nondualistic, rather than monistic.

Wolff regards Śaṃkara as "the *philosopher* Sage, par excellence,"[86] who wrote primarily for his *brahmin* class, who typically were priests, scholars, and introverts.[87] He insisted upon four qualifications for those worthy of entering into such discussion:

1. true discrimination of permanent and impermanent things
2. indifference to the enjoyment of the fruits of one's actions both here and hereafter
3. possession of *samā* (calmness) and the other five qualities
4. an intense desire of becoming liberated (from material existence).[88]

Because few could be expected to satisfy such requirements, these criteria define an elite group, which would imply that his teachings were not intended for the masses. Rather, Śaṃkara became a "Teacher of Teachers."[89]

Nikhilānanda states that "according to Śaṃkarācārya, the sole purpose of the *Upanishads* is to prove the reality of Brahman. . . . the Absolute, which transcends time, space, and causality. . . . and the phenomenality or unreality of the universe of names and forms and to establish the absolute oneness of the embodied soul and Brahman."[90] Although Wolff does not explicitly refer to any particular text in this regard, his avowed attraction to Śaṃkara's thought directs us to examples with which he would almost certainly be familiar. Consider, for instance, the discussion of the *Turīya* state in the *Māndukya Upaniṣad.*

> *Turīya* is not that which is conscious of the inner (subjective) world, nor that which is conscious of the outer (objective) world, nor that which is conscious of both, nor that which is a mass of consciousness. It is not simple consciousness nor is It unconsciousness. It is unperceived, unrelated, incomprehensible, uninferable, unthinkable, and indescribable. The essence of the Consciousness manifesting as the self [in the three states], It is the cessation of all phenomena; It is all peace, all bliss, and nondual. This is what is known as the Fourth (*Turīya*). This is *Ātman*, and this has to be realized.[91]

Since this ultimate truth is incomprehensible to the bare intellect, escaping adequate formulation, only direct experience under a competent teacher is capable of revealing it.[92] Wolff contends that Śaṃkara derives his system from his own mystical Realization, and that "the logical presentation of his system is incidental to a primary insight."[93]

Ramlal Singh supports A. C. Mukerji's position that Śaṃkara's epistemology is rational intuitionism, rather than antirational mysticism.*[94] Mysticism is more correctly regarded as nonrational rather than antirational (irrational). The antirational is the antithesis of the rational, whereas the nonrational may be thought of as a synthesis from a more inclusive perspective. Śaṃkara presents his philosophy "as a clarification and explicit logical development of the Vedic meaning," but the fundamental understanding of the Veda is of "the innate Wisdom resident in the depths of all consciousness,"[95] prior to all formulation. Superior formulation requires the combination of "*yogic* penetration, scholarship and the development of intellectual acuity and profundity,"[96] namely, the mystical genius of a Śaṃkara.

He sees the central problem in terms of ignorance, specifically, taking the phenomenal appearance for the ultimately real,

---

*"An Advaitic Emendation of Kant: A Study in Comparative Metaphysics," *Indian Philosophical Quarterly* 6 (October 1978):175–83.

the solution of which is the attainment of Knowledge of the Self (*Ātmavidyā*), which results in Liberation (*mokṣa*). Liberation is release from *karma* (the necessary reflexive effects of one's actions) by the Realization of identity between pure self and the ultimate, nondual reality. The phenomenal world appears as illusory from this perspective, insofar as it purports to be ultimate to ordinary, unillumined consciousness, but is Realized to be nonultimate. Ramakant Sinari claims that this "knowledge founded on the self-luminosity of pure consciousness represents the central quest of his Vedānta method."[97] For no other figure, so far as Wolff knows, "is the noetic element in the *yogic* consciousness so fundamental."[98] The common thesis advanced by both Wolff and Śaṃkara is that mystical insight provides knowledge in the sense of Gnosis, which, in this context, means esoteric knowledge based on intuition, rather than reason. Similarly, conceptual thought has a high place for each. Wolff calls it the "Royal Path of Yoga,"[99] in which the concept serves as viceroy to the Introcept.[100] For Śaṃkara, it "represents an unavoidable stage of discipline leading to the highest form of experience in which the ultimate reality becomes self-luminous and self-revealed."[101]

Wolff's Independent Formulation

Wolff honors Śaṃkara's thought as the overshadowing influence catalyzing his breakthrough[102] and "had spontaneously looked to him as to a *guru*,"[103] for he felt great rapport with his thought and temperament.[104] He found his writings to be of the highest potency,[105] his analysis of consciousness clear and convincing.[106] He says, "I found myself in striking agreement with the more fundamental phases of his thought and quite willing to apply the highly intellectual technique that he had charted."[107]

His uncanny affinity for this philosophy and methodology seems only partially explained by its appeal to the introverted intuitive-thinking psychological type (according to the Jungian typology),[108] which ideally suited his character. However, his distancing from Śaṃkara in his later work would appear to be the greater mystery, for his connection to this sage was stronger than to any other. Wolff explains that it was *because* of this attraction that he feared becoming a mere continuation of the Vedānta philosophy.

Therefore, he decided to unfold his indigenous expression based on the five realizations.[109]

Moreover, it would be accurate to characterize Śaṃkara's influence on Wolff's thought as the final impetus to his mystical breakthrough of the first Fundamental Realization. This effected a transformation in consciousness without essentially altering his conceptual understanding. Shortly thereafter, the spontaneous advent of his second Fundamental Realization so vastly superseded the first that it required a radical revision of his entire philosophy, reoriented to this base. The Vedāntin model, as he then understood it in terms of the Realization of the Self (*Ātman*) as ultimate, did not easily lend itself to this more profound viewpoint.

MINOR INFLUENCES

Wolff also holds Plato, Carl Jung, the Buddha, and Śrī Aurobindo Ghose in high regard, although their philosophical influence on him is far less appreciable. Plato and Plotinus (as well as Neoplatonists generally) are exceptions to the sensuous-materialistic orientation of Ancient Greece.[110] Wolff traces the historical roots of idealism in the West to this source, for "with Plato we have the clear emergence of the conception of ideal elements as ontologically significant and determinant."[111] Even so, Plato owes much to Pythagoras, and though it was largely through him that the Pythagorean influence developed, Wolff values more highly the original source.

Similarly, Jung was strongly influenced by Kant, and it is the latter who most impressed Wolff. Jung's indispensable role lies in supplying a psychological viewpoint that is compatible with the Kantian philosophy. This makes his psychological influence quite significant, for not only does it provide a general theoretical understanding, but it is also of practical benefit in transforming consciousness. In addition, his treatment of symbols underlies Wolff's development of techniques for expressing and communicating his Realizations.

In Wolff's estimation, Gautama Siddhartha, the Buddha, stands as the outstanding exemplar of the balance between knowledge and compassion.[112] Most notably, the Buddha's selfless renunciation of an ecstatic withdrawal from the world so as to assist humanity resolve the problem of suffering inspired Wolff to adopt and advocate the Bodhisattva Vow. In so doing, the individual thereby renounces permanent Salvation (the state of *Parinirvāṇa*) until all sentient beings whatsoever have been saved (Liberated). He had not personally made this vow before his realizations, but he believes that it was his compassionate commitment to be of service to humanity that effectively determined his return from both Fundamental Realizations. In this light, the influence of the Buddha seems to be primarily ethical, rather than philosophical—but, without it, Wolff might never have written his philosophy.

Aurobindo, a contemporary influence, only came to Wolff's prominent attention several years after he had completed his central works, so he is not relevant to Wolff's early development. His primary significance is to reinforce and confirm certain insights that Wolff attained independently. For example, Aurobindo's discussion of Knowledge by Identity[113] exhibits a close parallel to Wolff's notion of Knowledge-through-Identity, and his universal realism tempers and balances the otherworldliness of Śaṃkara's universal illusionism.[114]

SUMMARY

Wolff began in the Pythagorean spirit as a philosopher-mathematician seeking wisdom through the fusion of science and religion. Within Pythagoras's theoretical, conceptual, and mathematical orientation, he found numinous value, and in mathematical analogy he discovered a valuable tool for expressing experiences that defy description. Kant supplied the element of critical thought in his attempt to establish sound foundations by grounding metaphysics in epistemology. Wolff integrated Kant's critical approach, as well as his epistemological focus on the subject, rather than the object. Ultimately, he would extend Kant's revolution in philosophy by proposing that primacy belongs neither to the subject nor to the object, but to consciousness itself. Wolff's penultimate Realization, inspired by Śaṃkara's doctrine of *Ātmavidyā*, resulted from his intentional radical inversion of the natural object-oriented direction of conscious awareness. He thus Recognized the intrinsic identity of the Self as the Pure Subject. Consequently, he credits Śaṃkara with pointing the way to mystical transformation, and the attainment of the metaphysical knowledge that Kant allowed was theoretically possible.

Notwithstanding the seminal value of certain elements of Oriental thought in catalyzing his realizations, Wolff regards Eastern means as inappropriate for Western culture. He generally agrees with F. S. C. Northrop that the East is oriented to the aesthetic, to direct feelings, whether sensuous or emotional.[115] Wolff acknowledges that the dichotomy of East and West is not so clear-cut in the case of India, for its Aryan ancestry and the presence of diverse discursive schools of philosophy are more characteristic of the West. However, he notes that Indian conceptuality is primarily metaphysical, rather than mathematical—an important distinction.

Pythagoras, in contrast, exhibits a great love of knowledge or scientific wisdom and strikes the keynote of the West, which is mathematical and theoretical.[116] This explains Wolff's return to the essence of Pythagoreanism in his attempt to develop a truly Western approach oriented to the concept. He believes that it is important to adopt a method that is attuned to the psychical structure of the individual and that therefore Oriental methodologies generally will be unsuccessful when applied to Occidental culture.[117]

Nevertheless, emphasis on the highly developed intellect does not mean exclusive restriction, for otherwise Enlightenment would remain one-sided. He claims that one needs both Eros and Logos for full Enlightenment, "for the one-sided Enlightenment through the understanding is weak in Compassion, and thus falls short of the highest possibility."[118] Because the intellect dominates in the West, love requires cultivation if it is to rise beyond mere sentimentality. Fortunately, one may use attainment in wisdom to assist in the development of compassion.

Wolff incorporates mathematical, epistemological, metaphysical, and ethical elements into his own philosophical system, using his aptitude for analysis, but devoted to dynamic synthesis. The power of his personal mystical insight infuses his formulation, and however much affinity he feels for other systems, he has found none that coincides in all significant respects with his own. Nonetheless, he recognizes a certain essential identity with every authentic philosophy that is also ultimately rooted in Transcendental Realization—that which Wolff refers to as "Primordial Consciousness," "Root Consciousness," or "Consciousness-without-an-object and without-a-subject."

CHAPTER 3

Realization

THE NATURE OF MYSTICAL REALIZATION

One might surmise that for the spiritual aspirant Wolff's narrative account of his realizations and the aphorisms that he formulated from them comprise his greatest legacy. In contrast, the philosophical scholar most likely will prefer to contemplate and evaluate his systematic philosophy. In any event it would be a mistake to treat it simply as a system derived from philosophical speculation, for he explicitly emphasizes that it is a conceptual expression of his Realizations (or Recognitions), which constitute the fundamental ground for his philosophy. He asserts that "the essential elements of the formulation could not be derived by a reference to experience in the sense of sensuous experience, nor on the basis or the purely logical necessity, nor finally by a combination of these two."[1] For the proper understanding of Introceptualism it is absolutely necessary to be aware of the nature of its foundation in what he terms "Fundamental Realization." He states its importance unequivocally:

> It must be borne in mind that without these realizations there would be no reason for the writing or dictating of this philosophy. They are fundamental to it. It has been pointed out that other material has a place within the philosophy, but the realizations are the prime epistemic determinants. That point must not be forgotten, if one is to understand the bearing of the present statement.[2]

Wolff insists that "it is because of this cycle of Recognitions, and only because of them, that the resultant philosophy stands on a much more fundamental basis than mere speculative system-building. It is not a philosophy of mere arbitrary concepts, but a reflection in the form of a philosophic symbol of a realized Reality."[3] He contends that whatever is given in experience is, in some sense, real and that concepts designed to mediate an experienced reality are grounded in that experience. Thus it is far more likely to be adequate to that domain than would be a schema that is purely speculative. This is even more true when the process of concept formation *results from* the experience in question, and where such experience appears to transcend our ordinary range of awareness in a positive or exalted sense. He further holds that the nature of the apprehended reality is the determining factor in whether a conceptual system can describe, only symbolize, or altogether fail to represent it. Therefore, Wolff's philosophy must be understood to be grounded, in this sense, on his realizations—his own immediate, mystical awareness.

His conceptually mediated account of these realizations is the indispensable prerequisite for considering its philosophical implications. Furthermore, we can determine the status of the knowledge claims about the nature of Wolff's experiences, or grounded in it, only after presenting a descriptive formulation of the relevant biographical material, as well as his critical reflections on the process of its interpretation.

He designates only his final two Realizations as Fundamental. The other three, which were propaedeutic or preliminary, are mental. For the most part, he distinguishes between mental realizations and Transcendental (Fundamental) Realizations by approximating Aurobindo's treatment. Whereas the meaning of the essential content of the former permits adequate conceptual formulation, the immediate quale of the content of the latter is incommunicable.[4] Mental realization is characterized by a flash of insight that internalizes a conceptual content and illuminates it in a manner that mere intellectual acknowledgment of its correctness lacks. "In analyzing the difference between the recognition and the theoretical acceptance without recognition, it seems that in the latter instance there is a quality that might be called mediative distance, while in the case of recognition there is the closeness of immediacy."[5] It is an intuitive flash or conceptual breakthrough (a "Eureka!") that impacts upon the person with the force of a religious revelation. The inspiration that produced St. Anselm's Ontological Argument, and Descartes's Cogito are examples of this sort of occurrence. Transcendental Realization, such as the Buddha's Enlightenment under the bodhi tree, involves a "fundamental shift in one's essential orientation (as, for example, in the basic sense of 'I') . . . a radical surrender, sacrifice or mystical death."[6] Not only is Fundamental Realization Illuminative, but it is also existentially transformative. In addition, it carries a supernal value that far exceeds anything arising from ordinary experience. Wolff testifies that "only Transcendental Realization is worth any price."[7]

DESCRIPTION AND INTERPRETATION

Wolff's initial purpose in writing a descriptive narration of these episodes, the conditions and circumstances leading up to and surrounding them, and their subsequent effects is to provide an autobiographical dimension that is usually lacking in mystical literature. He intends thereby "to establish a ground of knowledge upon which the body of subsequent interpretation is largely based. This mainly descriptive-narrative statement is to be understood as having the same methodological significance that attaches to the laboratory record in the development of scientific theoretical interpretation."[8]

In theory we may easily resolve the problem of discriminating between descriptive and interpretative statements concerning an individual's actual experience. Description is limited to the phenomena of which the person is immediately aware. Interpretation goes beyond what is directly presented to consciousness by introducing such considerations as explanations, causes, consequences, implications, inferences, and further experiences to be expected. In practice, however, Wolff explains how interpretative elements may be introduced, not only upon subsequent reflection, but as part of the experience itself.

> It has come to my mind that the reader might be inclined to question whether this account may be called a narrative description, . . . since so much of the writing is manifestly discursive. However, it really is narrative description, on the whole, since it is a record of a process of thought that took place and had vitally determinant

> effects in the past. Only in subsidiary degree is this autobiographical material related to the objective life of a physical personality. In much higher degree is it an autobiography of intellectual steps and processes. Thus the discursive material that appears here is primarily not interpretative after fact, but rather part of a process in which interpretative factors were traceably determinant in my own consciousness as it became more and more oriented to the transformation. These interpretations were pragmatically effective agents. Whether or not they have a larger objective truth-value is not the question that is before us at present.[9]

Wolff has expressed explicitly his intention to relate this primary material as free from interpretation as possible. Thus it is reasonable to regard his narrative, including what seem to be interpretative passages, as primarily descriptive of his actual awareness of these central episodes in his process of transformation.

What distinguishes Fundamental Realization is that it transcends adequate conceptual understanding, which implies that no verbal formulation can be strictly descriptive, but this does not imply that it is meaningless. We shall defer until chapter 5 full consideration of the problem of mystical language. For our present purposes it will be sufficient to adopt the presumption of meaningfulness for language when used in an extended sense as metaphorical or analogical, where the intent is still to provide an uninterpreted account of immediate awareness.

Wolff's inclusion of the reports of his realizations is unique in the development of a mystically based philosophy. Our primary objective in this chapter is to present the essential features of Wolff's five realizations, out of which he developed his philosophy. The truncated version presented here has selectively deleted all but the most relevant features of his accounts, supplemented by appropriate commentary.

I AM *ĀTMAN*

One evening[10] a friend was outlining a systematic method for discriminating between self and not-self, showing that the Self, as such, is identical to the *Ātman*. Wolff had personally employed this method in the past and had previously accepted its logical soundness in theory. In fact, he considered its culminating judgment, "I am *Ātman*," to be a virtual tautology. He had understood *Ātman* to mean "a spiritual 'Self' conceived as being the irreducible center of consciousness on which all knowledge or consciousness in the relative sense depended."[11] In addition, he regarded the 'I' as identical to the 'Self',[12] not the ego.[13]

According to the approach of the Vedānta, the principle of individuation is *ahaṃkāra*—literally, "I-maker"—which Wolff equates with egoistic consciousness. "This is the consciousness of one's self as distinct from other selves. The feeling of 'I am I and none other'."[14] One might understand this as the sense of ourselves related to personal identity. It is based on the identification with the phenomenal self or empirical ego and is the objective referent of the pronoun *me.* In contrast, based on his first and fourth Realizations, he defines the *Ātman* as "the 'Self', the 'I', the 'I AM' and the 'subjective moment of consciousness'."[15]

> I have heard that *Ātman* has had a different meaning with others who have thought about the subject. I want to make it perfectly clear that this is the meaning given by the first realization and the fourth realization. It is the pure subject to consciousness, which in its first appearance is like a point surrounded by the universe of objects, both subtle and gross.[16]

Wolff stresses that he uses the term *I* to indicate the pure subject-to-consciousness devoid of any objective elements whatsoever. The point is that 'I', the "*Ātman,* the Pure Self or subject to consciousness . . . can never become an object before consciousness,"[17] no matter how gross or subtle. He acknowledges that defining *Ātman* as the subjective moment of consciousness is nonstandard but regards his realizations as taking precedence over any scholarly source because they provide immediate certainty, before interpretation.

Wolff uses the concept of a mathematical point to help convey his understanding of Self-Realization.

> This Realization of the Self may be represented by a point which has position but has no mass or volume. In other words, mass and volume can suggest an objective existence, something that can be objectively known; that being a pure point symbolizes the fact that it can be known only through identity and not by being aware of an object in any sense before consciousness. It is a subtle other way of cognition; I am the pure subject. Everything else that may be associated, no matter how intimately, with this person, is an object before this consciousness and therefore is not I.[18]

Positionality here is not to be construed objectively in the sense that the position of an object is determined by its relations to other objects. The 'I' need not be aware of any actual object, only that all objects (actual and possible) would appear as 'other' and would be viewed from a certain perspective. It is part of the awareness that the Pure Subject has of itself as subject.

On the occasion of his first realization, he recognized it as a profound truth of the highest significance. He avows that "in this case I suddenly seemed to Realize, with certainty, that, in fact, 'I am Identical with the *Ātman*'."[19] The realization had been prepared by theoretical approval, but was vastly different in nature and effect, though he experienced no change in thinkable content.[20] The difference was that between a quality of immediacy and one of mediative distance.[21] He felt an overwhelming assurance that was lacking in the case of conclusions reached by ordinary intellectual labor, such that "I knew the truth of the thought and did not merely *believe* in it."[22] Belief resulting from persuasion by discursive argument is always vulnerable to more complete evidence or better reasoning. Because fundamental conviction is grounded in insight (a religious phenomenon), it has absolute authority for the individual's orientation within its apprehended domain, and only a more profound or comprehensive realization can modify it. Naturally, this applies only from the viewpoint of the mystic. There was something added that was nonlogical, though not antilogical (illogical), for there was "an increased clarity in the apperception of the logical implications that followed."[23] He says that it is neither conceptual nor perceptual in nature, for it "belongs to some other dimension of consciousness."[24] There is a new Light that clarifies much that was previously obscure.[25] This additional Somewhat is known directly, but not as an element of the content of thought. Yet something of its nature may be conveyed by considering its effects upon the personal consciousness.

Most remarkably, Wolff found as an objective effect "that the thought flowed more spontaneously, more acutely, and with much greater assurance. The thought developed of itself, in high degree, without the sense of conscious labor."[26] As a result he found himself thinking what were essentially fundamental propositions of the *Bhagavadgīta,* with which hitherto he had only a bare acquaintance and not much sympathy.[27] He now "Realized them as obviously true, . . .

a source of Light and expansion,"[28] and found "a joyous and freedom-giving value."[29] Whereas it might just as easily manifest in new discoveries, the additional something that is added in Recognition would not be revealed by analyzing the stream of thought that led to it.[30] Wolff regards this "change in the base of thought" to be the most significant consequence of the Recognition.[31]

He found the value dimension in consciousness most radically affected, deepened, and intensified. Without the sense of supernal value that is aroused, one remains aware only of the surface configuration. According to Wolff, those who have awakened to this value dimension in consciousness will be aware of a depth to the form "over and above the concept, . . . that makes all the difference in the world!"[32] The effect upon his mind, along with the transcendental values, was of an "insemination," a vitalization and rejuvenation.[33] Consciousness was enriched, but although there was joy, it was not "the Current of Joy."[34] The effect of this momentary flash of insight persisted in both intellect and valuation, although feelings and actions would later often prove to be inconsistent with this recognition because not all aspects of the personal being were equally affected.

I AM *NIRVĀṆA*

Wolff's second premonitory recognition occurred (around November 1935) while he was meditating on the concept of '*Nirvāṇa*'.[35] It suddenly dawned on him "that *Nirvāṇa* is not a field, or space, or world which one entered and that contained one as space might contain an external object, but rather that 'I am identical with *Nirvāṇa*, and always have been and always will be so'."[36] It is the "Real Self,"[37] the inmost sense of I,[38] that is thus identical: "All that the individual . . . achieves is Recognition of this eternal fact."[39]

It is significant that unlike his first realization, the judgment in which it expressed itself did not conform with an antecedently held position. Rather, it constituted a new cognitive discovery that corrected his error of thinking of *Nirvāṇa* as another world separate from that of relative consciousness. Wolff now saw clearly that *Nirvāṇa* could not be in the relative manifold because it is, like "the inner core of the 'I', . . . not an objective existence but is, rather, the 'thread' upon which the objective material of consciousness is strung."[40] He now saw that the contrast between *Nirvāṇa* and *saṃsāra* reflected the contrast between the subject-to-consciousness and the object of consciousness, so that not merely was there a correspondence between the self and *Nirvāṇa*, but an identity. "*Nirvāṇa*, like the 'I', cannot be located anywhere, as in a distinct place, for it is at once everywhere and nowhere, both in space and time."[41] It is that upon which all experience and all forms that structure experience within relative consciousness depend. It would follow that attaining *Nirvāṇa* could never be the result of causes or conditions set up within the relative realm of *saṃsāra*, but the paradox of attainment dissolves when one realizes that the inmost sense of Self is already identical to the goal that one seeks. Wolff detects in this insight the hidden meaning contained in the subtle wisdom of the ancient Greek maxim "Know Thyself."[42]

Even though this recognition, like the first, was mental, rather than fundamental, it had effects that persisted in his personal or egoic consciousness.[43] There was "a deepening and illumining effect in the dimension of value"[44] and a realization of Joy in the sense of a Current, which for some time he could invoke at will.[45] He also noticed the capacity to trust spontaneous formulation while lecturing, during which time the attention of the audience was held in a deep stillness.[46] Finally, he experienced an intellectual rejuvenation partly resulting from this episode.[47]

SUBSTANTIALITY IS INVERSELY PROPORTIONAL TO PONDERABILITY

Wolff regards his third mental realization (c. 31 July 1936)[48] as the turning point in preparing his consciousness for the ensuing Illumination. "It altered the base of thought and valuation in a profound way and in a direction confirmed by the subsequent realization."[49] Initially, he afforded it the lesser status of an important idea, but as its full conceptual elaboration unfolded, a process spanning several years, he came to appreciate its true nature.[50] This implies that one may not immediately identify a mental realization as such.

For several weeks before this event, Wolff had developed a strong assurance and expectation that his search was near a successful outcome. Desiring solitude, he found time to penetrate deeply into *The System of the Vedānta* while prospecting near Michigan Bluff, California. While standing on the bank of a creek, looking at the sky above the mountains, it occurred to him that we seek the Real in the direction of the content of sensuous experience, and the immediate pointing of our concepts to that which we immediately perceive.[51] However, it is a fundamental error to attribute Reality to the object of cognition,[52] insofar as "ponderable matter . . . is, in fact, a relative absence of substance, a sort of partial vacuum."[53] He reports:

> In my reflecting upon the idea that this universe of things is derived from and dependent upon a primordial plenum, it suddenly struck me that in the midst of the bare and original fullness there could be nothing to arouse discrete or concrete consciousness. . . . Now, if it is relative emptiness that arouses to activity concrete consciousness, then it follows that actual substantiality is inversely proportional to sensibility or ponderability.[54] Sensible presentments and conceptual representations in that moment acquired the value of voidness, surrounded by a fullness that is forever hidden to a consciousness operating *exclusively* under those forms.[55]

Whereas the content of previous realizations were Vedāntin in nature, this one exhibited a strong theoretical component.[56] Wolff quickly found that the insight "Substantiality is inversely proportional to ponderability" (or "Reality is inversely proportional to appearance") readily lends itself to the mathematical formulation $S = 1/P$ where S is Substantiality and P is Ponderability, or $R = 1/A$ where R represents Reality and A stands for Appearance. This is equivalent to the general formula for the equilateral hyperbola $PS = 1$. His mathematical interpretation of what is essentially a metaphysical insight is nonlogical, for neither substantiality nor ponderability is scientifically quantifiable. Instead, it functions psychologically to give a thinkable analogue. What is more important, it helped to catalyze the process of transformation and integration through the subsequent development of his mandala (a visual representation of this insight, employing symmetrical geometric forms).

This realization appeared as a major new discovery, impressing itself upon him with the force of a delightful revelation and effecting a psychological conversion.[57] He experienced deep assurance and an affective quality of "Light."[58] Of greater importance than the idea was the effect on consciousness, loosening his habitual world view and coming to experience the world more in accordance with this insight. Wolff thus was able to surmount the final "residual barriers to the complete identification of the self with the supersensible and substantial world, accompanied by the thorough divorcement of the self-identity with the phenomenal world."[59]

He found three psychological points of interest concerning this realization:

1. His work during this period required that he spend considerable time underground. He later discovered that it was a common Oriental practice to place within caves those preparing for the process of transformation, often for considerable periods. According to the Jungian theory, this has the "value of entering the womb of the Great Mother Unconsciousness, preliminary to the Rebirth."[60] It makes no difference whether it is spontaneous (for example, hypnogogic vision or dream) or induced through ritual. For Wolff, this appears to have been an effective catalyst.
2. The subsequent unfoldment of his mandala exemplifies the process of integration of consciousness with the psychological unconscious.[61]
3. At the time of the realization, he believed it to have no theoretical antecedents, but later found that previously he had read the following passage in *The Voice of the Silence*: "Thou has to study the voidness of the seeming full, the fullness of the seeming void."[62]

I AM *THAT*

On the evening of 7 August 1936, approximately one week after his third realization, Wolff made the "breakthrough" into Transcendental Consciousness—his first of two Fundamental Realizations. After having returned from seclusion he "remained in a state of considerable mental detachment and continued brooding."[63] As he began reflective meditation upon Śaṃkara's discussion on Liberation, it suddenly dawned upon him that he had been making the common error in meditation of "seeking . . . a subtle object or experience. . . . [which] remains a phenomenal time-space existence and therefore is other than the supersensible substantiality."[64] He concluded that the goal was a state of pure objectless subjectivity, but that this did not require the absolute cessation of subject-object consciousness.

Consequently, he attempted to abstract by discriminative isolation, and focus awareness within, the purely subjective side of relative, subject-object consciousness. Discriminative isolation is essentially the same process that his first realization involved: the 'I' is really experienced as distinct from the 'not-I'. He simply adapted his practical method from Śaṃkara's technique of *Ātma-vidyā*, knowledge of the Self. The traditional method involves a gradual disidentification of the self from all objects, gross and subtle, by successively coming to experience all else as other than I, in the sense of the Pure Self. Since Wolff's actual procedure varies in specific ways, we should consider his most comprehensive account.

> The one essential principle of conscious method, insofar as the seeking of realization was concerned, was the use of self-analysis for the identification of that which I really am. . . . The isolation of the self, the *Ātman*, involved certain subtleties that were not uncovered and understood until after the passage of some years. The breaking of self-identification with anything that is objective proved to be quite easy, but the identification of that which, in reality, I am proved to have certain real difficulties. Usually in the action of our consciousness we may think of it as a flow from the subjective pole, which ordinarily we know only by inference, toward an objective content. To know is to have a content in consciousness such as an idea or a sense impression. It would thus appear correct to say that consciousness in this relative sense, that is, our common reference in the use of the term, has a vector quality, a direction of flow. The ultimate secret to the discovery of the self lay in a step which we might describe this way: Conceiving of this relative consciousness as a vector flow from an inferred subject to an object of consciousness, then reverse that vector flow by turning it through the angle π, so that it returns toward its source without projecting an object in consciousness, no matter how subtle. It becomes a consciousness concerned only with its source, and with this step it is possible to isolate the pure subject-to-consciousness, not, bear it well in mind, by a projecting of it outwardly as an apparent object, but resting in it as a pure subject. It is as though that inversion of the directedness of the consciousness flow animated unconscious contents so that there was a build-up of an energy potential. The subject is realized, not as an object, but through a principle which we may call "Knowledge

> through Identity"—a knowing by being identical with that which is known.[65]

According to this view, relative or subject-object consciousness exhibits a polar structure in which attention is almost exclusively caught by the object-pole. Wolff's technique involves the deliberate withdrawal of attention from the object, allowing awareness to sink back, as it were, into the subject-pole. It would be misleading to say that it *focuses upon* the 'I', or Pure Subject, for this would suggest that the subject-pole (by whatever designation) is really an object of a different sort. This he takes pains to deny.

The preliminary phase culminated in the "very clear realization that *there was nothing to be attained.*"[66] He resolved this apparent paradox of Enlightenment by this transitional realization, "I am already That which I seek, and therefore, there is nothing to be sought."[67] He distinguishes this transitional phase as a mental realization,[68] quickly deepening to the Fundamental Realization represented here by the aphorism "I Am That." Mystics generally report that the culmination of their quest comes as a seemingly passive bestowal, or act of grace, rather than as an active achievement. Wolff contends that the causal efficacy of willed action lies solely within the *saṃsāric* state (relative consciousness), which is the domain of causality. No such means can lead to the *Nirvāṇic* state, which can only be Realized, because 'I' abide there already as the Self. Thus attainment is to know this in a sense that is immediate, and not merely conceptual.[69]

For Wolff this was a moment of profound insight: "I saw that genuine Recognition is simply a realization of Nothing, but a Nothing that is absolutely substantial and identical with the SELF."[70] He found that it constituted a more profound reaffirmation of his first realization, "I am *Ātman*,"[71] differing more in affective value than in cognitive content. Whereas his initial realization had provided a portentous mental insight, this Realization constituted a real transformation involving "self-surrender, self-sacrifice and the mystical death."[72]

Here he broke through to a nonconceptual cognition. At the threshold, Wolff found the capacity for description strained to the utmost. "I found myself at once identical with the Voidness, Darkness, and Silence, but realized them as utter, though ineffable, Fullness, in the sense of Substantiality, Light, in the sense of Illumination, and Sound, in the sense of pure formless Meaning and Value."[73] The Light and Sound are clearly sensuous concepts employed with an exceptional meaning to suggest something of the nature of a state of consciousness that is radically nonsensuous. Beyond that point lies the ineffable, where language is simply incapable of describing the Transcendent.

This common difficulty of relating mystical experience is due to its intrinsic lack of multiplicity or distinguishable elements. Wolff notes that "this realization, as it is in itself, was wholly undifferentiated."[74] Yet such implications and consequences as follow from it may be formulated.

> The immediate noetic and affective values of the insight, while they may be directly realized, cannot be conveyed by any formulation or representation whatsoever.
>
> *A definite line of demarcation must be drawn between the transcendental state of consciousness itself and the precipitated effects within the relative consciousness.*[75]

Whereas the transcendental state of consciousness is a timeless Recognition or Awakening, and strictly speaking is beyond words, Wolff affirms that effects that are precipitated into the experienced spatiotemporal world of relative consciousness permit satisfactory formulation. "This realization . . . when reflected through the differentiated consciousness, had certain very discernible qualities."[76] His list of the salient features that he describes lends itself to the following arrangement.

Transcendence and Transformation

Shift in Base of Consciousness

Wolff calls the final step a "leap into Nothing." By the well-known psychological process of enantiodromia,[77] it immediately becomes utter Fullness apprehended noetically and affectively as the Real. By comparison, the relative world seems unreal, as if a dream. The result was a permanent transplanting of the roots of consciousness from the relative field to the supernal region.[78]

Transformation in the Meaning of 'Self', or 'I'

The process of discriminative meditation reveals the 'I', which is never an object, having position but no dimension, which he symbolizes as zero or "point-I." "The Self is no longer a pole or focal point, but it sweeps outward, everywhere, in a sort of unpolarized consciousness, which is at once self-identity and the objective content of consciousness. It is an unequivocal transcendence of the subject-object relationship."[79] At the critical stage of this Realization, he was aware of a discontinuity whence the I spread into unlimited thickness as all of space—as "Space-I." We must understand the sense of I here to be not merely individual, but universal—the Subject of all Consciousness.

Beyond Time, Space and Law

"As the substantial, spatial, and transcendent 'I' "[80] he 'knew' that the whole phenomenal universe or space-time manifold depended upon, and was sustained by, the Self—and that space, time and causality are forms that are imposed to make possible the experience of relative consciousness.

Identity with the Root of All

The transcendence of the forms of experience is also a Recognition of their Source. "Rising above space, time and law means fusing in identity with That from which space, time and law are derived. . . . [It] is, in some sense, ascension to the Root from which one's own being was derived."[81] In reality, nothing whatsoever is, or could be, separate from the Root of all, so it is not a matter of becoming reconnected with it, for one is already identical with it.

> The significance of this realization, therefore, means a re-establishment, as a conscious fact, of individual identity with the Root of all. In one sense, nothing has happened, for that identity is original and eternal, in point of fact, but has been forgotten as a truth for our surface consciousness. The realization therefore is an establishment in the surface consciousness of knowledge of an eternal fact. . . . But it makes all the difference in the world to

> know that I, along with every other self that there may be, is one with the Root source of all.[82]

Wolff prefers philosophical expression, but it is not implausible to equate its inmost meaning with that of several formulations from specific mystical traditions, for example, "*Ātman* is *Brahman*," and "Union with God."

Noetic Illumination

Illumination of Consciousness

Perhaps, above all, one could represent the state of consciousness as luminous. "In special degree, this is a consciousness that is fully luminous. The mind seems filled with light, and light pours through the being, illuminating it through and through."[83] Although the state virtually compels the use of light metaphors, it is important to note that this does not refer to a sensible light, as reported by St. Paul and St. John of the Cross, for instance.

Depth Penetration

There were two distinct phases of the initial stage of insight. The first, though highly noetic, is so extremely abstract and universal as to be superconceptual. Wolff characterizes it as "the compacted essence of thought,"[84] the objective unpacking of which would take eons. He was aware that he KNEW in this massive cosmic sense and felt its value.

The second phase absolutely transcends the extreme limits of both noesis and affection, even though a series of greater profundities is distinguishable. His self-identity remained intact as he plumbed "an impenetrable Darkness," which he knew as "the very essence of Light itself."[85]

New Base of Reference

It established a new epistemic ground in consciousness, insofar as "it determines a base of reference from which, henceforth, all is viewed—a new base quite different from that which had existed before."[86] From this new perspective, Wolff found

> a state of unbroken harmony, where all parts stand in perfect blending, a perfect relatedness. However distorted, crude, dissonant and even discordant may be the seeming of the play on the surface in the *saṃsāric* world, yet, behind that veil, there is a harmony unbroken and unbreakable—and this one knows. It is an experience of absolute perfection. All, everywhere, is as it should be in absolute completeness and beauty.[87]

From this new supermundane base of reference, the world appeared as a "mere phantasmagoria, having no substance, no reality. . . . worthy of no serious attention."[88] This felt devaluation of the *saṃsāric* realm would be rectified by his fifth Realization.

Knowledge through Identity

A nonanalytic sort of cognition spontaneously arose that was immediate, intuitive, and highly noetic, a "kind of intellection in which the concept is born spontaneously and has a curious identity with its object."[89] The resulting Knowledge is not mediated distance between a concept and its denoted object, but is rather "original and coextensive with a Recognizable, but nonexperiential, Reality."[90] Wolff suspects that personal orientation to cognition, rather than to affection or conation, induced the emphasis of this Realization on the noetic dimension of consciousness, because mystical literature supports this sort of correlation.

Metaphysical Resolution

All important metaphysical questions, including those posed by Kant concerning immortality, freedom, and God, are resolved here clearly and unambiguously. I know immediately that I am eternal, where *eternal* does not merely mean *everlasting*. "It says only that I, in my essentiality, am above the process of development and decay that are characteristic of time and all that is conditioned by time."[91] The question of freedom concerns the possibility that our actions are conditioned by external circumstances and by internal psychological factors, so that we wonder if we are truly free. This realization gives a positive answer, for one "finds himself identical with that which conditions all forms that are. The universal conditioner is not bound by its own conditioning."[92] As to the existence of God, psychologically the Realization was of a Supreme Value that had the character of a Principle or Law, although supremely beneficent and warmly intimate, as a friend. However, there was nothing to suggest the existence of a being corresponding to any theological conception of God, so the question becomes irrelevant.[93]

Radical Change in Significance and Value of Information

Formerly, acquired information was instrumental to the quest. Afterward, it was making manifest what was already known in a superconceptual sense, for "it seems as though, in an unseen and dark sense, I already know all that is to be known."[94] The value is one of revelation, to Wolff as well as to others, and the process serves to bring the cosmic thought to experiential clarification and elaboration.

Affective Exaltation

Liberation

"There was this deep sense that here Liberation had been achieved."[95] Wolff felt the transcendence of the law-governed space-time manifold as a release from bondage, and he accords the value of Freedom the highest importance within the affective range of experience.[96] Such a "feeling of freedom" might be interpreted as consistent with natural law, because mystics usually argue that their higher consciousness includes, without negating, what is rational and good in lower forms.

Release from Guilt

From the Self as the new base of reference, the feeling that the effects of one's past actions restrict one's future possibilities, the sense of guilt (sin; karmic bondage)[97] of the individual personality was totally dissolved. This affective value was instantaneous and immediate.

Solution of the 'Wrongness' of the World

The human condition of solitude and incompleteness, which Wolff believes to be the "driving motif of the religious quest,"[98] was overcome in a "fusion in identity" with what is sensed as Transcendent Otherness. This resolution to the sense of wrongness was a state of profound rest and contentment where full enjoyment required nothing more than the awakening within the knowledge of one's essential Divinity: "I saw one great Tragedy, the cause of all the rest, the failure of man to realize his own Divinity. I saw but one solution, the Realization of this Divinity."[99] However, because he experienced it as only a personal solution, the awareness of the suffering of the vast majority who had not yet attained this state prevented it from being wholly satisfactory.[100] His compassionate commitment to the ideal of actively striving for a general solution prevented Wolff from drifting into the "*Nirvāṇic* withdrawal" at that point.[101]

Calmness and Serenity

The affective qualities of calmness and serenity enveloped him, and no disturbance within the world-field had any power to destroy them. It was as if such events were irrelevant to his real being.[102]

Felicity

Wolff considers the state of felicity, the experience of supernal delight or Joy, to be the most notable affective quality precipitated from this Realization. It was a state of inconceivable, incommunicable delight![103] Within it he discerned the more specific qualities of inconceivable sweetness, self-existent beauty, and absolute purity—all quite beyond the comprehension of relative consciousness. Attainment is simply a matter of "turning from the object of, to the subject to, all relative consciousness, *plus the spontaneity of the SELF.*"[104] It manifests as a "Current of Joy," subtle, highly potent, and identical with virtue itself, appearing as a dynamic directionless force flowing through. He says, "It induces a sense of physiological, as well as emotional and intellectual, well-being."[105] He emphasizes that "in the Current lies the highest possible value which, from the relative standpoint, we call enjoyment."[106] Its value may only be inadequately suggested by his appraisal that "no cost could be too high as the price of its attainment."[107]

Benevolence

Associated with the Joy, he found Benevolence, "a spontaneous affective state born out of the very nature of the consciousness itself, without thought of an ethical imperative."[108] He characterizes it as "the consciousness of that which we designate by the word *love,* in its state of ultimate purity and completeness—a quality that is more than benevolence and compassion, though these qualities are derived from it, but is the absolute richness of this supreme quality of our feeling, too pure to be imagined. . . ."[109] The increase in impersonality results in the dissolution of the "conflict between self-interest and altruism."[110] There remains solely the interest that good be achieved.

Other Features

Bimodal Consciousness

One outstanding feature of the entire event that Wolff could find reported nowhere else in mystical literature is what we might call "bimodal consciousness." He found that ordinary relative consciousness and transcendent mystical consciousness operated simultaneously throughout the event. Although he had withdrawn energy and focus from the autonomously active relative mode of consciousness, it continued to operate as witness.

> I was at all times aware of my physical environment and could move the body freely at will. Further, I did not attempt to stop the activity of the mind, but simply very largely ignored the stream of thought. There was, however, a "fading down" of the objective consciousness, analogous to that of a dimming of a lamp without complete extinguishment. The result was that I was in a sort of compound state wherein I was both here and "There," with the objective consciousness less acute than normal.[111]

Even though Wolff's relative consciousness was attenuated, it did not cease functioning or lose contact with the intensified nonrelative consciousness, which was the locus for the process of transformation. The material that precipitated, as it were, from the nonrelative into the relative consciousness formed the basis for his subsequent reports, but at the time, it remained unreflected. For the most part, it was his spontaneously discovered capacity for maintaining a dual mode of consciousness that permitted such extensive articulation of his Fundamental Realizations.

Because this technique is a noteworthy feature of Wolff's spiritual methodology, and because it is a valuable resource that one aspiring to mystical realization might wish to cultivate, it is worth elaborating. Much of the Oriental literature with which he was familiar links the attainment of Fundamental Realization to *samādhi,* a trance state that he believes implies a blackout of relative consciousness. He had heard that some who had entered deep trance never returned. Wishing to avoid the danger of becoming locked into such a state, he had made a deep commitment to resist its attraction. This may have been the key factor that allowed him to maintain conscious connection to the phenomenal world.

> In place of this, there was a technique which somehow I knew, though I had never learned it, and that was to effect a certain division in consciousness, or in the mind, whereby one part stood upon the sidelines and witnessed the process, while another part went through the process. Somehow I knew how to do this, and in that there lies a mystery. At any rate, the witness self, in this case, the lesser consciousness, not the higher, as it is sometimes employed to mean, stood upon the sidelines, as it were, while another portion of the consciousness went through the process, which seemed like an ascension followed by a descent. This sense of "I" was present in both phases, and to distinguish them I suggested calling that portion that stood upon the sidelines the "witness self," and that portion that ascended and descended the "escalator self." I do not know of any similar report in the literature at the present time, but, at any rate, this technique had the advantage that there was an avoidance of a blackout trance, and at the same time a capacity to recall what happened, and to place it in the memory on the part of the witness self. The witness self was at all times cognizant of the environment. There was thus no loss of external or ordinary awareness, but the value of the environment, the value of the objective world around, seemed to be so far reduced that I have little or no memory of the external world of that time when penetrating deeply within.[112]

The inversion of the normal orientation of consciousness within the context of Fundamental Realization also inverts the sense of *witness.* In our usual habitual manner of engaging in everyday activity, we lose ourselves in the world. Developing the witness self in this context refers to becoming more fully and pervasively self-aware, so that we intensify the nonrelative consciousness. It is quite possible that this capacity for bimodal consciousness is widespread, if not universal. Furthermore, it is likely that other mystics also have remained aware of their environment during their experiences. However, because of the relative unimportance of this feature compared to the transcendental component, they probably did not consider it worth mentioning.

Ecstasy

Wolff reports that his realizations were not of the sort involving trance and that trance is not generally a necessary condition for mystical states. As a rule, he considers it of far greater significance to classify a state according to its inner "consciousness-value" than its external symptoms.[113] This is correct, inasmuch as there is no essential correlation between states of consciousness and external appearance.

Other Phenomena

Certain phenomena that are often associated with mysticism, such as automatisms (mediumistic activity), clairvoyance, and photisms were noteworthy by their absence. Wolff uses the term *Light* figuratively to express that quality of higher consciousness that is an illuminating force. It is not the experience of light, as in waking, dreaming, or hypnogogic states.[114]

Ensuing Effects

Wolff distinguishes effects occurring at the time of Realization from those enduring beyond the occasion itself. Several factors present during the period between his Fundamental Realizations are worth noting.

Fundamental Transformation of Consciousness

Because timelessness is a characteristic of mystical experience, it makes sense to inquire concerning the duration of the episode only from the standpoint of ordinary relative consciousness. In the case of Enlightenment, there is also something of a permanent transformation of consciousness. Consequently, Wolff reports that the onset was sharply defined, but there was no corresponding single moment that he could distinguish as its termination. "A different base of life and valuation has become normal, so that, in one sense, the recognition has remained as a persistent state. Yet there are notable differences of phases."[115] He experienced two major phases in his subsequent orientation. During the next month (that is, between this and the final Realization) his consciousness was focused on the Transcendent. Afterward, the Transcendent became the base as he focused on the relative world.[116]

Noetic Fecundity

At the end of this time, acting on Sherifa's suggestion that he record the account of his transformation, Wolff began writing. He remarks, "While the effort at formulation was a little difficult at first, the writing soon acquired momentum, and presently I found ideas developing in my consciousness faster than I could give them expression."[117] He gradually adapted to the higher noetic level until the end of the primary period lasting until the completion of *Pathways* in November 1936.

Increased Will

During the month between his two Fundamental Realizations, his desire for physical and sentient existence declined drastically, so he required a deliberate application of will, which had become more effective, to supplement it. On the one hand, he found the spontaneous inclination toward survival replaced by an inclination toward Transcendent Consciousness.[118] On the other hand, he felt a growing sense of power and could consciously control forces ordinarily operating below the threshold of conscious awareness.[119]

Temporary Bodily Strain

Within the first ten days of the succeeding period, he oscillated in and out of the 'Life-force' field,[120] or Current. However, he soon found it necessary to exercise restraint because of the strain he felt within his body.

THE HIGH INDIFFERENCE

Wolff's second Fundamental Realization, which occurred on the night of 8 September 1936, is of overriding importance because it constitutes the deepest grounding of his philosophy. He had exceptional difficulty in formulating a satisfactory account of the episode, discarding his original attempt in favor of the reformulation made at a time of exceptional intellectual lucidity thirty-three days later.[121] This version in *Pathways* was in turn superseded by that in *Consciousness*, which exhibits greater precision and detail. It is a model for conveying a sense of mystical consciousness, despite Wolff's disclaimer that this level of consciousness exceeds the valid use of language.[122]

He reports that his state of mind on the day of his ultimate Realization was "exceptionally clear and acute. In fact, the intellectual energy was of an unusual degree of potency, and his mood was decidedly one of intellectual assertion and dominance."[123] At the critical moment of transition, his "intense mental tension and exceptional intellectual activity"[124] contrasted starkly with the stillness that preceded the other recognitions, and that seems a general prerequisite for mystical experience. Unlike his other realizations, the sense of power was strongly emphasized.[125] In this case it was not a matter of inducing quiescence to capture something subtle, but of arousing the full resources of active consciousness to face an overwhelming power. "A force suddenly came that was commanding and even required the resistance of an active mind to maintain a certain balance or capacity to maintain one's entityhood against a force that could dissolve it."[126] Instead of the subtlety that typified the other realizations, the power principle, distinct from and complementary to both the knowing and feeling principles, accentuated this state. It was oriented to will, or conation, rather than to cognition and affection, and balanced the three psychological functions dynamically, not allowing self-possessed awareness and discrimination to dissolve—an otherwise irresistible tendency. He believes that without this forcefully active mental state he might not have been able to report more than an "inchoate Thatness."[127]

After retiring for the night, a mode of consciousness arose that initially produced a deepening effect of a predominantly affective nature.[128] Wolff considers the terms *unfolded, superimposed,* or *burst forth* not quite satisfactory as descriptions.[129] In a more recent formulation, he says, "A new consciousness walked into my consciousness . . . just took me over."[130] From the relative standpoint, the episode lasted several hours, during which time, according to Sherifa, the room was filled with a golden light.[131] Wolff was able to trace its progressive deepening through four distinct stages, although these were not distinguished by sharp discontinuities. He describes them as

> 1. a state of Universal Satisfaction,
> 2. a state of Indifference,
> 3. a state in which the Subject and Object vanished, and only Consciousness remained, and
> 4. a movement into darkness [that relative consciousness could no longer cognize] . . . from which I awoke in the morning with a sense of a still vaster Beyond.[132]

Satisfaction

Wolff describes the initial stage as somewhat of "a recapitulation of the values of the previous Fundamental Realization."[133] In particular, he notes the quality of delight that he found to be characteristic of all realizations—a quality that was here self-existent, not an attribute of some substance.[134] It is not accurate to regard the experience as a State that was satisfactory; rather it *was* 'Satisfaction'. The usual usage of the term "implies the idea of relationship or qualification. . . . [This] radically falsifies the essential nature of these inward States of Recognition."[135] He reports that " 'Satisfaction' and the *state* of satisfaction possess a substantial and largely inexpressible identity. Further, this 'Satisfaction', along with its substantiality, possesses a universal character. It is the value of all possible satisfactions at once and yet like a 'thick' substance interpenetrating everywhere."[136] Thus Satisfaction here must be taken to mean a substantial Actuality. It is not a mere abstraction derived from experience, but a pure self-existence that is real and substantial, prior to all experience.[137]

It resulted in a total elimination of desire, for it is only possible to desire when there is a felt need to fulfill a lack of some sort, or attain a goal without which one senses an incompleteness.[138] "When to wish for is to have immediately, it is impossible to isolate desire from possession. The awareness of desire necessarily vanishes."[139] Only the memory of the desire that others should become aware of the State could effectively awaken his will to resist remaining in that State.[140] To have absolute and complete fulfillment obviates desire, and he experienced in a passive but "profound balance in consciousness, a state of thorough repose with no drawing or inclining in any direction."[141]

Indifference

After a protracted period, the Satisfaction dimmed or faded, gradually to be fused into, enveloped by, or transformed into the more profound State of Indifference.[142] Satisfaction now lay below, so to speak, along with all other affective values, but with no sense of loss. All were potential and could be willed into effect, isolated from the total blending of value, but there was no desire whatsoever to render this potential kinetic.[143] The State was perfect and in no need of change,[144] for it was, in a mysterious sense, 'more' than desirable.[145]

> On the level of the High Indifference, there is no desire whatsoever, but simply unlimited potentiality. To find the Real, it is absolutely necessary to transcend desire. But it is impossible for the desire-bound consciousness to imagine the supernal value of that Consciousness which is free from desire. In the whole notion of desiring Desirelessness there is an inherent contradiction until somehow one has Realized that superior State and thus Knows directly Its superiority.[146]

Obviously, from the relative point of view, this state could not appear as attractive or even imaginable, but identity with the supernal State transcends relative consciousness and all valuation from that orientation.[147] Although it seems utterly strange from the relative perspective, from its supernal level, it is the only completely adequate State.[148] Thereafter one has a vastly more comprehensive base.

The Indifference was utterly distinct from an attitude of apathy. It was instead a condition of balanced aloofness in total equilibrium at the "zero-point" between the lofty positive values realized in the prior Recognition (and in the earlier phase of this one) and their negative opposites. "I feel that I am centered in a Level from which I look down upon all objects of all possible human desire, even the most lofty. . . . On Its own Level, It is the one State that is really complete or adequate."[149] He found as self-evidently true that this was the "nature of the All in its essential organization."[150] It is a dispassionate state above any inclination or preference, unattached and aloof. However, this does not imply that Wolff's personal consciousness was indifferent; it definitely preferred the positive values—such as delight to suffering, good to evil. The concept of 'Equilibrium' points to but does not fully capture the noetic value of the State, which is at once both the initiation and the termination of all possibilities.[151] Of the High Indifference everything whatsoever may be predicated, so long as it does not imply that any other predicate is excluded. From it all dualities are derived, but in itself it transcends all duality, "for in It are blended, at once, all qualities, all dualities."[152]

Whereas the Satisfaction was the acme of the affective and conative functions of Consciousness, the High Indifference was akin to affective-conative silence. Nevertheless, certain supernal values of this sort were involved, in particular, "utter Fullness beyond the highest reach of the imagination."[153] Wolff uses a mathematical analogy to contrast his first Fundamental Realization to our usual awareness, that "as the transfinite is to the finite, so is the value of this Consciousness to ordinary consciousness."[154] He extends this analogy to indicate that, relative to the other Transcendental states, the High Indifference is like a higher order of infinity (that could be called "INFINITY") that comprehends lesser orders.[155] Each of these, however, must be sharply distinguished from any finite range.

He also became aware of a strange sense of authority, which again occasionally manifested spontaneously during later periods of writing. "As an intimate part of that supernal consciousness, there is a sense of power and authority literally of cosmic proportions."[156] All worldly achievements, no matter how impressive, "inhere in a field of consciousness that in its very roots is subject to that Higher Power and Authority."[157] Here, the very forces of nature as well as all human endeavor depend for their existence upon this Transcendent Consciousness, which seems but the Void.

Wolff not only articulates the prominent features of the State itself, but also provides an account from within his personal, relative consciousness. Several points brought to light have considerable import.

Bimodal Consciousness

Similar to his other Fundamental Realization, this one manifested the phenomenon of consciousness that was simultaneously aware in both relative and Transcendent modes.

> Throughout the whole period of this supreme state of consciousness I was self-consciously awake in the physical body and quite aware of my environment. The thought-activity was not depressed, but on the contrary, alert and acute. I was continuously conscious of my self-identity, in two distinct senses. In one sense, I was, and am, the primordial Self and co-terminus with an unlimited and abstract Space, while at the same time the subject-object and self-analyzing consciousness was a sort of point-presence within that Space.[158]

However, there was a continuous shrinking of the personal consciousness concomitant with the deepening of the state until finally, in the fourth stage, the relative consciousness was extinguished.[159]

Expansion

Meanwhile, he witnessed an indefinite expansion of the I, or Pure Self, which spread everywhere, "identical with a kind of Space that embraced not merely the visible forms and worlds, but all modes and qualities of consciousness . . . blended, as it were, in a sort of primordial and culminating totality."[160] Even though it appeared that he could will to project into manifestation any of these modes or qualities without disturbing in any way the perfect balance, he found himself completely indifferent to such an effort.

To be able to formulate any account of it whatsoever, Wolff was obliged to extend basic concepts beyond their normal range of meaning.

> The Primordial Consciousness cannot be described as conceptual, affective, or perceptual. It seems that all these functions are

> potentially There, but the Consciousness as a whole is a blend of all these and something more. It is a deep, substantial, and vital sort of consciousness, the matter, form, and awareness functions of consciousness all at once.[161]

It might be characterized as a thick consciousness where consciousness and substance are "interpenetrating modes of the whole,"[162] as opposed to mere terms in relation, which is characteristic of relative consciousness.

Objectivity

The movement in consciousness was "toward objectivity, but not in the sense of a movement toward the relative world-field. The final State is, at once, as much objective as subjective."[163] This is entirely consistent with the nature of a state that transcends all dichotomies whatsoever—all opposites are timelessly coexistent. Thus the High Indifference is equally the terminal Value attained by penetration of the subjective pole, or I, and the culmination of what appears at the objective pole (the world-field).[164]

Divinity

The experience involves identification with supernal religious value.

> The Godless secular universe vanishes, and in its place there remains none other than the living and all-enveloping Presence of Divinity itself. So, speaking in the subjective sense, I am all there is, yet at the same time, objectively considered, there is nought but Divinity spreading everywhere. . . . The sublimated object and the sublimated self are one and the same Reality, and this may be represented by the judgment: "I am the Divinity."[165]

It is only by realizing that neither the Self nor the Divinity is subordinate to the other that individual integration may be maintained in the face of the awesome force of dissolution that is that Presence.

Logic

Wolff found that the logical principle of noncontradiction was simply irrelevant—inapplicable rather than violated. In spite of this factor, he maintains that there was "evidence of a perfect logic behind it."[166] The State itself is the result of the autonomous process according to Hegelian logic. It was the synthesis of desire-conditioned consciousness (as thesis) and the State of Satisfaction (as antithesis).

> For to isolate any phase of the State was to be immediately aware of the opposite phase as the necessary complementary part of the first. Thus the attempt of self-conscious thought to isolate anything resulted in the immediate initiation of a sort of flow in the very essence of consciousness itself, so that nascent isolation was transformed into its opposite as copartner in a timeless reality. Every attempt I made to capture the State within the categories of relative knowledge was defeated by this flow effect.[167]

This dialectical flow leads to the mystical fusion where all is One—a process that we can better apprehend by using Hegelian, rather than Aristotelian logic.

Ethics

Wolff also found that the moral imperative no longer applied. Duties and offices of compassion seemed wholly unnecessary due to the Recognition that, in Reality, there is no suffering whatsoever or any creature in need of assistance.

> The essential consciousness and life of all beings are already in that State, and both never had been, and could not be, divorced from it. The world-field with all its striving and pain, seemingly lasting through billions of years, actually is, or seems to be, a dream occurring during a passing wink of sleep. I simply could not feel any need or duty that would call me back to action in the world-field.[168]

Because Wolff found himself identical with All, there could be no question of departing, or of deserting anyone or anything. He was simply indifferent to the human drama in the world-field and saw all the evils of the world, no matter how tragic or catastrophic they might seem, to be insignificant.[169] What is more important, no external moral criterion had any validity while in that State.

> The imperative of the moral law no longer existed, for there was not, and is not, either good or evil. It seemed I could invoke

> power, even in potentially unlimited degree. I could choose action or rest. If I acted, then I could proceed in any direction I might select. Yet, whether I acted or did not act, or whether I acted in one way or another, it all had absolutely the same significance. It was neither right nor wrong to choose anything, or putting it otherwise, there was neither merit nor demerit in any choice. It was as though any choice whatsoever became immediately Divinely ordained and superior to the review of any lesser tribunal.[170]

Consequently, it would be impossible while in that State to act immorally or to err in choosing a course of action or inaction, for everything was authorized by Divine autonomy. In the High Indifference, all dualities—including right/wrong—"are completely absorbed in the nonrelative."[171]

This perspective, though transitory, superseded all relative valuation. Mystics commonly consider such a state supramoral rather than amoral. Wolff's personal system of valuation seems to have remained intact and continued to operate within the relative mode of consciousness, but he found himself identified with the Transcendent mode. The schema where the mundane reality appears to be but a play, where the participants are not self-consciously aware of the transcendent dimension of their consciousness, is an experienced element of interpretation having ethical implications. If Awakening is the sole release from the dream of life in the world-field, then the highest ethical ideal is to Awaken oneself and assist others to Awaken. Whatever proves effective in attaining this goal is thereby justified.

Within the State, the crux of the matter for Wolff involved an actual life or death decision concerning his personal existence—a crisis for the personal consciousness, but having no impetus for decision within the High Indifference. He witnessed the struggle dispassionately. During the conflict his will remained neutral, since there was neither reason nor desire for choosing either course. In his previous studies, he discovered that it might be possible to abandon the relative state permanently. Because of his compassionate vow to assist those who were still suffering, he had resolved to renounce personal Liberation, if it involved disregarding the world of suffering creatures. This orientation of his personal consciousness was, he concluded, the decisive factor in his return—

since he ultimately fell asleep, to awaken the next morning, with the issue obviously resolved. He concludes, "I cannot say that in the ultimate sense there was either victory or defeat. The choice was right, *for no choice could possibly be wrong.*"[172]

Dissolution of Subject and Object

The third stage of Wolff's most profound Realization resulted in the deepest penetration that still had determinate cognitive impact on his relative consciousness. Due to its singular significance in revolutionizing Wolff's philosophical position, and the progressive shading into total ineffability of the final stage, it should prove exceedingly helpful to compare his three most revealing accounts.

> I moved about in a kind of Space that was not other than Myself, and found Myself surrounded by pure Divinity, even on the physical level when I moved there. There is a sense in which God is physical Presence as well as metaphysical. But this Presence is everywhere and everything, and, at the same time, the negation of all this. Again, neither I nor God were There; only BEING remained. I vanished and the object of consciousness vanished, in the highest, as well as inferior, senses. I was no more and God was no more, but only the ETERNAL which sustains all Gods and all Selves. Is it any wonder that SILENCE is the usual answer to the question: What is the High Indifference?[173]

It is particularly advantageous for understanding the nature of the state to compare the preceding formulation, composed shortly after the Realization, with versions written after years of reflection. We shall also gain insight into the way language must be extended when employed to convey mystical experiences of exceptional profundity.

> There finally arrived a state wherein both that which I have called the Self and that which had the value of Divinity were dissolved in a Somewhat, still more transcendent. There now remained nought but pure Being that could be called neither the Self nor God. No longer was "I" spreading everywhere through the whole of an illimitable and conscious Space, nor was there a Divine Presence all about me, but everywhere only Consciousness with no subjective nor objective element. Here, both symbols and concepts fail. But now I know that within and surrounding all there is a Core or Matrix within which are rooted all selves and all Gods,

> and that from this lofty Peak, veiled in mists of timeless obscurity and surrounded by thick, impenetrable Silence, all worlds and beings, all spaces and all times lie suspended in utter dependence. On that highest Peak I could Know no more, for the Deeps of the deepest Darkness, and the SILENCE enshrouded in manifold sheaths of Silence rolled over me, and self-consciousness was blown out. But o'er this I heard as the faintest shadow of a breath of consciousness a Voice, as it were, from out a still vaster BEYOND.[174]

Another more recent formulation indicates the degree to which this Realization supersedes the others.

> There came a time when the whole object of consciousness, the world about, the total universe of all possible objects, dropped away, and 'I', the Self, dropped away, and only the Eternal and unchanging underlying Consciousness remained, and beyond this I was enveloped in Darkness where I plumbed to Depths, where Darkness merely became a greater and greater darkness of noncognition, and returned again to outer life—and at that point, and not before, I took to myself the doctrine of *anātman.*[175]

In the High Indifference, Wolff found a perfect Equilibrium between all pairs of opposites. However, the process of deepening continued until it presented "the supreme pair of opposites . . . represented by the subject-to-consciousness and the object of consciousness."[176] Here both were exalted to a supernal status equivalent to his first Fundamental Realization: The Pure Subject, I, was the Self or *Ātman,* whereas the Object was the Divine Presence or God. The awareness of their mutual dissolution as they vanished into the Pure Consciousness Itself or Consciousness-without-an-object and without-a-subject constituted the third stage of the Realization. This is the "foundation stone, a transcendental base"[177] of Wolff's philosophy.

Descent into Darkness

In the final stage, Consciousness deepened to the point where relative consciousness could not follow. Wolff reports descending through progressively deeper stages of noncognitive Darkness—then ascending. He initially interpreted the "descent into darkness," which was a darkness of noncognition, as revealing an unknown, unexplored possibility yet to be integrated into our understanding. The relative mode of consciousness actively witnessed and monitored the "higher consciousness whose only impact was that of a darkness of noncognition with deepening stages of cognizing noncognition."[178] Much later he reinterpreted it as "a view of the Absolute Consciousness in its impact upon the relative consciousness . . . in the form of . . . the darkness of noncognition in any sense."[179] The conviction that resulted was that this was the highest possible integration of which he was capable at this time, but not the final Truth. The transcendence of the first Fundamental Realization by the second, along with the progressive penetration to untraceable Depths, inclined him to accept that even more ultimate Realizations might be possible, but that this could not yet be determined.[180] He intimates that just as the High Indifference transcended his penultimate Realization as one order of infinity may transcend a lower order of infinity, the hint from Beyond suggests that there may be no insuperable limit to mystic penetration, no final highest State of Consciousness.[181]

Ensuing Effects

We must first understand mystical experience by studying the occurrences themselves as psychical events within the history of an individual. Of much greater significance, however, is their effect in radically transforming the individual in ways that are typically quite permanent. Let us consider the personal effects of Wolff's final Recognition, which was the culmination of the entire cycle, as well as his realizations as a whole from his perspective "as an individual center of consciousness, thinking, feeling, and acting within the relative world."[182]

Reversal of Overly Sensitive Condition

The preceding Recognition, "I Am THAT," had produced a condition of organic supersensitivity. His final Recognition reversed this, replacing it by an organic hardiness, which was "a radical change of phase in the individual consciousness."[183]

Intellectual Revitalization

Wolff noticed a definite intellectual revitalization that enabled him to "sustain creative and analytic thought activity at a higher level than formerly and for longer periods of time,"[184] while more easily comprehending difficult concepts.

Increased Impersonality

His affective nature manifested a deep and abiding Compassion. He continued to "care deeply for the growth of durable well-being,"[185] not only for himself and those with whom he had personal contact, but for the collective as well. Yet he sensed an increasing impersonality, an outright indifference to the trivial problems that comprise the vast preponderance of human existence.[186] When not indifferent, he would experience disgust or indignation, but recognized this as the result of insufficient detachment. As a result of his increased clarity, he also found his appraisal of the intelligence of the ordinary individual somewhat lowered.

PERMANENT RESULT OF THE FIVE REALIZATIONS

The entire set of realizations produced two related effects that Wolff considers exceptionally meaningful.

Shift in Base of Consciousness

He not only became aware of a way of consciousness that transcended and grounded the mundane order, but he experienced it as a permanent shift at the foundations of his personal consciousness.

> Probably the most important permanent effect of the whole group of Recognitions is the grounding of knowledge, affection, and the sense of assurance on a base that is neither empirical nor intellectual. This base is supersensible, superaffective, and superconceptual, yet it is both conscious and substantial and of unlimited dynamic potentiality.[187]

It is this foundation upon which he developed his philosophy, whose ultimate perspective "cannot be comprehended within the forms that assume time, the subject-object relationship, and experience as original and irreducible constants of consciousness or reality."[188]

View of Ultimate Reality

The first four realizations had led Wolff to hold the position that the ultimate reality was the Self, for the awareness of the Pure Subject did not require space, time, causality, or the subject-object relationship. However, his fifth Realization revealed both the Self (or subject-to-consciousness) and the object of consciousness to be comprehended by a more ultimate (nondualistic) Reality. "I saw with the eye of the mind the disappearance of the object and the subject into Consciousness itself, and this is the basis of Consciousness-Without-an-Object and Without-a-Subject."[189] So this Realization revealed the Self to be dependent upon a more Primordial Consciousness, which is ultimately responsible for the experiences of the Self and the conditions necessary for such experience.

PHILOSOPHICAL IMPLICATIONS

Process of Wolff's Transformation

A summary overview of the progressive unfoldment of these realizations will assist us to clarify their nature and significance. A sharp distinction is evident between the first three, which are neither Transcendent nor ineffable, and the latter two, which are both. The impact of the two Fundamental Realizations is transformative, and their essential nature inherently transcends language and conceptual categories. Wolff's three mental realizations produced a clear understanding that the referent of "I" is the Pure Self or *Ātman,* which is totally other than objects of any sort. Rather, it is identical with *Nirvāṇa,* which is consciousness of the absence of objects, the full Realization of which constitutes Enlightenment. Further, it is the realization of the substantial nature of reality—in contrast with the appearance of ponderable objects, which are relative voids. This prepared him psychologically for the shift in orientation of consciousness that was the key to Fundamental Realization.

The first of two, "I Am THAT," was the mystical fulfillment of the insights of his three premonitory realizations. Even though, in itself, Fundamental Realization is utterly Transcendent, the effects that coalesce within relative consciousness are conceivable, allowing for understanding and philosophical development. The process leading to Wolff's attainment of Fundamental Realization involved the abstraction or discrimination of the I, as subjective pole of consciousness, from everything that is not-I, including subtle objects and experiences. He found that full Recognition of the Self confirmed the world view established by his mental realizations, which essentially harmonized with that of Śaṃkara's nondualistic interpretation of the Vedānta. He regards everything preceding his fifth and final Realization as generally consistent with this view, which equates Transcendent knowledge with Knowledge of the Self. This became the illumined base from which he wrote *Pathways.*

When the High Indifference unfolded a few weeks later, everything changed. This Realization was spontaneous—its occurrence and nature utterly unsought and unexpected. Wolff calls the state the "High Indifference" because it is absolutely neutral between all polar concepts (including subject-object). This means that it could not be strictly described in terms of any of them. Thus we should consider all reference to what he immediately 'knew' as a result of its effects to be only symbolic of THAT which is neither subject nor object. It was not merely a conceptual insight, but an immediate awareness wherein both the subject-to-consciousness (in its highest manifestation as the Self) and the object of consciousness (in its highest sense, as God or the Divinity) vanished into Pure, Primordial, Field Consciousness. "The *Ātman* vanished into something more ultimate: Consciousness-without-an-object and without-a-subject."[190] Consequently, the theoretical and experiential view that the Self or Pure Subject (*Ātman*) is ultimately real Wolff found to be superseded by nondualistic Consciousness, which is the Source for both objects and selves.

Although he alludes to It as a fusion of matter, form, and awareness, as functions of consciousness, he denies that ultimately It was any more consciousness than nonconsciousness. This is his most subtle attempt to extend conceptual understanding to grasp the most profound depth of mystical penetration. The result is consistent with its nondualistic Transcendence of all conceptual distinctions, even the notion of the presence or absence of consciousness. So, we most assuredly must not subsequently attempt to substitute any other positive characterization, for here we have altogether exhausted the resources of conceptual distinction. He symbolizes this Transcendent base primarily as "Consciousness-without-an-object," but employs alternate designations as well—in particular, "the GREAT SPACE." It constitutes both his experiential terminus in mystical penetration and the source or ultimate foundation for his more systematic philosophy.

Transcendental Ground for Philosophy

Philosophically, the High Indifference is the keystone in the system of thought born out of the entire process. For Wolff, that which is symbolized by Consciousness-without-an-object constitutes both an epistemological and a metaphysical Absolute. Furthermore, his previous position (that the subject-to-consciousness transcends the object of consciousness) is in the spirit of Kant's Copernican Revolution, which directs primary philosophical attention to the knowing subject, rather than to the object known. His final position (that Consciousness Itself, or Consciousness-without-an-object and without-a-subject, transcends both object and subject), giving Consciousness the ascendant status over both subject and object, Wolff advances as his own Copernican revolution.

One important consequence is that *Nirvāṇa* is no longer conceived as the ultimate attainment. The insight of the mental realization "I am *Nirvāṇa*," which was fully Realized in "I Am THAT," lies in polar opposition to *saṃsāra*—the phenomenal realm. It is awareness characterized by the absence of objects, whereas the presence of objects pervades ordinary consciousness. When the entire subject-object structure dissolves, the resulting state is Pure Consciousness Itself—corresponding to *Parinirvāṇa*—that is prior to, and neutral concerning the presence or absence of objects. It is neither *saṃsāra* nor *Nirvāṇa*, but allows absolute freedom to enter either domain. Hence we may attribute a correspondence between subject, object, and Consciousness, on the one hand, and *Nirvāṇa*, *saṃsāra*, and *Parinirvāṇa*, on the other.[191]

Although Wolff's philosophy is grounded on that base, he regards its expression as only one of innumerable possibilities authentically derived from mystical experience. His unique formulation points beyond its conceptual content to the Reality of the ground, but he denies that it is, or could be, the only valid symbolic statement. He claims absolute assurance concerning such knowledge, prior to verbal representation, but denies that such certainty pertains to the literal truth of any proposition as such, due to the transcendent, nondualistic nature of the ground. Against the background of the painstaking record of his actual experiences, these enigmatic conclusions call for further elaboration and a more precise determination of their significance.

CHAPTER 4

Mysticism and Philosophy

The fundamental importance that Wolff's mystical realizations have for the grounding and development of his philosophy suggests that his contribution can be understood and appreciated only by considering the relationship between philosophy and mysticism. This justifies a general discussion of mysticism that attempts to develop the appropriate methodology for its understanding and to determine the possibility and nature of its adequate definition. The requisite starting point is the testimony and insights of the mystics themselves, especially those such as Wolff who have addressed these problems. Ideally, the investigator also should be a mystic, because firsthand acquaintance with any subject matter is an optimal condition for its mastery.

Several central issues help to focus our inquiry. Is there a common essence to mystical experience that makes it the same everywhere (the essentialist view), or are there, at best, only diverse typologies derived from clusters of typical features? Moreover, to what extent is the experience itself influenced, or even determined (the contextualist position) by the contingencies of the mystic's context or background—the culture, language, religion, and so on that frames her spiritual path? How can the experience itself be described apart from contextual influences on its interpretation? What is the significance of the mystic's claim that the experience was objective, despite its alleged ineffability? It will be suggested that resolution best lies in a new interpretation of essentialism based on the implications of ineffability.

Since mysticism challenges the presuppositions of every method of investigation, philosophy itself must become self-reflective, inquiring into its deepest nature and its relationship to the domains of science and religion. More specifically, we shall explore the import of mysticism for philosophy, not merely as a unique and exceedingly fascinating subject, but as transcendent ground and source of renewal for philosophy. Finally, we shall consider how the growth of philosophy from diverse experienced "indefinables," resulting in apparent conflict, leads us to a synthetic pluralism.

MYSTICISM

Characteristics of Mystical Experience

Mysticism initially is to be understood in terms of mystical experience, but besides qualifying it as religious, in the broad sense, a comprehensive definition remains elusive. Ninian Smart attributes this both to

1. the diversity of doctrinal interpretations coloring descriptions given by mystics from different backgrounds, and
2. the difficulty in distinguishing mystical from numinous, and other exalted types of experience, in a succinct formulation.[1]

Ronald Hepburn admits that "attempts to define mystical experience have been as diversified and as conflicting as attempts to interpret and assess its significance."[2] Even though exact definition may not be possible, he believes that some discriminations are.

Despite these inherent difficulties, a number of diverse studies besides Wolff's have proven helpful. We are indebted to the pioneering work of William James[3] and Walter Stace,[4] the careful, lucid treatment of James Horne,[5] and the following statement by Leon Rosenstein:

> The term "mysticism" lacks an adequate definition. . . . Primordially and essentially it refers not to a doctrine or a method but to a state of being. Physiologically, its etymological roots denote a

> closing of the eyes and mouth effected by a nonexperiential sight and a silence (or unintelligible mumbling). Psychologically, it is understood as a condition of trance, ecstasy, and disorientation. Experientially, it constitutes an act of apprehension of or encounter with (though more usually expressed as an attunement to or melding with) the unifying source of what-is such as to be of monumental human concern. This "source" is sometimes referred to simply as the "Divine," or the "Holy," as "God," as "Being," or equally as "Nothing." Though clearly "religious" in some sense, it is also irreligious in that it is neither a ritual, an attitude of faith, nor a doctrine—nor can it be made to conform to one, though of course it can be and usually is accounted for subsequently by and adjusted to a particular religion. Though it is also "philosophical" in the broadest sense of the term, it is essentially unphilosophical in that it constitutes neither an analysis of what-is nor a synthetic comprehension of what-is. It is neither the acquisition nor expression of information (and is for that reason "unteachable") because it has no definite method and no definite subject matter. It is in fact always "in the negative" that it operates and is expressed, though it takes this as most fully "positive." It claims truth, a truth hidden from either everyday, scientific, philosophical, or religious understanding and investigation, viewing science and logic not even as servants to its process but rather as inhibitors to its success.[6]

The perplexity that Rosenstein's somewhat paradoxical account engenders may be explained partially if we take seriously the widespread reports by mystics that what is essentially mystical about their experience is ineffable. Whatever might be conveyed concerning it should not obscure the point that what makes it mystical cannot be understood discursively. This suggests that a unique methodology is necessary for a satisfactory conceptual grasp of mysticism and that ultimately all attempts might well fall short.

In particular, the object-oriented methods of empirical science are severely limited in this regard. Nils Kvastad exemplifies the strictly empirical approach to determining the defining characteristics of mystical experience. This consists in collecting a comprehensive set of reports and accounts (which ideally would include all time periods, cultures, and religious contexts) from which to compile their common features.[7] Stace's comparison of the lists of William James, R. M. Bucke, and D. T. Suzuki illustrates the degree of variance resulting from this approach.

> James lists four common characteristics, namely: (1) noetic quality, by which he means the immediate feeling of the revelation of objective truth which accompanies the experience and is part of it, (2) ineffability, (3) transiency, and (4) passivity. (William James, *The Varieties of Religious Experience* [New York: Modern Library, Inc.], pp. 371–72.) R. M. Bucke gives the following: (1) the subjective light, or photism, (2) moral elevation, (3) intellectual illumination, (4) sense of immortality, (5) loss of fear of death, (6) loss of sense of sin, (7) suddenness. (R. M. Bucke, *Cosmic Consciousness* [New York: E. P. Dutton, 1923], pp. 72–73, 79.) D. T. Suzuki gives the following list of the common characteristics of *satori* . . . (1) irrationality, inexplicability, incommunicability; (2) intuitive insight; (3) authoritativeness; (4) affirmation (positive character); (5) sense of the beyond; (6) impersonal tone; (7) feeling of exaltation; (8) momentariness (roughly equivalent to Bucke's "suddenness"). (D. T. Suzuki, *Zen Buddhism: Selected Writings of D. T. Suzuki*, ed. by William Barrett [New York: Anchor Books, Doubleday & Co., Inc.], pp. 103–8).[8]

This shows why the task seems disheartening, for the inventories compiled by these researchers contain no single defining element and only partial overlap. More detailed research only tends to reinforce the conclusion that there is no single objective factor universally reported in mystical experience, suggesting that none may be cited as a defining characteristic.

Stace attempts to combine a family resemblance model with a defining common core in his proposed twofold typology.[9] In the family resemblance model, no single element is a necessary condition for membership in a class. Here the criterion of selection is the presence of a sufficient (but unspecified) number of a set of elements that are usually present. This implies that inclusion is a matter of degree and implies the existence of borderline cases. He distinguishes between extrovertive and introvertive mysticism according to the experienced presence or absence of empirical contents. These two types generally, but not invariably, share the following characteristics:

1. a sense of objectivity or reality;
2. feelings of blessedness, joy, happiness, satisfaction, peace, and so on;
3. feeling of apprehending the holy, sacred, or divine;

4. paradoxicality;
5. ineffability.[10]

Clearly, none of these alone is a defining characteristic of mystical experience because each occurs in other kinds of experience as well. Furthermore, they are not jointly sufficient, for something more essential is lacking.

In Stace's typology, introvertive mystical experience is essentially a distinctionless unified consciousness. However, no one should take this to mean that the contents of consciousness have been integrated into an organized structure, inasmuch as there is no longer any multiplicity of elements to organize. It is "the Unitary Consciousness, from which all the multiplicity of sensuous or conceptual or other empirical content has been excluded, so that there remains only a void and empty unity. This is the one basic, essential, nuclear characteristic, from which most of the others inevitably follow."[11] The second defining characteristic, implied by the nature of distinctionless unity, is that it is nonspatial and nontemporal.[12] The mystic reports the transcendence of time and space as a matter of direct awareness.

According to Stace, extrovertive mysticism usually occurs spontaneously within the context of ordinary sense experience. In these cases the objects of the world remain perceptible but reveal their true nature as an inner reality or depth dimension that pervades everything. Stace lists the corresponding central characteristics as

1. The Unifying Vision, expressed abstractly by the formula "All is One." The One is, in extrovertive mysticism, perceived through the physical senses, in or through the multiplicity of objects.
2. The more concrete apprehension of the One as being an inner subjectivity in all things, described variously as life, or consciousness, or a living Presence. The discovery that nothing is "really" dead.[13]

The phenomenal appearance of the world is not—or at least, need not be—altered, but its significance takes on a profundity that permanently affects the mystic's world view.

Stace regards the unifying feature as essentially the same in both introvertive and extrovertive mysticism, and as constituting the defining characteristic of mystical experience. He interprets the extrovertive variety as an incomplete type that finds its purity in the introvertive type. He considers extrovertive mysticism an incomplete form of introvertive mysticism because multiplicity is still present, whereas the distinctionless unity of Unitary Consciousness is the most central feature of the experience.[14] Moreover, he contends that undifferentiated unity is essential to introvertive experience.[15]

Notwithstanding the general value of Stace's work in providing an organizational framework for understanding the vast diversity of the mystical domain, several objections arise. William Wainwright adopts Stace's introvertive/extrovertive distinction in mysticism while rejecting the notion of an essence. He lists monistic and theistic mysticism as two distinct forms of introvertive mysticism and proposes four varieties of extrovertive mystical experience. However, he cautions that we should take all typologies "with a grain of salt."[16]

In India and the West, it is predominantly true that extrovertive mystical experiences tend to arise spontaneously, whereas introvertive mysticism is usually the result of a deliberately chosen path of spiritual development. In the Far East Zen Buddhism[17] would seem to be a notable exception to Stace's position, for Enlightenment occurs in the midst of the world. Zen is essentially a path of natural integration of mysticism with everyday life. Its technique of Zazen meditation makes no effort to suppress or eliminate the natural contents of consciousness, but even this unstructured practice is sometimes regarded as too unnatural. Hence it is a fully developed and intentionally chosen path that is extrovertive in nature, neither monistic nor theistic, yet complete. Indeed, because its context and development remain grounded in the world, it may exhibit greater completeness than some forms of introvertive mysticism that obliterate empirical contents from consciousness.[18]

Wolff's Fundamental Realizations comprise a more topical refutation of Stace's dualistic typology, for he explicitly states that through the resources of bimodal consciousness he never lost awareness of his external environment. Yet the mystical dimension of these experiences accords well with accounts of introvertive mysticism. His awareness of the external world remained mundane, though seeming less real than usual. Had it not been for his commitment to provide an exhaustively accurate report, he very likely would have ignored this aspect of the episodes altogether. The simplicity of his technique (isolating the pure subject or self and allowing awareness to sink back into it, as it were) makes it likely that bimodal consciousness is not rare in mystical experience, but that it mostly goes unreported.[19] In any case, Stace's analysis of mysticism cannot easily accommodate it.

The point of introducing these exceptions to a simple introvertive/extrovertive dichotomy is not to proliferate typologies, but to seek a common essence or core to all mystical experience. There is merit to Stace's focus on the One as Unitary Consciousness, so long as it is not interpreted as merely one phenomenal characteristic that stands out among others. If taken literally as a positive description, it is misleading. Rather, its significance is to indicate that when all empirical contents are removed from consciousness, what remains must constitute the essence of mysticism, for there is nothing else left in terms of which to define it. Furthermore, because the structures of space, time, and causality no longer apply here, this mystical quintessence could not have *arisen* in the process of, or been *produced* by, the dissolution of empirical contents within the mystic's awareness. To develop a truly comprehensive understanding of mysticism, it seems necessary to ground it in an awareness in which the presence *or* absence of empirical contents is irrelevant—namely, in THAT which is, in itself, nonphenomenal or unconditioned. The acknowledged diversity of empirical elements that may be found in mystical experience does not (and cannot) by itself establish the case against a nonphenomenal common core.

Typologies of Mysticism

Before supporting a positive case for this interpretation, it is only just to consider the view that denies any common essence to mystical experience and approaches mysticism solely through phenomenally grounded typologies. Several scholars claim that there are irreducibly diverse types of mysticism, while often upholding the superiority of religious mysticism within their own tradition. However natural it may seem to attempt to establish a hierarchical structure of types of mysticism, the criteria that are used often incorporate other than phenomenological considerations. Where this results from personal attachment and cultural conditioning, the individual is often unaware that the analysis has been compromised. For example, Henri Bergson, who developed a deep appreciation for Catholicism, states his case enthusiastically, but with obvious bias:

> The mystical impulse, if operating anywhere with sufficient power, was no longer going to be stopped short by the impossibility of acting; it was no longer to be driven back into doctrines of renunciation or the systematic practice of ecstasy; instead of turning inwards and closing, the soul could open wide its gates to a universal love. . . . We may therefore conclude that neither in Greece nor in ancient India was there complete mysticism. . . .
>
> For the complete mysticism is that of the great Christian mystics.[20]

In response, one might point out that the monastic tradition within Christianity appears as quietist as some forms of Greek or Indian mysticism. Furthermore, even if Bergson had correctly characterized Greek and Indian mysticism, he would need a separate argument against the fully integrated mysticism of Zen before designating Christian mysticism the consummate form.

More recently, R. C. Zaehner[21] and Martin C. D'Arcy,[22] who share Bergson's religious affiliation, oppose Stace, claiming that there are several distinct types of mystical experience, the most complete and exalted of which is theistic. Of course, it would be fallacious to reject their view solely because their conclusions coincide with their personal religious commitment. Rather, some have found evidence that they fail to distinguish adequately between description and interpretation of mystical experience. No doubt mystics tend to understand and express their realizations according to antecedently accepted doctrinal interpretation, particularly within traditions that stress adherence to orthodoxy. However, the radical transcendence that is typical of the mystical often revolutionizes commonly held views.

Wainwright lists the criteria that the Christian (in particular, Catholic) tradition has developed for judging and accepting the authenticity of mystics' claims:

1. good consequences for the mystic
2. good consequences for others (the community)

3. depth or profundity
4. agreement with orthodoxy
5. similarity to experiences accepted as paradigmatic
6. pronouncements of authorities.[23]

All of these requirements are obviously question begging. Mystics often serve the beneficial function of reformer by challenging the accepted values, beliefs, and practices of their group. A community does the mystic and itself a disservice by imposing conformity to the status quo as the standard for validating mystics and their messages. Even though it may not be possible to devise completely neutral criteria, a conservative bias must not be allowed to distort our appraisal of the legitimacy of a mystic's pronouncements.

Contextualism

A nonsectarian challenge to essentialism comes from Steven Katz, who disputes the notion of a common core by arguing that all experience, including mystical experience, is mediated. He bases his contextualist view on a simple epistemological assumption.

> *There are* NO *pure (i.e. unmediated) experiences.* Neither mystical experience nor more ordinary forms of experience give any indication, or any grounds for believing, that they are unmediated. That is to say, *all* experience is processed through, organized by, and makes itself available to us in extremely complex epistemological ways. The notion of unmediated experience seems, if not self-contradictory, at best empty.[24]

Accordingly, he holds that the concepts, beliefs, and doctrines that underlie the mystic's world view comprise the form and interpretation of his experience and provide ample scope for all sorts of religious and nonreligious mysticism.

No doubt, if Katz is merely assuming the truth of his position, then a mere denial is sufficient to reject it. Can it be more than an assumption? How could this sort of categorical claim be justified without having personal acquaintance with the entire range of possible awareness—human and otherwise? It is doubtful that anyone would wish to claim this sort of omniscience. Furthermore, the method of extrapolation from common experience would be fallacious, for there are crucial discontinuities in nonordinary ranges of experience. Rather, Katz appears to be arguing as follows:

1. The term *unmediated experience* is self-contradictory.
2. Even if it were not, we are so constructed that it would be factually impossible.
3. Even if unmediated experience were possible, such an experience necessarily would be empty, for any attempt to represent it would involve mediation.

Let us consider these propositions in turn. It will not do to claim that mediation of this sort is logically necessary. It is not analytically true that *conceptually mediated* is part of the meaning of the term *experience* (in the comprehensive sense) in the way that *unmarried* is part of the meaning of *bachelor.* Of course, one might stipulate or restrict the meaning of the term arbitrarily. However, where such a stipulative or precising definition has been given, this restrictive sense of *experience* does not exhaust all possibilities of awareness. Thus we require a complementary term (Wolff suggests *imperience*) to refer to mystical awareness, or Fundamental Realization. We may conclude that there is no inherent self-contradiction in the pregnant sense of the term *unmediated experience.*

Also, it is not factually necessary that experience, as such, be mediated in the complex pervasive manner that Katz claims. There is such an experience as pure perception, entirely prior to the normal autonomous activity of consciousness to distinguish, identify, conceptualize, synthesize, and constitute a meaningful world. Such experience lies totally apart from any sense of reflective self-awareness, that is, as a person having the experience. Those of us for whom such an awareness is not simply philosophical speculation, but an experienced actuality, may simply testify to the fact of unmediated experience. In addition, because of its overwhelming intensity, the experience of excruciating pain would tend to prevent conceptual mediation, independent of any antecedent or subsequent interpretation. Consequently, we do in fact find cases apart from mysticism that would count against contextualism.

Were Katz to reply that these examples are not *absolutely* unmediated, insofar as some positive description may be given afterward, this would already admit that they were originally unmediated in the pregnant sense, that is, such experiences are independent of language, conceptual framework, or cultural conditioning. Moreover, even though there are some elements in accounts of mystical experience that do appear contextually determined, the mystic's general claim that it is utterly ineffable testifies that in its inmost nature it is absolutely unmediated. More articulate mystics leave little doubt that it is beyond words and concepts; beyond time, space, and causality; beyond distinction; beyond form and content. Such reports are found in diverse cultures and throughout history, so they cannot themselves be regarded as culturally determined. No doubt, many unsophisticated mystics fail to transcend their own cultural and psychological frameworks in expressing and interpreting their experiences. Wolff states that "Transcendental Consciousness as it is on its own level is inevitably stepped down and modified by the [mystic's] psychological temperament,"[25] but he draws a sharp distinction between the two. Also, because many of the mystics who make the same point have been intelligent, thoughtful, and careful in their use of language, it would be unwarranted to claim that they all were misdescribing their experiences. It is far more reasonable simply to acknowledge that unmediated experience is not only possible, but actual.

We have interpreted Katz's use of *empty* in this regard not just to mean that—despite its logical possibility—no cases of unmediated experience really exist. Rather, it means that whether it occurs is irrelevant, insofar as nothing could be said about it apart from conceptual mediation. There is also a sense of subtle denigration implied by the term that suggests that it thereby would be unimportant or inconsequential. Whereas we shall deal with the problem of ineffability more fully in the succeeding chapter, suffice it here to note that the common core of mystical experience that grounds its universality does not require the existence of an objective, describable element.

Consider also that the strict transcendence of form and value that might be true of the core certainly does not apply to the relative consciousness of the mystic, who generally finds the experience of exceptional significance and value. Furthermore, the interpretation simply may not be mediated by the mystic's cultural conditioning and understanding. There is incontrovertible evidence that mystical experience may result in a radical transformation, not only of the mystic personally, but of his or her world view. As we have already seen, Wolff's Realization of the High Indifference required a fundamental revision of his philosophy from the new base. Due to these considerations, we must firmly reject contextualism as a universal thesis.

Essentialism

According to Horne, the problem of defining mysticism results from one of two factors:

1. the uncritical (or necessary) entanglement of description and interpretation
2. the failure to distinguish different types of mysticism, each having its distinctive characteristics.[26]

While these are genuine factors, he discounts a more central difficulty, namely, the actual ineffability that mystics claim. Many intelligent, articulate mystics who are steeped in long-established spiritual traditions that are adept at exploring consciousness have emphasized strict ineffability. Notwithstanding whatever else they may have reported, it would require an overwhelming argument to show that they all were in error. Wolff contends that it is the nature of the experience, rather than the lack of skill at formulation, that accounts for the sense in which mystics assert ineffability. He personally verifies that in the depths of Realization lies a residue that is innately impervious to all forms of conceptualization.[27]

Wolff's realization that what is most substantial is also least ponderable would suggest that if there is a universal essence to mystical experience, it would lie beyond words and concepts. Let us entertain the possibility of an ineffable 'core' that is the sine qua non for mystical experience. The term *core* must be taken in a special sense, such that it does not refer to anything definable, whether gross or subtle, that might be detected alongside the diverse empirical elements that mystics typically report. Since it is not identical to any of this cluster of discriminative phenomena, it cannot be rendered in terms of them. To be sure, distinguishing it would be problematic, as Wolff acknowledges concerning the High Indifference.

> Any possible report of the state of *nirdvāndva* [a nondualistic state beyond the contrast of opposites] inevitably seems to the relative consciousness as nothing at all. This adequately explains why the unillumined psychologists view the highest of mystical states of consciousness as identical with unconsciousness. There is a serious error in this interpretation, but only he who has known the actuality immediately can know, and he cannot tell what he knows to one who does not also know. One can only categorically affirm: "It is not unconscious."[28]

We must be content to advance this view as the most plausible account of the nature of mysticism and the most fruitful approach to its comprehension—not as a proof or demonstration because none can be given.

However, even though the view that an essential common core constitutes the underlying quiddity of mysticism cannot be proved or disproved, there are good reasons for preferring it. For one, it would explain why the mystic often seems able to say so much about what she claims is ineffable. Whereas the core or essence lies entirely beyond words and concepts, certain features intimate to it (such as timelessness), or phenomena that may attend it (for example, a feeling of joy, bliss, holiness or peace), are not. Phenomenal elements do not constitute what is mystical about the experience, for none of them is invariant in the accounts of mystical experience, and any might occur in other kinds of experience. Furthermore, the ineffability of the core implies that they lack determinate relation to it, although in its Presence they may become exalted and imbued with a special significance. Thus, unable to describe the Absolutely Transcendent, the mystic attempts to convey something of it by discussing the phenomenally immanent![29]

Another advantage of this account is that it would harmonize Stace's apparent inconsistency. The essence of mystical experience is the nonphenomenal core, whereas the phenomena that accompany it are best understood as having a family resemblance, without any single characteristic necessary as a defining criterion. It also places his two-fold typology in perspective: it is valuable for classifying mystical phenomena, but irrelevant concerning its ineffable essence. Discussion of typologies is not only legitimate, but necessary to develop a comprehensive understanding of mysticism. Nevertheless, whenever this approach ignores the Transcendent reference point of the essential core, the baby has been lost in the analysis of the bath. Consequently, we shall avoid preoccupation with detailed scrutiny of typologies so as to emphasize that which is intrinsically mystical.

Many mystics and philosophers lend support to this view. Stace's insight that there is an essential core of mysticism, however much his expression of it may be flawed, is somewhat consistent with it. William Earle's intuitive grasp of Evelyn Underhill's study[30] supplies additional confirmation: "If one impression is that mysticism is infinitely various, another is that remarkably enough through that variety, the *same thing* is being expressed."[31] In contrast to Katz, Ninian Smart gives credence to the notion of a mystical core when he says that "the inmost rapture which is imageless and locutionless is in my view the heart of mysticism, and correlates with some main uses of negative language and theology."[32]

Wolff also takes an essentialist approach transcending the empiricist framework. Because he is a mystic, his statement advocating this thesis carries considerable authority.

> Very few human beings have conscious familiarity with the zone in question, but there are a few who do, and they understand each other when they meet. This latter fact is of the highest significance, for it reveals that the subjective realm is not something absolutely unique in an individual. Unquestionably there are detailed features of the subjective zone that are unique, as one individual is contrasted with another individual and as one type of individual is set off by another type. However, these variants grow less and less with the depth of penetration, while there is a progressive growth in congruency of insight that in the end tends to become absolute. At the very center stands Enlightenment, which is fundamentally the same for all men. I must leave this statement in dogmatic form since it can neither be proved nor disproved in objective terms.[33]

Wolff's final claim concedes too much, for dogmatic assertion is not the only alternative to strict objective demonstration. He might have made a stronger case by citing a few examples—the most relevant from his own firsthand experience—where mystics who have engaged each other from diverse traditions overcame their differences. This would counter the belief that mystical experience is either purely subjective or essentially diverse, having no common core. Of those nonmystics who have provided philosophical accounts of mysticism, Stace seems most compatible with Wolff on this point. This passage definitely is consistent with Stace's notion of transubjectivity—the mystical transcendence of the dichotomy between subjectivity and objectivity. Stace considers the nonmystic fully justified in accepting the argument from unanimity, "that there is a basic agreement of mystical experiences all over the world in spite of many and great differences of interpretation."[34]

If the essentialist position has merit, then it follows that these restrictions inherent in empiricism make it unsuitable for providing a comprehensive account of mysticism. An empiricist methodology deals exclusively with phenomena in an objectively physical or perhaps psychological manner, but where psychology is still treated as a positive science. Because the essence of mysticism is nonobjective, nonphenomenal, and indeterminate, it transcends this approach. If any meaningful account is to be given of this *je ne sais quoi* that constitutes its ineffable essence, we must adopt a methodology that is oriented to the primacy of consciousness instead of phenomena.

Objectivity

Perhaps the most crucial problem arising from the nature of mystical experience is its objectivity, for it is intrinsically private, but claims universal validity. Mystics generally claim to experience a "sense of objectivity," that is, of a revealed reality presented as transcending the mystic's personal psychology. It does not deal with the disposition of the objects of ordinary experience, but with the nature of the world as a whole. It is not surprising that a common objection to the serious study of mysticism is that because mystical experience is not objective its claims should be dismissed as merely subjective, having no significance beyond the mystic's life.

Unfortunately, the problem of objectivity is muddled due to inconsistent usage of the subject/object distinction in Western philosophy.[35] Initially, the term *subject* referred to a real existent independent of the knower, while *object* designated that which is intentionally related to consciousness. The Kantian revolution reversed these meanings so that the subject became identified with the Transcendental Ego (or alternatively, the Pure Ego or act of consciousness). The object was expelled from subjective awareness—to become thought of as an external independent existent. Edmund Husserl and Alexius Meinong resisted the modern acceptance of this reversal. Wolff also departs from Kant on this point, distinguishing between the object (which is intentionally related to, and dependent upon, the consciousness of the knower) and the thing (which is the supposed independent reality existing apart from our awareness).

Mystical experience at its core is not objective in the sense of presenting an intentional object to consciousness, even though the mystic is aware of objects in extrovertive mysticism and some occurrences of introvertive mysticism. Therefore, neither is it merely subjective in the sense of an awareness that is restricted to some sort of private object(s), such as visions or dream images. There is mystery enough in the notion of the Pure Ego or Self in the individual sense, but, according to Stace, the mystic reports

> that this self, which seems at first to be his own private self, experiences itself as at once becoming one with or becoming dissolved in an infinite and universal self. The boundary walls of the separate self fade away, and the individual finds himself passing beyond himself, and becoming merged in a boundless and universal consciousness.[36]

This awareness is characteristic of the introvertive type, which Stace regards as a more complete form than extrovertive experience. Yet, without recourse to any empirical contents of consciousness, there is no principle of individuation. He introduces the term *transsubjective* because this awareness is neither objective, in the modern sense, nor subjective.

The sense of objectivity that mystics report has considerable philosophical import once it is clarified. It does not concern objects, as such, but refers to an experienced revelation of an underlying Reality superseding the mundane. Not only is it a common feature of the experience itself, but afterward the mystic does not repudiate the overriding validity of this insight. Care must be taken here to avoid any metaphysical hypostatization, as when Stace claims that the mystic has reached "the pure ego of the universe."[37] If she interprets it metaphysically, she will typically claim that its reality value transcends that of our normal awareness, much as the latter is held to transcend that of the dream state. The epistemological problem of determining the force of the mystical perspective cannot justly be preempted by the nonmystical consensus for the reason that it is the mystic who has the more extensive range of experience. Thus, we must inquire not only into mysticism as a subject matter for philosophy, but into the significance that mysticism has for our understanding of the philosophical enterprise.

PHILOSOPHY

Metaphilosophy

Wolff's philosophical significance extends beyond the detailed accounts of his realizations and his articulated philosophy of Introceptualism. He finds mystical experience to be the ground for an immediate, nonphenomenal, noetic content. It may be known with absolute assurance through identity, but its essential ineffability allows only nonexclusive symbolic formulations. This sense of assurance is of the nature of an intense and profound affective state, not an epistemological guarantee concerning the objective truth of any proposition that may issue from it. It follows that his proposed Copernican revolution, which would shift philosophical emphasis from the subject-object structure to Consciousness Itself, involves more than the treatment of new subject matter by the application of traditional methods. It requires a personal Awakening to a different way of consciousness as the immediate base from which to philosophize. Because Wolff's vision of philosophy challenges current understanding and practice in the West, we cannot properly assess his importance without considering the nature and meaning of philosophy itself, the role that mysticism plays in philosophy, and recent developments in the philosophical treatment of mysticism.

A completely definitive answer to the metaphilosophical[38] question concerning the nature of philosophy may be unattainable. What is at issue, however, is the role of a religious—specifically mystical—dimension for philosophy. Naturally, what is most relevant in this regard is a personal transformation of consciousness, not the mere study of religious phenomena as subject matter, nor the adoption of any particular religious doctrine.

Wolff distinguishes between comprehensive and restrictive approaches to philosophy. In contrasting philosophy to religion and psychology, he relates them to meaning, value, and fact respectively, the "fundamental zones of human interest and concern."[39] In contrast to what he calls "philosophy proper," a detached academic study devoid of practice or personal involvement, he advocates a synthetic approach that combines rather than isolates these disciplines. He emphasizes the conception of philosophy as a Way of Life—not the mere study of terms-in-relation.

> A real philosophy is a Way of Life, however much it may also be a system of notions. . . .[40] The office of great philosophy is to be a *Way* of Realization, and not solely a monitor of *doing*. This the ancients knew well, but in these later, more sordid, days this truth is all but forgotten. . . . For the eternal function of the Divine Sophia is to supply the knowing that serves *being* first of all and *doing* only in so far as action is instrumental to that being.[41]

Hence he rejects the strict compartmentalizing of philosophy and religion, as well as philosophy's adoption of the scientific ideal of the neutral observer who remains aloof from his subject matter.[42]

Philosophy and Religion

Consider that until very recently Eastern philosophy has been inseparable from religion, while in the West the original meaning of the term *philosophy* is "love of wisdom." For Pythagoras and Plato, care of the soul is paramount, and the contemplative function of philosophy promotes that end. Their introvertive, intuitive emphasis complements the predominantly extrovertive, sensuous orientation of the preponderance of Greek philosophy.

The interrelationship between philosophy and religion is mutually beneficial, but only when each preserves its integrity within a harmonious balance. Kenneth Schmitz claims that equilibrium between philosophy and religion requires that philosophy neither relinquish "its autonomy and its powers of criticism,—the power to frame its own questions, establish its own criteria and seek out its own methods [nor seek] to transform, erase or ignore religion."[43] Even so, a penetrating study of religion has profound implications for philosophy. Schmitz states:

> Reflection is transformed by what it feeds on. . . . A philosophy is changed by the regions it invades in its philosophical exercise . . . in its structural principles, its aspirations, motivations and criteria, and even in the way in which it seizes and understands itself. . . .[44]
>
> The philosopher who ventures into the philosophy of religion may think that he is going to add a new application to his basic principles; but if he takes seriously the modality of experience and behavior exhibited by the religious man,—then he may find that he will have to retrace his steps and recast his entire philosophy.[45]

This is because of the formative nature of religious language. It is formative of consciousness insofar as it requires involvement with its subject matter in a manner radically different from the aloof detachment of the propositional attitude found in science. Eliot Deutsch explains that contextually grounded religious language embodies an entire view of reality and conditions consciousness accordingly. How is this so?

> Thinking about reality, talking about the divine, is . . . a *projective* act of the mind; it is, at this level of being, the manner in which the mind engages reality. Spiritual being is not grasped by our thinking or talking about it; it is not in this way reduplicated in our consciousness; rather, in our thinking and talking about it, it becomes the locus of consciousness, the place where consciousness is *at.* And consciousness *becomes* where it is at. It takes on the structure of relationships that it projects—and is thereby formed.[46]

Schmitz believes that the development of modern Western philosophy has led to a fatal one-sidedness that makes an authentic (that is, open and nonreductive) study of religion imperative, for only by risking this challenge can philosophy regain its balance.

Philosophy and Science

Schmitz contends that a well-balanced philosophy should exhibit both aspects of reason, which we could describe as thinking and apprehending, or the logical and the noetic. *Logos,* or *ratio,* represents the strictly formal expectancy, which is discursive and systematic, emphasizing argument, method, and precision. By comparison, *nous,* or *intellectus,* indicates the flexible rationality, which is intuitive and apperceptive, stressing open discrimination of what is given in evidence.[47] Schmitz is reacting against a powerful orthodoxy in philosophy, going back to Descartes. When Descartes introduced a dichotomy between extended substance and thinking substance, he advanced the implementation of the Pythagorean ideal of a true mathematizing of nature. His dualistic metaphysics, which allows science to study matter independently from mind, made possible the revolution of Western science. The ensuing scientific requirements of precision and method have produced a conception of rationality equivalent to logically conceptual thinking supported by empirical verification,[48] a view that came to dominate philosophy as well. As a result, philosophy swung strongly toward the formal facet of reason, overbalancing away from *nous* toward *logos*. Wolff expresses similar concern when he argues that "the present sad estate of much philosophy is largely the result of a critical acumen that has run far ahead of the unfoldment of balancing insight."[49]

This distancing of philosophy from religion, and its rapprochement with science, with its positivist rationality, has had profound consequences. The rapid advancement of the physical sciences has led to the neglect of the inner, conscious side of experience, even for psychology. This extroverted attitude, which has been endemic in the West, has tended to reduce the study of humankind to what is publicly observable—namely, physiology and behavior. It has come to view consciousness either as epiphenomenal or nonexistent and ignores private experience as too subjective to be scientific. Consequently, by patterning itself after the successful physical sciences, psychology has abandoned its proper domain.

Ian Watson sounds a timely warning that the rise of the secular-materialist mind in the West (and rapidly spreading to the East) is dehumanizing, severing philosophy from its roots. The result is "a breakdown in *understanding* of what is meant by 'wisdom'."[50] Because 'wisdom' is intimately related to the values of our inner being, the real existence of which modern philosophy has largely ignored or denied, "'wisdom', it is thought, no longer has anything of moment with which to relate or be about."[51] Philosophy is faced with the crisis of its threatened disappearance as an independent discipline unless it is able to reestablish connection with its roots. Wolff regards his philosophy of Introceptualism as diametrically opposed to materialism and as a practical antidote to this malaise.

Nicholas Maxwell makes a similar point concerning the whole domain of intellectual inquiry, as academically institutionalized. He decries the dominance of the "philosophy of knowledge," the view that rational inquiry must ignore human needs, values, and social concerns to contribute to the store of objective knowledge. He proposes a revolution to the "philosophy of wisdom," that is, inquiry based on the orientation to human value. This not only would intrinsically conform to a more adequate standard of rationality, he contends, but also produce more desirable results. In spite of the self-perpetuating influence of the scientifically oriented approach upon the academic community, Maxwell finds recent evidence that the new philosophy is gaining ground.[52]

Mysticism Renews Philosophy

Mysticism is more than a curious and elusive subject matter for philosophy. More fundamentally, it functions as a preontological source of renewal to ensure an inexhaustible fount for philosophical rejuvenation. Wolff's account of Realization implies just that: One experiences an identity with the source of all value, as it were, wherein a primordial, self-authenticating wisdom may manifest innumerable variations of philosophical expression.

Similarly, from within a Heideggerian framework, Leon Rosenstein regards mysticism as a state of being in which the mystic experiences an apprehension of, or unification with, the source or ground of reality, and that the mystic regards as of overwhelming significance.[53] He entertains the "claim that philosophy in some sense necessarily requires or presupposes a rejuvenating and primordial foundation which either is or approaches mysticism."[54]

In particular, this orientation maintains the ontological priority of the question of Being. *Dasein* (human being—literally, *being there*) already has a preontological understanding of Being, which makes possible this fundamental questioning. *Dasein* must question the Being of things, or what is manifest, to recapture authenticity from everydayness (traditional or commonly accepted ways of doing and thinking).

> This going beyond by going towards is only possible because of man's preontological comprehension of Being. Philosophy itself is

> only possible because of this, for its fundamental questions could never be asked were it not for some vague awareness of what it is which is asked about. Yet it is precisely in this deepest probing that philosophy must leave itself and become mysticism.[55]

This will not result in a determinate theoretical formulation, for while the mystery of Being reveals itself in this questioning, it conceals itself from conceptual categorization. Philosophy is renewed, not by adding to its store of information or by advancing yet another systematic world view, but by returning to its ontological roots, seeing things anew, finding novel modes of expression, authentically challenging the philosopher to open to creative possibilities, rather than retrace worn and familiar paths. Nonetheless, the philosopher must renounce permanent residence in the mystical, if he is to continue philosophizing.

Apart from Martin Heidegger's adherence to the Thesis of Intentionality, there is substantial overlap with the notion of mysticism that Wolff exemplifies. However, whereas Wolff penetrates the subject-to-consciousness by discriminating the self so as to Realize the Self, Heidegger penetrates the object of consciousness by questioning the being of things so as to Realize Being. In the High Indifference, however, both the Self and Being are Transcended.

Awakening as Philosophical Paradigm

Wolff concurs with the commonly reported "sense of objectivity" characteristic of mystical experience—that is, that it is given as more fundamentally real than what is perceived in ordinary waking consciousness. Neal Grossman believes that the existence of this "superconscious state" requires an understanding based upon a new philosophical paradigm.[56] On his account, how reality appears according to the "old paradigm" depends upon our fixed state of mind, whereas in the "new paradigm" there are possible fundamental alterations in mental states that make possible various ways for the world to appear. Specifically, he asserts that there is a hierarchy of such states where a superconscious state (I_s) stands in the same relation to our normal awareness (I_a) as our waking consciousness stands to the dream state (I_d). This implies that one who has attained the perspective of I_s would be in a privileged position in regard to understanding the experience of I_a. He rightly concludes that adoption of the new paradigm would "fundamentally alter the nature of philosophy as practiced today." The goal would be "not the analysis or synthesis of conceptual edifices, but rather, the attaining of I_s."[57]

Vedānta is a traditional system that professes a similar ideal. Even so, whereas it regards attainment of this state as the goal or end, philosophically it also serves as a means to establish conceptual understanding on the basis of immediate awareness. Grossman contends that there is really nothing new about the paradigm and that Plato, for example, sought consciousness expansion as the goal of his philosophy, set out metaphorically in the Allegory of the Cave.[58]

Plato's allegory reminds us that there are two complementary phases to the process, for it is satisfactory neither to live in the cave in ignorance nor to enjoy individual Enlightenment in the sunlit realm while others remain in bondage. We now see how the philosophical paradigm of Awakening is both subtle and complex. There is in the phase of Awakening a transformation of world view that might be given philosophical expression, but ultimately philosophy (as a construction of words and concepts) also must be transcended in radical immanence. In the phase where the superconscious philosopher returns, formulation serves not only to convey an Enlightened view of reality, but also serves as a conceptual ladder that others may use to assist their ascent out of the cave.

Thus the Enlightenment process has profound philosophical implications. H. Gene Blocker explains the "three mountains" metaphor of Zen as a progression from naive realism, through idealism, to direct experience free from interpretation. Ch'ing Yuan says,

> Before I had studied Zen for thirty years, I saw mountains as mountains, and waters as waters. When I arrived at a more intimate knowledge, I came to the point where I saw that mountains are not mountains, and waters are not waters. But now that I have got its very substance I am at rest. For it's just that I see mountains once again as mountains, and waters once again as water.[59]

Blocker concludes, "In the end, we are brought back to the everyday world of sense experience, though our attitude toward this everyday world and its 'givenness' is radically altered."[60]

Louis Nordstrom characterizes the nature of Zen mysticism as "simply to unite with whatever is happening, completely to remove any trace of separation from the content of one's experience."[61] This "radical immanence" involves a "transcendence of transcendence," which is obviously not the same as no transcendence at all, but is "devoid of ontological content."[62] Philosophy, on this view, can have at best a heuristic value, as a raft or ladder to be discarded after it has served its purpose.

John Visvader borrows the Gnostic and alchemical symbol of Oroboros to characterize this type of therapeutic philosophy.

> Some of the drawings remaining from these schools depict a serpent, Uroboros, bent in a circle swallowing its own tail. Sometimes Uroboros is shown transforming itself into a salamander, and in this representation are portrayed two important aspects of uroboric philosophy. The first is the swallowing of one's tail, the throwing away of the raft or ladder, the erasing of one's footprints, and the second is the transformation into a salamander, the achievement of a state that is often discontinuous with and profoundly different from one's original philosophical stance.[63]

He states that Oroboric philosophies "do more, however, than merely refute themselves. They seem to transcend themselves in a profound way and leave the student in a place he was not in before. Philosophy is used as a means for putting an end to itself in a nontrivial way."[64]

Wolff doubtless would agree with Grossman's priority: The attainment of Realization is of supreme importance; the conceptual elaboration of a derived philosophical understanding is secondary. Even so, he strongly opposes the restrictive orientation of Zen to the domain of sense experience,[65] for he contends that it unnecessarily devalues abstract thought. He would deny that poetry can replace philosophy because the concept has more than a purely instrumental value.[66] The "Royal Road" lies *through*, not around the conceptual function, and while he acknowledges the efficacy of other paths, he questions whether they achieve the same result.[67]

The paradigm of Awakening faces a more practical problem, namely, convincing the skeptic that it presents a desirable alternative to the present dominant view. Wolff acknowledges the difficulty inherent in conveying the reality and superiority of Realization to the nonmystic.

> There is something here that can be realized immediately, but which defeats every effort of the intellective consciousness to capture and represent in really intelligible terms, but there can be no doubt of the superior authority of the State of Realization itself, for the individual who has acquaintance with it. To be sure, intellectual dialectic may confuse and veil the memory of the immense authority of the Realization, but this veiling process has no more significance than the power of the ordinary dream to veil the judgment of the waking state. Whereas the dream is generally something inferior to the waking intellectual judgment, the Realization has a transcendent superiority with respect to the latter. But can the intellectual consciousness of the man who has had no glimpse of the Realization be convinced of this? It is certainly quite difficult for the dreamer, while dreaming, to realize the purely relative existence of his dream. Has the waking intellectual judgment a superior capacity with respect to the acknowledgment of its own Transcendental Roots?[68]

The resistance of the nonmystic is primarily psychological. It is clearly philosophically insupportable to insist that there is no domain of human awareness beyond one's personal experience, or that whatever lies beyond it could not be superior to it. With unshakable conviction, the mystic "claims a greater reality-quale for the content or value realized through the mystical sense than for that possessed by all the other senses."[69] How could the nonmystic effectively challenge this? It is the mystic, rather than the nonmystic, who is in the better position to compare and evaluate their respective viewpoints, since only she has an immediate awareness of both.

Wolff illustrates the situation by considering the analogy of a person born with the sense of sight amidst a race born blind.[70] Such a person would know with absolute certainty the existence and superiority of her capacity to apprehend reality, even though convincing others would be quite uncertain. Whatever one might offer as evidence could always be interpreted to conform to an explanation based on the established world view, so it might seem unnecessary to introduce the hypothesis of a new faculty. Furthermore, even if it were accepted, those not possessing it could never know its immediate nature. Let us extend the analogy by assuming that a process were discovered by which the blind could be made to see. Could a skeptic in good conscience continue to reject the claims of those having sight while refusing to undergo this process to gain sight himself?

The foregoing metaphilosophical critique shows the need for philosophical renewal: redefinition of its nature, methods, and goals. Its role as "handmaiden to science" has resulted in the unwitting adoption of presuppositions that have restricted both its methods and its scope of investigation. In addition, the linguistic turn in philosophy—the shift of focus to the analysis and clarification of language—has tended to preempt the discussion of substantive issues. This does not at all imply that a philosophical renewal through mysticism would return the discipline to its medieval role as "handmaiden to theology," where the task of reason is limited to supporting religious doctrines antecedently held on authority. Wolff, Schmitz, Grossman, and others reject dogmatism of any sort. The ground for philosophical renewal is religious—more precisely, mystical—in nature, in the sense that it requires existential, rather than a merely theoretical, commitment. Here knowing and being are apprehended immediately and pretheoretically. This must involve the whole person—not merely the disinterested intellect. In this spirit, as Wolff recommends, philosophy would genuinely become a Way of Life.

Synthetic Pluralism

Wolff conceives philosophy "to be a conscientious effort to arrive at as comprehensive an understanding of reality as possible, whatever that reality may prove to be."[71] He regards the development of incompatible philosophical schools as the necessary result of the direct awareness of what he terms "indefinables," by which he means that which is immediately apprehended prior to interpretation. Thus "in the logical sense, any datum of experience must be regarded as an original and indefinable term."[72] Although his discussion of indefinables, per se, remains general, it is reasonable to infer that he is justifying his philosophy as primarily derived from indefinables unique to mystical experience. This substantial, though transempirical, "base is supersensible, superaffective, and superconceptual,"[73] hence indefinable. Wolff wishes to point out here that each is indefinable and ineffable as it presents itself to our direct preconceptual awareness.[74]

At this stage of awareness one has not yet articulated any propositions that go beyond immediacy. Therefore, Wolff contends that the indefinables themselves are logically immune to challenge—although it is possible to criticize the adequacy of subsequent formulation. He proposes that diverse indefinables lead to disparate philosophies. However, for the sake of completeness, he should further allow for different interpretations of the same indefinable to account for some heterogeneous philosophical development.

> The decisive part of indefinables as determinants of philosophical outlooks is becoming increasingly evident. It seems quite clear that these indefinables are known through immediate apprehensions and cannot be logically derived as a result of discursive process. . . . Where the immediately given indefinables for two or more individuals are largely disjunctive, . . . the inevitable consequence is the development of diverse and incommensurable philosophical systems and outlooks.[75]

This belief admits a relative validity to every school of philosophy whose emphasis is based upon the insights provided by the partial perspectives it embodies.[76] Wolff specifically refers to naturalism, neorealism, pragmatism, and idealism, as well as his new philosophy of Introceptualism, but his clear intent is that this synthesis should extend to all philosophies. He holds that "all these systems or ways of thinking bring into relief by accentuation authentic elements or complexes which are to be found in actual human experience or consciousness. Therefore, none may be wholly neglected, and a truly synthetic philosophy, when and if it is ever written, must do justice to, or at least find room for, the positive values of each."[77] Wolff's appraisal of philosophy is thus to be understood partially as a synthetic pluralism founded upon the total possible range of immediate awareness.

Given his notion of the primary source of diverging viewpoints, it follows that philosophy must attempt a higher integration of these perspectives by expanding our awareness of the range of indefinables. This compels us to go beyond mere analysis to achieve the most comprehensive synthesis. He maintains that "the most complete apprehension of reality can be attained only by him who has realized the widest immediate recognition of indefinables. . . . The awakening to progressively wider ranges of recognition of indefinables . . . , becomes the prime philosophic need."[78] Again, the notion of awakening is thematic, but here the objective focus (the indefinables of which one becomes aware) complements the subjective emphasis (the altered state of consciousness that permits a new range of awareness).

Even though awakening may occur spontaneously, it is the business of philosophy to make a self-conscious effort toward it. In either case, one attains a more inclusive understanding. "There may be an awakening to new immediately given indefinables and, in this case, a broadening of philosophic outlook becomes possible. In fact, for an individual who has had such an awakening, schools of thought that had stood in incommensurable relationship for him, now attain a more or less complete reconciliation within a higher integration."[79] Even without such an expanded personal comprehension engendered by the direct awareness of indefinables, an open encounter with alternative conceptual systems is valuable, principally to induce us to become more self-critical regarding our own.

Without firsthand acquaintance with the indefinable(s) grounding an alien philosophy, there may be an inclination to resist their introduction. For example, certain principles of empiricism, combined with the attitude that common sense is the criterion (or at least a necessary condition) for truth (or even meaningfulness), would erect a formidable barrier to the acceptance of the indefinables that ground Wolff's system. This point is illustrated by C. O. Evans, who upholds two principles introduced by C. D. Broad, namely, that if other things are equal we are to prefer a theory that need not "postulate anything of a kind which is not already admitted as a fact and found to be readily intelligible, . . . [or] suppose that all men are fundamentally mistaken on certain matters with which the whole race is and has always been constantly concerned."[80] Though these principles appear plausible and innocuous at first glance, their practical application will almost certainly effect a question-begging rejection of anything incompatible with the prevailing antecedent world view.

In contrast to these restrictive assumptions, Wolff advances only two conditions necessary for defining knowledge as scientific:

1. "The interpretative theory must be a logical and self-consistent whole from which deductive inferences can be drawn."[81]

2. The theory must not only provide inferences, but "suggest an empirically possible experiment or observation that can confirm or fail to confirm the inference."[82]

An interpretative theory of some kind is necessary to give meaning to the raw data that has been collected. The first condition is necessary for science per se; the second constitutes a necessity solely for empiric science. Wolff further acknowledges that in practice a third principle, whose only justification is psychological, operates "that serves convenience and even prejudice rather than logic. This is the requirement that the interpretative theory shall be congruent with already established or accepted scientific points of view, unless it is well proven that this third condition cannot be satisfied without violating the first or second."[83] Wolff is correct in insisting that this principle cannot be used as a criterion of the *truth*[84] of an interpretation. Its function is essentially psychological, serving the need for security. Anything that does not harmonize with an already extant *Weltanschauung* threatens its coherence and hence the security of anyone whom it confronts.[85]

The principles advanced by Broad and Evans are clearly variations of this third condition and thus are dispensable for the purpose of scientific (or philosophical) rigor. Other things are rarely equal, and it is bad philosophy to assume that what does not seem readily intelligible (on the basis of one's current view of reality) is incoherent from every perspective. We must aspire to *make* it intelligible in a way that does not violate its inherent nature.

Wolff feels the need to make a special appeal to avert this sort of offhand a priori rejection of the significance of mystical realization. He justifies the introduction of the indefinables in question both on theoretical and on pragmatic grounds. Theoretically, the degree of firsthand availability of an indefinable is not an essential factor in determining its legitimacy. In practice, the indefinable that is apprehended as "a timeless and nonphenomenal consciousness" has already demonstrated its value in the profound effect it has had upon Western, but especially upon Eastern civilization.[86] Thus not only is a mystically grounded philosophy permissible, but it is required, if we are to advance the ideal of synthetic pluralism.

To conclude, we have found that neither mysticism nor philosophy is definable, for they play complementary roles in humanity's ongoing quest for ultimates. The direct grasp by way of mystical realization is transformed into a conceptual representation of limited understanding, which in turn helps guide others in their efforts. Furthermore, as mystics, we seek immediate awareness of the ground from which to live, so as to apply it authentically in the infinite diversity of life. As philosophers, we seek the synthetic unification of all immediate contents of awareness into a comprehensive world view. Both projects are essentially open-ended, and contemporary philosophy now has come to accept generally the futility of constructing a single absolute and insuperable conceptual system.

Wolff's striving for foundations and his attempt to integrate contrasting perspectives does not imply that he believes that there is a single, ultimately correct philosophical formulation. On the contrary, he inveighs against all forms of reductionism in philosophy, insisting that "Justice demands that we accept these differences of adjustment as relatively valid and renounce the hope and desire for universal philosophic conformity. The conflict of philosophic schools is both desirable and necessary."[87] However, to avoid an empty eclecticism, philosophy must be grounded in an irreducible experiential base—not mere conceptual constructs. Unity may be mystically Realized, but it gives rise to a wealth of philosophical expression that must acknowledge the legitimacy of the full range of indefinables.[88]

CHAPTER 5

Mystical Language

Mysticism is difficult to comprehend due in part to the pervasive difficulty of trying to say something meaningful about an awareness that mystics universally allege is ineffable. We have assumed thus far that mystical discourse conveys some sense of the mystic's immediate awareness. Due to the philosophical weight of the role of language and logic concerning the understanding, formulation, and communication of mystical experience, we must now address this issue more fully. Not only are we obliged to show that it is *possible* to say something intelligible concerning mystical awareness, but that what mystics say *is* generally intelligible. If the claim of ineffability is literally true, we must delimit its application and inquire into the significance of the various ways in which mystics use language in practice. This involves a study of the strategies employed to express and communicate these experiences, as well as an analysis and evaluation of the language used to accomplish it. In particular, we shall investigate the nature of symbolic language and its suitability for the task. Finally, we shall apply our subsequent understanding to several examples of Wolff's most central modes of expression.

Wolff is keenly aware of the semantic problem that mysticism presents. He acknowledges the strict ineffability that lies at the core of his Fundamental Realizations, but he feels that, despite the unavoidable distortion of language when applied to this domain, the value even of its imperfect communication is warranted.

> I do not see any practical escape from what might be called a coloring of the colorless, just so soon as the Inexpressible is reflected in expression. The most perfect vehicle of expression is, inevitably, a distortion in some measure. The alternatives are, therefore, either to refrain from all expression, or consistently to employ the instruments of expression which the individual has actually evolved, being careful, however, to warn all that the expression is only a reflection of THAT which on Its own level remains ever inexpressible.[1]

Clearly, a discussion of mystical language is necessary, both to justify further philosophical consideration of mysticism and to guide those who would seek personal understanding.

The alleged ineffability of mystical experience is a most perplexing problem. Mystics consistently maintain that it is inexpressible, indescribable, incommunicable, inconceivable, and so on, but then usually go on to give some sort of account using language that is more or less intelligible. Several objections arise that might undermine the mystic's case for interpreting ineffability as literally true. On the one hand, it is suggested that the claim is simply mistaken, or more plausibly that the ineffability involved is no different than in the case of some common experiences, such as intense bliss or awe. If so, then there would be nothing further about mystical experience that would elude satisfactory empirical description. On the other hand, if the mystic's claim is correct, then silence would seem to be the only appropriate response, since any verbal formulation must result in nonsense. A critic who subscribed to this false dilemma would thereby regard mystical language either as sloppy literal description (because what can be said can be said clearly) or as utter nonsense (attempting to say what cannot be said at all).

In response, let us elaborate the view introduced in the preceding chapter. We shall argue that the most reasonable interpretation of the mystic's testimony is that there 'is' an essential, nonphenomenal 'core' common to mystical experience, and it is only to this that ineffability strictly applies. The obvious semantic difficulty in advancing this notion requires that key terms—such as *core*, *is*, and *point*—be taken symbolically, rather than literally. This is because the core cannot be identified with any phenomenal elements of the mystic's awareness nor any definable terms that are used to attempt to convey it. This core is irreducible to any of the phenomena, either gross or subtle, that they report. In its purity, it is absolutely beyond words and concepts, although language may be used symbolically when attempting to 'point' to it. Even though some mystics choose simply to remain silent, most attempt to express and communicate their Realizations by using such diverse means as universal negation, paradox, and positive formulations. We shall discuss and evaluate these strategies, especially the use of symbols (and consider the problems that they engender) to determine the extent to which language and logic are adequate to the task.

INEFFABILITY

Wolff dramatizes the difficulty by asking, "How do you communicate the truth, or at least indicate the truth, when the only tools you have to work with are all of them lies? . . . [It is] the problem of trying to communicate the consciousness of the nondualistic reality in terms that are essentially dualistic."[2] His personal reports of several realizations, as well as the manner in which he grasps and deals with this problem, are instructive. More concretely, we shall focus attention on Wolff's aphorisms on Consciousness-without-an-object[3] and on the SELF,[4] his symbolic use of mathematics and his mandala.[5]

Definition

Ineffability is a complex issue. What does *ineffable* mean? What, if anything, is ineffable? How could this be indicated? How can it be explained? What is the status of formulations concerning that which is deemed to be ineffable? Let us begin by considering the definition of this term. Its central meaning is related to the adequacy of verbal expression or description. To say simply that *ineffable* means "inexpressible," or as Wolff does, "unspeakable" or "incommunicable,"[6] is misleading. In principle, everything whatsoever is minimally expressible because the issue of adequacy of reference or communication has not yet been raised. One might arbitrarily choose any linguistic form or nonlinguistic behavior to express any awareness whatsoever.

Although the term *ineffable* also means "unspeakable," the sense of this latter term carries the implication of taboo—one is proscribed from saying what *might* otherwise be said. Leonard

Angel believes that it is possible to defend the mystics' ineffability claims,[7] but that the truth of the essentialist thesis is incapable of fully accounting for their silence. He contends that there are instances that are not (merely) logically inexpressible, but praxiologically inexpressible—that is, where the mystic could speak if she wished to do so, but prefers to remain silent for other reasons.[8] These might include piety and maintaining the secrecy of the teachings of an esoteric tradition. Such cases no doubt exist, but the preponderance of examples where mystics cite ineffability as the reason for their silence are not explainable by such factors.

Similarly, the term *incommunicable* is ambiguous. Is something incommunicable because it is intrinsically indescribable, or because a particular language happens to lack the required tools (for example, as Swahili lacks the means to communicate the concepts of higher mathematics)? It seems reasonable to conclude that 'ineffable' is best equated with 'incapable of adequate representation or formulation,' either in language or otherwise, where adequacy is related both to that which is expressed and to the nature of representation.

This proposed definition parallels that which J. Kellenberger attributes to William James: To say that something is ineffable means that it "*defies expression, that no adequate report of its contents can be given in words.*"[9] He claims that this meaning would involve the semantic paradox, that "we could not describe *at all* mystical experience or any other mystical object to which the sense was applicable."[10] Kellenberger's analysis suffers from a pervasive reference to "the mystical object," which is intended to indicate in a general way that which is ineffable. However, this is misleading because it implies the applicability of the subject-object structure. Wolff is clear on this point: in "the *Nirvāṇic* state of consciousness . . . there are no objects, for the simple reason that in that State there is no subject-object relationship."[11] Hence the mystical core must not be conceived as one objective element among those that mystics report, for it is not an object at all.

The Semantic Paradox

A great deal of confusion is dispelled once we distinguish the ineffable core of mystical experience from attendant phenomena. Reports of joy, photisms, and so on indicate elements that are not strictly mystical, and that would not make our ordinary experience mystical. Wolff takes such reports as evidence of some degree of blending of the *Nirvāṇic* state (as consciousness of the absence of objects) with ordinary relative consciousness. He contends that *Nirvāṇic* Consciousness "is the culminating point of the mystical path into the *subject pole* of consciousness."[12] Because this is a rare mystical attainment, he believes that most mystical states are only partially transcendent and thus somewhat capable of objective understanding. The degree of intelligibility of the mystic's account thus would seem to depend on the purity of the state, although other factors also are involved. Insofar as mystical experience is even partially transcendent, however, "always, with the mystic, there is an ineffable substratum that he never succeeds in more than suggesting in his expression."[13]

Wolff emphasizes the absolute distinction "*between the transcendental state of consciousness itself and the precipitated effects within the relative consciousness.*"[14] His distinction is explicitly grounded in direct awareness, as opposed to mere conceptual reasoning. If valid, it circumvents the semantic paradox, for what the mystic is describing is not the ineffable core itself. Description here relates only to the most sublime modifications of relative consciousness catalyzed by Fundamental Realization, as well as reports of attendant phenomena. This would further support the essentialist thesis that there is a common core that constitutes what is mystical, while explaining to some extent the diversity of mystics' verbal formulations. The mystic may assert, but cannot describe, the universal essence. By comparison, there may be considerable variation in the forms of precipitated material as well as in the symbolism employed to convey it and to indicate the core.

Ineffability of Ordinary Experience

One anticipated objection to the foregoing position is that no unique transcendent core (element) need be posited to account for the mystic's avowal of ineffability. We might easily accept that much of ordinary experience is also ineffable, so a skeptic could easily suspect that it is no more than this to which the mystic refers. In reply, let us first acknowledge that there are many things that are ineffable, for instance, the aesthetic quality of a sunset or a sense of the sublime while watching a space shuttle launch. In addition, mystics undoubtedly report some ineffable phenomenal elements, such as indescribable bliss. It may also well be true that in some sense no experience can be captured fully by description. Wolff remarks that we cannot adequately communicate the experiential quale of one sense organ in terms of another and that "there is something fundamentally ineffable in the relationship between percepts and concepts."[15] However, he introduces these examples so as to contrast them with the ineffability peculiar to the mystical, which is in no way reducible to any of the foregoing considerations.

Ineffability of Mystical Experience

We may take as paradigmatic of mystical ineffability, in the pregnant sense, Wolff's Fundamental Realizations, concerning which he explicitly rejects the adequacy of language for communicating their true nature. His first Fundamental Realization initially shifted into a conscious but ineffable identity with Voidness, Darkness, and Silence. These he realized immediately as Fullness, Light, and Sound—in the sense of Substantiality, Illumination, and "pure formless Meaning and Value,"[16] respectively. Immediately following this he became aware of an inconceivable deepening of consciousness that was

> quite beyond the possibility of adequate representation. To suggest the Value of this transcendental state of consciousness requires concepts of the most intensive possible connotation and the modes of expression that indicate the most superlative value art can devise. Yet the result of the best effort seems a sorry sort of thing when compared with the immediate Actuality. All language, as such, is defeated when used as an instrument of portrayal of the transcendent. . . . The immediate noetic and affective values of the insight, while they may be directly realized, cannot be conveyed by any formulation or representation whatsoever.[17]

We must interpret this categorical statement as explicitly intended to apply only to the transcendent core, not the attendant phenomena arising within relative consciousness.

Wolff's second Fundamental Realization, like the first, quickly became ineffable, yet quite differently. The preliminary deepening effect in consciousness became an affective state of Satisfaction, which he found to be identical with the word *Satisfaction* and the abstract universal concept 'satisfaction' that it normally represents.

> Here there enters a strange and almost weird feature. Language, considered as standing in a representative relationship to something other than the terms of the language, ceased to have any validity at this level of consciousness. In a sense, the words and that which they mean are interblended in a kind of identity. Abstract ideas cease to be artificial derivatives from a particularized experience, but are transformed into a sort of universal substantiality. The relative theories of knowledge simply do not apply at this level. So "Satisfaction" and the *state* of satisfaction possess a substantial and largely inexpressible identity. Further, this "Satisfaction," along with its substantiality, possesses a universal character. It is the value of all possible satisfactions at once and yet like a "thick" substance interpenetrating everywhere. I know how weird this effort at formulation must sound, but unless I abandon the attempt to interpret, I must constrain language to serve a purpose quite outside normal usage.[18]

We usually think of general terms, such as *satisfaction*, as referring to a universal quality abstracted from all particular instances (of satisfaction), and for this reason we tend to regard the reality as residing only in the particular case. The word stands at a distance from its referent, so to speak, unreal and insubstantial. Wolff experienced a collapse of the representative relationship such that the particular state of satisfaction was at the same time universal, the term *satisfaction* substantial.

Bear in mind that his account is of the awareness within the Realization itself—not a metaphysical theory. He cautions that the words are meant in an extended sense, rather than according to standard usage. His comments express serious concern that his formulation not be taken strictly literally, as if it were a straightforward scientific report of a wholly determinate subject matter. It would be wise to exercise similar caution when interpreting apparently unqualified accounts by other mystics.

How then are we to understand why the core of mystical experience is absolutely ineffable? Wolff explains that language, in its purely descriptive function, must necessarily fail to represent mystical consciousness because the latter is not subject to the principle of contrast, which is prerequisite for description. He found, in his first Fundamental Realization, that the 'I' transcended its normal position in the subject-object structure to become identical with all of space, conceived as "degrees of freedom," rather than physical space.

> It is an unequivocal transcendence of the subject-object relationship. Herein lies the rationale of the inevitable ineffability of mystical insight. All language is grounded in the subject-object relationship, and so, at best, can only misrepresent transcendent consciousness when an effort is made to express its immediately given value. . . .[19] Thus, consciousness that transcends that relationship cannot be truly represented through language built upon that base. Therefore, the expressions of the mystics must be regarded as symbols, rather than as concepts that mean what they are defined to mean and no more.[20]

These passages suggest that, as mystics often have asserted, what is directly Realized in mystical experience is *radically nondualistic.* This explains the source of the difficulty in employing language. The point is that the awareness itself is not reported as the sole source, but awareness is unified with more than awareness, as is language. In this case, what is reported is a unity that is undifferentiated, and where the principle of contrast does not apply, the descriptive function of language is impotent. That which is symbolized, he concludes, "cannot be conceived, but must be realized directly to be known."[21]

A deeper application of this principle involves concepts, which are more fundamental than language because intentional meaning is genetically prior to linguistic form, and the same concept may be expressed in a variety of languages. The development of language beyond a rudimentary level depends upon our need to express and communicate conceptual understanding, for which the resources of natural and artificial language would seem to be theoretically adequate. A concept is thinkable only in contrast to, and distinct from other concepts, but absence of multiplicity precludes conceptual determination just as surely as it does description. Thus it is that although the definition of *ineffable* is couched in linguistic terms, Kellenberger asserts that "what may be the most pregnant category of mystical ineffability [is] that *it transcends our concepts.*"[22] The mystical core is absolutely ineffable, inasmuch as it is inconceivable as well as indescribable.

Spiritual Blindness Theory

Having established that mystical experience is uniquely ineffable, we now seek a further clarification of the nature and limitations of our means of representation (concepts, logic, language, art, etc.) within a mystical context. For this purpose it will be helpful to critically discuss several theories that dispute the claim of literal ineffability. Let us first consider the spiritual blindness theory, which Stace says likens the difficulty in communicating mystical experience to nonmystics to that of communicating the nature of color to a person blind from birth. It concludes that ineffability is not intrinsic to the experience, but is due to "spiritual blindness."[23] That is, the difficulty in communicating the mystical lies entirely with the listener's incapacity to understand the message because she lacks a common base in experience.

Stace rejects this theory for two reasons. First, it reduces the problem of ineffability of mystical experience to the general difficulty that applies to every sort of experience. He objects that "the ineffability of mystical experience is plainly understood by those who speak of it to be a unique characteristic possessed only by that kind of experience and not shared with other kinds."[24] Our preceding discussion has strongly supported this view. Second, he claims that it is the mystic who experiences the impossibility of describing the experience, even to herself, whereas the person with sight has no difficulty expressing his color concept.

In some passages Wolff seems to confirm the view of the spiritual blindness theory.

> Now, the mystic knows an ineffable content or quality in the case of communication to a nonmystic, but in general, the concept, the sign, or symbol will convey this content, more or less adequately, to a fellow mystic. It is just a case of the concepts, signs, or symbols having a different kind of reference and of two or more individuals having common acquaintance with the relevant referents.[25]

His use of "reference" and "referents" in this context must not be taken as indicating something objective or determinate that might be described by using other resources. It follows that communication by this means is not a result of a literal interpretation of the terms involved. However, the following excerpt holds the key to the correct interpretation of his intended meaning.

> Yet always, with the mystic, there is an ineffable substratum that he never succeeds in more than suggesting in his expression. Often his effort to do justice to this substratum leads to formulation that simply does not make sense, when judged by the canons of subject-object language. The result is that only a mystic really understands another mystic.[26]

Wolff's reference to an "ineffable substratum" irrefutably locates the difficulty of expression within mystical experience itself, not in extrinsic contingencies. The problem of communication with other mystics is ameliorated insofar as their firsthand acquaintance with this core or substratum presumably would constitute a common ground in immediate awareness. Because they would personally know that it could not be described, they would interpret language symbolically, rather than literally.

Within the determinate-indeterminate zone, however, the spiritual blindness theory applies in varying degrees. Inasmuch as Fundamental Realization precipitates diverse content relative to the individual mystic, no two are likely to be exactly commensurate. Those who lack immediate awareness of the referents generally find symbolic language opaque, grasp it only with great difficulty, or mistakenly regard it as descriptive. Firsthand awareness of the core along with common overlapping elements would make communication far easier than if one party were personally limited solely to the mundane. We must sharply distinguish the sense in which the nonmystic may find such accounts ineffable from the ineffability that the mystic contends applies to the core itself. Having an essentially identical Realization would dispel the ineffability in the first sense, but not the second.

Deficient Language Theory

Kvastad disagrees with Stace's argument, essentially maintaining that the rarity of mystical experience implies that no language has yet been adequately developed to describe it. Thus he concludes that the mystic's difficulty is practical and contingent, rather than theoretical and essential.[27] The resolution, he contends, lies in the enhancement of language (Sanskrit, for example) to extend the normal range of discourse to include mystical experience. Doubtless, this is relevant to the mystic's difficulty in communicating the actual awareness, both to mystics and to nonmystics. However, it is rash to claim that this is the *only* factor—or even the central one.

Wolff insists that problems in formulating and communicating mystical experience cannot be attributed entirely to lack of linguistic skill of the mystic, nor is it because of some corrigible deficiency in the particular language. Rather, ineffability is due to a linguistically impervious element intrinsic to the experience.

> The ineffability of the genuinely mystical consciousness is not due to an imperfect knowledge of language on the part of the mystic. While many mystics have had a very defective knowledge of language, and are consequently especially obscure, yet others have not been so limited in their equipment. However, in either case, the ineffable and obscure element remains. The fact is, this ineffability can never be conveyed through language, any more than an irrational number can be completely equated to a rational number.[28]

Again we find that the proper application of the deficient language theory is restricted to the precipitated effects within relative consciousness—not the ineffable substratum. Wolff found the need to supplement the extensive terminology of Western philosophy by incorporating numerous terms from Eastern thought and inventing several more. Nevertheless, he makes it clear that even an ideal language designed to communicate the mystical domain still would *necessarily* fall short of describing the transcendent nonrelative consciousness. Of this, in itself, nothing can be said.

His status as a mystic certifies the basis for his refutation of both the spiritual blindness and deficient language theories in favor of a subtle essentialist position. Neither of these theories can provide a *sufficient* explanation for the ineffability that mystics report. There is something intrinsically indescribable, unintelligible, and so on, in the awareness itself. Notwithstanding the root of this difficulty, the resources of language, the mystic's skill at formulation, and the degree of experiential familiarity that others possess are important factors in communicating whatever is possible. However, whereas one might overcome these subsidiary problems in principle, this is not true regarding the strict ineffability of the core.

Mirror of Language Theory

Richard Jones follows Arthur Danto[29] in advancing the linguistically based thesis that the mystic's problems with ineffability stem from their tacit acceptance of the theory that holds that language functions as a mirror of the world. Succinctly stated, this is the view that there is a one-to-one correspondence between the structure of language and the structure of the world. He claims that mystics "who do discuss the mystical are seduced by the mirror theory"[30] into making ontological commitments based upon grammatical structure. Jones adopts Danto's position that all metaphysical systems presuppose what he calls "Grammatical Realism," according to which the logical structure of language mirrors that of the world. Mystics discover that this is not true of the world, but due to their belief concerning the nature of language, conclude that what they experienced was ineffable. Danto contends that "there are philosophers who realize that the world does not have a grammatical structure as its ultimate armature, but draw from this insight the desperately wrong conclusion that the world as it is must therefore be ineffable: for effability would require it to have, contrary to fact, a grammatical structure."[31]

Is language then absolutely incapable of rendering any true proposition concerning the mystical (except perhaps to say that it is ineffable)? Jones concludes: "Can something from the everyday world (that is, language) reveal something true about the mystical? To maintain that all claims must be false is to accept the mirror theory of language. Much about the mystical may not in fact be encodable, but some is."[32] We may infer from this that Jones opposes the mirror theory of language and that he also rejects the view that mystical experience is totally ineffable.

We should question, however, whether mystics do hold the metaphysical view that language functions solely to mirror the world. Moreover, even if a mystic were to adopt this linguistic theory, we still may dispute the claim that this is the explanation for her regarding the experience as ineffable. The central objection to Jones's account is that mystics rarely theorize about language, and whatever implicit understanding they may have concerning how language is related to the world reflects that of their culture. Yet, in spite of great cultural diversity—from East and West, ancient and modern—the claim of ineffability is universal. Therefore, it is far more plausible to attribute it to an *experienced* failure to describe—or even to conceptualize—the mystical. This is reinforced by their reports that, in its purity, not only does it have no grammatical structure, but it has no structure at all.

Jones further attempts to link the particular kind of response the mystic makes to his attitude toward the mirror theory.

> This survey of the four types of reactions to the mystical shows differing relations to the view that linguistic structures mirror the reality referred to. Silence and the way of negation affirm it; paradox shows perplexity concerning it; and the positive descriptions involving indirect reference implicitly reject it by accepting a commonality of some features comprising the mystical and the ordinary world.[33]

In practice, this correlation breaks down, inasmuch as few mystics restrict their response to a single strategy. For example, Wolff uses all but silence, which he acknowledges would be the strictly proper response to that which is wholly indeterminate—for "only in the Silence can the SELF be Known as It is."[34] Even Wittgenstein's original position, which overtly advocates silence on all nonscientific discourse, demonstrates in itself a positive "pointing" technique. We are led to conclude that the mystic's claim of ineffability is strictly true (when it refers to the core). However, it results not so much from his theory of language (explicit or implicit) as it does from the nature of his awareness as intrinsically incommensurable with language as such. His strategy (or strategies) of expression more closely reflects the balance between his emphasis on conveying something of great importance versus misleading others concerning its determinateness.

The three theories we have been considering do not account for the ineffability of mystical experience or refute the notion of a common universal nonphenomenal essence. To be sure, we must acknowledge that neither strict proof nor disproof of the reality of the core is possible. In such matters, however, proof is too strong a criterion to require or to expect. Even so, those who would wish to claim that it is possible that two strictly ineffable mystical experiences are (or could be) essentially different undertake the greater burden. Either this statement is logically empty or there must be some theoretical means by which they are to be distinguished. However, all distinction lies on the side of relative consciousness. If there is no awareness beyond the relative, then it is not mystical; if it is mystical, then what makes it so is ineffable because it transcends all distinction. Reports by reliable, qualified mystics provide overwhelming testimony of the reality of nonrelative consciousness that is uniquely and absolutely ineffable. It is reasonable to adopt the notion of a common nonphenomenal core to point to that which is immediately Realized.

STRATEGIES OF EXPRESSION

Even though they are faced with the inherent problem of ineffability, mystics who feel motivated to share the value of their experience often give it some kind of expression. We shall best deal with the issue of the meaning of mystical language by considering the mystics' major strategies of communication, which Jones gives as silence, negation, paradox, and positive formulation.[35]

Silence

If we assume that the mystic is telling the truth when she claims that her experience is indescribable, then the most logically precise response would be silence. Wittgenstein seems to recommend this solution at the conclusion of the *Tractatus*: "What we cannot speak about we must pass over in silence" (7).[36] Although some have cited his work in an attempt to discredit mysticism, his treatise appears inconsistent with its own conclusion. He claims that only the propositions of natural science (which are all other than philosophy) can be said (6.53) and that the propositions of the *Tractatus* are nonsensical, that is, cannot be said (6.54). Therefore, at face value, his advice is self-contradictory because had he followed it he would not have written the book. Consequently, his text demands more than a superficial interpretation.

The key to the matter is Wittgenstein's notion of elucidation, which is his implied justification for producing the work.

> My propositions serve as elucidations in the following way: anyone who understands me eventually recognizes them as nonsensical, when he has used them—as steps—to climb up beyond them. (He must, so to speak, throw away the ladder after he has climbed up it.) He must transcend these propositions, and then he will see the world aright (6.54).

Jerome Bickenbach finds that Wittgenstein contrasts elucidations with

1. genuine propositions (those of natural science),
2. 'senseless' propositions ("primarily tautologies, contradictions, and mathematical propositions that have the identity sign as a syntactic component"),[37] and
3. nonsensical pseudopropositions, some of whose signs lack reference (for example, in metaphysics, ethics, religion, etc.).

Bickenbach further explains the central importance of the notion of elucidation for Wittgenstein.

> Elucidations are nonsensical propositions, but they are recognized as such only after they are understood (6.54). These propositions serve to show the meanings of primitive signs (3.263); and given this function, it follows for Wittgenstein that philosophy is (or should be) the activity of presenting elucidations (4.112). But most importantly, the propositions of the *Tractatus* are elucidations (6.54).[38]

He interprets Wittgenstein's distinction between elucidations and nonsensical pseudopropositions not by what they say, for neither of them says anything, but by what they show. Only the former are able "to show us important features of language and the world."[39] Furthermore, once we have grasped that which has been shown, the means are disposable.

Positivists generally take the *Tractatus* to be an outright rejection of traditional metaphysics, which purports to say in propositional form what can only be shown—namely, the mystical. They simply accept as final the admonition to remain silent on such matters. K. T. Fann and Ignace Verhack elaborate a more explicitly mystical interpretation of this work. Fann contends that although

Wittgenstein rejects the traditional methods for attempting to express the inexpressible he does not discount the reality of the mystical nor the metaphysical enterprise itself. "There are, indeed, things that cannot be put into words. They make *themselves manifest.* They are what is mystical" (6.522). Fann finds that Wittgenstein holds that "the inexpressible (mystical) is everything that is important in life. The whole point of the *Tractatus* is precisely to show the inexpressible by exhibiting clearly the expressible."[40] He contends that Wittgenstein has the deepest respect for the mystical, so an antimystical, antimetaphysical reading of his work is mistaken.

Verhack, in the light of the recently acknowledged mystical dimension of Wittgenstein, views the *Tractatus* as an attempt to show the limits of natural science and, by implication, what lies beyond its boundaries. Besides its therapeutic value, Wittgenstein's philosophical activity also possesses a critical significance. Philosophy should clarify the limits as well as the possibilities of the factual domain of natural science. Moreover, it is by pointing out these limits that philosophy also should be able to manifest the existence of a dimension of unsayability. When considered according to this definition, the logical theory and critique of language no longer appear as the main goals of the *Tractatus.* It is employed instead as a method in function of the act of pointing toward a dimension of unsayability—that which defeats the logical grasp of language. In virtue of this method, the *Tractatus* also is able to pronounce an ontological difference between the sayable facts of the world in logical space, on the one side, and the inexpressible, on the other.[41]

Verhack notes that Wittgenstein's treatment of the world exhibits a polar structure: how it appears, "the totality of facts in logical space,"[42] which are capable of linguistic representation in the propositions of natural science; and that it exists, which is unsayable. "It is not *how* things are in the world that is mystical, but *that* it exists" (6.44). Wittgenstein's critique of language grounds this ontological difference. Thus Verhack contends that "Wittgenstein's critique of language was the method and work tool of a new *deictic* or 'pointing' metaphysics."[43]

Let us reconsider the conclusion that silence is the only alternative to the discourse of natural science. When Wittgenstein talks about the correct method in philosophy, it relates primarily to clarification of discourse. We should notice that he is not personally adopting, or even advocating, this approach, but talking in the logical sense—where precise criteria are possible. However, to restrict all philosophical activity in this manner would be to reduce philosophy to a technology. This he does not do. Instead, his method in the *Tractatus* uses language to point to the mystical, but since there may be an indefinite number of ways to point, its value as elucidation is more art than science. In addition, it would be inconsistent to say that we *ought* to restrict our human endeavor to exclude the ethical (or the mystical), for example. Because such statements are value judgments, they would thereby exclude themselves. It follows from his definition of the world as the totality of facts (1.1) that there is no value in the world (6.41). So, to operate as a strict positivist would be to adopt a procedure that would lead to sterility in the realm of values. We should therefore interpret Wittgenstein's purpose as demonstrating by his example that philosophy is the art of elucidation, and though it is possible for one to discard the ladder once one has climbed it, at least part of the business of philosophy is to construct such ladders.

It is of little moment that, unlike Wolff, Wittgenstein does not personally report specific mystical episodes. As a rule, mystics present the results of their insights and realizations, rather than intimate autobiographical data. It is reasonable to attribute to Wittgenstein at least mental realization. In any case, the overriding issue concerns the possible use of language in realms purported to be ineffable. To conclude, the *Tractatus* allows for, and demonstrates, the effective use of language for this purpose. It justifies such use so long as its formulations are not confused with the propositions of natural science.

This approach more adequately addresses the concerns that led positivism to adopt the verification principle, while avoiding the defects and excesses of verificationism. The principle itself is self-contradictory, for the claim that a sentence (used to express a statement or proposition) must be verifiable to be meaningful is not itself verifiable. Hence it is meaningless according to its own standard. More to the point, deciding the verifiability of a proposition already *presupposes* its meaningfulness and therefore cannot be a condition for it. Furthermore, consistent application of this principle not only would exclude metaphysics as nonsense, but also would exclude ethics, aesthetics, religion, poetry, and much else central to human value and concern. Eliminating all such discourse would devastate culture and impoverish humanity. Finally, actual verification is obviously too strong a requirement, but the weaker versions, involving verification (or falsification, confirmation, etc.) in principle, cannot exclude metaphysical propositions without the further question-begging condition that the only acceptable method of verification is that of natural science. On the contrary, there are other standards that are more appropriate to nonscientific domains of discourse. These defects in the verifiability criterion show that it is too crude a tool to employ for determining whether something is meaningful.

Since the meaningfulness of mystical language cannot be effectively ruled out in advance, the mystic is not simply compelled by logic to be silent. Even if silence is the response that is most faithful to the essential nature of the mystical core, there are pragmatic reasons to choose to speak. Wolff's position is that even though "there is no word-combination that is strictly true to the meaning intended—straining the common medium of language to suggest a most uncommon content"[44]—the importance of communicating what the mystic has encountered outweighs the risk of engendering misunderstanding.

Jones relates an example where silence, as the condition most beneficial for inducing the mystical state, is used as a strategy for instruction. "Bahva, who when asked to explain the self, said, 'Learn *Brahman,* friend' and became silent; when the questioner persisted, he finally exclaimed, 'I am teaching you, but you do not understand. Silence is that self.' "[45] The point seems to be that silence, because of its inherent ambiguity, in itself is incapable of conveying anything. Some further means must be employed in order to explain the significance of the silence, so silence, per se, fails as an adequate response if the mystic intends to express and communicate his awareness.

Negation

Both mystics and commentators often claim that whereas positive affirmations do not apply to the mystical, negations do—that methodological rigor allows us only to deny specific attributes. For example, Wolff says, "THAT, which is here symbolized by 'Consciousness-without-an-object' . . . when defined exactly rather than represented symbolically, is designated only by the negation of every possible predicate."[46] This strategy of the *via negativa* is intended to avoid altogether any misunderstanding that might arise from attempting a positive characterization of some sort. It discourages metaphysical speculation and demonstrates the futility of trying to grasp conceptually what can be known only directly.

According to Jones, this technique appears in at least three traditions: Advaita Vedānta, Theravāda Buddhism, and Neoplatonism. Śaṃkara's philosophy is explicitly nondualistic, which entails that *Brahman*, the ultimately Real, is unconditioned or unqualified. Consequently, the terse "not this, not that" (*neti, neti*), found in the *Upaniṣads*, serves "to remove all terms of name, form and action"[47] from what is in itself undifferentiated. Jones attributes the technique of fourfold negation to Theravāda Buddhism. In response to any speculative metaphysical question, each of the four logical possibilities is denied. Reduced to its formal essence, the response is as follows: It is not *A*; it is not *not-A*; it is neither *A* nor *not-A*; and it is not both *A* and *not-A*. Knowledge based upon all experience subordinate to *Nirvāṇa* is irrelevant to determine the answer, so all affirmations are negated.[48] Plotinus, in spite of saying much of a positive nature, ultimately concludes that it falls short of description. Jones explains that "with regard to the mystical, Plotinus says the same: any property (for example, being in motion or at rest) is a characteristic of being, not the One, and so all are denied."[49]

Although the strategy of universal negation is not as rigorous as that of pure silence, it is more informative, for one learns that the mystic is aware of something to which no attribute applies. However, this introduces the danger that one might take the negative formulation as a positive description, ignoring the strict meaning of the mystic's claim of ineffability as transcending both language and concepts. If the mystic's intention is to guard against misunderstanding concerning the mystical, then substituting negations for affirmations may not go far enough. It may be necessary to deny the applicability of both affirmations and negations, as does Dionysius the Areopagite.[50]

Paradox

Many mystics employ paradoxical locutions in their account of the mystical. It is important to determine whether such paradoxes are real or merely apparent, for if they are real then the basic laws of logic would appear to fall short of universal application. The evidence would seem to indicate that not all paradoxes of this sort may be dissolved and that their ultimate genesis lies in the nature of the mystical core.

Stace argues persuasively against several theories that hold that the paradoxes are not real, for paradoxes are not simply rhetorical devices, inasmuch as the thought content remains paradoxical even after paraphrasing it.[51] Even though the hypothesis that mystics are describing their experiences inaccurately cannot be conclusively refuted, it lacks credibility in the absence of similar criticism among mystics. The mystics themselves, many of whom are well qualified, are in the best position to know.[52] The mystics' general claim of ineffability implies that there is widespread agreement that this sort of experience is intrinsically indescribable. They do not tend to criticize each other for presenting paradoxical formulations by giving instead straightforward, nonparadoxical formulations that would be more accurate. It is more likely that they would object to using language at all. Then, too, it will not do to claim that each of two contradictory attributes applies to two different objects or to different aspects of a single object. There are indigestible counterexamples—for instance, that God is both identical to and different from the world.[53] Similarly, the pantheistic paradox is a stumbling block to the theory of ambiguity.[54]

Jones relates Paul Henle's theory, which would explain paradoxical utterances in terms of the contingencies of the mystic's language or conceptual scheme. Henle holds that the experience is not ineffable, but the mystic's expression is ill-formed because his language is inadequate.[55] Jones counters that mystics have not attempted to construct a new (more adequate) language, as one would expect if this theory were correct. We do find mystics introducing new terms (Eckhart's *Godhead,* Bucke's *Cosmic Consciousness,* Wolff's *Introception,* etc.) to capture distinctions transcending ordinary consciousness, but no suggestion that an entirely new language should be devised for the purpose. In any event, the theory cannot account for the overwhelming testimony of mystics who find language, as such, inadequate to represent the absolutely Transcendent. Thus we must firmly reject theories that attempt to show that the mystic's use of paradox can always be explained as merely apparent.

Are we thereby forced to accept Stace's alternative, namely, that these formulations are literally true, that the attribution of contradictory predicates is an accurate *description* of mystical experience? This would imply that mystical experience is not truly ineffable and that the mystic errs on this point. Stace contends that the mystic "is in fact mistaken. The paradox which he has uttered has correctly described his experience. The language is only paradoxical because the experience is paradoxical. Thus the language correctly mirrors the experience. . . . He confuses the paradoxicality of mystical experience with ineffability."[56] This would entail a clear contravention of the laws of logic, for if "it is both *A* and *not-A*" is literally true, it would violate the Law of Noncontradiction, which states that "*X* cannot be both *A* and *not-A*, at the same time and in the same respect."

Stace's position sets up a false dichotomy, for there is a third alternative. Wolff's account of his second Fundamental Realization contains a rare, if not unique, experiential report of an attempt to conceptualize the mystical state from within it by employing the resources of bimodal consciousness. The basis for rejecting Stace's conclusion rests upon an interpretation of this passage.

> While in the State, I was particularly impressed with the fact that the logical principle of contradiction simply had no relevancy. It would not be correct to say that this principle was violated, but rather, that it had no application. For to isolate any phase of the State was to be immediately aware of the opposite phase as the necessary complementary part of the first. Thus the attempt of self-conscious thought to isolate anything resulted in the immediate initiation of a sort of flow in the very essence of consciousness itself, so that the nascent isolation was transformed into its opposite as copartner in a timeless reality. Every attempt I made to capture the State within the categories of relative knowledge was defeated by this flow effect.[57]

According to Wolff, the High Indifference—which most clearly revealed the mystical core—is ultimately ineffable. In attempting to conceptualize it in discrete terms, and thus describe it, he failed. His "defeat" refers equally to his attempt to characterize it positively according to a single category, *A*, as it does to the combination of a category and its opposite, *A* and *not-A*. None of them would be more applicable than any other. He says, "Everything can be predicated of it so long as the predication is not privative, for in the privative sense nothing can be predicated of it."[58] To deny privative predication means that only an absolutely infinite list of predicates, along with their opposites, can be applied all at once—or none at all! Naturally, in either case, actually constructing the formulation is impossible, for one can either never begin or never complete the task.

Consequently, even if we merge the strategies of universal affirmation and universal negation,[59] it does not produce a description. On the contrary, it evinces that a description that communicates the whole truth about mystical Realization is impossible, which would explain Wolff's denial that the Law of Noncontradiction was violated. He states that insofar as Consciousness-without-an-object is the Source of all, including all law, it is not Itself determined by law. One who Realizes It thus finds that it Transcends the application of the law of noncontradiction, for "here no affirmation is a denial of the possibility of its contradictory. Also, Consciousness-without-an-object is that excluded middle that is neither *A* nor *not-A*. Hence, the actuality that Consciousness-without-an-object symbolizes is unthinkable, and so in order to think toward IT, a thinkable symbol must be employed."[60] That a paradoxical formulation has been generated from the attempt to represent the mystical in terms of our relative conceptual categories does not mean that logical contradiction becomes literal description. Although selected paradoxes may be helpful in symbolizing the state of consciousness directly aware of the mystical core, the ultimate referent remains absolutely ineffable and, strictly speaking, even beyond symbols.

Positive Characterization

If the mystical is truly ineffable, then the status of overtly descriptive formulations calls for explication. Two considerations already noted complicate the situation. First, the mystical state is rarely pure or totally devoid of attendant phenomena, so it is possible to describe much (if not all) of its objective content. For example, one might be aware of photisms, exalted feelings or moods, physical surroundings, and so on. Second, the values that precipitate into relative consciousness are at least partially amenable to description, or at least symbolic reference, although some may be ineffable for other reasons (for example, intensity or uniqueness). Our task is made more difficult because mystics usually do not make these distinctions explicit.

Most often, because of its overriding significance, it is the core to which the mystic refers as ineffable, in the absolute sense. Angel points out that the term *ineffable* is not a first-order predicate, so it cannot be used to describe that which is supposedly beyond description. Rather, it serves to deny that any description is possible. When the mystic uses descriptive language to strive to indicate it, such language always functions symbolically to direct our focus of attention, more than to inform. Remember that *mystical core* and all such verbal designations in this context symbolize whatever it is that transcends not only the merely phenomenal, but also the partially discernible material precipitated within relative consciousness. If one correctly takes the ineffability claim seriously, it is necessary to be sensitive to the mystic's problem of conveying an exceptional meaning. Some terms (used as symbols) are more effective than others for this purpose. For example, Jones gives *real* and *unitary* as more helpful characterizations than their opposites or most other terms. He warns that

> some descriptions are more accurate than their opposites, but the danger of misunderstanding the nature of the mystical is of tantamount importance. The device mystics use to avoid the reduction of the mystical when employing positive descriptions is to maintain that these remarks only "point to" rather than "directly describe" the mystical.[61]

When mystics use descriptive discourse without qualification, then it is reasonable to assume that they are treating peripheral phenomena. Such accounts are unqualified if they do not say that what they are talking about is ineffable and therefore that their formulation is not to be taken literally. When the mystic makes this qualification (and often when it is clearly implied), what would appear to be descriptive terms are best understood as functioning symbolically.

SYMBOLIC LANGUAGE

Signs and Symbols

The possibility of this sort of symbolic use of language raises several related issues. Discussions dealing with signs, symbols, and metaphors often are complicated and confusing,[62] but devising a detailed comprehensive theory would be a project well beyond our primary area of concern. Our priorities do not permit us to unravel this Gordian knot completely, but neither can we merely slice through it in a single stroke. We must treat symbolic language in sufficient depth to show not only its legitimacy, but also its indispensability. This will involve identifying the central issues, drawing crucial distinctions, and offering key definitions and examples. Our sketch will illustrate an approach to symbology that should prove fruitful for understanding mysticism in general and Wolff's concepts in particular.

There are advantages in regarding the sign as the widest generic category, including language and symbols. Though strict definition of a sign is problematic, we may identify two essential features:

1. It is a relationship between two elements such that one of them stands for or signifies the other, rather than itself.
2. Its significance necessarily depends on consciousness, insofar as signs are only meaningful for consciousness.

There is an important difference between signs that arise naturally (for instance, the formation of cumulonimbus clouds as a sign of impending thunderstorms) as opposed to artificially (such as linguistic systems). The former are indications reflecting correlation grounded in causal connections, whereas the latter are established as a result of conventional understanding. A third basis for functional signification is direct resemblance between a sign and that which it signifies, as in the case of icons.[63]

Symbols would seem to qualify as signs, according to the broad definition we are using. In addition, as Haig Khatchadourian affirms, a symbol conveys some idea(s) independently of its referent. "To symbolize something is precisely to present that thing to our imagination and/or intellect (or to direct our imagination and/or mind to it)."[64] The meaning of a symbol may be given either in terms of its intrinsic ideation or by a description of its referent.

Even if symbols are signs, two noteworthy difficulties arise. First, there are often complex interrelationships between symbols themselves, as well as in relation to (1) psychic states, (2) the causal connections within the physical world, and (3) language. For example, red does not resemble danger, nor is there a direct causal relation, but it symbolizes it better than does blue. This is because it more easily attracts our attention and it has a physiologically stimulating effect—both of which are of practical value in dangerous situations. Thus its intentional use is conventional in a manner that is not arbitrary. A symbol's adequacy in such cases involves the capacity to elicit the appropriate response, which varies according to the contingencies of the world and ourselves.

Second, where that which is symbolized cannot be adequately defined, the symbol's meaning cannot be strictly specified. Some would argue that the legitimacy of symbols extends only so far as its verbal equivalence, but we shall show that this view is unnecessarily restrictive. At seemingly opposite extremes of its application lie the domains of science and religion. "In religious thought and practice, symbols are commonly regarded as sensuous representations of a transcendent reality. In systems of logical and scientific thought the term is normally used in the sense of an abstract sign."[65] The former are intensive and qualitative, the latter, extensive and quantitative. Between the two lies the central category of what Erich Fromm calls "universal symbols."[66] It should prove edifying to survey this spectrum.

Scientific Symbols

Wolff contrasts the use of symbols in science and metaphysics by characterizing the theoretical constructions of science as models of what is not in itself thinkable. "The model, then, is . . . a thinkable and logical pattern that corresponds to the observed relationships in the referent. Such a pattern is . . . a symbol of relationships. In the transcendent sense, the symbol would represent substantialities."[67] This preliminary distinction is generally accurate, but not absolute, for there are exceptions, so this calls for a more detailed treatment.

At the outset we should separate normative science (symbolic logic, pure mathematics, etc.) from empirical science (astronomy, physics, chemistry, biology, etc.). To simplify, let us ignore the so-called social sciences (political science, sociology, economics, etc.). Scientific symbols typically are conventional and permit a non-symbolic, literal equivalence. To illustrate, the symbol π is both conventional (in the sense that mathematical constants are represented by letters of the Greek alphabet) and arbitrary (concerning the choice of this particular Greek letter). Its literal meaning is the ratio of the circumference of a circle to its diameter.

The generally rigid attitude manifested by positivism toward religious symbols might be ameliorated by pointing out that even in a scientific context the reality of the referent of a symbol may overflow its specified literal equivalent. For instance, a black hole—or whatever astrophysical symbol is used to mark its location on star charts—may be given a nominal verbal definition. We could define it as a region in space in which matter vanishes and there is an intense, self-sustaining gravitational field produced from a collapsed star having a mass greater than 1.4 times that of our sun. Scientists in general have accepted Stephen Hawking's definition, namely, "the set of events from which it was not possible to escape to a large distance."[68] Attempts to interpret these literally obviously are perplexing. Apart from the vague and unscientific tone of Hawking's definition, characterizing physical reality solely in terms of events is one-sided and incomplete, for it implies the existence of something to which the processes occur. It would make sense to specify physical objects or radiant energy as that which may or may not escape—but in relation to what? If we say, "a black hole," then the definition is circular. If we attempt a more positive characterization similar to the first definition, then what does it mean for matter to vanish? Of course, it disappears from all capacity for direct empirical observation, since not even light can escape from it, but the deeper meaning intended here is actual annihilation. Science has established that matter and energy may transform into each other. However, under the conditions present at the center of a black hole, matter and energy are thought to become *nothing*![69] According to our most advanced physical theories, general relativity and quantum mechanics, theoretical physicist Roger Penrose states that "there must be a region inside a black hole, a region of infinite curvature, called a space-time singularity at which the known laws of physics break down."[70] Indeed, according to John Archibald Wheeler, "when it comes to small distances either in the here and the now or in the most extreme stages of gravitational collapse, space-time loses all meaning, and time itself is not an ultimate category in the description of nature."[71] It was such unnerving implications that led Sir Arthur Eddington to reject the notion of a black hole as a *reductio ad absurdum* when the astrophysicist Subramanyan Chandrasekhar first presented it. He objected, "I think there should be a law of nature to prevent a star from behaving in this absurd way."[72] Nonetheless, the existence of black holes is now beyond serious dispute, and, as singularities, they are essentially both empirically and theoretically indeterminate. This means that no adequate literal equivalence may be given for this symbol. Consequently, the scientific symbol functions in this context to point to a mystery transcending the framework of science.

In normative science, symbols also may elude literal definition. In mathematics, $\sqrt{-1}$ (also symbolized by i) is translated as "the square root of negative one" or "the number that, when multiplied by itself, equals negative one." If challenged, we can specify no *real* number as an equivalent, since both positive and negative numbers yield positive squares. Nevertheless, this does not prevent its legitimate use in equations having a wide range of practical applications.[73] Similarly, ∞ symbolizes infinity, for which there is no straightforward, nonparadoxical equivalent. Wolff notes that Dedekind defines the infinite as a manifold in which the number of elements in some proper part is the same as in the whole. To illustrate, there are as many even numbers as there are integers.[74] This is clearly paradoxical.

What these examples illustrate is that, unlike simple signs such as = (numerical equality) and + (addition), many others have cognitive value that cannot be captured wholly in rational terms. Although scientific symbols serve a different purpose than mystical symbols, science has need for symbols as well as merely formally defined signs. Why not simply admit that in certain cases science, as well as religion, employs symbols to point to a hidden reality? The range of human experience exceeds our capacity for categorial understanding. Thus, even in science, language must be employed symbolically, as well as discursively, to express and communicate, at least partially, discoveries that transcend mundane reality and defy rational comprehension and expression.

Universal Symbols

In contrast to the specialized use of symbols in science,[75] we find the traditional domain of symbolism exhibited within poetry, art, mythology, metaphysics, religion, psychology, and so on. Herbert Read notes that the symbolizing function is a universal feature of humankind, whose need has been increased, rather than eliminated, by science and technology. The symbolic and the historical are not mutually exclusive, but instead are complementary ways of understanding the world. Mircea Eliade explains that

> the two points of view are only superficially irreconcilable . . . , for it must not be thought that a symbolic connotation annuls the material and specific validity of an object or action. Symbolism *adds* a new value to an object or an act, without thereby violating its immediate or "historical" validity. Once it is brought to bear, it turns the object or action into an "open" event; symbolic thought opens the door on to immediate reality for us, but without weakening or invalidating it; seen in this light the universe is no longer sealed off, nothing is isolated inside its own existence: everything is linked by a system of correspondences and assimilations.[76]

The question of the legitimacy of such symbols thus is answered not merely by their actuality, but by their necessity and the value of their unique function.

The ground for significance of these sorts of symbols is not reducible to the three that have already been cited for signs in general, namely, (1) index based on causal relation to that which is symbolized, (2) resemblance (icon), and (3)convention. Circlot accepts Fromm's definition of the universal symbol as "the existence of the *intrinsic relation* between the symbol and what it represents."[77] We originally noted that the second general characteristic of signs involves an essential reference to consciousness. However, the sense in which it refers to consciousness here is to be understood in terms of the collective unconscious—the realm of archetypes posited by Carl Jung. He states that "the origin of the symbol is always derived from archaic residues, or imprints engraven in the very stem of the race."[78] Jung's use of the term *archetype* is ambiguous, referring both to primordial images and to unconscious psychic structures. Not all universal symbols are archetypes, in Jung's sense, but all archetypes are symbols. They are "those universal symbols which possess the greatest constancy and efficiency, the greatest potentiality for psychic evolution, and which point away from the inferior towards the superior."[79]

Rooting symbols in the unconscious has important consequences. It introduces the dynamic dimension related to psychological process, for "the psychological mechanism that transforms energy is the symbol."[80] In addition, Circlot notes that the unconsciousness "does not recognize the inherent distinctions of contraposition."[81] This accounts for what Marius Schneider considers the essential quality of the symbol, "its ability to express simultaneously the various aspects (thesis and antithesis) of the idea it represents."[82] These features make possible the symbol's most essential function—the systematic integration of all reality. Circlot mentions that Eliade considers the symbol to function so as to go "beyond the limitations of this 'fragment' which is Man (or any one of his concerns) and of integrating this 'fragment' into entities of wider scope: society, culture, the universe."[83] Throughout this integrative process, distinction and freedom of movement remain unaffected.

This process of symbolic representation and integration does not conflict with the findings of natural science—it supersedes it. This is because, as René Guénon points out, "the symbol must always be inferior to the thing symbolized, which destroys all naturalist concepts of symbolism."[84] Two factors make possible the symbolic integration within a holistic world view: (1) there are correspondences linking various orders to each other; (2) each part has the capacity to symbolize the whole. According to Guénon, "the true basis of symbolism is . . . the correspondence linking together all orders of reality, binding them one to the other, and consequently extending from the natural order as a whole to the supernatural order."[85] Circlot defines *symbolic function* as "the dynamic tendency of the object to link up with its corresponding equivalents in all analogous series."[86] It is this set of correspondences that constitutes the intrinsic relationship between universal symbols and what they symbolize. In contrast to the "horizontal" connections of natural science, symbolic science establishes "vertical" links between objects within different orders of reality, at points of "common rhythm."[87]

Moreover, there is a tendency toward unification of a symbolized object with the All, for the assumption underlying the meaningful interconnection of symbols is the "indissoluble unity of the universe."[88] We find the ground for this assumption in the innate and irrepressible tendency of consciousness to synthesize all of which we are aware into a meaningful whole—that is, a universe. The tendency of the symbol to link to the totality leads to the second, and related, feature of symbolic integration, namely, that the part represents the whole, or "each fragment restates the All."[89] Eliade explains this capacity in terms of a tree: "A tree, by virtue of the power it manifests, may become a blessed haven, without ceasing to be a tree; and if it becomes a cosmic tree it is because *what it manifests* restates, point by point, what the totality manifests"[90] This does not reduce the whole to the part, for that which is symbolized remains superior to the symbol.

Metaphor, Myth, and Metaphysics

Whether or not symbols are universal, they may be either linguistic or nonlinguistic. Though sometimes it has been said that all words are symbols, this excessively broad inclusion ignores important distinctions. Some words symbolize directly, whereas others use indirect reference via icons, archetypes, psychic states, or concepts. When language functions symbolically, in the pregnant sense, it is typically metaphorical.[91] Symbolic language is most obvious and most effective in myth, which may be considered an extended metaphor,[92] serving four basic functions, according to Joseph Campbell:[93]

1. mystical, revealing the transcendent mystery of the universe,
2. cosmological, showing the scientific understanding of the universe in such a manner as to become aware of its mysterious nature,
3. sociological, reinforcing and legitimating a specific social order, and
4. pedagogical, teaching us how to live.

Monroe Beardsley notes that "recently, the tendency has been to bring together metaphor, symbol, and myth under the same general heading . . . all species, or aspects, of the same general striving for a transcendental or supernatural mode of expression."[94]

In short, symbolic language, in all three of these modes, has an essentially metaphysical function. Circlot agrees with Guénon that symbols essentially function as pointers to metaphysical truth. Douglas Berggren contends that "metaphysics must be vitally metaphorical"[95] insofar as dualisms (for instance, mind-body), to be creatively resolved, must preserve the identity of each aspect. Kant notes that metaphysical questions (whether the universe is finite or infinite, whether our acts are free or determined, etc.) exhibit an antinomian character that pure reason cannot resolve. The capacity of the symbol to present incompatible elements within the same unified structure is a fortunate and invaluable resource.

Religious Symbols

Scientific symbols treat the empirical domain of the physical universe and the a priori domain of pure logical and mathematical meanings—both of which suspend concern for the human dimension. Religious symbols, however, are essentially concerned with what is ultimate and our existential relation to it. They may be linguistic (for example, God, or *Brahman*) or nonlinguistic (for instance, the *yin-yang* symbol ☯ or the cross ✝. Although Ted Peters allows that symbols are a subclass of signs,[96] he follows Paul Tillich's theory in explaining several important differences from conventional signs. They

1. are not arbitrary, but "are born out of real life situations,"[97] and hence reformulation implies some loss of meaning,
2. have surplus meaning, permitting new applications and insights,
3. thereby making new levels of reality accessible,
4. involve the subject, and thus carry existential significance,
5. "themselves must participate in the very reality they seek to represent . . . have ontological force and serve to reveal to us being itself"[98]
6. grow and die—either infusing new meaning or becoming relics of the past.

This account is compatible with that previously given of universal symbols, but his final point concerning the evolution of symbols brings to light a contingent process not yet explored.

Circlot also cautions that a symbol may become degraded such that its metaphysical function is arrested.[99] This may occur by way of trivial vulgarization, over-particularized interpretation, or over-intellectualized allegorical interpretation, as well as analogical 'identifications'. These share "the same basic falsification: the creative drive of the symbol—its tendency to revert to the Origin—is restricted, and it is made to bear labels which are over-concrete, too materialized or inferior."[100] In this manner, a symbol may die. By implication, the reverse is also true: If openness of meaning and vertical linkage are preserved, a symbol may grow.

The question of the meaningfulness of religious symbols arises most pointedly within a philosophical scrutiny of the religious context. Often this takes the slanted form of an implied constructive dilemma: Either religious symbols have a specifiable literal meaning, or they do not; if they do, then religious language is mere obfuscation, but if they do not, then religious language is nonsensical; hence, religious language is either obfuscation or nonsense. This assumes that meaning is restricted to a term's denotation and ignores its connotation. Donald Burrill presents Tillich's attempt to resolve the issue.

> Tillich's critics—most of whom on this point seem to be analytic philosophers—maintain that symbols are *substitution* words that "stand in place" of clearly specified literal equivalents. Tillich, on the other hand, contends that symbols are *participatory* terms that not only stand in place of referents but also "point to a hidden reality" that lies beyond.[101]

Tillich[102] claims that symbols are neither arbitrary nor conventional, but arise either from the individual or collective unconscious and thus must be acceptable to the unconscious to function as symbols.[103] Tillich is a Christian theologian, so his analysis of symbols emphasizes this perspective by focusing on God as the ultimate symbol. However, if his general approach to understanding religious symbols is correct, then it ought to apply equally to other religious traditions. He further contends that ultimate human concern (the essence of religion) can be expressed only symbolically, because "that which is the true ultimate transcends the realm of the finite infinitely. Therefore, no finite reality can express it directly and properly."[104] How can we know that anything corresponds to such symbols? In this context the skeptic might question how we can know that God exists. Tillich says that the problem of the existence of God (in which he assumes that *God* is a symbol) is misconceived, if by *existence* we mean that of a being like other beings within all of reality.[105] The ultimacy of our ultimate concern is revealed in immediate experience,[106] and the concrete imagery (or ideation) taken from experience that is used symbolically to relate ourselves to this ultimate may be known to be functioning *as* a symbol. Moreover, it becomes idolatrous when it is not so recognized.[107]

Pointer Concepts

In our discussion of symbolic language thus far, we have explored its representational resources from the perspective of ordinary human experience striving to understand the nature of, and interconnections between, all domains of reality. This is mystical in the sense of humanity attempting to transcend itself, to grasp and become existentially related to, and unified with, the totality, the whole, or the All.[108] Wolff's problem is the adequate expression and communication of full-blown mystical experience and its subsequent effects upon his world view. The material that precipitated or coalesced within relative consciousness is partially determinate, and linguistic approximation is possible to varying degrees, according to the skill of the mystic. "The Transcendent as such is inexpressible within the relative manifold, but there is an intermediate domain, between the Transcendent proper and the more restricted subject-object consciousness, where partial expression is possible."[109] In the symbolic sense of which we are now familiar, concepts may be used to *point,* as it were, toward psychic states having distinguishable cognitive content. "Assuming that a given individual has awakened to a transcendental realization, it is possible for him to reflect the transcendent through concepts, when the latter are taken in a symbolic sense."[110] This is the sense in which

Wolff talks about pointer concepts, such that the concept does not encapsulate the meaning, for the meaning overflows discursive articulation and understanding. Rather, it helps to orient consciousness to the immediacy of the content itself.

The question of a symbol's authenticity is distinct from that of its validity. Because symbols function in this context as an aid to the goal of Enlightenment for those still unillumined, a further criterion of a symbol's validity is its efficacy. Wolff points out that "there is no such thing as an exclusively true symbolic representation of an unthinkable Reality."[111] Insofar as the referent is ineffable, no symbol may even claim full adequacy in this regard, although some may serve as pointer concepts.

> No form, either conceptual or aesthetic, can possibly be an adequate representation of the all-containing Ultimate Reality, since such form is a comprehended or contained entity. But a form may serve as a pointer to a meaning beyond itself and thus fulfill an office in the human consciousness in the sense of orienting the latter beyond itself. The effective symbol must possess the dual character (a) of being in some measure comprehensible by the human consciousness, and (b) of reaching beyond the possibility of human comprehension.[112]

He draws the inference that the validity of a symbol depends on the contingent psychical character of the group and individual employing it. In particular, a symbol's potency is weakened in proportion to the degree of attachment to it—mistaking it for the goal, rather than a signpost.

Granting the legitimacy of symbols and symbolic language in this domain, we may evaluate them according to three criteria:

1. authenticity—generation by a person who has genuinely realized its referent;
2. fidelity—the degree of skillful approximation to the distinguishable contents precipitated within the originator's relative consciousness; and
3. efficacy—the power to orient and transform the consciousness of others.

These reflect the relationship between the symbol and the three essential factors in communication:

1. the originating conscious agent,
2. the objective content conveyed, and
3. the receptive consciousness.

In practice, the application of these standards may be problematic.

Where the mystical core itself is concerned, in contrast to the domain of precipitated contents, there is identity and lack of multiplicity, so 'It' is ultimately unconceptualizable and indescribable. Therefore, it would seem to be impossible even to symbolize it, in the strict sense in which symbols are usually meaningfully employed. If the mystical core is absolutely ineffable, then how could language, even as religious symbolism, function to point to it? It cannot be just a matter of signification, which we have seen involves a relation between a subject and two objects—where a subject intentionally employs a linguistic or symbolic object to identify or characterize a specific object of awareness. However, the mystic emphatically denies that the essence of mystical experience is an object of any kind. Moreover, if it is indescribable because it is distinctionless, then this implies that it is also nonrelational.

Even so, one might argue that since we can use *I* to refer to the pure subject or self, by extension *Consciousness-without-an-object* and *without-a-subject* refers to THAT which is neither an object before consciousness nor a subject-to-consciousness. Wolff states that "Consciousness-without-an-object is not merely an analytic abstraction from the totality of common consciousness. It is also a symbol of That which may be directly realized."[113] It is "the conceptual symbol of that forever inconceivable Reality that underlies and envelops all partial aspects."[114] His usage in such references is *That*, but occasionally he uses the fully capitalized *THAT* for superlative emphasis. In this connection, the role of 'THAT' (or even 'That') as a technique for referring is invaluable. Normally we use 'that' to refer to something of a definable nature, but it is also used in ostensive definition in cases where definite description or naming presents difficulties. It may be used as a bare, colorless pointer because its function is purely referential and independent of the content of the referent. The point of spelling 'THAT' (as with 'IT')[115] completely in upper case letters is to indicate that the intended referent is unique and wholly transcends all other referents whatsoever.

Psychic processes devoid of imagery, when construed as symbols, are notable exceptions to our general classification of symbols.[116] The conceptual content aroused by terms such as *mystical core* is not an end in itself, but a means to direct our awareness of whatever is symbolized. This allows us to distinguish *Consciousness-without-an-object,* as a linguistic symbol, from the corresponding psychic state transcending the subject-object structure. Wolff intends that this state symbolize THAT which is ineffable. Consequently, the locution *Consciousness-without-an-object* directly symbolizes the state and indirectly the ineffable core of the Realization itself. Along with verbal formulations and psychic states, his mandala presents an evocative visual image. He uses his primary symbol, Consciousness-without-an-object, as a pointer concept in this manner and takes pains to explain its function and significance.

> Consciousness-without-an-object is not an object on the level where it is realized. But just as soon as words are employed to refer to it, we have in place of the actuality a sort of shadowy reflection. This reflection may be useful as a symbol pointing toward the Reality, but becomes a deception just as soon as it is regarded as a comprehensive concept. Conceivable conclusions may be derived from the original symbol, but the full realization of That which is symbolized requires the dissolving of the very power of representation itself.[117]

Consciousness is a useful symbol because it indicates that the referent is Realized, not merely understood. The mystic is not generating mere metaphysical speculation that is solely a function of ideation, but is reflecting his personal awareness. The term is capitalized to indicate that the state of awareness is supernal or transcendent in nature, as opposed to normal empirical consciousness. *Without-an-object*[118] refers to the experienced transcendence of the subject-object structure, and the hyphenation emphasizes the nondualistic nature of the state.

The foregoing exegesis must not be taken as a nonsymbolic or literal description of the referent intended by Wolff's symbol, insofar as *nondualistic,* perhaps the most applicable term, is implicitly paradoxical. The meaningfulness of 'nondualistic' trades upon the dualistic(!) contrast to the term *dualistic.* It is more logically correct to deny that ultimately it is either one or many (or neither, or both),[119] and thus silence is the only strictly proper response (though it is much more efficacious *after* performing this dialectical process). The mystic must balance the desire—or even compulsion[120]—to communicate (or at least express) what she experienced with the realization that its essential nature is indescribable. Because anything she says to convey the mystical will not be strictly true, in the propositional sense, this sort of qualification should attend it.

As a logical consequence of this line of reasoning, the *pointing* function in mystical discourse supersedes mere reference, for it is designed to direct one to the threshold of Realization. If the mystic has discovered something of supernal value that is ineffable and must be personally experienced to be known, then her purpose cannot be merely to inform, but also to induce the other to attempt a personal verification. In the final analysis, we must understand that symbolic language functions in a mystical context primarily to evoke and induce, not simply to refer. It is designed to produce an existential, rather than solely intellectual, awareness that the mystical transcends words and concepts. It may be that the mystic often only dimly grasps the full nature of her efforts to communicate an exceptional meaning, but intuitively uses any available media. Here, pointing implies that to grasp the thought that is symbolically presented consciousness is led to a state that is conducive to Realization. At the point where one leaves the ladder behind, so to speak, one has already climbed it—but then, out of compassion for others, leaves in place other ladders that are perhaps stronger and easier to climb.

GENRES OF WOLFF'S FORMULATION

Once we accept that philosophy is legitimately the art of elucidation, at least in part, and that the meaning of mystical language is shown through its symbolic function, then we may better understand mystical literature. Carl Keller lists various forms of expression for universal mysticism: "aphorisms, biographies, reports on visions, commentaries, dialogues, instructions, prayers, religious poetry, and fiction."[121] Remarkably, except for fiction, Wolff uses them all, as well as allegory, exegesis of mystical writings, a mandala, and mathematical symbolism. Due to the nature of mystical experience and what is revealed through it, philosophical expression may not be reduced to a single mode if it hopes to encompass all relevant content. The variety of means that Wolff employs demonstrates his sensitivity to the unique difficulties and requirements of expressing and communicating the nature, value, and significance of Fundamental Realization. He states that

> the direct meaning of language does not express the actuality of the Higher Consciousness. We might say that the Actuality envelops the expression but is not directly contained in it. Thus the reader should strive not so much to understand the formal meaning contained in these writings, but to make a certain turn in his own consciousness toward a Matrix that surrounds the expression. . . . Hence it remains important to employ various means of expression. But if the expression is taken too much in the rigorous or defined sense, the real and deeper Meaning is lost. Therefore, the words of an Illumined Man should never be taken in the literal sense when He is giving a cross-translation from the Beyond.[122]

Although Wolff's methodology is multifaceted in its expression, his philosophy exhibits a single-minded purpose: "the tendency to drive toward the Root,"[123] or source, which is known directly through Recognition (or Fundamental Realization).

Autobiographical Reports

Let us now consider the function and value of the primary modes of expression within the context of Wolff's philosophy. The relevance of autobiographical material to mysticism is, as Wolff intends in *Pathways,* to provide a record of the process of transformation in consciousness. Descriptions of experiences and conceptual developments resulting as an immediate effect of the state allow others to evaluate the significance that the mystic attributes to these realizations. He says that *Pathways* "was, of necessity, more in the form of a stream of ideas, composed as they welled up into the foreground of consciousness, rather than a systematic development. The writing was true to the thought of the day or the moment and synoptic in form in so far as it was related to the development of conceptions."[124] It functions to place mystical experience within a wider human context, including preparation for Enlightenment and its subsequent effects. As the mystic becomes known as an exemplar, his account of his spiritual journey helps others to clarify their understanding of the goal and the dynamics of method.

The mystic's presentation of his experience(s) provides the ground for any further interpretation, explanation, significance, or doctrine. Admittedly, interpretative elements may enter into the content of the experience itself, so a wholly neutral formulation may be impossible. Nevertheless, we may treat phenomenal elements phenomenologically, and transcendent material symbolically. Ideally, the report indicates the point where we cross this line. Therefore, the reader is advised to be alert for any claim of ineffability and/or strained verbal formulation.

Wolff's account of his five realizations comprises the distilled essence of his autobiographical material. This description of his immediate awareness serves to ground his subsequent interpretation. He regards its significance as similar to the observational data upon which scientists develop theoretical interpretation. It differs crucially by consciously penetrating the conscious subject (the 'I'), rather than observing the object of consciousness (the 'not-I').[125] His comprehensive and articulate reports of these realizations, which we have already considered in summary form, are primarily phenomenographical,[126] rather than phenomenological. At this point, his foremost concern is to produce as accurate and intelligible a narrative as possible, suspending ontological commitment and avoiding metaphysical hypostatizing. In other discourses he goes beyond neutral description to consider significance and conceptual understanding of content, but here his first priority is to establish a clear record.

Commentary

Although Keller is correct in viewing commentaries on mysticism as primarily heteronomous,[127] Wolff's extensive and multifaceted commentaries are mostly autonomous. His purpose is to unpack aphoristic thought, explain paradoxical formulations, provide exegetical illumination of crucial notions, make connections to related material and disciplines, and so on. His commentaries function to clarify and to provide a background for comprehending the obscurities that seem inevitably to arise within other modes of expression.

Unfortunately, unless part of the analysis includes a disclaimer to the effect that no such complete understanding of the mystical can be provided, there is considerable danger one might interpret such formulation literally. One might assume that ordinary conceptual understanding is wholly sufficient—confusing the signpost with the destination toward which it points. Jones cautions that "we are still left in the realm of language and, as the Ch'an adage goes, 'Wordiness and intellection—the more with them, the further astray we go.' "[128]

Poetry

Keller argues that "we cannot take these products of creative invention at their face value as expressions of personal mystical experience."[129] Nevertheless, where it is obvious from either context or commentary that a certain poetical formulation was a mystic's intended expression of her experience, then it may be of great value. Wolff considers the poetical and intellectual functions complementary and believes that Awakening arouses the former. "He who knows the Awakening becomes something of a poet, no matter how little he was a poet before. No longer may thought remain purely formal. The poet pioneers, while the intellect systematizes. The one opens the Door, while the other organizes command. The functions are complementary."[130] In his case, this development was spontaneous and came much as a surprise, as he had neither previous inclination nor training in this direction before his transformation.[131]

Poetry serves as the more natural mode of expression of the transcendent states of consciousness. Where content is indeterminate, poetic language may convey it more effectively because it suggests more than it describes. The unrestricted form of poetic creation is necessary, at least as a partial means of expression, to indicate thought that overflows the boundaries of analysis and logical relation—much as a continuum cannot be adequately represented by a definite manifold. Satprem (Aurobindo's biographer) believes, "Poetry is the most convenient means of explaining what these higher planes of consciousness are, for in the rhythm of the poem the vibrations are easily caught."[132] Wolff takes pains to add cautionary notes on the use of language in this context.

Overuse of superlatives, as often found in Sufi expression, should be avoided because the nonmystic might consider it a sign that the mystic has lost critical perspective. However, such restraint is difficult, "especially as one realizes that all superlatives, as they are understood in the ordinary range of experience, are, in fact, understatements."[133]

In opposition to the extravagance of this style, haiku poetry requires austere (three line form), direct (plain verbal description) pointing by means of sensuous imagery. For example

> Overhead circles the hawk—
> Below the lizard
> Lies still on shimmering rocks.[134]

R. H. Blyth suggests that "life is an unwritten poem,"[135] but that Zen prefers to live rather than to utter. He says, "Writing haikus, and the desire for (more and more) enlightenment is the last infirmity of noble mind. . . . We must not aim at immortality or even timelessness; we must not aim. Infinity and eternity come of themselves or not at all."[136] It prefers prereflective silence to the *intention* to formulate. Zen writing, then, derives solely from the mode of thought that Wolff characterizes as autonomous and effortless. It is directed toward clearly and simply expressing whatever manifests in the aesthetic continuum as a means of evoking the self-luminous awareness of the consciousness to which it is present.

Aphorism

Keller considers the aphorism (whether prose or poetry) to be "the most elementary and perhaps the most authentic form of mystical literature. . . . [It is] always didactic, giving terse expression to a moral or a religious truth. . . . [It is] the product of intellectual activity at its very best."[137] Wolff reports that his aphorisms arose from a mode of consciousness similar to that of his spontaneous poetical expression.

> The best of poetry has much of this kind of thought. It is the poetry that stirs the souls rather than the senses of men. It is the poetry of content rather than of form. But most of all, from this level of thought are born the aphorisms, that strange kind of thought that is both poetry and something more. For it stirs the

> thinking as well as the feeling and thus integrates the best of the whole man. Mystery is an inextricable part of this thought.[138]

His were produced from a state of consciousness between autonomous self-flowing thought and self-directed, conceptual thought and flowed so effortlessly that they virtually wrote themselves.[139] "The aphoristic thought is the child of the transcendental and the conceptual. This is the highest form of articulate thought. He who would understand cannot do so with his conceptual powers alone. He must also let the understanding grow up from within him."[140] By comparison, Wolff's commentaries on the aphorisms "often called for the severest kind of intellectual effort."[141]

The most profound set reflects his deepest penetration of the High Indifference, the direct value of which is inexpressible and inconceivable.[142] "The aphorisms on Consciousness-without-an-object constitute such a projection on a level of exceptional abstraction and universality, whereby the unthinkable becomes, in some measure, the thinkable."[143] The aphoristic function, Keller maintains, consists in refining the formulation of traditional thought, rather than expressing individual achievement. However, Wolff's aphorisms are a symbolic representation of the universal truth revealed through individual attainment.

He considers his aphorisms to function in two ways: practical and philosophical. Their mystical value consists in their employment "as seeds to be taken into the meditative state, in which case they will tend to arouse the essentially inexpressible Meaning and Realization which they symbolize."[144] This is effective even without grasping their conceptual meaning. They also have conceptual value "as primary indefinables upon which a systematic philosophy of the universe and its negation, *Nirvāṇa,* may be developed. In this case, they may be viewed as a base of reference from which all thought and experience may be evaluated."[145] The thought presents itself as authoritative according to its own nonobjective logic expressed in apparently dissociated aphoristic statements. Wolff contends that its role is analogous to the sets of axioms upon which formal mathematical systems are based. Unlike mathematics, however, "the aphorism is a spontaneous production out of an illumined state . . . authentic *axioms** and not

---

*Italics Wolff's from his original manuscript.

merely . . . *fundamental assumptions.*"[146] Logically, they may be considered solely as an arbitrary set of fundamental assumptions from which consequences could be deduced, in a manner similar to mathematical systems. The ground of direct mystical insight provides the central criterion of evaluation. In addition, there are two other appropriate bases for appraisal:

1. coherence, that is, internal consistency—but because the law of noncontradiction was found inapplicable,[147] it must be held in abeyance in appraising the aphorisms; and
2. human value, that is, found to be worthwhile as a reference point for integrating understanding.

This latter standard for judgment relates to both mystical and philosophical functions.

We may entertain it merely as a conceptual system, but if our concerns are exclusively intellectual, we will fall short of THAT which the aphorisms symbolize.[148] How is it then that symbols, which are necessarily dualistic, can be so organized as to lead consciousness into a nondualistic state? A pervasive theme within the development of these aphorisms is the transcendence of duality, represented in a manner similar to the triadic dialectic (Hegel's logical model of thesis → antithesis → synthesis). First, a central organizing concept (such as Time) is introduced as applying to the phenomenal world (*saṃsāra*). Then it is shown how it implies its opposite (in *Nirvāṇa*). Ultimately, both are negated in the Transcendent Consciousness-without-an-object. For example,

12. Within Consciousness-without-an-object
lies the seed of Time.

•

13. When awareness cognizes Time,
then knowledge of Timelessness is born.

•

14. To be aware of Time is to be aware of
the Universe, and to be aware of the Universe
is to be aware of Time.

•

15. To realize Timelessness is to attain Nirvāṇa.

•

16. But for Consciousness-without-an-object,
there is no difference between
Time and Timelessness.[149]

The effect of following and contemplating these aphorisms affects consciousness by loosening the automatic presumption and operation of the dualistic framework, cultivating instead a nondualistic mode of awareness.

Wolff's primary positive symbol for THAT is Consciousness-without-an-object (more precisely, Consciousness-without-an-object and without-a-subject), which is oriented to the subjective or noetic pole of consciousness. He introduces an alternative, complementary symbol of the GREAT SPACE, which is oriented to the objective or noematic pole. "Consciousness-without-an-object is such a symbol for the more subjective orientation of human consciousness, while SPACE is a corresponding symbol for the more objective orientation."[150] Its referent, the Sole Reality (a subsidiary symbol), is identical to that of Consciousness-without-an-object (Aphorism 54).

Perhaps unintentionally Wolff has arranged his aphorisms in a somewhat Neoplatonic manner. Beginning with the singular, nondualistic, ultimately Real Consciousness-without-an-object comes an account of manifestation—the genesis of the Universe. Then, from consciousness aware of objects, and hence also self-aware, comes the process of Liberation through Realizing its identity as Self. Yet the terminal point lies in the GREAT SPACE, beyond all duality, where none of the categories of relative existence apply.

51. Consciousness-without-an-object
may be symbolized by a SPACE that is
unaffected by the presence or absence of objects,
for which there is neither Time nor Timelessness;
neither a world-containing Space nor a Spatial Void;
neither Tension nor Equilibrium;
neither Resistance nor Creativeness;
neither Agony nor Bliss; neither Action nor Rest;
and neither Restriction nor Freedom.[151]

The end is identical to the beginning, in a sense unifying all between. "*1. Consciousness-without-an-object is.*"[152] "*56. Beside the GREAT SPACE there is none other.*"[153] Only the final aphorism appears without commentary—suggesting that words and concepts have taken us as far as possible and that further Knowledge requires another Way of Consciousness.

Mathematics

Wolff sometimes refers to his philosophy as a yoga of mathematics[154] based upon his contribution of the conception of the indeterminate theoretic continuum.[155] He follows Northrop in distinguishing between the aesthetic continuum and the theoretic continuum, which are the respective orientations to reality of Eastern (especially the Far East) and Western consciousness. In either case, ordinary consciousness is differentiated—hence determinate—whereas mystical consciousness (whether spontaneous or the result of yoga or other spiritual paths) is indeterminate. Typical Oriental consciousness oriented to the differentiated aesthetic continuum may be characterized as nominalistic, phenomenalistic, and positivistic, such that human experience may be likened to images on a soap bubble. Yogic discipline reorients consciousness to the indeterminate aesthetic continuum, so that one not only experiences the play of images, but also Realizes the underlying Reality supporting the images.

The development of Western science is the result of a far different approach, namely, consciousness oriented to the differentiated theoretic continuum. The sine qua non for its success has been mathematics: in normative science—conceptual proof; in empirical science—the quantification of natural phenomena as a means to formulate general natural laws as mathematical equations. Wolff's introduction of the indeterminate theoretic continuum also depends upon the resources of mathematics, but functioning as pointer concepts. Consciousness of Realization is of the latter sort, so it may be illustrated by mathematical analogies and symbolism, particularly the mathematics of the transfinite.[156] The symbolic use of mathematics is also central to understanding the significance of his mandala.

Mandala

A mandala is a unique symmetrical or quasi-symmetrical archetypal symbol of wholeness, generally having a concentric, counterbalanced geometric form.[157] It functions as an aid to unify disparate elements and to center consciousness in a nonspatiotemporal Oneness. In its proper sense, it "takes its inspiration from the mystic longing for supreme integration."[158]

Wolff's mandala (see figure 5.1) originates in the mathematical interpretation of the conceptual representation of his third realization, "Substantiality is inversely proportional to ponderability." However, its symbolic significance derives from the nondualistic Consciousness of his final, supreme Realization—the High Indifference.

Its geometrical composition required several years to complete, not due to complexity of form, but rather because of its psychological function—as the outward manifestation of an inner integrative process. It is composed of a circle containing an inscribed square and contained by a circumscribed square, as well as two exterior conjugate hyperbolas. All these are perfectly symmetrical about both horizontal and vertical axes,[159] manifesting an elegant formal simplicity.

Even so, it is highly exceptional. In the lengthy process of its unfoldment, Wolff added each element inward in concentric sequence. In light of the essential centering function of mandalas, the importance of each element is thought to be related to its proximity to the center.[160] However, in Wolff's mandala, the reverse is true, for it is oriented to infinity in all directions, and the transcendental significance increases as one moves outward. Indeed, since each of the arms of the hyperbolas is of infinite length, the entire mandala cannot be fully drawn, so relative consciousness cannot completely grasp it, either visually or rationally. He notes that although it satisfies the conditions for a mandala of fourfoldness and circularity, it is atypical, inasmuch as it is not an aesthetic projection, but only a pointing to the concept. Hence it is conceptual and theoretical, rather than aesthetic.[161]

Its symbolism is comprised of the three different geometric forms—each representing an orientation of consciousness—and their interrelationships. The circle represents the phenomenal realm; the hyperbola, the transcendent nonphenomenal domain. The square indicates conceptuality—the capacity to rationalize, organize, categorize, articulate, and understand human experience. The circle and the square are both well-known archetypes. The square stands for the determinate processes of dualistic conscious-

Figure 5.1

ness—for example, measurement, definition, distinction, and precise conception. The circle symbolizes the eternal timeless domain transcending dualistic or relative consciousness. The relationships of the square within the circle and the circle within the square are quite familiar. Both reflect the subtle significance of the function of a mandala as the attempt to square the circle—the quest for the union of opposites in a higher synthesis.[162] Wolff interprets this ancient problem symbolically as the attempt to "bring into the relative, dualistic consciousness that which belongs to the Transcendent."[163]

Overall, the significance of each element must be understood in relation to the whole, as interpreted by the person who originates the mandala. Here, Wolff regards the circle as representing the dynamic processes of the natural order, the time-conditioned realm of periodicities. Whereas the circumference is correlated to the ceaseless flux of the manifest world, he relates the center to the point of pure subjectivity—the self, I, or *Ātman*—having position, but no magnitude. This perspective (the implied center) from which consciousness views phenomena, lies in relation to—but utterly other than—the objective domain (the circumference).

The square represents systematic organization, conceptual distinction, determinate relationships between contrasting elements within a duality. As opposed to the circle, which is dynamic, the square is static. This contrasts the dynamic empirical domain with the a priori realm of forms, whose definitions and relations to each other are fixed and eternal. He views the inner square as representing complete determinateness of measurement and specification by completely defined concepts—the basis for science. Its limited position within the circle suggests that this mode of thought is inherently incapable of cognizing the entire natural domain as a whole. The outer square involves a more subtle conceptuality, for it comprehends the circle (all natural phenomena) and touches the hyperbolas (the realm of indeterminate transcendence). Thus it represents a zone that is conceptually thinkable in part, but where complete determination is impossible. Consequently, the two squares signify the distinction between scientific and symbolic modes of thought and language. That which is represented by the larger square is vaster in scope than the smaller, yet lacks its determinateness.

The hyperbolas merely touch the circle of the world. "A circle occupies the unique position as having a . . . perfectly balanced symmetry with respect to its center. The center therefore is emphasized."[164] In apprehending the circle, consciousness is drawn toward the center, surrounded by the circumference, representing the phenomenal world. In contrast, the hyperbola, because it opens to infinite space and its arms meet at infinity to close the curve, is centered in and embraces infinity. Thus, in apprehending the hyperbola, consciousness is drawn outward toward infinity. Symbolically, "the circle, therefore represents a circumscribed zone of consciousness centered in the self. . . . The hyperbola may be viewed as the state of consciousness oriented not to the center, but to space."[165] Similarly, it touches, but lies outside the outer square, so it is not even partially determinate, although nondeterminate expression may be possible. The hyperbolas represent consciousness that is no longer bound to the world, superseding the polarized structure of a centered consciousness aware of phenomena. This is completely discontinuous in nature from the centered relative consciousness represented by the origin point. Instead, it is oriented to infinity, to Space as inexhaustible possibility, and symbolizes Liberation, as well as the transcendent, nondualistic Field Consciousness—that is, Consciousness-without-an-object and without-a-subject. The hyperbola is the crucial symbol that inverts the usual significance and function of the mandala and infuses Wolff's with a subtle potency.

CRITICAL EVALUATION

Due to its nature, mysticism is exceedingly difficult to comprehend, especially for the nonmystic. Our discussion has made the case for the presence of a transempirical dimension to mystical experience that may be designated as its core. The notion of an ineffable, universal essence to mystical experience provides an organizational touchstone by which to connect superficially disparate accounts. The essentialism that we are advocating here, however, stands in sharp contrast to the empirical method that seeks a common *objective* element, or elements, in all mystical experiences by which to define it. Failing to locate anything of this sort, one may assume erroneously that every version of essentialism has been refuted and fall back on an approach that relies on general typologies of mysticism, or attempts to understand each individual case solely in terms of the particular mystic's external context. Whereas this may be useful for making cross-cultural comparisons, a danger lies in assuming that the cluster of objective features available for analysis is all there is to the mystic's awareness. That which is of overriding importance could thereby easily escape detection. Universal reference to a Transcendent core of mysticism makes possible a unified view from which to understand particular typologies as well as unique expressions.

Granting this, one might yet question whether it can be shown to be unique, that it is truly the same for all mystics. Upon reflection, we find that this question is unintelligible, for it misconstrues the significance of the term *core*, as though it applied solely within the domain of relative consciousness. To the contrary, the notion of a mystical core explicitly transcends these boundaries in the strictest possible sense, such that an absolute indeterminacy prevents any positive characterization or categorization. In a distinctionless unity it cannot simply be that the core of two mystical experiences might be different, but that we lack the means to determine what it is. Rather, there is no conceivable basis upon which to posit any sort of difference. Detectable differences in the accounts of various mystics are traceable to distinctions within relative consciousness. The core refers to the mystic's awareness Transcending the relative domain. It is the strictly ineffable Somewhat that constitutes what is mystical in mystical experience. Admittedly, our entire discussion necessarily takes place within relative consciousness, but in such a manner that, by allowing our attention to play along its frontier, as it were, we begin to sense a Beyond—the true referent of our most Transcendent symbols.

In summary, we are justified, at least on pragmatic grounds, in accepting the notion of an essential core of mystical experience, which the mystic truly claims is ineffable, for it is absolutely indeterminate. However, silence is not his only option, for although he cannot *say* (describe) what it is like, he can *show* (using symbolic language or other means) the direction in which it may be directly known. Besides this indescribable Somewhat, the mystic is also usually aware of objective elements that may not only be described, but used symbolically, as pointers to the Transcendent. The mystic's use of language is meaningful, for, as Wolff has shown, much may be communicated by skillfully employing a variety of language functions. Nevertheless, THAT which is the essence of mysticism ever eludes linguistic formulation. Only by Realization can it be Known.

CHAPTER 6

Transcendence of the Self

FOUNDATIONS OF WOLFF'S PHILOSOPHY

Wolff's Three Fundamentals

The central focus of our critique highlights the cardinal theses of Wolff's philosophy. After years of reflection, he distilled it into three primary principles that he calls "Fundamentals":

1. Consciousness is original, self-existent and constitutive of all things.
2. The subject-to-consciousness transcends the object of consciousness.
3. There are three fundamental organs, faculties or functions of cognition.[1]

The first two of these basic propositions sets out his metaphysical and epistemological position concerning consciousness and reality. The former asserts the ontological primacy of Consciousness, in the primordial sense—THAT to which Wolff refers by *Consciousness-without-an-object* and *without-a-subject.* He states that the most fundamental principle of this philosophy is that consciousness, as such, is original and primary, and thus not merely an attribute of something else."[2] The second affirms both the epistemological and ontological primacy of the self (or pure subject) over the object, within the domain of relative, subject-object consciousness. This means that whereas the self-aware 'I', or subject, is both epistemologically and ontologically prior to its object of awareness, both are ontologically derived from transcendent Pure Consciousness, which Wolff calls "Consciousness-without-an-object."[3] He claims to know this through the noetic aspect of mystical Realization, which he calls "Introception," where knower and known are experienced as identical. His third fundamental proposition, the noetic thesis, proclaims the existence of this cognitive function.

We shall consider these propositions in turn from an epistemological, metaphysical, and methodological point of view in chapters 6, 7, and 8, beginning with the second Fundamental. The present chapter primarily deals with his claim that the subject transcends the object within the context of relative, subject-object consciousness. We shall defer until the following chapter the investigation of his more central assertion that nonrelative Consciousness has ontological primacy and present the full discussion of the noetic thesis in chapter 8.

Subject Transcends Object

It is advantageous to begin with Wolff's second Fundamental, for it involves a mode of awareness that is more widely known than the Primordial Consciousness that grounds his first Fundamental. It states that the subject-to-consciousness (the self or "I") transcends the object of consciousness (within the subject-object structure). Thus it is to be understood to apply solely to the context of relative consciousness, where subject and object are distinct. Another reason why it is more accessible is that it proceeds from Wolff's penultimate fourth Realization (the first Fundamental Realization). By comparison, his first Fundamental is based on his culminating fifth Realization (the second Fundamental Realization), which transcends the fourth in depth and profundity. In his first Fundamental Realization, "I am That," the pure subject, or self, became self-aware independent of any objective content. He reports that the subject-object structure of awareness remained intact, but the object-pole became empty, leaving the subject-pole as a bare "point" of awareness—aware of itself "through identity." In addition, he also argues his case using the resources of ordinary awareness. Because it involves the domain of relative consciousness, we may plausibly expect that various treatments of the nature of the self and its relation to the object are already extant. Part of our strategy, then, will be to compare Wolff's account with independent sources.

The second Fundamental asserts the relative primacy of the self. Consequently, it should prove fruitful to begin our study by considering the epistemological and methodological primacy of consciousness so as to lay the groundwork for ontological determinations.[4] Initially, we shall show that the issue of determining the ontological import of psychological material is best resolved according to phenomenological principles, rather than the methods and procedures of natural science. Furthermore, given the ubiquity of the notion of consciousness in Wolff's philosophy, and the intrinsic relation it has to the self, a primary goal of this chapter is to give a clear account of consciousness. During this exploration, we shall find independent corroboration of Wolff's contention that a definition of consciousness is neither possible nor necessary and that the self (the purely subjective 'I') is not the empirical individual (the objective 'me'). We shall be led to conclude that reductionist theories of consciousness (and the self), which attempt to account for it in terms of something other than consciousness, are fundamentally misguided and must fail.

Method of Critique

Wolff intends that his claim of the transcendence of the subject over the object not be taken merely as a descriptive report having purely individual, psychological significance. It also has import for our understanding of the nature of consciousness and reality, raising methodological, epistemological, and ontological issues. At the outset, we may take the notion of the self as necessarily involving consciousness, so the primacy of the self over the object implies the primacy of consciousness over the object. According to this picture, we may interpret the thesis of the primacy of consciousness in methodological, epistemological, and metaphysical senses. Whereas it may be established easily on phenomenological grounds that consciousness has priority for the method of investigating and knowing reality, establishing its primordiality is more challenging.

A brief introduction to phenomenology will assist us in determining the nature of the relationship between psychology, as a natural science, and ontology. This issue has significance for determining the philosophical implications of Wolff's realizations in particular and mystical experience in general. Specifically, a phenomenological account of the procedure of natural science will show the latter to be inapplicable to the study of consciousness, per se. It will also reinforce Wolff's view that the subject-object structure of ordinary, relative consciousness is not a relation between two independently existing things.

As we examine the viability of consciousness-oriented philosophy, we shall verify that the self (the referent of the indexical "I") is purely subjective and that self-knowledge (through self-identity) consists in nothing other than self-awareness as this pure subject. Further, we shall find that the pure ego and serial theories of the self fail because they both erroneously assume that the self is an object of some kind. This will lead us to acknowledge the irreducible reality of consciousness and the need for a first-person approach to provide a proper notion of the self—hence also of the Self.[5] It will be crucial to determine the merits of a consciousness-oriented methodology for the general inquiry into the nature of reality.

Wolff's philosophy of Introceptualism lies at the opposite extreme from naturalism (as well as realism). Thus, much of the argumentation introduced to support it will counter both the metaphysical and the positivist versions of naturalism and expose the covert metaphysical claims of realism. His second Fundamental receives independent corroboration from several contemporary approaches, thereby establishing that object-oriented philosophies are intrinsically incapable of treating satisfactorily either consciousness or the self.

We must first clarify methodological considerations and come to grasp the notions of consciousness and self by reflecting upon our immediate awareness. Only then can we sort out the relationship between subject and object and the sense in which Wolff's second Fundamental is sound. Wolff claims that subject and object are interdependent, but whereas the *existence* of the object is dependent on the subject, its *being* is not. This implies that neither realism (which holds that objects exist prior to, and independent of, any conscious subject) nor idealism (which, at least in some versions, holds that the being of the object is dependent on the subject) comprises an adequate view of reality.

PHENOMENOLOGY

Descartes's Legacy

Wolff began philosophizing early in the twentieth century within the Western tradition. This is reflected in his quest for certainty (in the spirit of Descartes's mission to overcome skepticism) and his attempt to establish foundations for philosophy (the Kantian influence). Central to this endeavor is Wolff's choice of focal point—the consciousness of the knowing subject, a perspective that was increasingly vindicated as he became more familiar with Eastern thought.

The difficulties encountered by Cartesian dualism have led many Western philosophers to repudiate the approach to philosophy that begins with one's own case, which places the consciously aware subject at the center.[6] Consequently, Wolff's approach requires clarification and argumentation. The certainty that Descartes finds in the Cogito lies in the self-guaranteeing nature of the existence of conscious thought.[7] Wolff concurs "with the fundamental discovery of Descartes, i.e., that when everything is submitted to critical examination, it still remains impossible to doubt one's own being, however little one may be able to understand the nature of that being."[8] At the moment when thinking is self-aware, it is impossible that it does not exist, and this impossibility is known with unshakable certainty.

Wolff also follows Descartes in claiming certainty for the awareness of what appears—purely as appearance. It is this part of the Cartesian legacy that inspired Edmund Husserl to approach philosophy as a strict science—a science of immanence. Philosophy as phenomenology would retain its rigor by avoiding all ontological and metaphysical presuppositions and simply describe the essential structures of whatever appears to consciousness. Wolff also strives for epistemological rigor, yet holds out the possibility of the legitimate reintroduction of metaphysics grounded in immediacy—consciousness directly aware of a content that transcends phenomena.

Epistemological Primacy of Consciousness

Wolff's theory, which obviously has idealist predecessors, also has contemporary analogues. Wolff maintains that nothing may be known apart from some sense of consciousness and that speculation is pointless concerning that which forever remains beyond it, insofar as "every element that is brought into any speculation is, of necessity, within the field of consciousness."[9] Phenomenology accepts as fundamental the truism that anything that is to be known will be known by some kind of consciousness. In the same spirit, Wolff also acknowledges and embraces the epistemological implications of the egocentric predicament, namely, that it is impossible to know anything that lies beyond consciousness in every sense. The egocentric predicament is "the problem that we wish to know and interpret the world, and must do so from the perspectives available to us, perspectives centered in ourselves or our egos."[10] However, it is critical that we interpret it so as to avoid unwarranted ontological presuppositions. In particular, we should be careful to avoid Descartes's mistake of hypostatizing the ego into an entity of some sort—as a "thinking thing."

To evaluate Wolff's insights and formulation effectively, let us first introduce Aron Gurwitsch's succinct account of the phenomenological approach to philosophy.[11] Although Gurwitsch is not the founder of this school of philosophy, he accepts Husserl's fundamental principles. Yet, according to Frederick Kersten, he goes beyond Husserl in developing his own theory of intentionality.[12] We shall supplement it by Quentin Lauer's critical summary of the development of Husserlian phenomenology.[13] Although there are egological approaches to phenomenology as well, it will be more interesting to develop the one with which Wolff would have most affinity. Since both egological and nonegological versions suspend commitment to ontological presuppositions, they serve equally as a base from which to critique positive science. In addition, the discussion of the primacy of consciousness will lend support to the nonegological view of consciousness. This comparison will explore the philosophical implications of their common ground for the primacy of consciousness thesis—particularly the relevance of psychology to a strict philosophical treatment of epistemology and ontology, and the inadequacy of the naturalistic approach to psychology.

Circularity of Natural Science

According to Gurwitsch, the first move in the phenomenological critique of naturalism is the distancing of phenomenology from psychology by showing that consciousness, per se, is not part of the so-called real world. Therefore, consciousness transcends the domain of natural science. This point has immense import! The phenomenological approach to consciousness is radically different from the psychological approach,[14] inasmuch as psychology is to be included as one of the positive sciences. Although the latter has propriety within its domain, its *significance* is seen to be fundamentally altered. "From the psychological point of view, acts of consciousness are considered as events of a specific nature occurring in the same real world and in the same objective time as events of other kinds, e.g., organismic processes (especially of the nervous system), and physical processes of all sorts."[15] Acts of consciousness, physiological and physical processes are all considered to be causally and/or functionally related. Sense organs are stimulated by external physical events, and this is thought to cause corresponding conscious experiences. It follows that psychology, seen as fully integrated with the mundane realm, uses physics and the biological sciences as part of its methodology for the study and understanding of consciousness.

Gurwitsch contends that the origin of this view is the natural attitude (our usual uncritical awareness, in which we simply believe that objects have the kind of existence they appear to have). This attitude is engendered by the prereflective acceptance of our object-oriented existence. In this mode of consciousness, we unquestioningly take the variety of objects within our perceptual world as real.

> All those objects, things and animate beings appear and are accepted as real existents, pertaining to the *real* world encompassing all existents including ourselves. Living in the "natural attitude," the attitude not only of every-day-life experience but also of any activity, with the sole exception of radical philosophical reflection, we simply accept the existential character with which the perceptual world and its constituents present themselves.[16]

This implicit general thesis concerning mundane reality becomes explicit when we seek scientific explanation, for the natural attitude typically still prevails there.

Because, in the natural attitude, we base natural science on correspondence to perceptual experience, these beliefs come to pervade the scientific interpretation of the world as well as our prereflective view. It follows that we will then see ourselves as one among many mundane existents that "must be reformulated in terms of the human organism exposed to external stimulation which causes certain processes in the organism. Such processes are, in turn, correlated with the experience of sense-data."[17] Hence the formulation of psychological problems and the theories proposed to resolve them are circular because they *presuppose* the conception of the universe given by physical science.[18]

Lauer argues that Husserl's critique shows naturalism to be self-contradictory because, although it regards only the physical as real, it must presuppose an objectivity that is ideal. Natural science requires some means for determining the validity of its concepts, but "the question then, of scientific knowledge of what experience presents, cannot be answered by experience."[19] Science oriented to facts requires a normative foundation that cannot be derived from the study of facts, and its attempt to do so is circular! Furthermore, empirical psychology, because it refuses to deal with psychical data directly, falls short of psychology—which properly means the study of the psyche.

Consciousness Transcends the World

In contrast, phenomenology, though also object-oriented, has a radically different subject matter and methodology from that of any positive science. Gurwitsch explains that knowledge properly includes both the originary, pretheoretical knowledge arising from, and applied within, the lifeworld and the theoretical and scientific knowledge derived from the pretheoretical. Phenomenology aims to provide not only ultimate clarification, but also justification for both.[20] His point is that insofar as positive science stands in need of this sort of clarification and justification, it would be circular to employ its methods and concepts in this project. To be sure, it is often objected that phenomenology is also circular, but phenomenologists believe they can show that neither their methodological nor their epistemological circularity is vicious.[21] However, the ontological and metaphysical presuppositions of positive science, particularly psychology, demand scrutiny from a more radical perspective. Verier Smitheram suggests that by basing objectivity within subjectivity, phenomenology is able to provide this much-needed critique of science.[22]

Phenomenology thus holds that consciousness has both methodological and epistemological, but not necessarily ontological, primacy. No object appears except to consciousness, and knowledge is achieved only through the acts of consciousness. The phenomenological goal is to provide a presuppositionless descriptive account and ontological classification of objects of all sorts. As a consequence, "we are referred to the respective acts through which these objects present themselves in their sense and significance in our conscious life."[23] Therefore, consciousness has a unique, transcendent status. Gurwitsch concludes, "If *consciousness* is a unique realm of absolute priority, it is because it is the *medium of access to whatever exists and is valid.*"[24] As that to which the world appears, it cannot be one among the objects that appear.

> From the phenomenological point of view, consciousness cannot be regarded as one mundane realm among others. To whatever mundane realm an object belongs, it necessarily involves, implicates and, in this sense, presupposes consciousness, namely, those acts through which the object in question appears and displays itself as that which it represents in our life. Consciousness thus reveals itself as the universal domain or medium of presentation of all objects, a domain to which every mundane realm necessarily refers. Herein consists the privilege and the priority of consciousness to every mundane realm. The mundane nature of a realm purports its insertion as a part into the whole of the total reality. In this sense, mundane nature must not be ascribed to consciousness.[25]

Accordingly, phenomenology may be seen to provide a rationale independent of mystical experience that, to a great degree, justifies Wolff's assertion that consciousness transcends mundane reality.

Wolff's Phenomenological Attitude

Wolff's position resembles the phenomenological approach regarding its restriction of existence to phenomena—that is, to objects present to consciousness (in whatever modality). This implies that the *existence* of an object presupposes and therefore depends on consciousness.

> No object requires more than *seeming* in order to exist for consciousness. Existence conceived in any other sense, than as for consciousness, is entirely meaningless. For that existence is found to be dependent upon *being conceived*, which, of necessity, is a conscious act or state. In the strictest logical sense, therefore, all objects rest upon the same base, i.e., that of *seeming*.[26]

It would be more precise to relate the existence of an object to its mere presence to consciousness, for it may not yet be conceptualized. Within the now, he notes, objects may have a temporal index as past, present, or future (as a re-presentation from memory, a presentation in the moment, or something imagined, respectively). Nonetheless, they all may be considered to exist equally.

Wolff insists that even the attempt to posit an existence apart from consciousness in every sense presupposes consciousness. Positing the existence of *X*, imagining that *X* exists independently of consciousness, and coming to know that *X* exists (by perceiving it, for example) all involve the activity of consciousness. Therefore, they presuppose the reality of consciousness. All this, to be sure, does not prove that the reality of *X* is derived from the individual self in an ontological sense—nor would Wolff wish to trust the security of an impenetrable but sterile solipsistic citadel. In the succeeding section we shall investigate his claim that Consciousness-without-an-object and without-a-subject provides the ultimate ground for both subject and object.

If our interest is philosophical, and we wish to avoid circularity, then we are clearly prohibited from proceeding in the manner of positive science. This is because it views consciousness as integrated into a physical world that is assumed to have ontological primacy. In particular, we cannot account for perception in terms of objective physical processes, which are themselves dependent on our account in terms of perception.[27]

Lauer's phenomenological basis for ontology—that "to be is to be given to consciousness,"[28] accords well with Wolff's position in this respect. However, in neither case is this equivalent to George Berkeley's position that "to be is to be perceived,"[29] which would restrict being to the range of awareness of the present moment. Furthermore, for both philosophers the relevant focus of inquiry must go beyond psychology as a natural science, insofar as it either ignores as unreal whatever is psychical, or attempts to reduce it to physical terms. Lauer characterizes the psychical as a realm of monadic beings whose relations are acausal and where being is identical to appearing.[30] As such, the problem of objectivity arises.

Suspending the Natural Attitude

Gurwitsch claims that resolving the problem of objectivity requires that we suspend or bracket the natural attitude and acknowledge that objectivity is essentially related to subjective experience. This involves the phenomenological reduction to radically justify philosophical knowledge. We simply withhold assent to, rather than doubt or deny, the existence of the world.[31] Once we acknowledge that objects are essentially referred to acts of consciousness, "the first step consists of explicating this reference, and thus disclosing consciousness as a unique and uniquely privileged realm, prior to every domain, including the perceptual world."[32] On this basis, the reduction of data is the necessary methodological step that severs consciousness from the world[33] so that both are apprehended with radically altered significance. "Under the phenomenological reduction, in consequence of the suspension of the existential belief, the real world as a whole as well as particular real existents are no longer simply accepted as existing, but are taken merely as representing themselves and appearing as existing."[34] The original existential belief remains intact, but with the added index "meant and intended" as existing. Gurwitsch says, "The existent in question is taken as an existent meant, and meant as what it actually presents itself through a given act of experience."[35] As a result, "we find only things and objects meant and intended which, accordingly, have to be *taken as they are meant and intended,* that is, *exactly as they present themselves in* actual or potential *experience.*"[36] Our philosophical concern requires that we carefully ground ontology by shifting from the natural to the reflective attitude.

Ontology

Because we may consider potential, as well as actual experience, existence is not dependent on present perception. Yet orders of existence may be distinguished according to the thematic field containing whatever object appears. Gurwitsch asserts that every object "*presents itself within a certain order of existence and as a member of that order. To experience an object amounts to being confronted with a certain order of existence.*"[37] Each order, or "natural grouping," is unified by *specific relevancy principles* that constitute it.[38] This sort of classification of objects amounts to regional ontology.

To illustrate, material objects such as rocks share the structures of time, space, and causality and appear as independent of the knower. Abstract objects such as numbers and universals also appear as independent of the knower, but are not subject to the three primary structures that frame material objects. Objects that are dependent on the knower include memories, images, feelings, and so on, and the body is a unique region that combines both material and psychical structures. Just as every ontological region has specific laws of constitution for its objects, the manner by which they are known also may be described according to unique structures. For instance, we perceive material objects perspectivally—in glimpses, as it were, that are synthesized in consciousness (through what Kant calls "apperception"). Consequently, knowledge of a material object is necessarily always incomplete, for there are always an infinite number of possible perspectives remaining. In contrast, an abstract object, such as the general form of a triangle, is grasped by intuition all at once. A complete account of reality would require a full description of both objective (noematic) and subjective (noetic) structures for all ontological regions.

Questions arise here concerning the metaphysical significance of phenomenological ontology and the possibility (even necessity) of extending it beyond this framework of investigation. For instance, Heidegger gives ontology precedence over epistemology because Being is a more fundamental phenomenon than the object of consciousness.[39] Marion Tapper explains that the rationale for Heidegger's break from Husserl may be traced to Heidegger's "argument that the being of any possible object, including consciousness, always exceeds both what is given and what is meant."[40] Heidegger pursues the implication Husserl ignores, namely, "that ontology, that is, the enquiry into the meaning of Being, is more fundamental than epistemology, and that epistemology always presupposes an ontology which may not have been made explicit, clarified, or justified."[41] This "surplus of being," so to speak, raises the question of Being. For Heidegger, this remains unanswerable "within a framework of a theory concerning the relationship between conscious intentional acts and the objects of such acts."[42] He distinguishes the *ontical* being of things from the *ontological* being proper to human being (*Dasein,* or *Being there*). *Dasein,* as Being-in-the-world, is already involved with things and thus does not transcend the world, as would the transcendental ego posited by Husserl. As Heidegger considers Being thoroughly phenomenal, he concludes that "radical disengagement from the world is impossible."[43] William Vallicella says that Heidegger believes that "ontology is only possible as phenomenology"[44] because "Being is phenomenal through and through."[45] However, Vallicella casts doubt on the viability of Heidegger's phenomenological ontology by arguing that, for Heidegger, only Being is dependent on *Dasein*; being*s* are not, and thus he is unable to avoid something like a Kantian thing in itself. Unfortunately, pursuing these issues, as well as working out the relevancy principles and interrelations of the various orders of reality, is a massive undertaking that need not, and will not, find scope here.

In any event, there are widely divergent views held on phenomenology's orientation to metaphysics. Edward Farley remarks that the idealist interpretation of phenomenology results in an antimetaphysical position, but that through the integration of a theological perspective, he "sees metaphysics as its appropriate telos and not its limit and contradiction."[46] Richard Holmes, by comparison, asserts that "Husserl's transcendental phenomenology, which he labels transcendental idealism, is epistemologically idealistic but metaphysically neutral."[47]

This brief outline cannot hope to do full justice to the depth of insight and complexity of issues within and related to phenomenology. Even so, since we are not employing this approach, either strictly or exclusively, nor is there any evidence, apart from a similar attitude toward phenomena, that Wolff was even aware of this school, we may forego a more elaborate comparison. Suffice it to say that just as empirical science enjoys success and legitimacy within its purview in spite of its deficiencies, phenomenology too has provided a powerful tool for articulating the structures of human experience without exhausting its total range. However, because the latter is restricted to intentionality, it regards its domain as the definite manifold comprised of all phenomena.

Intentionality

The thesis of intentionality, which Franz Brentano advanced and Edmund Husserl developed, claims that *all* consciousness is intentional, or object-directed. Wolff's two Fundamental Realizations provide firsthand evidence that disputes this thesis. He reports that "the Primordial Consciousness cannot be described as conceptual, affective, or perceptual. . . . It is not a consciousness or knowledge 'about', and thus is not a field of relationships."[48]

Moreover, within the phenomenological approach, a penetrating application of the technique of free variation would reveal that the intentional structure of consciousness applies only to a subcategory of consciousness. Therefore, it is not essential to consciousness per se. The method of free variation determines the essence of an object by systematically altering it in various ways through active imagination to discriminate between what necessarily belongs to it and what is accidental or inessential.[49] This procedure cannot be applied strictly to consciousness itself, which is not a phenomenon, but rather is that which is aware of phenomena—and thus can never be an object presented intentionally to itself. Yet, nonintentional consciousness remains a bare logical possibility until actually discovered directly through Introceptive Realization.

Norman Melchert explicitly points out the implications that the accounts of (at least some) mystical experiences involving undifferentiated unity have concerning the thesis of intentionality.

> It is not and cannot be an experience of something. For the "directedness" of intentional experiences requires that an object be "focused on" or "picked out." In this mode of experience we always experience *something*, and we always experience it *as* something—even if only as an otherwise uncharacterized "something." Thus, the object is brought under concepts and can be made an object of experience only through concepts. But if the unitive experience is empty of all sensuous or conceptual content, it follows that it is not an intentional experience.[50]

Thus the mystics' claims imply that no account of consciousness, in its most comprehensive sense, can be satisfactory that holds that consciousness always must be directed toward an object. On similar grounds we also may refute the thesis that intentional consciousness is *always* conceptually mediated. For example, if one interprets the realized goal of Zen Buddhism as perceiving directly without perceiving *as* something or other, then it would verify that the state of unmediated awareness may be attained. These points deserve emphasis, for they undercut the view that consciousness is to be identified with its empirical contents.

Wolff and Phenomenology

As previously established, Wolff is oriented to nonphenomenal awareness, whose nature he suggests by employing the notion of the continuum, rather than the definite manifold. Consequently, it requires a treatment not wholly restricted either by natural science or by phenomenology. Much of the relevance of phenomenology revolves around the independent support it provides for Wolff's second Fundamental (and partial support for the first Fundamental) from the standpoint of a philosophically rigorous point of view. Still, the phenomenological approach would be wary of his first and third Fundamentals, which involve a nonphenomenal metapsychological base and a metaphysical interpretation. Phenomenology restricts its activities so as to forego metaphysics and metapsychology until it compiles an exhaustively comprehensive network of descriptions detailing the structures of the relevant kinds of objectivities. Note that whereas Wolff tends to regard the self as relatively substantial, phenomenologists such as Gurwitsch prefer to talk only about consciousness, the acts and modes of consciousness, and the objects of consciousness. Nevertheless, we might interpret Husserl's general principle, "to the things themselves," which broadly refers to the lifeworld as lived (*lebenswelt*), as allowing legitimate investigation within areas of awareness that go beyond "things."

Let us summarize the area of general agreement between Wolff's philosophy and phenomenology. Consciousness is that to which all objects appear and is presupposed in any ontological or metaphysical inquiry. As such, it never itself appears as an object and thus may be considered to transcend the objective domain, although its acts, states, moods, qualities, and contents are objectivities that do appear within the world. However, an object is always an object *for* consciousness, in some sense. If we accept the phenomenon/noumenon distinction, then objects must be considered strictly phenomenal, not noumenal, so they have a necessary relation to, and dependence upon, consciousness. Without consciousness as the necessary field within which objects appear, it would make no sense to talk about objects. What there might *be* in the total absence of consciousness is unknowable, since knowing requires consciousness, and sheer speculation concerning its absence is, at best, pointless. Therefore, at least in this sense, consciousness transcends any object of consciousness.

Wolff does not deny that we must treat the world as an empirical reality for practical purposes—*as if* things were self-existent. However, in opposition to naturalism and realism, he rejects the view that phenomena, as such, constitute ultimate reality. An adequate critique of reality requires that we suspend the attitude of naturalism and forego the insupportable assumptions of realism. At the other extreme, a thoroughgoing phenomenalism[51] would lead to an unacceptable degree of skepticism, for it would restrict reality entirely to the domain of phenomena or appearances. Finally, even though phenomenology also avoids these defects, and its methodology is better suited to the task of describing objective structures, mystical reports establish the fact of nonobjective, nonintentional consciousness. Consequently, a wholly adequate philosophy must supersede the limitations of phenomenology as well.

CONSCIOUSNESS

Consciousness is Indefinable

The etymology of the word *consciousness*[52] shows it to originate from the Latin *con* (with) and *scire* (to know). Wolff avoids the term *mind*, which has taken on various meanings (specifically, as a metaphysical substance that contrasts with matter, as the individual conscious subject, as well as that which contains all that we regard as unconscious) and has thereby become burdened by well-nigh insoluble problems. More to the point, perhaps, is his insistence upon a first-person, rather than a third-person, point of view, which consciousness entails, but mind does not.

Because the importance of consciousness to Wolff's philosophy is primary and central, it is a focal point for our investigation.

He claims that consciousness is knowable but not definable, for there is nothing more fundamental in terms of which to define it.[53] It is "that which is in no need of definition. We are most intimately acquainted with it. It is that which is presupposed in every definition, but not itself defined. We have only to remind one of the fact that they already are conscious and know what it is."[54] Furthermore, we are simply inclined to indicate consciousness, since everyone concerned with its definition is already directly acquainted with it. "We can point to consciousness by saying that it is that which becomes less and less as one sinks into dreamless sleep and that which becomes more and more as he or she slowly returns to waking consciousness. No one who has never had this experience or its equivalent could ever possibly know what consciousness is."[55] This reminder evokes more than defines its meaning by referring directly to an experience that can be identified only by one who has had the experience. Wolff's account accords well with that found in the *Dictionary of Philosophy*:

> Consciousness is generally considered an indefinable term or rather a term definable only by direct introspective appeal to conscious experiences. The indefinability of consciousness is expressed by Sir William Hamilton: "Consciousness cannot be defined: we may be ourselves fully aware what consciousness is, but we cannot without confusion convey to others a definition of what we ourselves clearly apprehend. The reason is plain: consciousness lies at the root of all knowledge." (*Lectures on Metaphysics*, I, 191.) Ladd's frequently quoted definition of consciousness succeeds only in indicating the circumstances under which it is directly observable: "Whatever we are when we are awake, as contrasted with what we are when we sink into a profound and dreamless sleep, that is to be conscious."[56]

This does not refer to any change in content, but to the attenuation or intensification of awareness of these contents. Moreover, according to mystics' reports, no such content need always be present to consciousness. It follows that any definition that asserts or implies that consciousness is identical with some objective, definable content is in error.

Consciousness is a completely indefinable notion that must be known by immediate awareness or not at all. Wolff distinguishes between a conception and a notion. The meaning of the former may be completely given in a conceptual definition, but the latter is partly or wholly indefinable. Notions "are used as pointers to a meaning that is entirely outside the process of conceptual cognition."[57] Whereas to know consciousness it is sufficient to be conscious, an act of reflection is necessary to know as a fact that one is conscious.[58] What it is to be conscious, however, eludes definition.

C. O. Evans makes the same point in a somewhat different manner than Wolff, but he stresses the utter absurdity of requesting or attempting to give a *real* definition of consciousness. Defining descriptions have point, he affirms, only if one is unfamiliar with the phenomenon in question. However, it is logically impossible that a person be unacquainted with consciousness, or that a definition might be communicated to anyone lacking it.[59] Yet he fears that it is misleading to say only that consciousness cannot be defined.

> For the claim that consciousness is indefinable inevitably suggests that it is either too transparent to describe or too elusive to pin down, and neither of these is the right reason for concluding that consciousness is indefinable. . . . If we say no more than that consciousness is indefinable we leave the impression that the request for a definition was in order but simply could not be met. . . . Definitions of consciousness presuppose experience of what it is to be conscious on the part of both hearer and speaker. Consequently it is pointless to propose a definition as a substitute for encountering consciousness, and it is equally pointless to point out that no definition can substitute for an actual encounter.[60]

He concludes that only verbal definition is meaningful, but this is true solely as an assertion that two terms are equivalent in meaning.

Distinctions Concerning Consciousness

Even though Wolff contends that consciousness cannot be defined, he has formulated some valuable distinctions concerning it. His Fundamental Realizations constitute the ground for his characterization of relative and Transcendent Consciousness. Relative consciousness is that with which we are all familiar, "a relationship between a knower and a known, . . . that aspect of consciousness that is aware of phenomena."[61] In the nonrelative or Transcendent sense, Wolff contends that Primordial Consciousness (Root Consciousness or Field Consciousness) is self-existent. It is

> not the consciousness of a self or an entity, but a consciousness which pre-exists all selves or all entities, and as well all objects whatsoever. It is to be regarded as self-existent, as that which is unmade, which is, in a word, primordial and to be regarded in this system as the Root from which all comes. All selves and contents of knowledge are contained within this pure Field Consciousness as potential. When it becomes actual, there is a projection outward in which there is produced a consciousness as relationship between a knower and a known, but this latter consciousness is to be regarded in itself as an effect, and only in this sense of two types of consciousness could we say there is present in them the principle of dualism, but the consciousness as such in both cases is essentially incorruptible.[62]

Wolff has qualms concerning the legitimacy of extending the term *consciousness* in this way. Nevertheless, he feels that he must use it because nothing else conveys his meaning as well. The central point is that, although consciousness may be colored by objects, mood, and affect, pure consciousness as awareness is not at all affected by that of which it is aware. In itself it is "colorless" or "uncorrupted." Still, even though consciousness as such is indefinable, we may distinguish between the character of diverse states of consciousness and the nature of the objects of awareness.

Inasmuch as Wolff's formulation of these distinctions appears in metaphysical guise, it raises questions regarding the ontological relation between relative consciousness and Transcendent Consciousness and how this might be known. For the moment let us consider the meaning of the passage simply as Wolff's interpretation of his Realizations—an attempt to convey an understanding of an awareness that goes beyond straightforward conceptual accounts. His distinction between these states by the presence or absence of the subject-object structure appears to be descriptive. Nevertheless, we must determine the significance of the claim that Primordial, Root, or Field Consciousness *projects* all of relative existence. Is it metaphysical, mythical, or otherwise? It is best to defer this discussion until after the respective treatments of the nature of Introceptual knowledge.

Wolff further distinguishes consciousness in its immediacy as "the state of 'being aware',"[63] from self-consciousness, "the consciousness of being conscious."[64] He illustrates this state by contrasting it to the state of dreamless sleep. However, the phenomena of sleepwalking and night terrors appear to arise from this state, which provides indirect evidence for awareness, but no memory of any experiential content of these episodes. From a metaphysical standpoint, he asserts that everything is conscious (which would help to explain the phenomena we are considering), but the claim is neither directly verifiable nor falsifiable. In our normal waking state, consciousness is self-luminous, in that it takes no further act to be aware. Last, his use of the expression *consciousness of being conscious* does imply a further act of reflection, the capacity that (he agrees with Bucke) makes us distinctively human.

In a higher sense Self-consciousness may indicate the "consciousness of the subject to all consciousness," or "Consciousness of the Self."[65] Wolff explains that "it is extremely difficult to attain this consciousness, for very easily it reduces to consciousness of a subtle object. To attain consciousness of the Self in its purity is to Awaken to Cosmic or Transcendent Consciousness."[66] The phrase *consciousness of the subject to all consciousness* is best understood experientially—the state of pure subjectivity within which there is no basis for individuation. This is opposed to egoistic consciousness, which identifies with the individual uniqueness of the empirical ego in the "consciousness of one's self as distinct from other selves. The feeling 'I am I and none other'."[67]

"Relative consciousness"[68] is the same as "subject-object consciousness"[69] and stands opposed to "Cosmic Consciousness" and "Transcendent Consciousness." Wolff defines Cosmic Consciousness according to Bucke's use of the term to mean "any consciousness attained by awakening out of a crystallized subject-object consciousness."[70] Bucke considers that "the prime characteristic of cosmic consciousness is . . . a consciousness of the cosmos, that is, of the life and order of the universe."[71] Since it may involve experiential content, Wolff claims that it lies intermediate between relative consciousness and Transcendent Consciousness, which transcends experience (in the narrow sense) as a pure, timeless, formless Consciousness. We should stress that he upholds the reality of Transcendent Consciousness "on the basis of a direct mystical Recognition."[72] Whatever else may be doubted, his realizations show that a state of consciousness exists that transcends relative or subject-object consciousness. It is Transcendent Consciousness, symbolized by the High Indifference, which he later calls "Primeval Consciousness,"[73] "Primordial Consciousness,"[74] "Root Consciousness,"[75] "Pure Consciousness,"[76] "Absolute Consciousness,"[77] and "Consciousness-Without-an-Object."[78] The terms *Primeval, Primordial,* and *Root* suggest that the relationship between Transcendent and relative consciousness is that the former is original, the latter derivative. However, Wolff needs to show how this is known through Introception, and not simply as an interpretation of realization from an antecedently held conceptual system (such as Yogācāra Buddhism). He uses the term *Field Consciousness,* like *Absolute Consciousness,* in his tapes, but not in his formal writing. The terms *Pure, Absolute,* and *without-an-object* are more strictly descriptive, indicating the nature of the consciousness that he Realized. The term *Absolute,* while contrasting with *relative,* must not be taken in a restrictive sense, insofar as he maintains that there was nothing in his realizations that would indicate that further penetration is impossible.

The Unconscious

As part of Wolff's position concerning Transcendent Consciousness, he proposes that we redraw the distinction between consciousness and unconsciousness. Obviously, it would be impossible to prove either that there is or is not a domain that is absolutely unconscious, for if it were totally apart from consciousness in every sense, it could not be known at all. We are doubtless never—and could never be—aware of complete unconsciousness. He points out that the notion of the unconscious "is only indirectly inferred because contents enter into consciousness which cannot ordinarily be traced."[79] Dream images and waking phantasies are examples of such untraceable contents arising within relative consciousness. *The unconscious* is thus the term used for a posited psychical continuum akin to the processes of relative waking consciousness but untraceable by it.[80] Even so, we do not know that it is unconscious from its own viewpoint. Without self-consciousness, there would be no awareness of any difference between consciousness and unconsciousness, for "sheer consciousness that is not aware of itself, by reason of that very fact, would not know that it was conscious."[81] Consequently, Wolff's view seems consonant with panpsychism as well as the philosophies of Pierre Teilhard de Chardin and Śrī

Aurobindo Ghose.[82] Wolff agrees with Aurobindo that what seems unconscious to us is but another way of consciousness.[83]

> The real distinction should not be made between consciousness and unconsciousness but rather between self-consciousness and the absence of self-consciousness. When there is no self-consciousness in a given zone there is then no more valid basis for predicating sheer unconsciousness than there is for saying that it is a zone of consciousness that is not self-conscious.[84]

Thus he affirms that all is consciousness, although only one who has attained Enlightenment might be able to 'know' this by a capacity to penetrate into zones other than our relative waking state.[85] Establishing a universally agreeable criterion for determining who has attained Enlightenment is problematic, if not impossible. Nonetheless, what is important here is familiarity with nonrelative consciousness, whether or not this is a defining criterion. Also, it is well to mention that being in a *position* to know does not guarantee that one *will* know.

In brief, Wolff contends that the notion of consciousness is indefinable, but that each of us already knows it immediately. Distinctions based on differences in mode or content of consciousness are possible, the most important of which is between relative and Transcendent Consciousness. Furthermore, whereas the notion of the unconscious may be used in a psychological sense, this does not justify its metaphysical use.

SELF

Self-Knowledge

We seek to establish the irreducible reality of consciousness and demonstrate that consciousness is the most important prerequisite for the study of the self. It is also essential for a correct understanding of self-identity, as opposed to personal identity. By exploring the nature of self-knowledge, we shall confirm that *I* refers to the self, which is irreducible subjectivity.

Let us begin by contrasting empirical and phenomenological approaches to the self. From an empirical point of view, C. O. Evans agrees with Gilbert Ryle that consciousness is a polymorphous concept[86] and accepts James Mill's claim that it is a generic term referring to the actual perceptions, thoughts, emotions, and other mental contents that one experiences.[87] This list is not exhaustively specified, and there is no common property, that is, nothing more than these experiences. Wolff, who was not familiar with Evans's work, shares the view that a theory of consciousness is best grounded in experience, so long as it includes mystical experience. In Wolff's case, the High Indifference is the immediate ground for his notion of unprojected consciousness as Consciousness-without-an-object and without-a-subject, or Consciousness in a primordial state prior to 'projecting' either subjects or objects. The implication of an experience of consciousness that transcends the subject-object structure is that consciousness is known not to be exhausted by its intentional acts (such as paying attention). Therefore, *consciousness* cannot be regarded as a generic term referring to actually experienced thoughts and perceptions.

For Evans, the experiences of the self are identical to consciousness, but partly in the sense of unprojected consciousness—which always forms the background for its objects of attention.[88] He disclaims the possibility of proving his theory, but defends his "deliberate philosophical postulate" because it provides the most adequate explanation of our experience.[89] He employs a somewhat analytical method to establish his theory of self-awareness. Although he developed his theory independently of both Wolff and phenomenology, some similarities are to be found. By *unprojected consciousness* Evans means everything, at a particular time, of which we are conscious, other than our object of attention. One might say that as we concentrate on a particular object, it becomes thematic, and all the other elements of which we are aware form the context within which such a contrast becomes possible.

Using a phenomenological approach, Aron Gurwitsch more correctly distinguishes between the *theme*, the *thematic field*, and the *margin*. The *theme* is the focus of attention, the *thematic field* is "the totality of those data, co-present with the theme, which are experienced as materially relevant or pertinent to the theme and form the background or horizon out of which the theme emerges as the center,"[90] and the *margin* is those co-present data that are irrelevant to the theme.

The self, which Evans understands as the 'I', or *subject* of consciousness, and not as the empirical ego or 'me',[91] is the unprojected consciousness, which can never be an *object* of consciousness. Evans believes that this common feature vindicates his proposed equivalence, and that it explains why the 'I' is systematically elusive.[92] As soon as we pay attention to something, it becomes an object of attention and thus not part of the subject of consciousness.

Evans is correct that the 'I', self, or subject can never be an object, and (within the domain of relative consciousness) that consciousness is polarized. He errs, however, by placing the 'I' on the wrong side of the subject-object polarity. An object of attention stands out against a background of other objects—which remain objects so long as the subject remains aware of them. They are by nature wholly passive and lack any capacity to project themselves. In contrast, what is truly subjective performs the activity of perceiving, attending, reflecting, and so on. We see, then, that the pure subject can never be correctly identified with the objects of these acts. To illustrate, while engrossed in listening to a symphony, I may suddenly find myself attending to the flute. Here the flute music is thematic, standing out against the thematic field composed of the music of the other instruments. The margin of my awareness includes the audience, my own extraneous thoughts and feelings, and everything else in my awareness not directly related to the theme. If I were suddenly to reflect upon my act of attending, then quickly reflect upon my first act of reflection, and so on through an indefinite regress, I find that I can never catch my*self* (the 'I' or purely subjective moment of consciousness) as object. At each level of reflection I find only traces of its past activity, along with a pervasive, but indefinable, *sense of self* (a nonpolarized self-awareness) that is other than any object that I might isolate. Experientially, this account better explains how the 'I' is systematically elusive, without lapsing into either the pure ego theory or the serial theory, both of which Evans criticizes.

Pure Ego and Serial Theories

Evans correctly maintains that questions of personal identity and self-identity, though complementary, are distinct and require separate, nonreductive theoretical solutions.[93] He rejects the theoretical approach to the self that empiricist philosophers generally employ, which reduces self-awareness to the awareness by a self of its objective states at a particular time. Instead Evans contends "that self-awareness is the awareness of the self as the conscious subject of the states of the self."[94] Cartesianism, the epistemological method originated by Descartes, uses the immediate knowledge of our own direct awareness as the starting point for deriving inferential knowledge of whatever lies beyond oneself.[95] In contrast, the persons approach is an objectively oriented reductionism that claims that knowledge of self-identity extends no further than the sort of knowledge we obtain concerning the personal identity of others.[96] The only difference here is that the person in question is oneself. Evans's preliminary task is to show why it is necessary to avoid both of these theories.

The persons approach was devised as an attempt to circumvent the metaphysical problems of Cartesianism, which were mistakenly thought to attend unavoidably any method that starts with the philosopher's own awareness. However, this remedy goes too far. Upon adopting it, we would find it impossible to conduct a legitimate inquiry into the self, precisely because the persons approach "is an attempt, in short, to locate us among the furniture of the world,"[97] that is, as objects among other objects. As a consequence, self-awareness would necessarily reduce to possessing a *concept* or *idea* of oneself. In reply, C. O. Evans contends that awareness of something is experiential in a way that having a concept of something is not. Pointedly, we all have the "experience of being a self."[98]

> What the *persons-approach* seems to ignore is the awareness we have of ourselves and with it our knowledge that we have this awareness, which I shall call our *native knowledge of the self.* Knowledge of what we take the self to be is not such knowledge. Whereas the latter sort of knowledge is theoretical and hence propositional in nature, native knowledge of self is non-theoretical and non-propositional; it is the knowledge we have of a self because selves are what we ourselves are. In short, it is experiential knowledge of the self.[99]

There is a crucial distinction between a third-person and a first-person point of view: the former is appropriate to the study of persons and the problem of personal identity, whereas the latter is the perspective we have on our own experiences. As selves or subjects we are 'aware of' experiences; we 'undergo', 'enjoy', or 'suffer' them; they happen *to* us as the subject of experience.[100]

The traditional theories of the self fail to provide a satisfactory account of the self, for they share Hume's skepticism regarding the possibility of actually experiencing the self. The pure ego theory holds that there is a self, but that our knowledge of it is inferential—a result of its manifestations and accomplishments—rather than experiential. "What it is in itself remains forever a mystery. We call it the self, the mind, the ego, or the subject, but apart from dignifying it with a name, we cannot say what it is."[101] Descartes adopts this position when he inquires into the nature of the Cogito, inferring that he is a thinking thing. It is this hypostatized 'I', derived in a manner not wholly consistent with Descartes's avowed method, which is the source of his problematic metaphysical dualism. Evans contends that this view is an extension of the general doctrine of substance and attribute, where the substance is required as support for its attributes, but cannot be directly known as it is in itself.[102]

By comparison, the serial theory of the self rejects the notion of a self beyond all experience and holds "that the self is constituted by its experiences."[103] Consistent with this approach, David Hume's introspective search for a substantial self led him to conclude that we are nothing but a bundle of perceptions with no self apart from them. This view encounters difficulties because there is need to posit some agency apart from the elements themselves that is responsible for unifying them. More to the point, that which is aware of performing the investigation into the nature of the self is not found as an object in the bundle.

Although the pure ego and serial theories stand opposed, they both presuppose that an account of the self can be given that is of the same type as for material objects. Thus both theories "treat the self as an object."[104] It is this supposition that vitiates them. As Wolff insists, the self is irreducibly the subject-to-consciousness, not an object before consciousness, no matter how subtle. This neither implies a dualism of substance nor a distinction between different sorts of entities, but rather an experiencing subject (or self), as locus of awareness, and object, as that of which the subject is aware. We must firmly resist the coercive effect of language here regarding the terms *self* and *subject*, which superficially exhibit noun forms, but do not refer to a person, place, or thing.

This would seem to imply that the self, in the strict sense, has no objective qualities or characteristics with which to individuate or identify it—as *this* self. If we think of the self as a locus of awareness, its particular mode, contents of awareness, and perspective on these contents will provide practical criteria for individuation. Strictly speaking, only these objective complexes are distinguishable. Where there is no objective content, as in some cases of introvertive mystical experience, self (as Pure Self) is Recognized as universal.

Consciousness is Irreducible and Underivable

It is the irreducibility of self-knowledge that dooms in advance any attempt to resolve the problems of Cartesian dualism by eliminating mind. The denial of the existence of consciousness leads to far graver difficulties. It constitutes a *reductio ad absurdum* of this sort of reductionism because our immediate awareness is self-validating and irrefutable. As Thomas Busch claims, "None of the attempts by reductive metaphysics to explain away consciousness will ever convince, since every statement of such a metaphysics presumes the existence and validity of consciousness."[105] The proper understanding of human existence, namely ourselves, requires recognition of the reality and legitimacy of consciousness and the rejection of biological or mechanistic reductionism.[106]

Even the grudging admission of the existence of consciousness, when combined with the attempt to show that it is somehow derivative from something fundamentally unconscious, is flawed methodology. Wolff rejects the exclusively object-oriented approach of empirical science that attempts to account for the origin of consciousness from an assumed primordial background of matter, things, and/or relations. Inquiring how consciousness could arise from matter generates an inexplicable mystery,[107] he contends, for the problem has been misconceived from the outset.

> I affirm that this mystery is purely artificial and grows out of assuming an inadequate base of reference. For "matter," "thing," and "relation" are creatively constructed notions and by no means originally given material. On the contrary, consciousness is original and is presupposed in the very power to recognize and formulate a problem. . . . Thus every element that is brought into any speculation is, of necessity, within the field of consciousness. . . . This much we know, even though we know nothing else,

> "Consciousness is." For it is presupposed even in the acknowledgment of ignorance and in the agnostical and skeptical attitudes. . . . Consciousness is the common denominator underlying the possibility of any philosophy, world view, religious attitude, art, or science. I, therefore, affirm the systematic primacy of consciousness as such.[108]

This argument closely parallels the argument he gives for the Transcendence of the Self over the object. Because the self can never be an object, it cannot be derived from purely objective considerations, for example, the attempt to understand how consciousness could have arisen from an unconscious primordial material base.

> The fact is that a problem concerning nature has as its essential basis a conscious self that makes the apperceiving of the problem possible. In a purely blind and dead nature, there never could arise a scientific or any other kind of problem. Of primary importance, then, for the understanding of any problem concerning nature is a knowledge of the Self and of the knowledge-forms through which It acts in cognizing or sensing the world. The most primary fact of all is the Self that thinks and senses. Its presence is the one completely immediate reality that can neither be proved by logic nor found through experience, for it is the absolutely necessary basis for both these forms of consciousness. Thus it is only of the Self that we may properly predicate self-existence. It alone is that which is the original indubitable "given" on which all the rest depends. So the real problem is: How does the external universe come to have existence? It is a complete misconception to state the problem in the form: How did the Self come to be injected into the universe?[109]

An investigation of the self therefore requires a first-person standpoint. Wolff thus establishes the presumption that consciousness has primacy based on ordinary immediate awareness as well as his Realizations.

The difference between self and Self marks the distinction between our ordinary awareness of pure subjectivity within the relative manifold as opposed to a monadic awareness within a Transcendent Space (as in the Realization "I am THAT"). Furthermore, the term *self-knowledge* is preferable to *knowledge of the self* because syntactically the preposition *of* refers to an object of some kind. Thus the latter sort of locution reinforces the mistaken identification of the self with the empirical ego. The contrast between the terms *self-identity* and *personal identity* indicates a similar distinction. The former implies a first-person point of view; the latter, a third-person objectivity.

According to C. O. Evans, who also regards the self as underived from the object, our starting point for an account of self-identity is

> the self *qua* subject of consciousness. Such an account must begin with consciousness, for apart from consciousness no question about the subject of consciousness can arise. I cannot know what it is to be a self if I am not conscious. . . . Equally I cannot be a self if I cannot at least be conscious. Such native knowledge as I have of myself cannot therefore be divorced from the fact that I am conscious I am a self. Consciousness will therefore have to be subjected to an analysis if we are to give a philosophical account of the self.[110]

If this understanding of self and its relation to consciousness is correct, then it implies that physicalism (or more generally materialism) and psychological and philosophical behaviorism are all necessarily mistaken. Let us consider their refutations more closely.

Physicalism

For our purposes, materialism and physicalism shall be deemed to be essentially the same theory, and the distinction between the eliminative and reductive versions is of no moment. This theory essentially holds that only physical (or material) objects are real. Anything mental or spiritual is either denied altogether or its reality reduced to physical terms. Wolff explains why the West tends to attribute primacy to the subject matter of physical science.

> There seems to be but one fact of experience that affords the explanation of this attribution of reality-value to the material of physical science and that is that this material is relatively common and constant with respect to the vast majority of observers, and that so far as is commonly known, no individual can successfully act as though this material were not. Here there seems to be an objective somewhat with which the conscious being must come to terms if he is so to adapt his life as to live successfully. . . . But this fact by no means implies that that something or somewhat is an independent self-existent reality.[111]

For instance, the same facts of human experience would be equally compatible with the theory that reality was a projection from the collective unconscious. Whereas Wolff acknowledges the value of the general attitude of naturalism as a heuristic principle, in the sense of an attempt "to explain everything by reference to natural causes or processes,"[112] he rejects outright the materialistic version. This is the metaphysical theory that would restrict nature to the arrangement of physical bodies (matter) in three-dimensional space. Such a view cannot provide a satisfactory account of consciousness or the psychical phenomena of which we are aware.

Contemporary criticism reinforces this point. Thomas Nagel initially expressed qualms concerning the comprehensive capacity of physicalism insofar as it fails to encompass the "essential subjectivity of psychological states. . . . Nowhere in the description of the state of a human body can there be room for a physical equivalent of the fact that I (or any self) and not just that body, am the subject of those states."[113] More recently, he has brought this issue to the forefront of the debate on physicalism. His example of a bat illustrates that the interiority of awareness of any organism is the indispensable point of view of that organism's experience.

> If the facts of experience—facts about what it is like for the experiencing organism—are accessible only from one point of view, then it is a mystery how the true character of experience could be revealed in the physical operation of the organism. The latter is a domain of objective facts par excellence—the kind that can be observed and understood from many points of view and by individuals with differing perceptual systems.[114]

This discussion forcefully calls to our attention that subjectivity, the unique viewpoint the agent has on his experience, is intrinsically other than all objectivity. Therefore, because its description cannot be divorced from the subjective point of view, it necessarily transcends the domain of physical science. We must conclude that the 'I' can neither be reduced nor eliminated, and so physicalism fails.[115]

Behaviorism

C. Stephen Evans presents two responses to the challenge of behaviorism as advanced by its founder, J. B. Watson, who advocates that we "apply to the experimental study of man the same language of description that many research men had found so useful for so many years in the study of animals lower than men. . . . Man is an animal different from other animals only in the type of behavior he displays."[116] C. S. Evans regards the resulting reductionism as stemming from metaphysical naturalism, which is the view that a human is *nothing more than* an animal, combined with the causal or mechanistic model of explanation. This explanatory framework assumes "that human behavior is completely determined and the job of the scientists is simply to discover the laws which will account for that behavior."[117] Evans counters that human persons are responsible agents who are essentially conscious and self-reflective—they know, imagine, create, value, and make choices. Even though there is some sort of relationship of agency to body and environment, these are not identity and cause-effect respectively.

Wolff sees the rise of behaviorism as a consequence of the realist's assumption that consciousness is neither substantial nor determinative. As a result, psychology would consider consciousness, and hence introspection, to be irrelevant, inasmuch as the psychical realm is conceived to be observable as overt, objective behavior. He rejects this approach because it ignores our immediate experience and would not be able to satisfactorily account for it even if it did acknowledge it. In response, he admonishes, "The immediacy of inner consciousness does not cease being a fact simply because some methodological theory has no place for it."[118]

Philosophical Behaviorism

Philosophical behaviorism, the approach commonly attributed to the later Wittgenstein and to Gilbert Ryle, suffers from the same sort of defect as the other approaches that attempt to deal with consciousness exclusively from a third-person point of view. Launching a frontal attack upon the traditional Cartesian position, Ryle theorizes that "overt intelligent performances are not clues to the workings of minds; they are those workings."[119] This goes far beyond Wittgenstein's view that "an 'inner' process stands in need of outward criteria,"[120] for Wittgenstein at least acknowledges the existence of our mental life. " 'But you will surely admit that there is a difference between pain-behavior accompanied by pain and pain-behavior without any pain?'—Admit it? What greater difference could there be?[121] . . . And now it looks as if we had denied mental processes. And naturally we don't want to deny them."[122] Consequently, the ensuing criticism, based upon the incisive insights of Mark L. Conkling, will be seen as applying primarily to Ryle.[123]

Ryle would reduce mind and its operation to overt behavior, with nothing of interest remaining. "The styles and procedures of peoples' activities *are* the way their minds work and are not merely imperfect reflections of the postulated secret processes which were supposed to be the workings of minds."[124] In short, he rejects the "ghost in the machine" account of the relation between mind and body because it commits a category mistake. This error involves thinking of the mind as analogous to bodies, in the sense that there is assumed to be an inner spatially conceived viewing of ghostly performances caused according to determined mechanical laws analogous to those governing material bodies in external space. 'Mind,' according to Ryle, is a behavioral concept referring to our performances, dispositions, capacities, and the like. Whatever residue remains, he considers unimportant.[125]

Ironically, Conkling accuses Ryle of committing a category mistake himself—that of overgeneralizing from the valid point that ideas and images are not *in* the mind (e.g., as books are in a bookcase) to deny *any* place to a first-person account of actual mental processes. This is an error because "there is nothing that consciousness and dispositions *both are*,"[126] so they belong to different logical categories. Conkling reminds us that " 'consciousness' is not a behavioral concept" and that "our experience of our awareness takes different forms."[127] Consciousness is, he argues, a self-luminous intentional relation between a person and his experience.[128] This should be taken as his account of what consciousness is, and not one of its different forms. Concerning Ryle, he says, "I call the mistake of focusing upon the particulars of behavior, without acknowledging the *reliance upon* the subsidiary awareness of mind or consciousness, *The Fallacy of Losing Your Mind.*"[129] Whatever the merits of Ryle's insights, by ignoring the reality of consciousness, Ryle commits a serious error.

Wittgenstein too does not entirely escape this criticism. The point of his "beetle in the box" analogy seems to allow the reality of mental processes only to deny that we can say anything about them. "It is not a *something*, but not a *nothing* either! The conclusion was only that a nothing would serve just as well as a something about which nothing could be said."[130] The strict sense of "saying" that makes this seem plausible has already been discussed. Thus we have found that the capacity of language to *show*, as well as *say*, is considerably greater than this statement admits. Alan Paskow contends that Wittgenstein's argument against privacy is the result of assuming "inappropriate criteria of verifiability for the identification of private phenomena."[131] Reports on the contents of one's dreams would have the status of this sort of proposition. Wittgenstein's dictum concerning the necessity for public criteria overlooks the asymmetry between knowing the psychical activity of others and knowing my own. In the latter case I have direct, immediate access to the subject matter, so it would generally be inappropriate to take a third-person point of view toward myself. Even when we apply public criteria to others to determine the content of their inner awareness, the most reliable is their authentic first-hand reports, not mere inferences from overt behavior.

It is generally absurd to make unsolicited first-person knowledge claims concerning one's thoughts, feelings, moods, and so on (for example, "I know I am in pain."), rather than just expressing them ("I am in pain."). However, this is not because these statements have the same meaning, or that we do *not know* our inner condition, as some have argued.[132] The absurdity arises because we assume that normally (in standard contexts) a person *does know*—and does not merely *believe*—the truth of what she explicitly reports concerning her inner awareness. We may drive the point home by contrasting the preceding locutions with the statements, "I do not know that I am in pain," or "I am in pain, but I don't know it." If spoken seriously by someone who understands English, these statements are ludicrous. Furthermore, we are ordinarily justified in taking a person's honest report, "I am in pain," as sufficient to know that she is in pain. It would then be ridiculous for us to hold that *we* know that she is in pain, but that *she* does not know it.

Paskow contends that part of what we communicate is in propositions that denote essentially private experiences. They are true if they correspond to the facts of subjective awareness, notwithstanding the fallibility of such statements.[133] He also considers it important that we regard first-person accounts as descriptions, and not merely expressions of inner awareness, because of the profound difference it makes in our understanding of others.

> Such a view encourages the understanding of another's causes of and motives for action not through cognition of his linguistic and bodily responses and the subsequent generalization of such responses in the form of criteria for behavioral interpretation, but (primarily) through the reflection on our own causes and motives for action and through the formulation of hypotheses about others on the basis of what we discover about ourselves. We understand another truly and profoundly not by scientifically observing his behavior as though he were a strange creature in a zoo; instead we see in his movements and gestures, speech inflections and alterations in complexion, patterns of response that reflect our own ways of acting in the world—ways whose significance we can grasp because they are associated with, and manifestations of, the emotionally based pro-jects of our private lives.[134]

The attempts to deal with the philosophical problems of the psyche by ignoring its primary data are found to be no better than the flawed Cartesianism they hoped to replace. The fallacy of losing your mind is the downfall of these efforts, and shows them to lead to a philosophical cul-de-sac.

Appreciating the importance of this defect should prompt a fresh attempt to provide a satisfactory solution that acknowledges the irreducible reality of consciousness, while avoiding the pitfalls of metaphysical dualism. Accordingly, it is now time to deal directly with Wolff's second primary principle—involving the relative transcendence of the self.

SUBJECT AND OBJECT

Definition

To determine the nature of both subject and object, as well as their interrelationship, it will be necessary to discuss relevant methodological and epistemological considerations. Phenomenological reflection reveals that any consciousness of objects is polarized within a subject-object structure that frames the stream of lived experience and in which objects arise and are known. Wolff employs the terms *subject* and *object* with clarity and precision. The subject is the self or subject-to-consciousness, which, insofar as it is the actually aware pure subject (not as projected, conceived, or thought), can never be an object. In contrast, an object is any distinguishable somewhat of which consciousness, in whatever mode, is aware—at a distance, as it were.

We must resist equating *subject* to *person*, on the one hand, and *object* to *thing*, on the other, if we are to avoid confusion and ontological question begging. The pure subject is the perspective from which consciousness is aware of objects, but in itself is never an object. Persons are objectively identified entities composed of physical and psychical structures that mediate experience. These structures uniquely determine a person's identity, but the manner in which they are known differs between the person herself and the Other. Each person has an inner view of herself from a lived identity, whereas the normal point of view of the Other is external. In the natural attitude, we live the world through these intimate structures, whereas in the reflective mode each of them may be objectified. Things, like persons, are material, but lack manifest self-awareness. All things may be objects, but not all objects are things, for awareness of objects belonging to diverse ontological regions is possible. Succinctly stated, the terms *person* and *thing* are conceptually mediated and ontologically biased; *subject* and *object* are immediate and ontologically neutral.

Subject-Object Interdependence

Wolff's articulation of his second Fundamental begins within a quasi-phenomenological approach characterized by an analysis of experience that eschews ontological assumptions. Within subject-object consciousness (the domain of our ordinary, relative awareness, to which his second Fundamental applies), Wolff contends that the subject and object are *inter*dependent.

> The existence of a self implies the existence of objects, whether subtle or gross, and as well, the existence of objects implies the presence of a self that is aware of them. The object and the self are polar existences that are interdependent. The notion of a self that is conscious without being conscious of anything does not correspond to any possible actuality. The object may be very abstract, such as a bare field of consciousness viewed as an object, but analysis will always reveal a polar relationship. The subject is the inverse or complement of the object, or in other words, its "other."[135]

Subject and object are thus mutually implicative. However, to characterize their relationship as a polarity may be misleading, for it suggests an objective equivalence in some respect. This would be impossible for the subject or self, *in its purity,* which is radically other than objects of any sort. It is a locus of consciousness intentionally related to objects *through,* or by way of, certain noetic structures. It is this which gives the subject its unique perspective on objects of awareness and makes possible the distinction of one locus from another. These structures do not appear on the side of the intentional object, but only upon an act of reflection. As long as it is understood that these objects also remain radically other than the pure self or subject, the subject-object relationship may be viewed as a polarity.

Wolff's position supports the thesis of intentionality when its range of application is restricted to the domain of relative consciousness. He would hold that an object such as a tree exists empirically as an appearance, where *existence* (in its etymological sense as "emerging or standing out from") is necessarily related to consciousness. This is because the distinction between that which stands out and the background from which it stands out implies an awareness—that *to* which it appears, or *for* which it exists. At this point we have no reason to hypostatize the self, or subject, into a self-existent entity, so it is best to defer the question of its ontological status until we consider the first Fundamental. It is sufficient to note, as C. O. Evans has shown, that we have tacit or "native" knowledge of it and that it exists as the "other" of objects.

Notwithstanding their interdependence, or mutual implication, Wolff contends that the subject transcends the object. Epistemologically, the knowing subject is primary, for it constitutes the object—a point that Wolff would understand in the Kantian sense: the appearance of the object known depends upon the structures imposed by the knower. This has ontological implications. "To be known is to be an object. Since by 'universe' I mean the totality of all possible objects, it then follows that the universe is dependent upon being known for its *existence.* The universe exists for one who experiences or thinks, but for none other."[136] Taken in abstraction, the object, as such, is not a universe, but simply a multitude without interconnection and therefore not even a collection. The *universe* is the resultant of the interaction of the self and its object—

that is, it is a disconnected multiplicity integrated through the unity of the self.[137] What Wolff means by *Universe* in his aphorism "Consciousness of objects is the Universe [is] that domain of consciousness wherein a self is aware of objects, the latter standing as opposed to, or in contradistinction to, the self that is aware of them."[138] This range is far vaster than the totality of objects in the physical universe, which is the domain of Western science. Without the involvement of the knower, there may be a fullness of being, but no universe yet stands out from it. He regards the sense in which the object's existence derives from the individual subject to be the result of a psychological process, more in the nature of an unconscious projection than a consciously willed creation.[139] The notion of projection requires explication because the term has other unwanted associations. He would be wise to make his point by proposing that the process is conscious, but not reflectively self-conscious, and spontaneous rather than deliberate.

The statement *To be known is to be an object* does not imply, however, that the Being of the object is dependent on its being perceived. Phenomenologically, we might say that we constitute the meaning, or sense, but not the being of the object, which is not ontologically reducible to its actual appearance as a phenomenon. Some classes of objects present themselves as resilient to, and hence independent of, the self. Wolff distinguishes between being and existence in this way:

> To predicate that consciousness is original and self-existent does not imply that *Being* is dependent on *being known*. . . . On the other hand, "to know" does *imply* being, but the implication is of an antecedent, not of a consequent. To become aware of knowing is to become aware of the reality—in this case relative reality—of Being. The awareness of this reality is something achieved, but the achievement has not made the reality. However, to *be known* is to *exist*, and this is a true sequential or derivative existence. Being is *antecedent*, existence *derivative*.[140]

Simply stated, though subject and object are interdependent, the subject as knower transcends the object known. Furthermore, the object depends upon the subject for its *existence*, but not its *being*.

Wolff's position diverges importantly from subjective idealism, which holds that being (not merely existence) is dependent upon actual perception. Berkeley attempts to save his system from obvious absurdity—namely, that when no one is perceiving something, it disappears from the world—by simply positing God as all-perceiving. Without the unwarranted introduction of God, Berkeleyan idealism would reduce to solipsism—that all of reality is what *my* mind perceives. Wolff's thesis rejects the view that the primacy of consciousness means that all of reality is ontologically dependent on, and derivative from, the individual, or relative consciousness. The being of an object, distinct from its existence, cannot be characterized further, except that no account in terms of its phenomenal qualities could apply. Perhaps he could couch his distinction between existence and being by using the Kantian distinction between phenomena and noumena, which he seems to accept. Reality is multifaceted, and consciousness operates in diverse modalities, providing more than sufficient resources to account for the world we commonly experience—as well as more rarely encountered possibilities.

Consider also that because the subject-object structure is a polarity rather than a duality, we need not attribute separate substances to them. Consequently, Wolff is able to avoid certain problems of Cartesianism, although other problems may arise concerning his substantialistic interpretation of the nondualistic Primordial Consciousness.

Evidence from Realization

Whereas analysis, grounded in reflection upon ordinary experience, seems sufficient to establish that the knowing subject is ontologically irreducible to any kind of objectivity, Wolff's Realizations provide a more compelling argument. There he discovered consciousness (and, concomitantly, the subject or self) to be independent of the object of consciousness.

> When the Light of consciousness turns upon itself toward its source, the object vanishes. It would follow that if consciousness were dependent upon the object for its existence, then the resultant state would be one of complete unconsciousness. However, we find, to the contrary, that the resultant state is quite other than one of unconsciousness; it is, indeed, a state of greatly intensified consciousness. Thus if consciousness depends upon anything at all, it is exclusively dependent upon the subject or self.

> However, the vanishing of the object as consciousness sinks back into its source, as it were, thereby proves the contingency of the object. . . . At the first stage of the introceptive transformation, the object vanishes, while the subject persists. This minimally implies the transcendency of the subject relative to the object.[141]

This does not contradict his avowal of interdependence of subject and object because at this stage there is still awareness of the empty object pole (the absence of objects). Consciousness is aware through the positional focus of the self (which Wolff refers to here as "point-I") even after the object vanishes. Thus he believes he is justified in attributing relative primacy to the subject.

Within the subject-object structure, we experience the world as a definite manifold. The Self, understood as the purely subjective moment of consciousness, constitutes its primary reality. We should not confuse this with the pure ego theory of consciousness, which posits an independent nonphysical entity as the owner of consciousness. The egological view is akin to the pure ego theory discussed by C. O. Evans, but it does not regard the self as so crudely objective (as though one could discover it through introspection as an object of inner perception). Even so, it also considers the self to be an entity of some kind, which suggests that it is to be thought of as a subtle object. This view has now been shown to be mistaken.

Neither Realism nor Idealism

Insofar as the resolution of questions concerning what there is depends intrinsically upon our capacity and means of knowing such matters, it is naive to attempt to study metaphysics apart from epistemology and methodology. In the debate between realism and idealism, one point emerges with certainty. It is impossible to *know* whether there is anything beyond the range of consciousness in every sense. Thus the realist's claim that there is and the idealist's claim that there is not are equally unprovable. Such claims are metaphysical in the invidious sense. If there is something beyond all awareness, whatever might be said concerning it would be strictly speculative, at best. Both schools of thought appear one-sided, assimilating the object to experience or vice versa. Though they would seem equally vulnerable to criticism in this regard, Wolff points out that idealism has the advantage of preferring a ground that is accessible to investigation, so that predications of being and existence have meaning. Realist ontology, on the contrary, is based on an order of existence that can only be *assumed*, for it is necessarily beyond any human awareness.[142] To attempt to define it would thereby bring it into the range of consciousness. He suggests that the idealist may "quite reasonably contend that the burden of proof rests with the realist, since the latter is affirming a thatness beyond the range of direct epistemological determination, thus involving hypostatization beyond all possible experience."[143] Consequently, we should concede whatever edge there may be in this debate to the idealist.

What makes realism so appealing to common sense is that we all have ordinary experience of things such as rocks, trees, and stars that appear as independent of us, that is, as having a reality apart from our awareness of them. Our originary experience in the natural attitude is that we are already in a world with others. At the prereflective level, there is simply no relevance to the philosophical problems of the existence of the external world and of other minds. However, we cannot remain entirely undisturbed within the naive attitude, for experiences such as reaching into a pool of water generate cognitive dissonance because my arm both feels straight and looks bent. In this way the issue of the relationship between appearance and reality arises.

As we shift to the reflective level, there is a subtle but thoroughgoing difference between the realist and idealist approaches that is not captured within our practical, prereflective attitude toward the world, in which adherents of either school function equally well. The crux of their philosophical opposition lies in the role of consciousness in determining knowledge of reality. Consciousness of some kind is obviously an absolute precondition for knowledge. The idealist's investigation of the world is grounded in a way that the realist's is not because only the former takes this point seriously. The things of the world exist in and for consciousness, so all objectivities are meaningful only insofar as they are constituted by consciousness. In contrast, the realist understands the things of the world as self-existent, such that if there were no such thing as consciousness, then trees and rocks, for example, would still exist just as they do in our experience of them. This implies that consciousness is entirely irrelevant to the matter—a view that is quite impossible to verify. In short, the realist affirms, while the idealist denies, the self-existence of the world.

The realist errs in hypostatizing objects that appear independent of the knower into metaphysically self-existent things. Phenomenologically, all that we are entitled to assert with certainty is that a rock *appears* as independently real—not that it *is* independently real. The idealist, in acknowledging the indispensable role of consciousness in epistemological grounding, errs in hypostatizing it into a spiritual substance that is necessary, not only for the *existence* of the object, but also for its very *being*. The phenomenologist avoids these defects by refusing to hypostatize or engage in any sort of overt metaphysics, but at the cost of limiting all philosophy to description of phenomena—determining the essential structures of all appearances constituted in consciousness.

Wolff rejects realism because it assumes the existence of the independent thing and allows no significant role for consciousness. The reality of consciousness is immediately certain. Proof of a thing's independent existence, he contends, is an epistemological impossibility because all knowledge necessarily presupposes consciousness.[144] However, he is also careful to forego the classical idealist denial that there is anything beyond awareness. He agrees with Aurobindo that

> there is no such thing as an objective reality independent of consciousness; but at the same time there is a truth in objectivity and it is this, that the reality of things resides in something that is within them and is independent of the interpretation our mind gives to them and of the structures it builds upon its observation. These structures constitute the mind's subjective image or figure of the universe, but the universe and its objects are not a mere image or figure. They are in essence creations of consciousness, but of a consciousness that is one with being, whose substance is the substance of Being and whose creations too are of that substance, therefore real. In this view the world cannot be a purely subjective creation of Consciousness; the subjective and objective truth of things are both real, they are two sides of the same Reality.[145]

This position mirrors several features central to Wolff's philosophy: namely, the

1. distinction between relative consciousness and Transcendent Consciousness,
2. grounding of objective reality in consciousness, and
3. distinguishing an object's phenomenal existence from its being.

Neither Wolff nor Aurobindo may justly be accused of lapsing into subjective idealism, for neither holds that the being of a thing is reducible to its perception by an individual subject. Wolff explicitly characterizes his philosophy as "neither idealistic, in the subjective sense, nor realistic, but which may incorporate both idealistic and realistic aspects."[146]

Ultimately, Wolff maintains that the theory that an external world exists as an independent thing is unimportant and any attempt to demonstrate its self-existence necessarily must fail.

> Whether there is an external world existing as a thing, outside the relation of being an object for a subject, is really a matter of no importance. To predicate existence or nonexistence of such supposed independent thinghood is a meaningless judgment, since no meaning attaches to the notion of existence apart from consciousness. Anyone who attempts to define such existence inevitably finds that the very act of defining has transformed it into an object, that is, into a somewhat that exists for consciousness.[147]

Wolff proposes that "every predication concerning that which is totally outside of consciousness is not so much false as meaningless, because it is by its inherent nature unverifiable,"[148] insofar as all verification occurs within consciousness. This implicit acceptance of verificationism is benign in this context. Moreover, according to Wolff, the existence of the independent thing is necessary neither for thought nor for consciousness. It is simply irrelevant, and both the realist's affirmation and the idealist's denial are pointless. Wolff's philosophy "is neither realism nor idealism, since it is oriented to Consciousness Itself."[149]

Discovery of the self, or subject, through philosophical or phenomenological reflection differs drastically from its Realization. The egoistic sense of "I am I and none other" is Transcended in Realization of the SELF as "I am the One without a second or, more strictly, 'I am not-one and not not-one, and there is no second.' "[150] Intermediate between these is the sense of I that is also

We, the state "where I realize Myself as 'I am I and yet also others'."[151] Even in his first Fundamental Realization, the Self that is Realized is fully transpersonal. Wolff reports that "it is only from the egoistic point of view that the Transcendent Consciousness appears as an 'I' Consciousness. On the highest level, both the 'I' and the 'thou' disappear."[152] The SELF can never be an object, but it may be Realized and Known through Identity.[153] What Wolff (and the mystical view) adds is what he calls the "Transcendental Component," reference to an immediate, nonphenomenal (perhaps noumenal) awareness that pervasively alters the significance of the entire phenomenal realm.

Overall, we are justified in accepting Wolff's second Fundamental as he has defined it. Indeed, there seems to be no possibility of refuting it, insofar as existence necessarily presupposes consciousness, and any attempted ontology already presupposes the self, which itself can never appear in the objective domain. To be sure, the *being* of the object also may transcend this realm, but nothing further may be said intelligibly concerning it.

CHAPTER 7

Primacy of Consciousness

Wolff asserts that "the most fundamental principle of this philosophy is that consciousness, as such, is original and primary, and thus not merely an attribute of something else."[1] His first Fundamental, stating the primacy of Consciousness, is more straightforwardly metaphysical than the claim that the subject transcends the object. A central difference from his second Fundamental is that the meaning of *Consciousness* here is Consciousness-without-an-object and without-a-subject, rather than the relative subject-object consciousness.

> The basis of integration afforded by the aphorisms is that of the radical assertion of the primacy of Consciousness. . . . The radical element in my philosophic departure inheres in the "without-an-object." Herein lies precisely the difference between a state of consciousness that is only relative or saturated in raw immediacy and no more, and one that involves profound mystical realization. However, consciousness is the common denominator underlying the possibility of any philosophy, world view, religious attitude, art, or science. I, therefore, affirm the systematic primacy of consciousness as such.
>
> As soon as consciousness is concerned with objects, and inter-relations, other complexities are introduced and accordingly, all sorts of divergencies. Deleting content, only Consciousness-without-an-object remains as the common denominator. If approached in a purely theoretical spirit, this might have merely the

> value of an abstraction. I have demonstrated its actuality as a direct realization, but found it the most difficult of things to attain when starting from the basis of reflective consciousness. However, when realized, it is the simplest of all things.[2]

Accordingly, we would expect that the justification of the primordiality of Consciousness ultimately will rely on the ground of Realization. Nonetheless, the findings of reflective consciousness may bolster this position.

Wolff's second Fundamental Realization, the High Indifference, culminated in an awareness wherein both the subject-to-consciousness—Realized as Self—and the object of consciousness, in the most supreme sense—Realized as Divinity or God—dissolved into a more ultimate nondualistic Primordial Somewhat. Thus Consciousness Itself (that is, without-an-object and without-a-subject), as a field of awareness (Field Consciousness) prior to the subject-object structure, has a primacy that Transcends the relative primacy of the Self.

Consciousness in some sense is doubtless a necessary condition for it to be known at all, but any distinction between knower and known (or between any other pair of opposites) no longer applies. From this Realization, he understands as part of the significance of the High Indifference that the term *Consciousness,* taken in a Primordial (or Root) sense, may be used to indicate the underlying ontological ground for manifest reality. This is true to the extent that it is possible to use language meaningfully in mysticism to symbolize or point to what cannot be described.

To investigate the significance of Wolff's orientation to Consciousness, we need to distinguish between relative consciousness and nonrelative Primordial Consciousness. We must further discriminate between consciousness, the self (which is pure subject), and the ego (which is an object). Then we must explicate the notion of Consciousness-without-an-object to draw out its metaphysical implications. During this process, it will be especially illuminating to consider Earle's treatment of the phenomenology of mysticism, Sartre's phenomenological account of the ego, and other philosophical positions that treat consciousness as primary.

Because phenomenology is in theory neutral, and in practice often hostile to metaphysics, we shall include other points of view to determine whether consciousness has priority in this sense. For instance, we shall compare Wolff's metaphysical interpretation to Charles Hartshorne's panpsychism and the "Consciousness-Only" School of *Yogācāra* Buddhism, which also hold that consciousness is ontologically primary. Inquiring into the ontological primacy of Consciousness, we will attempt to resolve the critical issue of whether consciousness is egological. Both Wolff and Sartre advocate a nonegological position, so it will be instructive to compare them to each other, as well as to contrast them to the egological position.

Finally, we must clarify the distinction between consciousness and Consciousness-without-an-object to determine the sense in which the first Fundamental is acceptable.

PRIMORDIAL CONSCIOUSNESS

Transcending the Subject-Object Structure

The primacy of consciousness lies at the heart of Wolff's philosophy. It is crucial that we understand the distinction between Consciousness as Field Consciousness, which he calls "Consciousness-without-an-object and without-a-subject," and relative, or subject-object consciousness. So far, in our attempt to explicate the second Fundamental, we have been thinking of consciousness as a polarized subject-object awareness. However, this is not the most penetrating perspective from which Wolff derives his philosophy.

Even if the subject transcends the object, it remains to be shown that consciousness transcends the subject, rather than being dependent upon it. Thus the dispute between the egological and nonegological views of consciousness will comprise the first theme of this section. Empirical and phenomenological methodologies, appear inconclusive in this matter, but Realization provides a ground of knowledge that tips the balance toward the nonegological view as more ultimately correct.

Wolff contends that "any phase implies its other, and Consciousness-without-an-object is their mutual comprehender, or rather, the conceptual symbol of that forever inconceivable Reality that underlies and envelops all partial aspects."[3] He refers to the ultimate ground primarily by *Consciousness-without-an-object,* as well as *The GREAT SPACE,* but he also uses other terms. However, IT cannot be wholly characterized by these, or any other symbol, for it is *THAT* which is the ineffable essence of mysticism beyond all distinction. Hence it becomes necessary to discuss the adequacy of its representation in terms of Field Consciousness, awareness that transcends the relative domain, and determine whether his account of the High Indifference justifies this interpretation. For this reason the second important theme of this section deals with his interpretation of his Fundamental Realizations. In particular, we shall see to what extent it is appropriate to use the notion of consciousness—in the mystical sense of nonrelative consciousness, wherein the subject-object structure no longer obtains—to point to THAT which he Realized. What is most important, we shall consider whether, and in what manner, we may justify the claim that Field Consciousness, or Consciousness Itself, has ontological primacy.

Egological Theory

A fundamental bifurcation between the various attempts to understand the nature of the distinction between self and consciousness contrasts the egological and nonegological views. The egological conception of consciousness regards all acts of consciousness as emanating from a subject, self, or ego. The nonegological view, to which Wolff would subscribe, regards the self or ego as derivative from or dependent upon consciousness. A discussion of this issue is timely for assessing the first Fundamental.

Let us again turn to phenomenology as the most promising nonmystical approach within modern Western philosophy for dealing with the topic of consciousness. William Fowkes presents an elaborate account of the egological position, conferring primacy on the self, or transcendental ego, which he defines as follows:

> The transcendental ego is to be understood as the origin or originating point of the act of consciousness . . . the support for the acts of consciousness, the *center* of consciousness, the ultimate sense of the pronoun "I," the guarantee of the coherence of the world, or the agent of all free acts. . . . The transcendental ego is to be understood as something over and above the de facto or empirical ego . . . a really existing entity.[4]

The transcendental ego is concrete, rather than abstract, although "it cannot be made into an object of consciousness,"[5] individual, rather than universal, and the ontological ground for all acts of consciousness.

William Earle contrasts the egological view with Kant's notion of the self as a contingent and abstract unity.

> But the acts of the self cannot possibly *be* independently of the self. There can hardly be anything like knowing, loving, feeling or any other intentional act unless there is a subject or self which knows, loves, or feels. The subject obviously need not be conscious of itself; but it must be there actual and efficacious if there is to be anything remotely resembling the inner life with which we are acquainted. The self or subject is precisely *that* which acts, and therefore is not a unity of pre-existing acts.[6]

Others of note who hold the same essential position are Descartes, the later Husserl, and Alfred Schutz. Earle insists that the self is concrete, and no mere abstract essence, for it is temporal and "bears all sorts of actual relations to other selves, and to temporal and concrete objects. An eternal essence or an abstraction clearly is incapable of any such life."[7] Furthermore, whether or not it is independent of the physical conditions of embodiment, "the self is no epiphenomenon. The life of the self is a life permeated by choice; and if I do anything, what I am most clearly conscious of is that *I* am doing it, that *I* am the agent; my acts are mine either because they may be attributed to me, or correlatively, because I originated them."[8] However, what the self *is* is ultimately a mystery,[9] but "the self, in its cognitive dimension, is that to which reality can *appear*. The *self* to which something appears, thus, is a *cognitive subject*."[10]

Nonegological Theory

The competing view holds that Consciousness-without-an-object is the ultimate primordial invariant source and that selves as well as objects are derivative. Wolff's philosophy is a conceptual unfoldment from this viewpoint, grounded in his most profound Realization.

> This binding principle neither develops nor disintegrates. It is thus the invariant element associated with all variation. At certain stages in the analysis of consciousness, it appears as though the invariant element were the pure Subject or the Self, but at this stage the analysis has not isolated the subtle distinction between

> pure Subjectivity and consciousness, as such. It thus appears as though the pure Self were a sort of permanent atomic nucleus, which is persistent through all states. But, when analysis is carried further, this notion is seen to fail. Ultimately, it is found that the Self is derivative as well as the objective pole of consciousness. Thus, there remains as the sole nonderivative principle the Pure Consciousness Itself.[11]

The rarity of the nonegological theory in philosophical and spiritual literature may be explained in part because it is difficult to become aware personally of this depth of penetration into the nature of consciousness.

The strength of the egological theory is that it seems to accord better with ordinary experience. However, further study from analytic, phenomenological, and mystical perspectives brings to light serious difficulties. Let us elaborate each in turn. Thomas Natsoulas attributes to Wittgenstein the rejection of a substantial self by analytical philosophy. Wittgenstein denies that the possessive "my" has any legitimate use concerning primary experience (pain, for instance), for there is nothing to which it can contrast (inasmuch as *I* cannot feel *your* pain). Consequently, " 'I' when used to characterize primary experience is a *pseudo-subject*—analogous to the 'it' in 'it is raining.' "[12] Many contemporary thinkers consider the unity of consciousness to be no more than an assumption. How can we know that successive mental episodes are all the experiences of the same self? Consider: "The self that thinks is known to the self-aware human being—if he knows it at all—in terms of no properties beyond those of the mental episodes themselves."[13]

Gurwitsch also objects to the monadic view of consciousness, which is exclusively egological, on the grounds that we would not be able to account for the meaning of the social world and the sense of the behavior of the Other.

> According to the (analogical) theory, every experience is assumed to be *my* experience. Every sorrow, every joy, every pain is lived through as being *my* sorrow, *my* joy, *my* pain; every thought I have is given as being my thought. . . . It is . . . an essential characteristic of the traditional conception. Every experience is given *to me as being my experience*; in order for it to be an experience, it must necessarily and essentially include an index which determines it as *mine*. But then, our "shared-and-reciprocal" experiences . . . become incomprehensible.[14]

It would follow that *my* experience exhausts all that I may know concerning experience or subjectivity. The notion of "your experience" or "our experience" can have no meaning on this view. It follows that if the ego is thought to be an entity that necessarily *owns* or is the source of its experiences, then the problem of intersubjectivity seems well-nigh insoluble.

The problem of intersubjectivity is perhaps the most intractable residue of Husserlian phenomenology. The success of his ideal to do philosophy as a strict science depends upon the joint activity of a community of investigators. This in turn requires that each be able to constitute the Other as essential subjectivity, that is, as an autonomous center of consciousness in his or her own right. However, Husserl insists on radically grounding knowledge in the immanent presence of phenomena to consciousness—an approach inspired by Descartes. Unfortunately, this seems to lead to a sort of transcendental solipsism, which makes any authentic grasping of the Other as other impossible.

Gurwitsch's approach has the advantage in this regard, for this problem does not arise for his nonegological conception of consciousness. According to Alexandre Métraux, the phenomenological ground for the primacy of field consciousness is that the ego is essentially an object.

> The fact that in unreflective experience consciousness reveals a multiplicity of objects, relations between objects, persons, symbols, and "objective qualities," (27) and the fact that the ego *qua* stream of consciousness makes its appearance through reflection (and through it alone) (28) these facts place the ego on a par, in principle, with the Other or any possible noema as such. The ego is substitutable for an infinity of other themes (29) which are without exception governed by the laws of field organization.*[15]

Gurwitsch thus contends that "the ego exists neither *in* the acts of consciousness nor *behind* these acts."[16] There are several significant advantages to his theory: it

---

*Numbers in parentheses refer to the footnote numbers in the original text by Métraux. In my reference I have included the full reference to Aron Gurwitch, whom Métraux cites, and altered the style to conform to that of the present work.

1. makes the distinction between various aspects of ego (transcendental, empirical, onlooking, etc.) illusory,
2. avoids complex ego-metaphysics, and
3. brings me into the Other's field of consciousness, just as the Other is within mine.

Métraux is unreserved in his praise for this revolutionary viewpoint.

> Thus, the experience we have of each other is accounted for in terms of the organization of the social field which includes person as a possible thematic unity. We could, in line with Gurwitsch, define sociality as the reciprocity of thematized and thematizable fields. In other words: we no longer belong to a monadic universe each member of which is locked up within its window-less consciousness. Rather we belong to an interpersonal world in which I am there just as every Other is, i.e., as a noematic object.[17]

Field consciousness contains all persons equally, each of which may in turn be made thematic (that is, the focus of attention) in an act of reflection, myself included. Not only does Gurwitsch's theory of consciousness lay a more satisfactory groundwork for sociality than that of Schutz, but also it better accords with the more profound mystical insights transcending the individual.

Buddhism, at least in some forms, is a far different established tradition that too rejects the egological conception of consciousness on the basis of a rigorous analysis of experience. Its doctrine of *anatta* (*anātman* or no-self) holds that the self is a fiction. According to Edward Conze, "It is claimed that nothing in reality corresponds to such words or ideas as 'I,' 'mine,' 'belonging,' etc. In other words, the self is not a fact."[18] P. T. Raju states that the Buddhist position rejects the notion of a permanent and substantial entity corresponding to our use of 'I'. "The 'I' is not the *Ātman.* It is simply the unity of several aggregates that appears as the 'I' and is mistaken to be the *Ātman.* On proper analysis the *Ātman* shows itself not as a distinct entity, but as an aggregate of five aggregates (*skandhas*)."[19] His understanding of the *skandhas* is, in summary:

1. *rūpa*—the physical body, which produces its form;
2. *vedanā*—feeling (pleasure, pain, and other feelings and sensations);
3. *saṃjñā*—perceptions; conceptions, and other ideas;

4. *saṃskāra*—impressions (instincts, tendencies, urges, etc.); and
5. *vijñāna*—consciousness (as a series of moments).

Surendranath Dasgupta discusses these in much greater detail.[20] More practically, Conze shows how personal expressions, such as "I have a toothache," would be analyzed according to this schema. Impersonally, in terms of ultimate events, this experience is divided into

> 1. this here is the *form*, i.e., the tooth as matter;
> 2. there is a painful *feeling*;
> 3. there is a sight-, touch-, and pain-*perception* of the tooth;
> 4. there is by way of *volitional reactions*: resentment at pain, fear of possible consequences for future well-being, greed for physical well-being, etc.;
> 5. there is *consciousness*—an awareness of all this.[21]

The 'I' of commonsense parlance has disappeared; it forms no part of this analysis. A person is a series of impermanent states with no permanent entity above these states.

Ātmavidyā or Anātman?

Wolff wishes to harmonize Śaṃkara's doctrine of *Ātmavidyā* (the view that the ultimately Real is known by Knowledge of the Self) with the Buddhist *anātmic* doctrine (the unreality of the self). He attempts to reconcile the apparent contradiction between them by pointing out that "the *Ātman* of Śaṃkara is here spelled with a capital *A* while that of Buddha is spelled with a small *a*."[22] These practices suggest that the latter term refers to the personal (or empirical) ego, not the Self. Here, the 'I' obviously refers to the empirical ego (*ahaṃkāra*), rather than the Transcendental Ego (*Ātman*). Wolff contends that it is the personal ego, "that which I mean when I speak of myself as distinct from other persons, that which has various desires, inclinations, points of view, and so on, that differentiate me from other beings . . . that the Buddha affirms is impermanent."[23] If we understand the personal ego as "the power of subjective awareness,"[24] we may distinguish further between the concrete subject, conditioned by its forms of awareness, and pure subjectivity that is not so conditioned. The latter corresponds to the notion of the *Ātman*. Raju notes that the "Buddha's refusal to answer the question whether or not the *Ātman* existed was taken by his followers as a denial of its existence."[25] However, if the issue concerns only the empirical ego, then he easily could have given a definitive negative answer. His unwillingness to answer in this manner implies that the *Ātman* refers to a more profound sense of self, beyond clear conceptual determination. Perhaps the indeterminacy is due to the absence of criteria to individuate the Realized *Ātman* apart from the objective material that comprises the empirical ego. Similarly, without this material the question of its permanence (which means its persistence through time) does not apply. Wolff's later study of Buddhist sutras inclined him to believe that the more philosophical of them referred to a twofold egolessness. This corresponds respectively to transcending the egoic self and transcending the Supreme Self. The former is simply the detachment from the object of consciousness, as in "I Am THAT"; the latter involves a Transcendence beyond the perspective of the Pure Subject—to Primordial Consciousness, as in the High Indifference.[26]

He personally found that ultimately even the Self is transcended by the nondualistic Consciousness-without-an-object. Further reflection produced a helpful mathematical analogy, which likens the Self to a mathematical parameter.

> The Subject or Self occupies a position analogous to that of the parameter in mathematics. In simple and general terms, the parameter may be thought of as a local invariant that varies when considered over a larger domain. With respect to a specific case of a given curve, it stands as the invariant element, but in the generation of a whole family of curves of a given type, it is a variable. The ultimate invariant is the plane or space in which the curves lie. This supplies us with a thinkable analogue.
>
> With respect to a specific entity, the invariable identity is the Self, but with respect to all creatures and all modes of consciousness, the Self becomes a parameter that varies. Behind and supporting this parameter is the ultimate invariant, Pure Consciousness Itself. Herein we have a key for the reconciliation of the *Ātmic* doctrine of Śaṃkara and the *anātmic* doctrine of Buddha.[27]

One may conclude that each of the doctrines of *Ātmavidyā* and *anātman*, and hence the egological and nonegological theories of consciousness has a relative validity. However, in the deeper sense, derived from Pure Consciousness, the latter is by far the more profound truth. Wolff's philosophy is rooted in the more ultimate conception, due to the manner in which his ultimate Realization superseded the others. Still, at times, he uses the notion of egological consciousness to render his work more easily comprehensible. For our present purposes, it is the more ultimate viewpoint of nonegological consciousness that requires elaboration—yet also as related to, and as explanation for, our ordinary relative consciousness.

ORIGIN AND NATURE OF THE EGO

Wolff and Sartre

Wolff's account of the primacy of consciousness and the derivative nature of ego may be compared profitably to that of Jean-Paul Sartre's phenomenological account given in *The Transcendence of the Ego.*[28] This invites a critical comparison that should prove illuminating. Essentially, both find that consciousness is primary insofar as it transcends the empirical ego and constitutes (or, according to Wolff, "projects") it as object. However, whereas Sartre holds that consciousness, or subjective being (Being-for-itself), is ontologically dependent upon objective being (Being-in-itself), Wolff's second Fundamental denies that the pure subject is derived from any order of objective being. Inasmuch as Sartre adheres to the thesis of intentionality, he intends to restrict his analysis to this context, so his analysis remains within a dualistic framework. In contrast, Wolff derives his position from Fundamental Realization, during the first of which the object-pole of the subject-object structure became empty. Yet he admits that the being of objects transcends their existence as phenomena. Thus we may infer the logical possibility of relation (of a nature impossible to determine) between objective and subjective being apart from the actual awareness of objects.

He also would counter Sartre's attempt to reduce the transcendental ego to the empirical ego, as well as his acceptance of the standard phenomenological tenet that consciousness is always intentional. Despite their differences, due to diverse experiential bases of reference, they have produced accounts containing surprising similarities.

Genesis of the Ego

Wolff states the metaphysical problem by asking, "How is it possible, within a beginning-less and endless Primordial Consciousness, for transitory states to arise?"[29] He cautions that we must avoid thinking of this as a First Cause.

> It is unthinkable that the formless and attribute-less Primordial Consciousness, all of a sudden, at a certain point, started to project Itself into the subject-object series of states. Rather, no beginning or end to the series of states is thinkable, one state being always the consequent of a preceding state and the cause of the one that follows. Consciousness-without-an-object is not a First Cause; it is the substratum underlying all possible states and causes.[30]

This is implied by the nature of the Realization as transcending the structures of space, time, and causality. Consciousness-without-an-object is present in the Eternal Now. "Consciousness-without-an-object is not a cause that determines any particularization, but it is the Causeless-Cause whereby all particularization is possible."[31] Clearly, any account of the origin of either objective phenomena or individual selves, which are also derivative, will be problematic. These should best be considered as myth or allegory, as opposed to straightforward literal description.

Wolff attempts to trace his proposed genesis of the ego from Primordial Consciousness, or Consciousness-without-an-object and without-a-subject. Primordial Consciousness is Pure Consciousness without self-consciousness. In the course of projecting objects, it experiences these objects as a restriction, an irritation that arouses self-consciousness. The notion of an atomic ego as an object (sometimes referred to as an "entity" in an attempt to import some sort of objective identifying characteristic(s) into what is essentially subjective) is the result of an objectifying superimposition.[32]

> Out of consciousness of the consciousness of objects there is finally aroused the inverse realization of the subjective principle. We thus find the substratum on which all objects rest. By superimposing an objective character upon this substratum, we evolve the notion of an ego having an atomic existence analogous to that of objects, save that we give to it a fixed character in contradistinction to the ever-changing character of all genuine objects. The ego is thus produced as a compound of the atomic nature of objects and the relatively deathless persistence of pure

> subjectivity. But this atomic ego is a false construction, and not the genuine subjectivity. It is, in fact, but another object in the universe of objects; however, it is the peculiarly invidious object whereby consciousness is especially bound.[33]

This explanation is grounded in the High Indifference, the core of which is nondualistic, transcending any positive characterization—including relations. Because of this we must be careful to avoid a strictly literal reading of his account. *Primordial Consciousness* (and other such terms) is to be understood symbolically. *Projection* does not denote a real relation or activity of that which is beyond all distinction—including action/rest. Rather, it is a metaphysical (somewhat mythical) notion employed to resolve the ultimate question concerning the origin of the relative world field—that is, the genesis of the many from the One, and the manifest from the Unmanifest. However, his analysis (as is Sartre's) of the constitution of the ego appears genuinely phenomenological and open to confirmation or disconfirmation. Phenomenology, but not empirical psychology, is capable of this sort of radical reflection. Whereas personal acquaintance with mystical experience, though helpful, is not a necessary condition, suspending the natural attitude is.

Wolff regards the naive fascination with the object as the most pervasive impediment to the Realization of *Nirvāṇa.* On his interpretation of the notion of *Nirvāṇa,* the nature of his first Fundamental Realization, it is no different from "the purely subjective element of the subject-object consciousness"[34] (the self or pure subject). It is this self, the omnipresent invariant of consciousness that is impervious to every change of content, to which each of us refers by *I.* In this instance, Wolff is practicing revisionary metaphysics, inasmuch as it implies that most of common usage is erroneous. The use of 'I' to refer to the body or personality would produce false predication, as in "I am sick."[35] The natural attitude is uncritically intentional, or object-directed. Thus, "man has the power to see, yet he constantly projects himself into the objects seen, and complementarily, introjects objects into himself, thereby superimposing upon himself the limitations of those objects."[36] Ironically, *Nirvāṇa* lies too close, and reflective thought is preoccupied by the universe of objects (*saṃsāric* consciousness). "Man's bondage to subject-object consciousness inheres in the fact that, characteristically, his analysis of consciousness has succeeded in capturing only the *saṃsāric* element."[37]

Objectivity of the Ego

For Sartre, "transcendental consciousness is an impersonal spontaneity,"[38] and "nothing but consciousness can be the source of consciousness."[39] He takes great pains to deny that the ego is either *behind* consciousness—"the ego is not the owner of consciousness; it is the object of consciousness,"[40]—or *in* consciousness,[41] either formally or materially. Although Wolff at times refers to consciousness as a container, he intends its application to be a metaphorical characterization of the Transcendent sense of the term. He says, for instance, "Absolute Consciousness contains the cognizer, the thing cognized and the cognition . . . all three in itself and all three One."[42] Sartre identifies the ego as a transcendent object of a unique kind *outside in the world.*[43] Functionally, Sartre distinguishes between the *I* and the *me* as two polar aspects of the ego: "The *I* is the ego as the unity of actions. The *me* is the ego as the unity of states and of qualities."[44] In a word, Sartre's view of the ego is, "The ego is nothing outside of the concrete totality of states and actions it supports."[45]

He thus diverges completely from the formal account of the I, which he attributes to Kant and Husserl: "For Kant and for Husserl the *I* is a formal structure of consciousness. We have tried to show that an *I* is never purely formal, that it is always, even when conceived abstractly, an infinite contraction of the material *me.*"[46] Furthermore, both concepts of the I differ markedly from that of Wolff, who identifies the I with the pure subject or Self, which "must be so recognized as never to become a new subtle object . . . underlies all notions, but is never itself a notion,"[47] as distinct from the ego (or the me), which is an object in the world.

Like Gurwitsch, Sartre claims that the I never appears in unreflected consciousness, and on the reflected level only "appears at the horizon of states, (as) the spontaneous transcendent unification of our states and our actions."[48]

> The ego never appears, in fact, except when one is not looking at it. . . . As soon as I turn my gaze toward it . . . it vanishes. This is because in trying to apprehend the ego for itself and as a direct object of my consciousness, I fall back onto the unreflected level, and the ego disappears along with the reflective act. Whence that vexing sense of uncertainty, which many philosophers express by putting the *I* on this side of the state of consciousness and affirm-

> ing that consciousness must return upon itself in order to perceive the *I* which is behind it. That is not it: the ego is *by nature* fugitive.[49]

Certainly, the attempt to perceive the I as an object (thing or entity) *behind* consciousness (or before consciousness) is fundamentally misguided, both Wolff and Sartre would agree. However, based on his realizations, Wolff would insist that the 'I' is the subjective moment of consciousness and is essentially identical with it. It does not lie on the side of the objective 'me'—no matter how subtle or contracted. When consciousness turns back upon itself, it reveals the I directly by identity, through Introception (which is defined and discussed in the context of the noetic thesis). Because this technique is neither introspection nor phenomenological reflection, both philosophy and psychology have generally remained ignorant of its existence and import.

Pseudospontaneity of the Ego

Apart from this discrepancy regarding the nature of the 'I', Wolff and Sartre share an interesting area of overlap regarding the constitution of the ego and its pseudospontaneity. Wolff denies that the ego possesses genuine subjectivity, even though it appears to relative consciousness to be the author of our actions. Sartre provides a succinct account.

> The ego is an object apprehended, but also an object *constituted*, by reflective consciousness. The ego is a virtual locus of unity, and consciousness constitutes it in *a direction contrary to* that actually taken by the production: *really*, consciousnesses are first; through these are constituted states; and then through the latter, the ego is constituted. But, as the order is reversed by a consciousness which imprisons itself in the world in order to flee from itself, consciousnesses are given as emanating from states, and states as produced by the ego. It follows that consciousness projects its own spontaneity into the ego-object in order to confer on the ego the creative power which is absolutely necessary to it. But this spontaneity, *represented* and *hypostatized* in an object, becomes a degraded and bastard spontaneity, which magically preserves its creative power even while becoming passive. Whence the profound irrationality of the notion of an ego.[50]

Why is this so? What is the raison d'être of the ego? Sartre contends that the function of the ego is intimately bound up with the experience of existential angst—a profound anxiety or dread facing the continual awareness of the possibility of nonbeing or nothingness. He suggests that the ego's essential function is practical, namely, "to mask from consciousness its very spontaneity. . . . Consciousness is frightened by its own spontaneity because it senses this spontaneity as *beyond* freedom."[51] To escape the awesome awareness of its total freedom and the burden of acknowledging its ultimate responsibility for continually creating itself, consciousness makes it appear that a relatively permanent ego is the true agent. "Everything happens, therefore, as if consciousness constituted the ego as a false representation of itself, as if consciousness hypnotized itself before this ego that it has constituted, absorbing itself in the ego as if to make the ego its guardian and its law."[52] Sartre believes that without these limits or barriers that hide from consciousness its true nature as sheer active, upsurging spontaneity, it would experience absolute anguish, irremediable dread.[53]

The Ego Presupposes Consciousness

Fowkes objects that Sartre's notion of a nonpositional self-consciousness is no less mysterious than the transcendental ego.[54] Moreover, he needs to introduce a concrete ego as pseudosubject on practical grounds because consciousness would otherwise find itself "beyond freedom."[55] He also challenges Sartre to show how one could know the nature and motivation for this sort of projection.[56] Notwithstanding the plausibility of Fowkes's objections and purported advantages for positing a transcendental ego, he admits that his base is purely conceptual—an attempt to determine what is necessary for thought.[57]

By comparison, Charles Scott prefers an inferential, rather than a phenomenological methodology, since consciousness itself can never be given for description.

> All phenomena available for descriptive analysis presuppose self-relation and hence consciousness. The difficulty is not that a *description* of consciousness is conscious and therefore involves a circular situation. It is rather that *what* is described can never be

> consciousness as such, but is necessarily already a state of consciousness, an organized state, in which the self is related to itself in a particular way. . . . Consciousness is not a self-manifesting phenomenon, although one can develop *descriptive theories* about it by means of inferential thought.[58]

In contrast to Sartre, Scott adopts Dieter Henrich's definition of the ego as "an active principle of organization of the field of consciousness."[59] Even so, all phenomena presuppose consciousness, as does the self-conscious ego.

Intrinsically, consciousness must be considered nonintentional and egoless. The weakness of the egological position is particularly apparent concerning self-reference.

> The immediate certainty of self-reference presupposes consciousness, and if one attempts to describe consciousness fundamentally as self-consciousness his description is unproductively circular because he founds self-consciousness on self-reference. . . . Therefore . . . explanations of consciousness that give primacy to the ego are inadequate. They presuppose what they are designed to explain.[60]

This corroborates Wolff's thesis that consciousness has primacy for both the subject and the object. However, it does not address the psychological account that Sartre proposes for the genesis of, and identification with, the pseudosubject. It also fails to consider the possibility of discovering a ground for the theory of consciousness that goes beyond inference from the analysis of ordinary experience.

PHENOMENOLOGY OF MYSTICISM

William Earle uses a variation of the phenomenological method[61] to attempt to isolate and examine the essential core of mystical experience, which he regards as "*the experience of the identity of the soul and God*" or, more neutrally stated, "*the experience of the identity of myself with Absolute Reality*."[62] He defines his method precisely as "the attempt to reflect radically upon experience as that experience presents itself to the experiencer. It will be then mind reflecting upon itself, without presupposition, in an effort to discern explicitly what the structure and content of that experience is."[63] Because this does not purport to be a proof or objective demonstration, the proper procedure for confirming his findings is a similar process of radical reflection by the critic.

This contrasts starkly with Melchert's descriptive phenomenology of the central objective phenomena of what he designates as "unitive experience," namely

1. (intense) awareness;
2. "completely empty of all sensuous and conceptual content"; devoid of all multiplicity;
3. detachment; desirelessness; absence of anxiety;
4. bliss; joy; sense of release; "the peace which . . . passes understanding."[64]

Although Melchert's account has the merit of attempting to forego all interpretation, it ignores our view that what is essential in mystical experience cannot be detected by his method of investigation. It is not surprising that he concludes that there is insufficient support for the truth of any of the ontological claims that mystics typically make.

Transcending Space, Time, and Logic

Earle's approach should prove more fruitful. He uses the term *myself* to refer to the self-identity of any subject, or I, which is a potential self-awareness for any sentient being. Only the mystic, of course, is in a position to confirm by immediate awareness the identity with "Absolute Reality." Phenomenologically, Earle distinguishes the I (ego or soul) from the personality or anything else that another might encounter as the me. I am "that which grasps itself reflexively as a self, a self for itself. The ego or self then is taken here as a self, conscious of itself as a self."[65] Moreover, this awareness is primordial pure self-awareness that never can be an *object* of any sort. As such, "the I as it is for itself, is only *accidentally* related to its body, to the physical world, to other persons. . . . [It is] something that can consider the world but is not itself a part of that world."[66] It follows then that the I that perceives what is spatial is not itself spatial. "Neither I, the perceiving self, nor my act of perception, is a three-dimensional object. . . . The *I perceive* is a nonspatial act, *related* to a spatial object, but not in and of itself spatial."[67] Thus it clearly transcends the physical realm.

Similarly, if time is the "*flux and flow of the world*,"[68] as Earle contends, and the I, as we all know, is aware of time, then it also transcends time. Nothing that is wholly subject to time, and therefore wholly different from moment to moment, could apprehend this fact. He concludes that the I "is *related to* time but not itself temporal."[69]

Furthermore, according to Earle, the application of the law of noncontradiction, which is the central principle of logic, reveals the identity between the I and Absolute Reality. That which entertains contradictory possibilities is not captured by them, and this must be so if will, or volition, is to be able to choose between them.[70] Wolff makes the same point when he asserts that the I lies in the excluded middle between *A* and *not-A*, for neither *A* nor *not-A* applies to that which can never be an object.[71] Earle remarks that

> Anything whatsoever combined with its contradictory, exhausts the universe of discourse; anything whatsoever will fall into one camp or other. The contradictory therefore has precisely the same structure as Being itself; together, contradictories constitute a universe. Clearly there can *be* nothing which is not an instance of Being. Absolute Being then is not identical with any of its instances.[72]

As such, Absolute Being (Absolute Reality, or God) may be thought of as the coincidence of opposites—"the ocean in which all that *is* and all that now *is not*, are engulfed."[73] Because Being is not identical with any particular being, it is identical to No-thing-ness.

As we have noted already, Wolff found that the law of noncontradiction was inapplicable and irrelevant to the mystical state.[74] Stace notes that there is "a popular dogma among contemporary philosophers that no experience could ever conceivably contravene the laws of logic, and that these laws would be valid for any possible experience in any possible realm or world."[75] Wolff's report confirms Stace's conclusion that this prejudice is erroneous, but to say that the law of noncontradiction does not apply is not the same as conflicting with or contravening it. Earle contends that the proper domain of logic is "the finite and determinate world of particular things; it is false when applied without restriction to Being or Absolute Reality."[76]

Whereas contradictory premises imply every proposition whatsoever, this is an embarrassment only for the analytical attitude in trying to articulate mundane reality. Earle affirms that "for the metaphysical or mystic consciousness it is, on the contrary, a delight to arrive at an absolute principle from which everything indeed does follow. This would assure us of its infinite fertility, exactly what is needed for an ultimate principle which is understood to be generative of everything."[77] Since both the I and Absolute Reality share this principle, neither is to be regarded as finite. This strongly indicates their identity, which would be expressed by the *Vedāntin* equation, "*Ātman* is *Brahman.*"

The World

Earle has argued that the I must transcend the mundane phenomena of space, time, and logical distinctness to know them. He further claims that the world, because it is time-conditioned by ceaseless flux, is unintelligible without the mediation of mathematics and a priori conceptual categories, which are innate. "Number, . . . as well as the other innate ideas and categories, such as substance, actuality, eternity, and the rest, never exhaustively listed or listable, all derive their primary meanings from the self's own self-reflection, and are therefore innate, and not acquired."[78] It is God rather than the world that is intelligible, due to the structure of the transcendental ego, which is that of Absolute Reality. The world, to the contrary, is known only as a reflection dependent for its existence upon that Absolute, which in turn is independent and ontologically prior to every finite thing.[79]

Absolute Reality

Concerning Absolute Reality, which Earle proposes is identical to the I, he insists that we are misguided if we seek to understand it objectively, even as "an infinite or absolute Object," for "*no Object could possibly be absolute.*"[80] His argument rests upon Kant's epistemological shift of focus, placing the subject rather than the object in the position of priority.

> Absolute reality *can* not be considered as an object exclusively. By thinking of an absolute object, of which the natural cosmos might serve as a limited type, we have forgotten the inescapable fact, that to be an object at all, or a cosmos at all, is to be an object *for a subject*, a thinking ego. We have forgotten ourselves. In thinking of Absolute Reality then in objective terms, we have secretly introduced a limitation: it is considered *objectively*. When that last limitation is removed, it will appear that such an infinite object must be so *for* an equally absolute subject. Or, put otherwise, Absolute Reality must think itself, must logically have an *idea* of itself by which it reflexively grasps itself as object. And then it will be understood as self-dependent, or equivalently, independent or Absolute. Only the idea of the Absolute is Absolute.[81]

Insofar as the transcendental ego is also subjectivity that transcends the finite, he concludes that not mere isomorphism, but strict identity obtains between the I and Absolute Reality. It is "*Absolute Reality thinking* itself."[82]

Critique of Earle

We may question whether the egological perspective he adopts elsewhere is capable of complete harmony with his notion of Absolute Reality, which transcends the merely subjective as well as the strictly objective. Wolff's ultimate focus on Consciousness Itself (Pure Consciousness or Field Consciousness) provides a more satisfactory schema. Although the I or the pure subject is the point of contiguity through which knowledge of Absolute Reality manifests, in itself the Absolute transcends, while encompassing, all duality, including subject-object.

A more weighty criticism follows as a consequence of the limited applicability of the laws of logic. These laws apply only to finite, objective multiplicity; however, both the I and Absolute Reality transcend this domain. Consequently, the assertion of their strict identity has no definable *logical* meaning. Instead, the term should be taken in its phenomenological sense, as referring to an 'experienced' undifferentiated identity of the pure subjective moment of consciousness with THAT which is in itself ineffable, but which may be interpreted as the ground for all that is—"Absolute Reality thinking itself."

Besides the merit of Earle's exposition, his point of departure (the I, or self, or subject-to-consciousness) accords well with that of Wolff. Moreover, allowing for terminological differences, his conclusions may be seen to support the mystical point of view in general, and the primacy of Consciousness thesis in particular. However, Earle's account lacks Wolff's explicit firsthand grounding in mystical experience that would lend a greater authority to his rationally discursive argumentation.

METAPHYSICAL IMPLICATIONS

Ontological Primacy of Consciousness

Let us see to what extent Wolff's position involves metaphysical elements, and the sense in which mystical realization (as contrasted with speculative metaphysics, of which rationalism is accused) may justify it. His assertion of the primacy of Consciousness tends to conflate the methodological, epistemological, and ontological considerations, taking the indubitable evidence for the former as sufficient to establish the latter. His orientation to consciousness therefore has manifest superiority over approaches that either ignore or devalue the role of consciousness. Quite clearly, consciousness is the indispensable methodological and epistemological presupposition. Apart from consciousness, nothing can undertake an inquiry of any kind, and nothing may be known. The being of consciousness is self-evident—it is the one truth of which we are most certain. What remains at issue for Wolff is the ontological status of Consciousness-without-an-object, for this cannot be established solely on grounds common to most philosophical enterprise. Thus a more explicit justification is in order.

Wolff upholds the claim of ontological primacy nearly exclusively by appeal to his Fundamental Realizations. In "I Am THAT," he found the subject to be independent of any object, whereas in the High Indifference both subject and object vanished, as it were, into a more primordial Consciousness. This transcended both subject and object, but was, in itself, entirely unaffected by the presence or absence of either. This constitutes a mystical verification of the nonegological theory of consciousness. Thus he affirms the ontological priority of Consciousness-without-an-object on the grounds of his most profound Realization.[83] It is this Primordial Consciousness that is the common ontological ground of all forms of consciousness, regardless of content.[84]

Wolff identifies the experiential keystone of his philosophy as Consciousness-without-an-object and without-a-subject, stating that "the essence of the mystical state is a Consciousness that does not fall within the subject-object framework."[85] It appears as full, substantial, and the metaphysical ground for everything.

> Ordinary consciousness is a relationship of a knower and a known: it is thin, not having substance in itself. But underlying and supporting all this it may be realized that there is consciousness in another sense—a matrix supporting this, that which I have called Consciousness-without-an-object and without-a-subject or Field Consciousness, which unlike the relative consciousness is substantive—the container, source of all that is. It may be identified with the notion of space.[86]

When Wolff uses *space* in the sense of the GREAT SPACE—an alternative symbol for Consciousness-without-an-object, he intends that "the notion must be understood in the most abstract sense possible, as the root or base of every specifically conceivable space."[87] Consciousness-without-an-object is to be thought of as independent and self-existent, the unshakable base and container of all.[88] The first Fundamental of Wolff's philosophy essentially states that "Consciousness is the original and self-existent Reality."[89] Because this Consciousness is original, the Source from which both subject and object are derived, "the Primordial Consciousness is not to be regarded as the consciousness of some Transcendent being who is aware of some content."[90]

He develops this fundamental or primordial principle in terms of Consciousness for the reason that it is the phase of Fundamental Realization that may be known with immediate certainty. Even so, terms of positive characterization must be understood in a special symbolic sense.

> The Primordial Consciousness cannot be described as conceptual, affective, or perceptual. It seems that all these functions are potentially There, but the Consciousness as a whole is a blend of all these and something more. It is a deep, substantial, and vital sort of consciousness, the matter, form, and awareness functions of consciousness all at once. It is not a consciousness or knowledge "about," and thus is not a field of relationships. The substantiality and the consciousness do not exist as two separable actualities, but rather it would be more nearly correct to say that the consciousness is substance and the substance is consciousness, and thus that these are two interpenetrating modes of the whole. It is certainly a richly "thick" consciousness and quite other than an absolutely "thin" series of terms in relation.[91]

Inasmuch as "this Consciousness is both Substance and Life,"[92] these latter notions also might provide a reasonable basis for grasping the primordial principle and providing alternative philosophical expression. However, "Consciousness, Life, and Substance are not to be regarded as three distinct realities, but as merely three facets of the nondualistic Reality, as the latter appears to the analytic consciousness."[93]

It is important to appreciate that Consciousness-without-an-object is not merely awareness of an absence of objects, for its primordiality is prior to the distinction between awareness of objects and awareness of their absence.

> Consciousness-without-an-object is not simply consciousness of absence of objects. It is THAT which is neutral with respect to the presence or absence of objects. As such, IT stands in a position of Indifference to this presence or absence. In contrast, the consciousness of absence has a positive affective quale, just as truly as is the case with the consciousness of presence of objects, and this is not a state of indifference.[94]

Wolff contends that the distinction between Primordial Consciousness and our ordinary relative consciousness is the same as that between *rig-pa* and *shes-rig* in Tibetan Buddhism.[95] This reflects the difference between unconditioned and conditioned consciousness. The neutrality of this Primordial Consciousness includes all relative differentiation, whether affective, noetic, or otherwise. Thus, in itself, it represents all possibilities without being identified with any of them.[96]

> The final position is: The One, nonderivative Reality, is THAT which I have symbolized by "Consciousness-without-an-object." This is Root Consciousness, per se, to be distinguished from consciousness as content or as state, on the one hand, and from consciousness as an attribute of a Self or *Ātman*, in any sense whatsoever. It is Consciousness of which nothing can be predicated in the privative sense save abstract Being. Upon It all else depends, while It remains self-existent.[97]

Since it is neither subject nor object, it follows that it can be known only by mystical Realization of Consciousness aware of Itself through Identity.

The ontological interpretation of Wolff's first Fundamental also presents difficulties. In his Realization of Consciousness-without-an-object, both the Pure Subject-to-consciousness and the most exalted sense of the object of consciousness dissolved. "This implied that there was a principle more ultimate than that represented by the notion of Being, . . . that which we view as a quality, namely consciousness—which is viewed as a function of Being—is itself the ultimate substantial Reality, and that entityhood, an objective existence, became derivative with respect to That."[98] Let us clarify the meaning and justification of Wolff's first Fundamental, that "Consciousness is original, self-existent and constitutive of all things." It is an attempt to render thinkable that which lies beyond all concepts and symbols whatsoever by employing elements from relative consciousness that are both epistemologically grounded and symbolically effective. The notion of Consciousness, as Consciousness-without-an-object and without-a-subject, is explicitly intended to be symbolic of THAT. Of all the symbols that might be used, it has the unique advantage of comprising the ubiquitous epistemological ground that all knowledge requires. Insofar as consciousness must be presupposed in knowing that anything is symbolic of this Transcendent Somewhat, Consciousness Itself serves as a self-authenticating symbol.

It may be more logically precise to deny the application of all pairs of opposites, as in the Buddhist reference to the eighth and final stage of *dhyāna*, or meditative absorption, as "Neither Consciousness nor Nonconsciousness." However, Wolff is committed to positive, symbolic articulation because this is the mode most valuable in Western philosophy and for the general approach of the Western mind. We must guard against the constant danger that by attempting to accommodate the needs of relative, dualistic consciousness, we might forget that the *ultimate* referent is THAT which Transcends both language and concepts.

We must interpret the characterization of Consciousness as "original, self-existent and constitutive of all things" with great care. *Original* symbolizes the status of the ultimate source of everything, completely underived from anything within the dualistic realm. The problem here is in understanding how THAT which transcends all duality might be characterized at all, for besides transcending space, time, and causality, it would also transcend all relation. Hence we find some awkwardness concerning such traditional attempts that refer to it as the "Causeless-Cause" or "Rootless Root" and the process of creation as "emanation" (Plotinus) or "self-obscuration" (Wolff). Similarly, *self-existent* not only implies a denial of ontological dependence on anything other than itself, but also suggests that it is noetically self-manifesting. Lastly, *constitutive of all things* means that THAT which is symbolized by Consciousness-without-an-object is Reality that is itself underived, and from which all else is derived. In Kantian terms, this would be conceived as the noumenal ground for all phenomena. Insofar as our entire articulated account is a concession to relative consciousness, *Consciousness* is used symbolically, and it explicitly should be so understood.

Wolff introduces an alternative symbol, the GREAT SPACE, to make the same point from the objective side of relative consciousness:

> *54. The GREAT SPACE, or*
> *Consciousness-without-an-object, is the*
> *Sole Reality upon which all objects*
> *and all selves depend and derive their existence.*[99]

Naturally, the GREAT SPACE is not to be construed as objective, any more than it is subjective, for in this ultimate sense, Space comprehends both. So we must also avoid interpreting *Sole Reality* objectively. Moreover, because *sole* is a positive symbol (implying a oneness, as distinct from a manyness), it is primarily psychological, rather than metaphysical. In strict terms, nondualistic Ultimate Reality cannot be characterized as either one or many, but perhaps all that is thinkable is to correct the view that it is a multiplicity. Wolff explains that, even though 'sole' "is not an ultimate conception . . . we should think of the soleness as having a unity more like that possessed by the mathematical continuum than that of the bare number 'one'. For the continuum is a notion of a unity of a totality composed of infinite multiplicity but not involving relationships between discrete entities."[100] Similarly, *Reality* is equivalent to the Kantian notion of the noumenon, what is given through the Introceptive function, as contrasted with phenomena, or appearances given through the senses.[101] Irrespective of our ability to demonstrate this correspondence, the essential referent of this aphorism is the Realized Ground.

Even though other symbols may be, and traditionally have been, employed in this regard, there is good reason to prefer assigning primordiality to Consciousness. The phenomenal world is experienced by relative consciousness according to structures innate to the knower, whether these are conceived as Kantian or otherwise. Mystical experience shows the possibility of a nonphenomenal awareness by a Consciousness that is unconditioned, and prior to these structures. Consciousness Itself then is primordial in that sense. Furthermore, this Consciousness is nondualistic, transcending the subject-object structure. Whatever is known thus cannot be distinguished from the Consciousness that knows. In this case it would be natural to attempt to *characterize* it as Consciousness, even though no literal use of language can strictly apply. It is more accurate to regard Consciousness as *symbolic* of THAT which is Primordial, but, as Wolff cautions, ultimately even symbols fail. The terminal phase of his second Fundamental Realization reveals no ground other than Consciousness, for relative consciousness simply lost the capacity to trace any further depth of penetration.

Wolff's justification for claiming that Consciousness is primordial is that it is the most adequate conceptual representation of the way that this Realization transformed his relative consciousness. Its aphoristic formulation encapsulates the metaphysical essence of his philosophy. Although it is grounded in mystical insight, its expression reflects the philosophical integration of his world view subsequent to his whole cycle of five realizations. We must bear in mind here a key provision of this philosophy—namely, that no single formulation may lay claim to exclusive truth. So long as we appreciate the significance of his first Fundamental within a context that allows for the legitimacy of alternative symbols and expressions, then it is acceptable as true.

Panpsychism

The sense in which nonegological consciousness has primacy for Wolff differs from panpsychism as a metaphysical theory. For example, Hartshorne's version is a sort of inverted materialism that seeks to reduce the mind/matter dualism to mind only. He argues that metaphysical dualism is generally unacceptable to philosophers and scientists[102] and that "materialism (in spite of 'identity' theories) cannot effectively be distinguished from emergent dualism (for feelings and thoughts do occur)."[103] He states his position quite forcefully.

> My argument is: whereas mind as such is experienced (for each of us experiences the flux of his emotions, sensations, and thoughts and cannot really doubt that his neighbours have similar experiences), 'mere matter', taken as irreducible to any kind of mind, cannot as such be experienced or in any way observed. No observable property could show that a part of nature was sentient *neither as a whole nor in its constituents.*[104]

That is to say, it is impossible to demonstrate that anything is *not* conscious—we simply might be incapable of detecting it. Hence it is matter, rather than mind, that may be more justifiably viewed as epiphenomenal, and Hartshorne therefore concludes that panpsychism is the more plausible nondualistic alternative.

Unfortunately, his approach remains exclusively within what Wolff distinguishes as the relative domain. Assuming the objective universe as his frame of reference, Hartshorne asserts that a ubiquitous (mostly hidden) inward awareness comprises the essential reality, of which the phenomenal appearance of things is a manifestation. Lacking experiential grounding for this claim, for example, by way of extrovertive mysticism, it shares the same sort of status, qua rationalistic, metaphysical speculation, as the materialism it rejects. Its advantage would seem to lie primarily in its capacity to account for that of which we are most immediately certain—the fact of our own consciousness.

Storehouse Consciousness

Wolff considers the *Vijñānavādin* (*Yogācāra* Buddhist) notion of *ālayavijñāna* (translatable as "*Root* Consciousness"[105] or "Absolute Consciousness")[106] to be essentially synonymous with "Consciousness-without-an-object,"[107] and thus that it somewhat corroborates his positive formulation of the High Indifference. Yet there are discrepancies. For example, Wolff apparently allows pure abstract Being to be predicated of it and favors a substantialist (*aśūnya*) metaphysical expression,[108] notwithstanding his reporting it to be beyond both concepts and language. In contrast, Raju contends that, because the state of consciousness is indeterminate, the Yogācārins considered it meaningless to predicate of it either Being or Nonbeing—which are determinations—referring to it instead as emptiness (*śūnya*).[109] This Absolute Consciousness may be known only by a self-validating suprarational intuition.[110] Similarly, Wolff states that this Primordial Consciousness may be known only "through a Recognition transcending the *Nirvāṇic* State,"[111] and that it transcends the distinction between being and nonbeing. This shows that both agree when speaking from an ultimate nondualistic perspective. There are also surprising similarities when each attempts to formulate a positive metaphysics, for the Yogācārin model is that of a "Storehouse Consciousness" underlying phenomenal reality. This resembles Wolff's metaphysical interpretation of Jung's notion of the collective unconscious.

Wolff uses the term *Primordial Consciousness* to refer to Consciousness-without-an-object as the "rootless Root" and *Recognition* to indicate the quality of "Realization" that makes it seem that one is recollecting what one already knows. The Transcendence of the *Nirvāṇic* State (in the narrow sense implied here) means attaining the state of *Parinirvāṇa*, which he conceives as the dissolution of the awareness of the Self (*Ātman*) into Consciousness-without-an-object and without-a-subject. However, from that perspective, he found *neither* voidness (*śūnya*) *nor* plenum (*aśūnya*) to be ultimately valid interpretations. Consequently, he explicitly attributes a merely provisional significance to his preferred metaphysical formulation.[112]

Summary

Let us review Wolff's account of consciousness, its relation to Consciousness-without-an-object, and the nature of its primacy. Both consciousness and Consciousness-without-an-object are indefinable notions, but while everyone knows the former immediately, only mystics are aware of the latter. Within consciousness, our ordinary intentional experience is a polar relation between a subject (self, I) and an object, where the existence, but not the *being* of the object is dependent upon the subject. Moreover, the subject may gain self-knowledge independently of any object. Wolff, following Śaṃkara, found that the key to Enlightenment lies in the conscious penetration of the subject pole, distinguishing it in immediate awareness from everything objective.

At a certain limiting point there is a discontinuity of awareness, beyond which lies only a nonpolar Field Consciousness, which is, strictly speaking, indescribable—for it is strictly nondualistic. As conscious awareness, however, it is indisputably nonegological. Hence, although the subject has primacy concerning the object, Consciousness has primacy concerning both subject and object. Wolff thus characterizes the Pure Subject or Self as a transcendental phenomenon, which is "a component that is constant and primary only in relation to the object, but in relation to Pure Consciousness is derivative . . . a sort of transcendental phenomenon, i.e., transcendental with respect to the object but standing in something like a phenomenal relationship to Pure Consciousness."[113] Consciousness-without-an-object transcends ordinary awareness, and its impact upon the latter plausibly induces the interpretation that it constitutes the fundamental ground for our relative awareness. Yet any concept or notion (though some better than others) can only be extended beyond its ordinary usage to "point" to THAT (obliquely, as it were, since Wolff states that here even symbols fail). Wolff grounds this quasi-phenomenological statement in his immediate awareness in mystical Realization. However, his ensuing formulation of this Transcendent Somewhat as well as his metaphysical theory based upon it do not share this certainty. The former requires symbolic language to indicate a nonintentional awareness, while the latter involves interpretation and explanation. The status of his metaphysical interpretation of Realization is but a conceptual formulation that only "points" toward THAT which ultimately is beyond all duality. It is only relatively true to hold that all is Consciousness, for mystics (including Wolff) generally maintain that ultimate Reality transcends the distinction between the physical and the psychical—even beyond the distinction between Consciousness and nonconsciousness. It follows that neither Consciousness, Matter, Will, nor any other partial characterization can be completely adequate to the Reality.[114]

The articulated development of his philosophy, Wolff claims, is grounded in the Knowledge gained from his Realizations themselves. This presently leads us to consider his third Fundamental—the claim that mystical experience is a source of knowledge transcending sense perception and pure conceptual thinking. If mystical experience is a source of knowledge, what is its nature, how is it attained, and to what extent is its authority legitimate?

CHAPTER 8

The Noetic Thesis

If Wolff could show that he has realized a third major function of cognition besides perception and conception, his contribution to philosophy would be ample. Yet he goes beyond this by attempting to establish that the knowledge engendered is metaphysical in nature and by delimiting the significance of its conceptual formulation. He defines this purported cognitive function, articulates its method of operation, and illustrates three kinds of relative knowledge derived from it. What is more interesting, he shows how its operation extends cognition beyond the relative sphere. Our critical task is to evaluate Wolff's case for the existence of this function, define its nature, determine the sense(s) in which it yields knowledge and whether such knowledge is metaphysical.[1] Finally, we shall ascertain the extent to which its results constitute justifiable authority for the mystic, in whom it is active, and for the nonmystic, who must rely upon the testimony of mystics.

From a strictly epistemological point of view, Wolff's primary purpose is to establish "that mystical insight is a source of knowledge."[2] William James not only finds the noetic nature of mystical experience generally confirmed, but includes it as one of its four identifying characteristics.[3] Wolff, as both philosopher and mystic, explicitly emphasizes the importance of this claim: it is the crux of his formal philosophy.[4] *The Philosophy of Consciousness without an Object*[5] is a philosophical treatise whose central concern is the establishment of the truth of the noetic thesis: "The primary problem of the present work is the demonstration, as far as may be, of the actuality of noetic value springing from mystical or gnostic roots."[6] Wolff leaves no doubt as to the significance of this theme.

> In the present work there are only two points covered that are of a central importance:
>
> 1. the factuality of a third organ, faculty or function of cognition, which was called "introception";
> 2. the possibility, through the function of introception, of a metaphysical knowledge.
>
> The problem is fundamental.[7]

Wolff contends that the cognitive nature of his Fundamental Realizations was Introceptive, in contrast to both sensuous and conceptual cognition, and that Introception is "the organ, faculty or function by which metaphysical truths may be known."[8]

The painstaking descriptions of his five realizations comprise the experiential evidence for its operation. His attempts to formulate the knowledge attained through this function required aphorism and poetry, as well as his most highly developed and profound discursive thought. Still, he insists that only direct realization can verify its existence and confer authority upon its content. Consequently, he is "much more concerned that introception should attain recognition as a genuine psychical function than that this system of interpretative ideas should be accepted."[9]

Several interpretations of the noetic thesis might be proposed, the most interesting of which avers the propositional truth of metaphysical claims derived from realization. However, Wolff declines this straightforward approach because he finds that bare conceptuality is intrinsically inadequate to encompass and articulate what he cognized. Seemingly incompatible metaphysical formulations might apply equally to a distinctionless content, so language would better serve to point symbolically, rather than to attempt to define or describe.

The discussion of knowledge, as such, insofar as it is determinate and distinct from noncognitive functions of consciousness, belongs to relative consciousness. The more defensible versions of the noetic thesis are therefore grounded on the effects of Transcendent Consciousness upon relative consciousness. Wolff details the actual operation of an extraordinary cognitive function from his own firsthand awareness from within a highly noetic state, reporting a shift in consciousness at its base. In addition, he says that conceptual forms "precipitated," as it were, into (or crystallized within) the relative field. Furthermore, there is an obvious sense in which our knowledge is augmented by the discovery that a state of consciousness exists that permits solely negative predication. A more thorough scrutiny of these factors will lay the foundation for judgment concerning the significance of his third Fundamental.

We must then discover how he defines the term *Introception*—his designation for the third cognitive function—and understand how it works, as well as decide whether it results in knowledge. Not only will we find that it is noetic, but that it provides at least three items that legitimately qualify as additions to relative knowledge. Because Kant's critique of the possibility of metaphysical knowledge first inspired Wolff to seek it, any purported success should be evaluated, at least partially, in Kantian terms. Consequently, we must determine whether Introception gives metaphysical knowledge, or, otherwise stated, whether it is noumenal—that is, knowledge of the thing as it is in itself. Finally, we shall consider the scope of legitimate authority for statements grounded in realization.

MYSTICISM AND NOESIS

Interpretation

Wolff uses the term *noetic* to refer to knowledge not derived from experience, or observation, basing his interpretation on its original usage by the ancient Greek philosophers.[10] He would accept as a definition "those concepts which are nonsensuous and nonempirical but are conceived by reason alone . . .; the noetic aspects of reality are those which are knowable by reason."[11] However, *reason* here would have to be understood as implying intuitive apprehension, rather than logical ordering.

Minimally, Wolff intends "to prove . . . a way, if not *the* way, in which noetic mystical content is *possible in principle* and, in the negative sense, to refute the anti-mystical pretension of disproof of this possibility."[12] Thus the weakest version of the noetic thesis (hence the easiest to support, but also the least interesting) simply states that in principle it is possible that one may experience noetic value in mystical experience. Obviously, an argument assessing the burden of proof would work quite well for this purpose. To prove that it was factually impossible, an opponent would either need to show that Wolff's claim was logically self-contradictory, or to demonstrate omniscience concerning the total range of psychical possibility. In the first instance, the number and kind of cognitive faculties that a being possesses are a matter of contingent fact, not logic. In the second, even if one were omniscient, there would be no way to demonstrate it. In any event, there seems little point in contesting the modest proposal of mere possibility, for without some reason to believe that this means of knowledge is also actual, there is no advance beyond Kant.

A more substantial version could be based on an interpretation of reports of noetic value derived from such states. For instance, in the period immediately following Wolff's first Fundamental Realization, he found himself "in a state of deep brooding, thinking thoughts that were so abstract that there were no concepts to represent them. I seemed to comprehend a veritable library of Knowledge, all less concrete than the most abstract mathematics."[13] Bahá'u'lláh (founder of the Ba'hai faith), as well as other mystics, also have reported this supercomprehensive sense of knowing. We should assess such reports phenomenologically to avoid problems of interpretation.

Wolff certainly wishes to advance a stronger version of the noetic thesis than claiming its mere possibility, for his realizations revealed the existence of an actual cognitive faculty. Still, it does credit to his critical acumen and intellectual integrity that he acknowledges that he has not demonstrated the truth of his thesis. He carefully concludes only that he has been able to refute every significant attempt at *disproof* and to establish a strong presumption of truth.

> In principle, it must be admitted that the supposition of a nonexperiential or transcendent existence or reality can possibly be justified. Epistemological logic does not rule out this possibility; it simply establishes the point that by means of pure conceptions and logic alone, transcendental existences or realities cannot be proved.

> In the present philosophy, all effort to establish such a proof is abandoned. Logic and analysis of consciousness are employed simply to build a reasonable presumption, without laying any claim to coercive demonstration. It is, however, asserted that direct extralogical and extraempirical verification is possible.[14]

Thus he denies the possibility of a strictly logical proof that would convince any rational person by force—an achievement that would be exceedingly rare for any meaningful philosophical issue.

Of course, it is theoretically insupportable to restrict verification to these means. Determining that there is such a function is possible in principle by personally activating it, and credible reports by those who have done so also must be considered as evidence. Under these conditions, the *essential* requirements of science are not violated.

Leuba's Objection

Wolff takes some pains to defend the noetic thesis from James Leuba's criticism that the mystic brings nothing more out of the state than he brings into it. Leuba agrees with George Coe that "the mystic acquires his religious convictions precisely as his nonmystical neighbor does, namely through tradition and instruction, auto-suggestion grown habitual, and reflective analysis. The mystic brings his theological beliefs to the mystical experience; he does not derive them from it."[15] Wolff introduces weighty counterexamples that effectively demolish this claim. First, even though there is substantial evidence that tradition and religious instruction color the interpretations of the typical mystic, the reverse tendency in the case of the outstanding mystical geniuses (such as Buddha, Christ, and Śaṃkara) is impressive.[16] Notwithstanding their strong cultural ties and commitments, each brought forth revolutionary teachings. Mansur Al Hallaj, Meister Eckhart, and Bahá'u'lláh are other notable mystics who diverged drastically from orthodox doctrine, provoking responses ranging from charges of heresy to crucifixion with hands and feet severed. In all these cases, mystical realization transformed—not conformed to—their antecedent views.

What is more important, Wolff's case shows that realization is a source of knowledge: "I insist upon their cognitive value for I have so experienced them."[17] It was the High Indifference that most convincingly illustrates the impact on the noetic orientation of his philosophy. It "led to a real revolution in my philosophical outlook—all of which is a testimony to the fact that it is not true that the knowledge that one brings forth from a state of Realization is no more than that which he took into the state. States of Realization may produce consistent changes in one's philosophical outlook."[18] This shows that although mystical experience does not invariably involve a noetic impact of such magnitude, it does possess a noetic dimension.

Mystical Cognition

If humanity were restricted to subject-object consciousness, Wolff would uphold the validity of Hume's absolute agnosticism.[19] However, he claims to have verified the existence of a third cognitive function by direct awareness transcending relative consciousness and that such evidence is possible for others. It would seem, then, that the relevant question regarding the actuality of cognition through mystical experience concerns justification, rather than proof—evidence, rather than formal demonstration.

If the mystic is correct in maintaining that her experience is ineffable, and therefore beyond formulation, how is it even meaningful to claim that it is noetic? Wolff treats the matter explicitly:

> The fundamental issue here is whether we are justified in viewing a state of consciousness in which there is a coalescence of subject and object, of knowledge and thing known, as a case of knowledge. So long as the state stands in *complete* separation from relative consciousness, the response must be negative. However, we equally cannot predicate affection or conation of such a state. It is simply beyond all relative predication, so it can only be defined by universal negation.[20]

Purely, as THAT which is directly Realized, its absolute ineffability prohibits any positive characterization, either as knowledge or as anything else. Even universal negation (exceptionless denial of every positive attribution) is a concession to the desire by relative consciousness to understand. Such knowledge is possible because relative consciousness is modified by Transcendent Consciousness, including noetic effects.

> Fortunately the pure mystical state may impinge upon relative consciousness, in greater or lesser degree, producing effects for the latter. This results in a compound consciousness in which either the mystical and relative form an impure effect, or the two forms of consciousness exist side by side. In either case, relative consciousness is affected. It is relative consciousness that experiences Bliss or Beatitude, reorientation of the will, and a new noetic orientation and content.[21]

The term *mystical experience* refers to both the Transcendent consciousness and the precipitated effects, although, strictly speaking, the former is not experience as we normally understand it and the latter is not inherently mystical. This explains how a new cognitive value, as well as affective and/or conative value may arise from Introception. Since cognition is generally considered to mean knowledge in its widest sense, the cognitive effect of the noetic shift to which Wolff refers would qualify as knowledge attained by means other than perception or pure conception. Such cognition would be sufficient to vindicate the third Fundamental, independent of and prior to considering the truth of any proposition that might issue forth from it.

Wolff presents personal testimony concerning the nature of this new orientation and content, both generally and in his particular case.

> In terms of content, relative consciousness now knows, as an object, the state of consciousness in which merge both subject and object, as well as knowledge and thing known. This is an increase of relative knowledge having most profound significance, both in the theoretical and pragmatic senses, insofar as it tends to make an enormous difference in life and conduct, and in valuation and meaning. The new orientation is like changing the base of reference in mathematical analysis. The material of relative consciousness enters into a new perspective that tends toward radical difference in theoretical organization. In this way there is addition to knowledge in the conceptual sense, with respect to content as well as altered theoretical organization.[22]

Thus the new object that the relative consciousness knows is the Introceptual state of consciousness (where knower and known are identical) objectified and distinguished from other states of consciousness. The new orientation is a shift in the base of consciousness that pervasively alters the significance of all phenomena, without necessarily involving any change in their sensuous characteristics. The facts of the empirical world remain as they are, but the mystic no longer views the empirical world as the final point of reference.

Transcendental Thought

Wolff distinguishes "three senses in which noetic value may be predicated of mystical consciousness,"[23] and he contends that he has established at least a presumption for their acceptance as knowledge. Let us consider in detail the account given for each and evaluate the supporting evidence.

> Transcendental thought . . . , at a certain level of mystical penetration, is Realized as a self-moving process, in terms of a stream-like cognition incommensurable with the granular relative conceptions, which are capable of definitive differentiation. Using word conceptions this thought may be precipitated in such a way as to determine a pattern of relative thought, which, however, has an exclusively or predominantly transcendental, rather than perceptual, reference.[24]

This goes to the source of purported mystical knowledge, "the self-moving, inarticulate, flowing thought that constitutes the primary ground of the noetic aspect of mystical consciousness."[25]

Communicating the essential nature of this thought presents special problems inasmuch as it is essentially irreducible to either concepts or words. Nevertheless, relative consciousness must use these tools, and their use may be better or worse depending upon both the profundity of the mystic's Realization and her skill at formulation. Wolff illustrates the implied conceptual relativity by means of analogy:

> Concerning this supernal realm, the definitive concept may be likened unto a vessel immersed in the sea. The form of the vessel is the definitive concept, while the water that it contains is its substantive meaning. By analogy, just as the water, in its inherent nature, has not the shape of the vessel, the meaning overflows the form of the concept. The concept (vessel) has truth bestowed upon it by reason of the meaning (water) that it holds, but many vessels may hold water. The thought that is of identical nature

> with the sea is like the oceanic currents that flow from shore to shore, distinguishable as currents, yet not distinguishable from the whole ocean as water. In the end, the flow of any current mingles indistinguishably with the whole.[26]

This implies that no single conceptual scheme is, or can be, definitive. Even so, the testimony of mystics is exceedingly helpful in conveying everything of which they are aware that lies antecedent to the threshold of ineffability, and in providing effective symbolic pointers to guide others' personal firsthand Realization of THAT transcending it.[27]

Such is the case with Wolff's characterization of what he calls "*Nirvāṇic* Consciousness" (or "Transcendent Consciousness") as the inverse of "*saṃsāric* consciousness" (ordinary, relative subject-object consciousness).[28] He suggests that its unity is "better symbolized by the notion of the true continuum than by the finite number 1 (one)."[29]

> The inverse of the phantasmagoric series, which constitutes the universe of experience and thought in its purity as abstracted, is the true continuum. The one is a granular manifold, the other a flowing unity. . . . The unity of numeral one is an abstraction and not a concrete actuality. It is the unity of the continuum, in the true sense, that symbolizes the unity of the *Nirvāṇic* State. The *Nirvāṇic* Consciousness is not granular but flowing. It is without parts, in the sense of finite proper parts, but is a ceaselessly flowing and self-contained stream. It is not a stream from past to the future, that implies division by the point called the "present," but a flowing that comprehends the totality that appears in the universe of objects as the temporal series.[30]

The use of the term *flow* here is a notion symbolizing an atemporal awareness that is dynamic, but unchanging. Thus it cannot mean *change* in this context because awareness is not partitioned into elements that may be rearranged—and without change there can be no time.

At first impression it may seem self-contradictory to liken a timeless state to a flowing stream, and we must admit here a pronounced element of paradoxicality. However, according to Stace, paradoxicality is a common feature of mysticism.[31] From the time of the preSocratics, time and the problem of a logical understanding of change also have generated paradoxes for Western philosophy. Thus within the overlap of time and mysticism lies one of the greatest challenges to logic.

Whereas Wolff asserts the inseparability of motion and consciousness in some sense,[32] it is only consciousness-as-experience that is time-bound. In itself, consciousness is unconditioned by time, and hence superior to it. "Time is thus to be regarded as a form under which certain modes of consciousness operate, but not as an external existence, outside of consciousness in every sense. . . . In the terms of Kant, time is a transcendental form imposed upon phenomena. But, it follows, consciousness, in so far as it is not concerned with phenomena, is not so bound."[33] Time is a binding form in the phenomenal realm and cannot be thought as having a beginning, for "beginning" is a temporal concept. Where time is transcended in the depths of consciousness, it is an eternal possibility, and an instant has the same significance as incalculable eons. This is an unfathomable mystery![34]

Negation of Predicates

The first sense in which mystical Consciousness manifests noetic value pertains to the precipitated effects from the transcendental, self-flowing thought. The second relates to the stage of mystical penetration that appears transcendent from the viewpoint of an objective witness. Paradoxically, from the perspective of the state itself, there are further (perhaps unlimited) depths beyond the threshold. However, insofar as concepts have no application there, Wolff considers it unprofitable to inquire whether it is a state of knowledge *in itself.* In contrast, in its relation to relative consciousness, he finds it to be "the point of universal negation of everything relative," and therefore "it is genuinely knowledge because to know as negation is as truly knowledge as to know as affirmation."[35] He asserts that "the knowledge of the negation of all relative predication and of sensible presentation has noetic value. This is the noetic value, appertaining to the highest discernible ascension of mystical consciousness from the relative perspective, in its relationship to all relative cognition."[36]

We commonly accept negative propositions as knowledge, but a dissenter might point out that when we deny that a predicate applies, this is generally acknowledged to imply that some other predicate does. Universal negation entails the inapplicability of every predicate whatsoever, and that whatever state of affairs obtains is impervious to any effort at positive description. Even so, it is no less knowledge to know this than is the common relative negation.[37]

Base of Reference

The most significant noetic factor resulting from Introception consists in a total, pervasive, and permanent reorientation in the apprehension of reality. Wolff states that "noetic value grows out of the new birth, in the sense of change of base of reference, with manifold effects in the meaningful evaluation of all relative knowledge."[38] The mystical transformation, a mystical death and rebirth (as mystics sometimes characterize it), involves a shift to a new center of self-reference from the previous orientation to consensus reality (the world as commonly experienced). To be precise, it is not experience, because it "is not a change of content of cognition, but change of the base of orientation to cognition."[39]

> Henceforth, from the time of the new birth, when thinking in terms of his essential reality thought—but not in his more or less frequent "as if" thinking from the base of the old ego—the mystic integrates the whole of relative cognition about a new center or base of reference. This is equivalent to a radical alteration in the significance of the whole body of relative cognition. Shift in significance is a noetic alteration and, hence, accession of knowledge.[40]

Concerning the noetic thesis in this regard, Wolff initially focuses on the effect it produced upon relative cognition, disregarding the "*proper* content" of Transcendent Consciousness.

Wolff defends his view that this Copernican shift in base of reference is a change in knowledge on the grounds of the following noetic components: change in meaning, and "acquaintance with the fact of base of reference and its determinant place with respect to cognitive content; . . . [and] the possibility and actuality of more than one base of reference."[41] These are analogous, he contends, with

1. Copernicus's revolution in astronomy from the geocentric to the heliocentric theory,
2. Kant's Copernican revolution in philosophy that shifted the focus in cognition from the object to the subject, and
3. the mathematical concept of base of reference and the effect of changing to an alternative base.

If we are justified in noetic attribution in these instances, then it follows that the effects of the mystic's transformation that are essentially similar to these accepted cases also must be noetically significant.[42]

Wolff details the mathematical analogy and his argument that it constitutes knowledge as follows:

> Let us consider briefly the function of the base of reference in mathematical analysis. The analytic formulation of a problem invariably depends upon a base of reference, most commonly in the form of rectilinear Cartesian coordinates. Generally, this base is no explicit part of the analytic development but is implicit in the very form of the development. The expressions and equations are what they are partly because the chosen base of reference is what it is, and partly because of the specific nature of the configurations analyzed. A transformation of base changes the analytic development. If we think of the analytic development as thought content, then the base of reference does not appear explicitly in the content. Yet, the specific pattern of that content stands in functional relationship to that base. Furthermore, if the noetic element were conceived as exclusively the content, then the base would stand apart from knowledge. However, if the noetic is understood as including its roots as well as the content, then the base of reference is part of the noetic order. I believe the latter conception is the sounder, so in that sense we may affirm that the mystical change of base is noetically significant.[43]

The disanalogy here is that the base of reference in mathematics may be objectified and adequately represented in discursive form, whereas the mystically Realized base can only be symbolized.

Although Wolff declines to discuss the possibility of a new content becoming available as a result of this shift, such a development would constitute a more pertinent justification for its inclusion as knowledge. Where his purpose is solely to support the truth of the noetic thesis, he prefers to advance only his strongest arguments. Still, it is the content of Introception that so impressed him that he felt compelled to discuss it. Therefore, we need to address it directly as the focal point of the noetic thesis.

We are inclined to agree with Wolff that it is possible in principle for mystical experience to be a source of knowledge and that his realizations do provide evidential grounds for claiming noetic value. Nonetheless, he has yet to show that the purported knowledge attained in this manner is metaphysical in nature. It is also unclear that the noetic aspect of mystical experience constitutes a separate and unique psychical function—and, if it does, defining it is problematic. Let us see how he treats these issues.

INTROCEPTION

Definition

Wolff claims that the way of knowing that he found in Introceptive Realization is unique and irreducible to any cognitive function of which we are normally aware. Like perception, an immediate content requiring conceptual mediation is present. However, whereas sensation deals with a range of objects within a definite manifold, the essential content in mysticism is nonobjective and nonphenomenal. This suggests that the way in which concepts mediate it will also fundamentally differ. Of course, both functions differ from pure conception, which discovers a priori relationships between ideal objects.

The problem of devising accurate philosophical terminology to distinguish it from perception and conception prompted Wolff to invent the term *Introception. Introceive* is the corresponding verb form, and *Introcept* is the noun form referring to the content given via this function. His earliest definition, "to take in or into," is derived from the Latin *intro,* which means "within, into or in," and *capere,* which means "to take." This gives the meaning "the process or mode of consciousness which penetrates to profundity through the affective function."[44] He later revised his definition to better reflect the nature of this process: "The Power whereby the Light of

Consciousness turns upon Itself toward Its Source."[45] In his philosophy, "introception is given a dual reference, (1) to a function of consciousness, and (2) to the content or state of consciousness rendered accessible by the function."[46] The Light of Consciousness is simply "the cognitive factor in consciousness."[47] Wolff uses the word *consciousness* generically.

> In my employment of the term *consciousness* in the phrase *the Light of consciousness turning toward its source,* I am implying something more fundamental than either the noetic or the conative. Consciousness, in its total meaning, includes these two aspects, as well as feeling tone and more or less undetermined other qualities. Consciousness is the common denominator of all. Therefore, it is the best neutral term.[48]

Precisely stated, Introception is "the process whereby consciousness turns upon itself and moves toward its source."[49] As Realized, the Source of consciousness is Primordial Consciousness.

Method

Because it would be more strictly correct to define Introception as the cognitive aspect of mystical experience, it seems reasonable to interpret Wolff's definition functionally, as a practical instruction concerning its attainment. His professed method involves isolating "the subjective factor in consciousness" while "permitting the objective consciousness to continue through its own automatism."[50] This is simple, but not easy, for our natural direction of attention is toward objective content, and this tends to increase according to a person's intellectual development. He explains that "the effective focusing of consciousness is precisely in the diametrically opposite direction. It is toward the subjective moment in the subject-object manifold, and this possesses the simplicity of a point. It is often overlooked just because of its extreme simplicity."[51] Although Wolff exerted no effort to control or silence thought processes, he found it advantageous to quiet the affections.[52] He had previously adopted the practice of "stopping thought and closing out the senses, but the artificial state thus effected was barren of results."[53] He advises allowing the eyes to remain open during meditation to avoid drowsiness,[54] also noting that sensory deprivation experiments most often result in initiating psychical processes that produce much greater subjective distraction than the external distraction of ordinary states of consciousness.[55] Meditative balance requires relaxed alertness that succumbs neither to drowsiness nor to agitation. In addition, we already know how to focus attention upon any of a complex of objective elements. The essential difference here is that the subjective factor is radically opposed to any object, so the proper technique is difficult to describe.

Recall that Wolff initially activated this function in the course of his first Fundamental Realization. Subsequently, he seems to have been able to access it more or less at will by using the same technique. In addition to his account of the first episode,[56] already presented in chapter 3, he relates a second version concerning these further cases of Introception:

> My experience has always been in the form of a separation in the flow of consciousness so that a minor portion of the stream continues toward the object, with the result that objective consciousness is dimmed, but not extinguished. The object is extremely depreciated in that it loses all, or nearly all, relevancy, but always remains as sensibly or conceptually available. In contrast, the consciousness in the state of the reverse flow toward the subject is like a Light highly intensified. All objective consciousness is, relatively, only like moonlight contrasted with bright sunlight in a dry desert. I know that the introceptive state is anything but a dimming or disappearance of consciousness; rather, it is a radical intensification of it.[57]

A permanent shift results in relative valuation of the ordinary and Introceptive states. We must be careful to avoid interpreting "flow toward the subject" as though the self were a subtle object. More accurately, it is "ceasing the effort to discover it as an object, and sinking back into it."[58] Finally, "turning from the object of, to the subject to, all relative consciousness, *plus the spontaneity of the SELF*,"[59] is the "Current of Joy." Insofar as it is a latent faculty, Introception is a human potential that in principle may be developed intentionally.

Contrast to Introspection

The inward penetration that reveals the self through Introception must be clearly distinguished from introspection, which has a necessarily objective orientation.

> It is not the same as introspection wherein consciousness merely short-circuits itself to observe more subtle psychical objects that are generally unconscious for the extraverted attitude. Introception, when successful, leads to a state such that consciousness becomes its own content, that is, a consciousness that is divorced from its objective reference. By this means, the self as source of consciousness can be Realized, without being transformed into a subtle object, as a *me*.[60]

Recollecting the discussion in the previous chapters, one is not tempted to interpret the self as an objective entity of any sort. The term *Source of consciousness* here must be taken to mean the locus of awareness for individualized consciousness directed toward objects—not Consciousness Itself. Introception then may be understood as the conscious penetration of the self, or subject, in luminous self-awareness.

In contrast, the self can never be found by the method of introspection, which remains exclusively object-oriented, revealing only qualities, states, and processes of consciousness, as well as objects of personal (rather than interpersonal) awareness. This explains why Hume's attempt to locate a permanent self by this technique is misguided, for he is seeking to identify the self as an object.[61] His theory that the self is only a bundle of perceptions equates the self with the complex of objective elements of which it is aware—a defect that has plagued psychology to the present day. As a result, introspection is used as a method of internal observation to catalog our personal mental life. Even if this program is more successful than Hume's efforts, it remains squarely within the scope of the empirical ego. The self (or 'I') is reduced to the objective 'me'. Thus, in its true nature as pure subject, it remains inaccessible to the empirical methods that limit psychological research.

In contrast, Wolff suggests that Introception serves as the tool of "metapsychology." His analogy of a lighted lamp illustrates the difference between Introception and introspection.

> The being of the self, which for introception is more unequivocal than the being or actuality of perception, is like an unsupported Light. It is "the Flame that burns without wick or oil." It is so pure as to be quite without the taint of personality. One may conceive of it as like a self-supporting Light within a more or less differen-

> tiated lamp. The latter carries the individual characteristics of personality. There is thus something about the pure self that gives it the character of real impersonality. While in the rigorous sense it is highly subjective, it is not a personal subjectivism. This is a point of exceptional importance for philosophy, because the impersonality of the self gives it a universal value. It is the ground for something a good deal more than a merely personal philosophy.[62]

Thus introspection gives us only knowledge of the lamp; Introception reveals the Light itself. If we ask, "To what or to whom is it revealed?" the answer must be, "To the Pure Subject or Self." However, it would be more correct to extend his metaphor to say that the Light is revealed by shining *through* the Self or Pure Subject, but that it is known self-luminously (through identity) by the Self. Objective reference to a person is a secondary consideration, for the determination of personhood is extrinsic to the mystical state—even for the mystic. Self-identity is awareness from a certain position or point of view, but devoid of content; personal identity is the discrimination of one set of lived contents from others.

Transcending the Empirical Ego

We must concede that the empirical ego is encountered as a by-product of the investigation of the self, but such a study is, for the most part, irrelevant to the knowledge revealed by Introception. Furthermore, fascination with the personal nature involves a serious practical impediment to this vastly more profound unfolding.

> The initial and most superficial stage of the subjective penetration is, admittedly, intensely personal, for no man can start at any point save that of himself, a concrete individual living at some particular point in time and space. An early danger of the Way is that of becoming entrapped in this purely personal subjectivity for an indefinite period of time. But he who is caught at this point has scarcely taken the first step on the ladder. The real penetration lies beyond the personal self. Reaching beyond the personal stage, the 'I' rapidly grows in impersonality until it acquires the value of a Universal Principle.[63]

Often the allure of the vast multidimensional panorama of subtle phenomena traps the unwary. It is then likely that one will be caught within the fascination of transcendental empiricism and fall short of the goal.

Cosmic Introspection

Mael Melvin defines Introception, in contrast to ordinary introspection, as a sort of "cosmic introspection" where "the individual consciousness becomes cosmic while looking inward,"[64] in a state of detached witnessing. Superficially, one might take this to mean that the function is objective, especially since Wolff has discussed Introception in connection with objects of perception (including other people) as well as essential meanings. However, just as extrovertive mystical experience takes place while the mystic perceives external objects, Introception does not necessitate the obliteration of objective content. Wolff explicitly distinguishes between the content derived from objective perception of the sensible world and that attained by Introceptive penetration of the self.

> Almost immediately, consciousness acquires a new kind of content that is wholly of a sacred character and is not the world as formerly known. What is meant by this is very easily misunderstood, since it does not mean or, at least, does not necessarily mean that the photographic image of the sensible world is altered. . . . The transformation affects the attitude toward the sensible world, rather than its apparent form. It is the reality value that undergoes a radical alteration.[65]

By "the photographic image of the sensible world" he most likely means the sensuous image of shapes and colors (and similar preconceptual equivalents corresponding to the other senses) just as they appear. He leaves open the possibility that Introception might result in some altered appearance, but such change would not be required. The Introceptive transformation therefore need not affect the world's sensible form.

Bimodal Consciousness

It is generally believed that the deepest mystical penetration involves the cessation of relative consciousness. Even so, Wolff's Fundamental Realizations show how consciousness is able to operate in two modes simultaneously, allowing the subject-object structure to remain intact along with the Transcendent. Wolff successfully employs a technique whereby the thinking and experiencing power of consciousness is held in abeyance while the process of Realization unfolds. To maintain this subtle balance requires not merely the capacity for passive observation, but active monitoring and equilibration, where "the self-analyzing power functions with clear discrimination."[66] This allows a conscious correlation between the two levels.

> The success of introception means that at some point consciousness loses all content other than itself. Such a point, if absolute, is equivalent to the complete disappearance of the world of experience. It is also possible that the fundamental effect may be achieved by a sort of division of the major portion of the stream of consciousness so that it turns about toward its source, while a residual portion continues to flow toward its object, namely, the phenomenal world. In this event, objective consciousness continues in a kind of twilight in an inferior portion of the individual's total psyche. The diverted portion of the stream becomes a consciousness without objective content, but with an exclusive awareness of itself and its subject. Such a consciousness is clearly not a mere relation between two terms, a subject and an object, inasmuch as only one term remains. This point has very great epistemological importance, since it begins to undercut the whole conception of consciousness as exclusively a relation *between* terms.[67]

He uses the metaphor of a "flow" not only to characterize relative consciousness, where contents seem to "stream" through our awareness, but more fundamentally to suggest something of the nature of his Realization of Transcendent Consciousness.[68] This accords well with his view of consciousness as substantial, but radically nonmaterial in nature. For Wolff, Root Consciousness is substantial in the sense that it is "the substance of all things and the source of all cognition."[69] Normally, consciousness is intentional and may be understood as spontaneously upsurging activity oriented to constituting the phenomenal world. When instead, either willfully or spontaneously, it withdraws from its involvement with objects and reorients to the 'source' of the upsurge, its modality may bifurcate. It is possible for relative consciousness to continue somewhat autonomously, but greatly attenuated, such that it may progressively fade away. The resulting marginal awareness contrasts sharply with the increased intensity of the Introceptual mode. Herein consciousness apprehends itself immediately through identity and most emphatically is not entertaining a conceptual projection of itself. In this state, the Introceptual mode is dominant and of overriding interest, whereas the relative mode is of great practical assistance in providing the link through which memory and formulation are possible.

Volition

There is a striking parallel between the Light of Consciousness turning back upon itself and Schopenhauer's depiction of salvation as the will turning and denying itself. The latter is a nonvolitional process appearing to originate externally, "from mystical insight which wholly transcends the will and the world."[70] Wolff pointedly notes that Schopenhauer's avowal of something more fundamental than will and the possibility of nullifying the will is inconsistent with his voluntarism—the claim that the will is the ultimate ontological principle. On this evidence Wolff believes that Schopenhauer was quite likely personally acquainted with the function of Introception. There is a further parallel in the Buddhist sutras with "the turning about at the deepest seat of consciousness."[71] His firsthand appraisal of Introception is that "the 'turning about' does involve conative factors, so it may be viewed as an inversion of the will such that it denies itself in its habitual movement toward the object."[72] Nevertheless, he regards the process as of primarily methodological rather than ontological importance.

Intuition and Science

Wolff regards Introception as a form of intuition in the broad sense, insofar as "intuition is a general notion applying to all forms of immediacy reaching from the most primitive instinct up to the highest insight."[73] However, because of its metaphysical nature, it requires a special designation apart from other forms of intuition. Specifically, it has the character of a timeless, nonphenomenal (hence nonsensuous) immediacy.[74] Therefore, Kant's Forms of Intuition (namely, time and space), as well as the categories of the understanding (quantity, quality, relation, and modality), do not apply.

The content disclosed by Introception should not be confused with the subject matter of the empiric sciences; it is not in itself a psychic shortcut to the objective determinations of the world. Rather, the key to Introceptual methodology involves a penetration of the self, or 'I', which is purely subjective.[75] It is not a subtle object or objects of which only I am aware, but is that which can never be located in the objective field.[76] This contrasts starkly with the exclusively object-oriented approach of empiric science. Wolff maintains that the unnecessarily restrictive methodological presuppositions of Western science (including psychology and the preponderance of philosophy) preclude the possibility of transcendental knowledge. Thus "SCIENCE, in the sense of knowing fully, cannot be restricted to objective material, but must, as well, be open to other possibilities of awareness."[77]

Our phenomenological critique of empiric science has already given this point a theoretical foundation, but Wolff extends its range of application. For him, Introception is more than a theoretical possibility—it is a metapsychological reality. His personal testimony concerning its operation, contrasting and comparing actual modes of thought and tracing the process from its ineffable Root to its articulated interpretation, supplies ample evidence. How then does it function?

KNOWLEDGE-THROUGH-IDENTITY

Identity of Knower and Known

The nature of the knowledge attained through Introception is that of a fusion of knower and known in Knowledge-through-Identity, a notion that Wolff introduces to distinguish the function from other kinds of intuition.

> I have invented a term that seems much more satisfactory. I call it "*Knowledge through Identity.*" As it is immediate knowledge, it is intuitive in the broad sense, but as it is highly noetic, it is to be distinguished from other forms of immediate awareness that are

> largely, if not wholly, noncognitive. . . .[78] This is neither pure experience nor pure formal demonstration but a totally different kind of Knowledge. I have called It "Knowledge through Identity." It is Intuition, in the highest sense, but the word "intuition" covers other meanings; so the former term is less ambiguous. Genuine Knowledge through Identity is infallible and absolute. It is substantial and not relative. It does not merely mean something other than Itself, but is absolutely Its own Meaning. Knowledge through Identity is not possessed by any self but IS the SELF. It is not "knowledge about," not even in the sense of "about God," but is Divinity Itself.[79]

It possesses a far greater intimacy than does the knowledge gained by immediate acquaintance with objects in common experience, for there is no subject-object distinction, as there would be for knowledge concerning objects. Wolff contends that the quality of this consciousness is ineffable. Even so, it may be suggested by contrasting its substantial 'thickness', experienced as an immediate Realization of 'depth value', with the superficial 'thinness' of both percepts and concepts. We may understand this as meaning that percepts give only perspectival glimpses of the surface of things, while concepts divorced from content provide only an empty categorial framework. Knowledge-through-Identity "does not *represent* Substance, but *is* Substance Itself. So, it is true that 'I'—the self or *Ātman*—am not different from that Knowledge."[80] Wolff suggests that we understand substance in terms of Realized Depth in consciousness, where "the Depth quale is precisely the inexpressible element in all Gnostic and mystical Realization."[81] Thus substance, as a metaphorical (if not metaphysical) notion, might serve to distinguish Introception from phenomenal or intellectual apprehension.

Knowledge-through-Identity is not to be construed as some kind of transcendent subject-object knowledge, the existence of which empirically oriented philosophers would rightly deny. The basis for distinguishing it from Transcendent Consciousness is extremely subtle: "We might say that It is the Transcendent Consciousness as reflected through the knowledge quale. . . . The assertion of the Reality of this Knowledge implies that Knowledge may descend from the Transcendent to the relative domain."[82] Wolff equates this sort of knowledge with *vidyā*, knowledge of the noumenal, or ultimately real,[83] not the merely empiric knowledge, or *avidyā*. In itself it is ineffable.

Self-Surrender

Wolff contends that a major difficulty involved in actualizing this function self-consciously is the necessity of developing an attitude of self-giving or surrender to Truth or Wisdom—that is, an attitude of humility and devotion.

> Here, feeling, in the best sense, must fuse with the thought. Thus the thinker must learn also to feel his thought, so that, in the highest degree, he thinks devotedly. It is not enough to think clearly, if the thinker stands aloof, not giving himself with his thought. The thinker arrives by surrendering himself to Truth, claiming for himself no rights save those that Truth herself bestows upon him. In the final state of perfection he possesses no longer opinions of his own nor any private preference. Then Truth possesses him, not he, Truth.
>
> He who would become one with the Eternal must first learn to be humble. He must offer, upon the sacrificial altar, the pride of the knower. He must become one who lays no possessive claim to knowledge or wisdom. This is the state of the mystic ignorance—of the emptied heart. He who has thus become as nothing in his own right then is prepared to become possessed by Wisdom herself. The completeness of self-emptying is the precondition to the realization of unutterable Fullness. Thus mere "knowledge about" becomes transformed into Knowledge as Reality.[84]

Similarly, Richard Alpert says that we must "give up the knower to become the known."[85] He insightfully observes that Western culture is characterized by attachment to the rational mind, which disposes us to be exceedingly reluctant to allow this sort of self-surrender. Such aversion is unfounded, however, for nothing of real value is lost. Wolff discovered that

> to know THAT which the aphorisms symbolize is to be possessed by THAT and, then, to be one with THAT. Thenceforth, all thinking, all feeling, all particularization, and all selfhood lie below. To be sure, all these remain, but no longer as claimants to a Throne they could not possibly fill. They remain thenceforth as the actors in the Divine Drama, but no more.[86]

He affirms its Transcendent Value in unequivocal terms: "No cost could be too high as the price of its attainment!"[87] Renouncing the sense of oneself as controlling and directing one's thought processes opens the way for Transcendent Thought to become self-manifest.

Autonomous Thought

Knowledge-through-Identity contrasts starkly with analysis, which "achieves its results through a laborious and painful dissection of given raw material from experience and a reintegration by means of *invented* concepts applied hypothetically."[88] Analysis necessarily depends on experience and involves a distance between a concept and the object to which it is related, which entails the forfeit of epistemic certainty. However, in Knowledge-through-Identity the concept arises spontaneously, rather than as a result of willed effort, and is curiously identical with its object.

> The inner Thought is spontaneous in that it happens of itself insofar as the objective or personal thinker is concerned. It is not the product of a consciously willed effort by the personal ego. Further, it is not a content that stands out as clearly differentiated from the self. Rather, the self and content are blended in identity, a state that is very difficult to conceive from the objective point of view.[89]

Consequently, Wolff maintains that "Knowledge through Identity is not to be regarded as an analytic extraction from experience, but as a Knowledge that is original and coextensive with a Recognizable, but nonexperiential, Reality."[90] It is independent of experience, although valuable for rendering experience intelligible by providing "the fundamental propositions or 'indefinables' from which systems can grow at once by pure deductive process."[91]

The process by which Wolff formulated the aphorisms, comprising what he suggests we might view as the axiomatic framework of his philosophy, illustrates his claim. He reports that it involves the fusion of conceptual and Introceptual thought. Conceptual thinking, characteristic of cultural development in philosophy, art, and science, including mathematics, involves consciously directed effort, and its effective communication demands an extreme degree of skillful verbal articulation. In contrast, Introceptual thought is essentially nonconceptual and *sui generis*, flowing effortlessly from the utmost depths of consciousness.

> It is fluidic rather than granular. It never isolates a definitive divided part, but everlastingly interblends with all. Every thought includes the whole of Eternity, and yet there are distinguishable thoughts. The unbroken Eternal flows before the mind, yet is endlessly colored anew with unlimited possibility. There is no labor in this thought. It simply is. It is unrelated to all desiring, all images, and all symbols.[92]

This is what he refers to as "thought thinking itself." It contrasts with our usual experience of the spontaneity of thinking, inasmuch as it is predeterminative. It operates at a primordial level that is ontologically antecedent to the desire for any particular form or end, as well as for any specific representation in imagery, symbols, or language.

Transcriptive Thought

Between Introceptual and conceptual thought, but participating in each, lies what Wolff refers to as "transcriptive thought." This flows of itself, as it were, into conceptual form, expressing itself naturally in aphorism or poetry. He discovered it to be a distinct mode of thought—partially spontaneous, but also directed, integrating the two cognitive functions. At first, while immersed in the autonomous mode of thought, Wolff reports that whoever

> finds thought thus thinking within discovers no words therein nor concepts that his or her personal understanding can embrace, but knows the truth of the thought, and that remains.
>
> Then, later, out of this thought is born another kind of thought, which partly thinks itself, and partly one thinks with contributed effort. It is all exceedingly clear and employs word concepts, seemingly as one might speak or write. However, they are not yet speakable or writable. They are thoughts of which the words are the cream of human abstraction.[93]

In its purity, the Transcendent cannot be expressed in relative terms. Wolff makes this point unequivocally: "All language, as such, is defeated when used as an instrument of portrayal of the transcendent."[94] Nonetheless, there is an intermediate zone that is partially determinate where meaningful formulation may take place between the utterly ineffable and the subject-object consciousness.[95] This involves the genesis of a unique kind of concept that has no fixed definition, but is fluidic or functional. He describes this process as finding an idea spontaneously arising along with an immediate recognition of its counterpart. "Then the original idea takes on a sort of flowing quality which seems to proceed toward the level that synthesizes both it and the counter idea."[96] His formulation is obviously strained to capture the subtlety of the origin of aphorism.

> In high degree, this thought flows of itself, yet blends with verbal concepts. Here the conceptual thought and the transcendent thought combine in mutual action. . . . From this level of thought are born the aphorisms, that strange kind of thought that is both poetry and something more. For it stirs the thinking as well as the feeling and thus integrates the best of the whole man. Mystery is an inextricable part of this thought.[97] The aphoristic thought is the child of the transcendental and the conceptual. This is the highest form of articulate thought. He who would understand cannot do so with his conceptual powers alone. He must also let the understanding grow up from within him.[98]

This kind of thought carries within it a sense of authority. Though superficially the aphorisms appear as dissociated statements, the thought flows according to its unique logic, similar in nature to certain systems of formal mathematics.

> The genuine aphorism differs from most groups of mathematical postulates in that the latter are generally inventions of the unillumined mind, while the aphorism is a spontaneous production out of an illumined state. They could well serve as postulates from which systematic logical development could be constructed, in which case they might well be conceived as authentic *axioms* and not merely as *fundamental assumptions.*[99]

Because Wolff's aphorisms are immediately derived from Introceptual Realization, they are grounded securely in a way that speculative constructs are not. This is not to say that the latter are without value, or even that their value for enhancing our understanding is necessarily inferior. The advantage of immediate awareness of the source is that it provides an epistemological basis for judging the adequacy of ideational systems that purport to deal with it.

Aphorisms on the Self

Wolff exemplifies the process of developing this sort of axiomatic system in his aphorisms on Consciousness-without-an-object,[100] and aphorisms on the Self.[101] He prefaces the aphorisms on the Self by summarizing his Realization of the Self.

> It has already been stated that when introception is carried far enough, the self and the DivPine Other coalesce in a Self having a highly transcendent character. This is a radically unitary Self of so complete an aloofness that personality simply does not exist for it. It is equally aloof from the empiric world. It is the union of the subject-to-consciousness and its content. It is not contained by space, time and the world of sensible objects, but is like a Space that contains and comprehends all these. From this state of introceptive Realization certain consequences follow.[102]

Wolff lists "The Self supports the universe, yet is not conditioned by the presence or absence of the universe"[103] and ten other propositions that he derives immediately from the state itself. Due to their origin they have a unique status. He contends that these

> statements are not merely invented postulates from which one might proceed to build a hypothetical system, nor are they to be viewed as the necessary consequences of either empiric or pure objective thought. This is a very fundamental part of my whole thesis. Criticism that does not bear this point in mind misses the essence of the whole argument. *They are ideas in objective form derived from the Thought of the Self.* They are not themselves the immediate form of that Thought, which is inherently independent of the concepts and word signs of objective thought. That Thought, in its essence, is forever incommunicable in the forms of relative consciousness. Thus the primary postulates are, rather, precipitates within relative thought of a Meaning prior to the latter. They are subject to unavoidable distortion through processes whereby content identical to the Self is made to appear as an object of consciousness for the empiric subject. The Thought of the Self is not, and must not be conceived as, an objective or empiric thought, even to the point that, if realized by a nonthinking being, it would not appear as Thought at all.[104]

He is quick to disavow any claim to exclusivity of truth for these propositions because a necessary relativity attaches to any objective statement or set of statements concerning the Realized, nonrelative, nonobjective Reality. Wolff therefore affirms their truth, "but not as so exclusively true as to preclude precipitation in other patterns."[105]

Aphorisms on Consciousness-without-an-Object

His aphorisms on Consciousness-without-an-object, which he says "virtually wrote themselves" without effort, might be considered as axioms. The first five comprise his first Fundamental, and the next six his second Fundamental.

1. Consciousness-without-an-object is.

•

2. Before objects were,
Consciousness-without-an-object is.

•

3. Though objects seem to exist,
Consciousness-without-an-object is.

•

4. When objects vanish,
yet remaining through all unaffected,
Consciousness-without-an-object is.

•

5. Outside of Consciousness-without-an-object,
nothing is.[106]

Wolff notes that "this forms the primary principle of the philosophy. . . . the self-existent, nonproduced character of Pure Consciousness."[107]

The following aphorisms express the principle of "a quality of consciousness that remains unaffected by the presence or absence of objects within it and also by the presence or absence of a subject-to-consciousness within it."[108] Here both subject and object are potential projections from this Primordial Consciousness.

6. Within the bosom of
Consciousness-without-an-object lies
the power of awareness that projects objects.

•

7. When objects are projected,
the power of awareness as subject is presupposed,
yet Consciousness-without-an-object
remains unchanged.

•

8. When consciousness of objects is born, then,
likewise, consciousness of absence of objects arises.

•

9. Consciousness of objects is the Universe.

•

10. Consciousness of absence of objects
is Nirvāṇa.

•

11. Within Consciousness-without-an-object
lie both the Universe and Nirvāṇa,
yet to Consciousness-without-an-object
these two are the same.[109]

Although Wolff's aphorisms can be completely verified only by similar Recognition, partial confirmation is feasible using pragmatic means. Wolff proposes that we entertain them as metaphysical postulates that may be of value as integrating principles for rendering experience more intelligible. We need only "accept them *as though* they were true symbols of the Reality, and drawing the consequences that follow from them, finally noting how they affect the problems of life and thought as practically experienced."[110] Inability to imagine them presents no greater barrier to their acceptance than does our inability to imagine certain mathematical conceptions that have proven fruitful.[111]

KANT AND ŚAṂKARA

The Kantian Context

It is now time to consider more closely the metaphysical import of system(s) of thought grounded in Realization through Introception. For convenience, let us propose that the strongest version of the noetic thesis asserts that Introception results in metaphysical knowledge. To better place the issue within a framework that illuminates Wolff's philosophy, let us first explore the Kantian context, within which he originally conceived the significance of his quest. It will also be worthwhile to consider a contemporary attempt to resolve Kant's problem of metaphysical knowledge from the perspective of Śaṃkara's Advaita Vedānta—a tradition that strongly influenced Wolff's development.

Wolff regards epistemology, "the science of the nature and possibilities of knowledge,"[112] as indispensable for a grounded metaphysics. Its study is essential for delimiting the scope of relative, subject-object knowledge and suggesting something of the mystical knowledge that transcends this realm. He has a pronounced affinity for rationalism,[113] which formulates its metaphysics according to ideas that appear intuitively self-evident. He would prefer to write in that mode were he not aware of the necessity for treating the epistemological problem,[114] namely, grounding such statements. Thus he remains faithful to the Kantian inspiration that provided the impetus for philosophical development beyond the limitations of rationalism and empiricism. Wolff has concern for the critical evaluation of the authority of Realization, the philosophical training required to perform such a critique, and immediate acquaintance with Realization itself. These all comprise the unique combination of factors that allows him to extend beyond the Copernican revolution in philosophy that Kant began.

Metaphysical Knowledge

Kenneth Dorter claims that Descartes begins this movement toward epistemology as a condition for certainty for his scientific revolution. "Formerly, first philosophy was ontology or metaphysics, inquiry into the ultimate nature of being; in Descartes's hands it becomes epistemology, inquiry into the human conditions for experience."[115] Kant's expressed intention is to suspend all metaphysical activity pending the determination of the conditions for its possibility as a science. He does not wish to end metaphysics, but to ground it through critical idealism. The discovery of synthetic a priori judgments, he believes, provides the possibility of constructing metaphysics as a science.[116]

Wolff seeks another doorway, which Kant left ajar, yet has for the most part remained neglected by Western philosophy. Kant's *Critique of Pure Reason* establishes the existence of the two familiar means of cognition, but leaves open the possibility of other ways of knowing. Wolff's search for a third function of cognition was motivated by the hope that one could ground metaphysical knowledge by uncovering an immediate, nonsensuous content for consciousness. If we are restricted to the familiar forms of cognition, he contends, our knowledge of existing things is at best only probable. Thus the epistemic ideal of certainty spurred him to find (discover or rediscover) a way to indubitable knowledge.

Dorter warns that the general rejection of metaphysics, prompted by the widespread belief that Kant's conditions could not be met, has led to a crisis in contemporary philosophy. Its position as the "Queen of the Sciences" has deteriorated to the status of handmaiden to science. As a result, its relevance apart from certain narrow methodological concerns regarding logic, grammar, and certain technical matters is being seriously questioned.[117] He implores us to reexamine the philosophical presuppositions and assumptions that have led to the denial of the metaphysical quest. Otherwise our aspiration toward knowing appears doomed to frustration within the framework of the "egocentric predicament"—the legacy of modern philosophy.

> Man's inborn desire to know is not fully exhausted in the discursive knowledge of science, knowledge of the inter-relationships among entities; there are those who, now as always, seek ultimately a noetic insight into the unitary nature of the whole. Man seeks not only the knowledge that is power, but also the knowledge which gives meaning, and which, for example, enables the individual to see even the realm of science in a perspective more promising than that "whatever works" is true, beautiful and good.[118]

Wolff meets this challenge from a wider perspective. He recognizes these fundamental human aspirations within himself, yet acknowledges the force of Kant's prohibition. As a result, he attempts to provide a solution that is compatible with the Kantian tradition while going beyond the unnecessary, restrictive assumption that reason and sensibility are humanity's total resources.

Epistemological Noumenon

Central to Kant's epistemology is the distinction between the phenomenon and the noumenon, or between the thing as it appears and the thing as it is in itself. Henry Allison points out that there are several subtle inconsistencies in Kant's treatment of the thing as it is in itself, the noumenon, and the transcendental object, which would cast doubt upon their strict identification.[119] Nevertheless, for our purposes, using these terms interchangeably will have no adverse consequences. Kant holds the view that all that is (and can be) given to the senses is the phenomenon—never the noumenon. Furthermore, the thing only appears through certain fixed forms of intuition (space and time) and categories of the understanding.

It would follow that without the faculty of intellectual intuition, which Kant does not believe we possess, the thing-in-itself would be unknowable, and to posit it would violate his principles proscribing speculative metaphysics. Fichte, Husserl, and others reject the notion for this reason. However, some recent commentators defend Kant's inclusion of the thing-in-itself, or noumenon, because it is a necessary epistemological notion, not an invidiously ontological one. Allison, for one, adopts this approach.

> Properly construed, this problem is not, as is generally believed, that of somehow justifying the assumption of the existence of unknowable entities. Rather, it is to show the possibility and the significance of this act considering things *as they are in themselves,* which means apart from the conditions under which we can know anything about them. To do so, is to provide the only possible justification of the Kantian conception of the thing in itself, or, more properly, the thing as it is in itself.[120]

Nicholas Rescher concurs.

> All that Kant is entitled to on his principles, but also all that he needs within the framework of his commitments, and *all that he wants* is a mind-correlative *conception* of "things-in-themselves," an ultimately *epistemological* resource, and emphatically *not* an ontologically construed, altogether mind-inaccessible realm of "real things." The Kantian thing-in-itself is to be understood not as a part of the furniture of the real world as such, but rather as an instrumentality of our thought about the real world.[121]

Thus we are to consider the thing-in-itself as a conception that is thinkable—not an entity that is unknowable. However, in contrast to phenomena, it can be defined only negatively. Methodologically, it functions "to keep phenomena in their place as *phenomena,* to keep appearances in their status of being just that, appearances, by providing for the contrast between the appearance itself and a something that appears, thus blocking the way to idealism (in its phenomenalist configuration)."[122] Wolff also notes that Kant views universal, a priori forms as epistemological predeterminants, rather than metaphysical self-existences.[123]

On this interpretation of Kant, not only is it possible to think of things as they are in themselves, but it is necessary to do so "as a postulate of the human understanding."[124] The notion of a thing-in-itself, or a noumenon underlying a phenomenon, serves to delimit the bounds of human understanding. It stands as a constant reminder of "Kant's requirement to consider objectives in relation to the human mind and its conceptual scheme, which simply is the Copernican revolution in philosophy."[125]

Ontological Noumenon

Even if we grant that the epistemological interpretation of the thing-in-itself is central, this does not by itself exclude the possibility that it may also be understood in an ontological sense. Kant seems to allow for the possibility of nonsensuous intuition when he says, "We have not, indeed, been able to prove that sensible intuition is the only possible intuition,"[126] and "We are not entitled to maintain that sensibility is the only possible mode of intuition."[127] However, he does not believe that we possess it, that even though such an intuition may not be theoretically impossible, "it is so for us. But neither have we been able to prove that another kind of intuition is possible."[128] He believes that "such an intuition, that is, an intellectual intuition, is no part of our faculty of cognition."[129]

Furthermore, he denies that we can even conceive of an intellectual intuition: "We do not possess an intuition, indeed, not even the conception of a possible intuition,"[130] because "our concepts of understanding being mere forms of thought for our sensible intuition, could not in the least apply."[131] Nonetheless, his point here is not that there *is* nothing, or can be nothing, beyond sensibility—only that we cannot *conceive* of anything beyond it or how it would be possible to know it. He holds this on the grounds that our concepts are necessarily derived from sensible intuition and therefore could in no way apply to anything nonsensible.

Notwithstanding Kant's careful and guarded program of critical philosophy, when he speaks from an ontological, rather than epistemological, standpoint he makes an interesting assertion: "Doubtless, indeed there are intelligible entities corresponding to the sensible entities; there may also be intelligible entities to which our sensible faculty of intuition has no relation whatsoever."[132] Clearly, he uses the term *noumenon* solely in the negative sense on epistemological, not ontological grounds because he cannot satisfy the conditions he deems necessary for its use in a positive sense. To be able to describe these entities according to some positive knowledge of them is Kant's precondition for such attribution of the terms *noumenon* and *noumenal*. This he cannot justify.

Taking up this challenge leads to Wolff's point of departure from Kant. He quotes the key passage setting forth the requirement of a presentation through intellectual intuition as necessary for knowledge of the noumenon.

> In order that a noumenon may signify a *real* object that can be distinguished from all phenomena, *it is not enough that I should free my thought of all conditions of sensuous intuition but I must besides have some reason for admitting another kind of intuition besides the sensuous,* in which such an object can be given, otherwise my thought would be empty, however free it may be from contradictions.[133]

He interprets Kant as allowing the possibility of metaphysical knowledge, but denying that it is accessible within the capacity of human cognition. Quoting Kant, "Our consciousness of all existence . . . belongs altogether to a unity of experience and an existence outside this field cannot absolutely be explained away as impossible. But it is a supposition that we have no means of justifying."[134]

Wolff accepts this conclusion as correct if, and only if, it is meant to apply to the domain of consciousness proper to natural science or to experience in the narrow, objective sense of empiricism. However, he maintains that these principles do not logically rule out the justification of "the supposition of a non-experiential or transcendent existence or reality."[135] Still, he agrees that Kant has shown that proof based solely on logic and pure concepts (the overt metaphysical program of rationalism) is impossible. He acknowledges that pure reason by itself is limited to judgments of mere possibility, although it is able to predicate actuality in conjunction with sensuously given material. Even so, such knowledge remains at best only probable in its proper domain (empirical science) and speculative beyond this range. Wolff states, "I do not contend that the pure reason, either acting in a strictly formal sense or upon a material given by experience, can demonstrate a transcendental reality. On the contrary, this reality must be realized immediately, if it is to have more than a hypothetical existence."[136] In any case, if we are to overcome skepticism within the critical spirit, we need some reason for accepting that a nonsensuous intuition of the noumenon is not merely a logical possibility, but actually occurs—however rarely.

Introceptual Noumenon

Having established his case for the possibility of this further means of knowledge, Wolff goes on to make the strongest possible argument, not only for its possibility, but for its actuality through Introception. He further wishes to explicate its significance for Western philosophy and for humankind.

> I go further than Kant in maintaining that in the total organization of consciousness there are phases that are neither conceptual nor empiric. . . . The character of this phase of consciousness, as it has been represented in existent discussions and as revealed in my own contact with it, is of the nature of immediate awareness of an existential content or value. This immediacy is of a far superior order as compared to that given through the senses, for the latter is dependent upon the instrumentality of sensuous organs and functions. As compared to the experience through the senses, this rarer phase of consciousness gives a transcendent value immediately and renders possible the predication of its existence in a judgment without violating the fundamental principles laid down by Kant.[137]

The rigor and clarity of thought provided by Kant's critical approach to philosophy proved of great benefit to Wolff. It enhanced his capacity to appreciate and express the significance of his realizations, not only for religion (to which the relevance of mysticism in the West had hitherto been mainly restricted), but for epistemology and metaphysics as well.

Are we limited to passively recording the results of the autonomous functioning of Introception, or may it be actively directed? Wolff suggests that there is the capacity to engage it through a subtle solicitation or seeding process. The inner spiritual thought

> certainly is not under the direction or control of the personal ego. At the appropriate level of mystical penetration wherein both the personal egoic thought and the higher thought are conscious, within a common zone of consciousness, the personally directed thought may query the higher thought, either by a direct question or by tentative predication. This will initiate a responsive activity in the higher thought.[138]

This neither constitutes a method, in the ordinary sense, nor a demonstration that it reveals a noumenal reality. No matter, it reveals a dimension of human potential that demands further investigation.

Noumenon and Vedānta

Whereas Kant provides Wolff's point of departure within the tradition of Western philosophy, it was Śaṃkara whose thought prepared his philosophical understanding of how metaphysical knowledge was possible. Śaṃkara's account shows that the resolution to the Kantian problematic may lie in mystical or unconditioned consciousness, instead of the synthetic a priori. Wolff explicitly states that consciousness unconditioned by perspective is necessary for metaphysical knowledge.[139]

From an approach compatible with Wolff's, Ramlal Singh traces the philosophical relevance of Śaṃkara's Advaita Vedānta to Kant's project. Essentially, he focuses upon and establishes the importance of self-awareness as the key to transcendental knowledge.[140] Singh sees Kant addressing the problem of determining "both validity and limit of the universal principles of knowledge."[141] Like Wolff, he regards Kant's use of the phenomenon/noumenon dichotomy as successful for constructing "the metaphysics of experience but . . . unable to discover the nature of higher reality positively."[142] Kant's theory is essentially a theory of scientific knowledge, but it is in need of the Advaitic emendation to become a theory of knowledge in the full sense. Singh claims that

> Kant and Śaṃkara have the same epistemological problem before them, i.e. the problem of the knowledge of the unconditioned. Kant had solved the problem of the limit of the theoretical activity of reason in knowledge. He, as a matter of fact, defined the scope of agreed knowledge in philosophy and consequently put philosophy on the sure path of science. Kant admitted the philosophical knowledge, the knowledge of the unconditioned, as merely an ideal. He laid much emphasis upon the *aprioriness* of knowledge characterized by necessity and universality but he paid almost no attention to the realization of self as the sole and only reality in the intuitive awareness or any other form of higher experience.[143]

Kant thus sets forth the problem of metaphysical knowledge as a theoretical problem, but, because of his restricted assumptions, he can offer only a practical solution. He can do no more than justify statements concerning the noumenal by considering them as postulates of practical reason.

Singh contends that whereas Kant regards the human intellect as merely discursive, but the Divine[144] as fully able to know the reality of the noumenal, Śaṃkara considers human and Divine intelligence essentially identical. This prepares a full theoretical solution based on the idea that the unconditioned may be known only directly, never merely as an *object* of cognition. In addition, Śaṃkara would accept, and even insist upon, Kant's distinction between the empirical ego and the transcendental ego, inasmuch as it is only the latter that can never be known as object, and with which the self is identified.

> Both of them realized correctly that self is the presupposition of whatever is known objectively and consequently cannot be dragged to the realm of that which depends on it. It is at the back of all psychic activity and therefore psychically unknowable. But while Kant makes self unknowable and unspeakable, Śaṃkara would like to make the case for both these possibilities. Though the unconditioned or self is objectively unknown, it can be subjectively realized and though it is literally unspeakable it is expressible symbolically.[145]

From this point of view, which Wolff would approve, it is wholly arbitrary to restrict knowledge to the domain of objectivity, for it necessarily makes the unconditioned unknowable. It cannot be shown that knowledge extends no further than this. Singh remarks that "to think that all that is known and is knowable, is an object to a subject, is to insist on the phenomenalization of the noumenal."[146] He accuses Kant of lapsing into the objective attitude, thereby ignoring the noetic possibilities inherent in the self and leaving his Copernican revolution incomplete. It is necessary to look to the philosophy of Śaṃkara to fulfill its promise. "Śaṃkara, while denying the knowledge of the ultimate reality as an object, very clearly admits the possibility of its knowledge as the ultimate knower. In every act of knowledge, in every event of cognition, we are conscious of its existence but not as an object but as a subject."[147] Following A. C. Mukerji,[148] Singh distinguishes between Śaṃkara's epistemology and both rationalism (for example, Leibniz and Hegel) and agnosticism (Kant), characterizing it as "rational intuitionism." The Vedāntin philosophy of Śaṃkara is grounded in knowledge that is not objectively experienced, but subjectively revealed, such that "ultimate reality becomes self-luminous and self-revealed."[149]

From Noesis to Noumenon

Beginning from the Kantian approach to viewing the problem of metaphysical knowledge, Wolff's proposed solution seems to follow that of Śaṃkara, as Singh interprets him, for it is based on Self-knowledge. However, in Wolff's ultimate Realization, the High Indifference, both the Subject and the Object, in the highest sense, dissolved into the nondualistic Consciousness-without-an-object and without-a-subject, which transcends the Pure Subject or Self (the *Ātman*). This supersedes Śaṃkara's treatment in terms of *Ātmavidyā,* if interpreted as the perspective from a monadic consciousness. Wolff further considers his second "Copernican Revolution" an advance beyond Kant (who shifted the focus of Western philosophy from the object of consciousness to the subject-to-consciousness), for it is grounded upon pure Consciousness Itself. At the same time, he contends that it completes the Kantian program by showing how noumenal knowledge is possible.

Does Introception actually give this sort of knowledge? For many, the only acceptable proof would be to compare Wolff's Introception to noumenal knowledge provided antecedently and show that they were the same. Of course, this is impossible. Still, we can show that it satisfies the formal requirements for the noumenal, insofar as Introception

1. provides a nonsensuous content immediately to consciousness;
2. is atemporal;
3. is nonspatial;
4. is unconditioned, that is, acausal;
5. transcends the categories of understanding; and
6. transcends language and concepts.

There is, in addition, a heightened sense of 'objectivity' or reality—an enduring conviction that a more ultimate reality is being revealed. All of this counts in favor of Wolff's interpretation that Introception is noumenal and perhaps no more can be done.

Things-in-Themselves

Qualms may remain concerning the *ding an sich,* the thing as it is in itself, so we should also consider the problem in these terms. Wolff's approach involves a radical introversion. As such, it is difficult to see how it could be of any assistance in providing metaphysical knowledge concerning the inner reality of worldly phenomena. How can Introception be relevant to knowing what *things* such as rocks, trees, and coffee mugs are like *in themselves*? Is one able to use this faculty to discriminate between a particular rock, such as Barnacle Bill (the first rock analyzed by the Mars Rover) and a particular tree, for instance, Methuselah (the bristlecone pine that is the oldest living thing on earth)? If so, how would the accounts differ as to what they were like *in themselves*?

Although Wolff does not address these questions overtly, he hints at the direction whereby both a theoretical and a practical solution might be developed. He contends that the three cognitive functions—conception, perception, and Introception—may operate either individually or in combination, resulting in seven possible distinct fields.[150] In combination with conception, Introception results in a completely different way of apprehending the meaning of a concept. A concept normally indicates its meaning as a sign pointer directing attention to a perceptual experience and hence is of purely instrumental value. In contrast to this extraverted sense of meaning, the subjective significance of a concept is inherent within it, such that it enrobes its meaning, so to speak. Wolff explains that

> introceptive meditation is not merely a process of reflection about an object, whereby one deduces or infers consequences. It is a movement of consciousness such that a successful outcome implies a transcendence of both thinking and perception, so that consciousness enters something like another dimension. The inward penetration into the significance of a concept is the epistemological or psychological parallel of the introceptive movement toward the self, wherein the self is not transformed into a new object, but remains unaltered in its subjective character.[151]

This radical introversion reveals a meaning that is substantial, not instrumental. Based on the immediacy of the mystic's awareness, the greater reality is generally correlated to the concept's degree of abstraction.[152] "When a concept enrobes an inner Significance, it possesses thickness or depth."[153] The Introceptual thickness intensifies as the process of abstraction moves toward and beyond the limits of conceptual thought. First, words are transcended as an adequate vehicle for conceptual meaning—then symbols are as well. "Thought then deals with a disembodied Meaning. . . . This is an extremely pregnant Thought, for a single Idea, in this sense, may require literally volumes for its interpretation. Indeed, it is never wholly interpreted, since no objectively thinkable elaboration can ever exhaust its possibilities."[154] Intrinsically, the "pure introceptive Thought" is pure formless Meaning and, compared to objective thought, virtually infinitely thick.[155]

Wolff's philosophy unfolds from conception combined with Introception, oriented to the indeterminate theoretic continuum, but acknowledges that the path dominant in the East is oriented to the indeterminate aesthetic continuum. In Taoism, for example, Introception is combined with perception, while conception is held in abeyance. He proposes that the fusion of Introception with both perception and conception is the greatest task for synthetic philosophy.[156]

His mysticism focuses primarily on the mystical core in its purity, secondarily on the conceptual domain, particularly mathematical concepts, and is least concerned with ordinary perception. Just as the fusion with Introception revealed an inner depth to the concept, one would expect a similar finding for the percept. So let us examine the application of Introception to the spatiotemporal realm by drawing upon a few succinct examples of extrovertive mysticism compiled by Stace. According to Meister Eckhart, "All that a man has here externally in multiplicity is intrinsically One. Here all blades of grass, wood, and stone, all things are One. This is the deepest depth."[157] Jacob Boehme reports, "In this light my spirit saw through all things and into all creatures and *I recognized God in grass and plants.*"[158] Finally, consider a twentieth-century American mystic, to whom Stace refers as N. M.:

> The room in which I was standing looked out onto the back yards of a Negro tenement. The buildings were decrepit and ugly, the ground covered with boards, rags, and debris. Suddenly every object in my field of vision took on a curious and intense kind of existence of its own; that is, everything appeared to have an "inside"—to exist as I existed, having inwardness, a kind of individual life, and every object, seen under this aspect, appeared exceedingly beautiful. There was a cat out there, with its head lifted, effortlessly watching a wasp that moved without moving just above its head. Everything was *urgent* with life . . . which was the same in the cat, the wasp, the broken bottles, and merely manifested itself differently in these individuals (which did not therefore cease to be individuals however). All things seemed to glow with a light that came from within them.[159]

These typical cases illustrate the operation of the Introceptive function within the context of familiar things. Introception is the noetic aspect of mystical experience, wherein is revealed a Transcendent dimension to ordinary reality. Stace notes that N. M. emphasizes that "during the experience he felt that he was, as it were, 'looking through a keyhole' into the 'inner reality of things' and seeing them as everyone would see them if they could be awakened from the 'sleep or somnambulism' of our ordinary lives."[160]

Within the mode of Introception combined with perception and conception, we find both the apparent distinction between a multiplicity of particulars and their revealed underlying Oneness. On the one hand, there is the apparent distinction among ourselves, animate life forms (such as the cat and wasp), lower life forms (grass and plants), and inanimate things (stone, wood, broken bottles). On the other hand, we find their common inwardness or inner 'life' revealed through a depth of awareness. All of this is expressed conceptually by employing symbolic language in a manner that preserves the essentially mysterious nature of this awareness.

AUTHORITY OF REALIZATION

Whether Introception is pure or combined with other cognitive functions, problems arise with its ensuing formulation. Although it does not conflict with established fact, it is expressed in statements that are neither an extension of the compendium of scientific knowledge nor a parallel set of propositions based on the model of natural science. Furthermore, the various articulated systems that result from its operation may appear to be incompatible. Nevertheless, Wolff contends that they are 'true'. Mystics may very well acknowledge the veracity of diverse accounts, so the applicability of propositional truth here may not be assumed. What is more significant, the mystic makes her pronouncements with unwavering conviction. In what sense, then, and to what degree is Realization authoritative either for the individual mystic or for others?

The Ground of Certainty

Wolff contends that the mystic's Realizations are authoritative for the mystic alone. For anyone else, they constitute only presumption, to be rigorously tested, so he counsels others to regard no Realization as higher than their own. Even within the realm of analytic truth, as in logic and mathematics, infallibility remains an unattainable ideal. He contrasts the conviction produced by Realization with what he calls "convincement" resulting from rational argument. Conviction is a feeling of overwhelming assurance or certainty involving one's total being, essentially religious in nature and possibly involving a conversion from a contrasting viewpoint. Convincement is the result of a cool judgment, possibly based on discursive argument, instead of a change in psychological state. Wolff reports that

> introceptive Realization is a state wherein the subject and the object become so far interblended that the self is identical with its

> knowledge. This is a state of intimacy that pure rational demonstration alone can never attain. For this reason, the most rigorous logical proof, however far it transcends mere experience, nonetheless falls short of certainty. The subject can be absolutely certain only of that knowledge with which it is itself identical. This is characteristic of introceptive Realization.[161]

Because convincement relies on evidence and reasoning, additional evidence or improved reasoning may modify or overturn it. However, only a more profound or comprehensive Realization can modify conviction. Wolff asserts, "For me to change any point of view would require entering into a more transcendent Realization. . . . No argument whatever can modify the force of a given Realization."[162] To conclude, only Realization may effectively challenge Realization in determining a person's world view.

This leads to perplexing consequences. There arises an apparent contradiction that Realization is intrinsically infallible, providing legitimate certainty, while also vulnerable to the superseding Truth of a deeper Realization. Wolff remarks that "the conviction that grows out of a Realization can lead to a state where a deeper Realization is attained such that the earlier point of view is seen as valid relative to a limited zone, but not universally valid—that there are higher truths that change the perspective of that held in one's consciousness."[163] His notion of zones of application, which may be thought of as differing and more or less inclusive perspectives or levels of insight, resolves the problem.[164] Realizations may vary, and although each is completely authoritative for its particular zone, its truth is relative to that domain, so it may be transcended by more comprehensive Realizations.[165] The Transcendence of Wolff's penultimate Realization by the High Indifference illustrates the dynamics of this process. His fourth Realization had revealed that the Self is the primary reality, but the fifth Realization forced a revision of this view by revealing the more Transcendent Reality of Consciousness-without-an-object and without-a-subject. This did not falsify his former knowledge, but instead showed it to be true only within a certain zone of application. This relativity of Realization may greatly explain some apparent discrepancies concerning a mystic's pronouncements and also accounts in some measure for the legitimacy of metaphysical relativism.

A more central concern is the loss of certainty between the immediacy of the Realized content and its expression in conceptual form. Wolff explains why Introception manifests an absolute certainty that ordinary knowledge lacks.

> In the case of ordinary knowledge, the knower stands in a relation of distance or difference from the object of his knowledge. He has, therefore, no ground of certainty with respect to the content of his knowledge. But, in contrast to ordinary knowledge, introceptive cognition is in the form of an identity between the knower and the known. Thus the certainty-destroying factor of distance or difference is eliminated, with the consequence that introceptive cognition is absolutely certain on its own level. Undoubtedly, subsequent error can be introduced when one proceeds to a conceptual interpretation of the introceptive content, but such error does not attach to the pure introceptive cognition itself.[166]

Wolff believes that the importance of this knowledge justifies the risk of error involved in its formulation and communication.[167] He deals with this problem explicitly and is careful to point out the implications.

> Introception is the function whereby a human being transcends the limits of the merely human. It is the way to direct metaphysical understanding, but here sound criticism must be careful to draw the distinction between the pure metaphysical understanding and the conceptual framework that symbolizes it. What a person can think conceptually is not a true portrait of the transcendent, and never can be, for a conceptual order is objective with respect to a thinking self, while transcendental Knowledge is identical with its self-aware subject. As a consequence, the process of objectification inevitably implies distortion, no matter how great the skill of the thinker. However, the conceptual order is a symbol that means the transcendent order, and a defect resident in the symbol may not rightly be predicated of that which is symbolized.[168]

In place of a clear literal statement that would communicate this knowledge, we must be content with some kind of skillful, symbolic formulation that directs our attention toward the Transcendent and evokes our innate capacity to Realize its meaning.

Wolff explains why strict description is impossible, in conjunction with reporting how concepts unfolded from the mystical state. If the concepts that he employs in this manner comprise a metaphysical system, it must be understood as arising from immediate awareness, as opposed to intellectual construction. Knowledge-through-Identity yields certainty as well as knowledge so long as one remains within the immediately given, prior to formulation.

> As a result of this identity between the I and the content, there is no possibility of a content that is erroneous with respect to the self. Hence, there is a noetic certainty here, without all the problems and doubts that grow out of the trial-and-error method of empiric cognition. There is no question of knowing correctly until one seeks to achieve a formulation through the objective mind. However, the latter process can be more or less in error, and, withal, is never wholly accurate.[169]

Wolff's certainty is based on a higher (that is, transcending form and language) Meaning or Significance Realized in the immediacy of the state itself. It is not an objectively justified confidence that he has articulated an absolutely correct propositional determination. "The SELF is All Knowledge. . . . He who has Realized himself as the SELF is at once Omniscient . . . but the Knowledge is not of the subject-object type nor anything that could be conceived within the cognitive framework of the latter."[170] He suggests the gap between these levels by characterizing the Grand Formless Thought as Pure Significance packed tight "and, below this, a level where I form slowly and painfully in the words of this outer consciousness a small fraction of a fraction of a fraction of a Grand Formless Thought."[171] Consequently, he insists that any metaphysical formulation that is based upon this Knowledge does not share this infallibility and indeed cannot.[172] One may Know the Meaning with absolute certainty, but express it incorrectly. Wolff attests, "I Know with categorical assurance with respect to Meaning alone. I do not know that my formal expression is the most correct possible; nay more, I can find faults in that formal expression myself, but fail to see how it may be substantially improved."[173] In this manner, a mystic "shows himself to be quite fallible and yet Knows *what* he is talking about, however incorrect his expression may be."[174] Even so, if this be a defect it is a necessary one and is shared by all knowledge that is derived by conceptual mediation of an immediately given content.

> The validity of the present thesis rests primarily upon the actuality of the function of introception. Without at least assuming that actuality, the thesis loses its ground as a possibility. Moreover, even if the function is granted to be real, it does not therefore follow that the theoretical statement is necessarily correct throughout. It may be correct as a matter of fundamental principle and yet fall short of accurate interpretation in detail.[175]

Of necessity, the process of philosophical interpretation involves the introduction of an element of falsification, as well as a measure of skill in formulation, and this exposes it to criticism. Thus it is of considerable importance that we determine the nature and limitations of the alleged authority of mystical pronouncements.

Critical Evaluation

An anticipated objection is that the scientific method has exclusive validity for the determination of knowledge and truth and the authority of Realization must, at the very least, be subordinated to it. However, Wolff denies that there is any conflict between knowledge attained through Realization and the discoveries of science.

> I have not found that the Realization invalidates in any way scientific research in any field, but may delimit the value attaching to the conclusions drawn from them, for the Realizations are concerned with the very roots from which the processes of cognition which render an empirical science possible are to be found. . . . determining the range of valuation of any merely empirical determination. . . . [of] those facts that can be experienced through the senses and can be transformed into a logical conceptual system.[176]

He contends that both perception and conception are cognitive possibilities *derived* from this Root Consciousness or Primordial Consciousness, whereas Realization deals with it *directly*. Therefore, Realization is not subject to the criticism of discursive thought, which lies at a distance from its source. He concludes that Realizations "have an epistemic authority in the zones they cover transcending everything coming from the field of sensuous cognition and conceptual determination. This point is fundamental!"[177]

Nevertheless, he maintains that the authoritative nature of Realization does not entirely preclude critical evaluation. He warns that the lessons of critical philosophy require us to ask how we know what we claim to know, and thus we cannot simply accept "the impact of certainty at its face value . . . without falling into error."[178] Strictly speaking, that which is certain in Realization is incommunicable, for any conceptual mediation is already at a distance. Hence, error is unavoidable.[179] This introduces the necessity of epistemological criticism.

Mystical experience and the knowledge affirmed from this base require as neutral a context for investigation as possible. Moreover, the investigator ideally should be personally acquainted with the experience, particularly its noetic aspect. The central criterion for competency to perform such a critique is direct knowledge of the source, which would permit personal verification by means of mystical insight. According to Wolff,

> epistemological criticism is perfectly valid in this philosophy—in fact, it is insisted upon! But no individual who is outside the range of experience of Fundamental Realizations is in a position for their epistemological criticism for he does not know the material. No amount of knowledge based upon experience or epistemological analysis with respect to experience and logic is competent to judge the knowledge value of experience of the type called Realization, Enlightenment or Mystical Unfoldment.[180]

The epistemologist, far more than the psychologist, requires personal acquaintance with the pertinent material because her task involves the evaluation of its significance and value.[181]

The other salient requirement is training in critical philosophy. This implies that only the mystic who is also a critical philosopher is fully qualified to perform a "direct epistemological evaluation of the noetic content of the mystical insight."[182] Naturally, there may be mystics who attain Enlightenment, or Realization, but who are not interested in epistemological reflections on their experiences. Often their overriding purpose is to serve as guides for others. Even here, however, theoretical understanding may be an effective complement to practical method.

Rejection of Hypostatizing

Wolff's epistemological training is invaluable in guarding against making mystical pronouncements as knowledge claims that go beyond their grounding in pure immediacy of awareness itself, in which, he claims, lies our only certainty.[183] He reminds us that "all objects are equal in that their existence is a *seeming* to consciousness and no more."[184] The authority of mysticism does not extend to the interpretations based upon immediate awareness, and therefore metaphysical hypostatization of symbolized content is unjustified. However, he contends that physical hypostatization is equally vulnerable to this criticism.

> The predication of an external physical world, in the last analysis, is grounded only upon psychical immediacy. It thus rests upon the same base as the metaphysical world predicated by the uncritical mystic. The logical analysis that discredits the metaphysical existence, when applied consistently, equally discredits the objective physical world. The fallacy of hypostatization arises just as much in the one instance as the other. Strictly, then, the only thing we know beyond all doubt is immediacy. All else rests upon an "as if" basis. We can act *as if* there were a physical world that serves as the cause of certain immediate psychical states. However, we may also act *as if* a metaphysical reality, such as God, caused other of our immediate psychical states. The logical ground of either position is equally weak. . . . The one indubitably sound position is to repudiate all hypostatization, whether physical or metaphysical. Then we ground ourselves upon pure immediacy. Law becomes the necessary connection between various states of consciousness, both of a more objective and of a more subjective sort. . . . Here, we have retained only that which is strictly necessary and of which we can be justifiably certain. The immediate qualities of conscious states are their own existence; they do not depend upon or hang upon either a physical or metaphysical somewhat beyond themselves. Consciousness is the one self-existent Reality. The goal of religion and practical philosophy is not union with a metaphysical Being, but Realization of the state of consciousness known as "Enlightenment."[185]

Wolff's characterization of the contrast between physical and metaphysical hypostatization is misleading. Both the realist and the idealist may be equally accused of metaphysical hypostatization insofar as they each claim a substantial basis to reality that is not cognitively accessible. Wolff's quest for Truth does not permit unquestioned naturalist or realist assumptions, nor those of the idealist, as a starting point.

The nature of the noetic thesis that Wolff advances neither involves paranormal awareness concerning mundane facts nor the existence of a nonphysical spirit world (perhaps ruled by an awesome deity). Rather, he concludes that the mystic's claim is twofold:

> 1. Negatively, it is a denial of all substantial reality to all worlds, physical or metaphysical, and an equal denial of all selfhood in the same sense.
> 2. Positively, it affirms the indubitable reality of consciousness, and of all its immediately Realizable states. In the 'as if' sense, there may be all kinds of worlds, objective and metaphysical, with their corresponding kinds of beings and selves. This supplies everything that is necessary for innumerable possibilities.[186]

This consideration establishes a philosophical rationale for the three Fundamentals of Wolff's philosophy.

Anything that either mystics or nonmystics assert that goes beyond this bedrock of immediacy cannot share in the epistemological certainty of immediate awareness. Nevertheless, Fundamental Realization provides a grounding for formulations whose authority one may justly accept for oneself. Even though not immune to revision by more profound Realizations, they are more certain than any claims that are otherwise grounded. Thus even within the relative field, mystical penetration may contribute to knowledge.

CONCLUSION

Wolff's firsthand reports and analysis of the noetic value of mystical experience are sufficient to establish the basic interpretation of his noetic thesis. Thus we are entitled to accept his third Fundamental as true: Introception constitutes a third means of cognition not reducible to sense perception or conceptual cognition. He has shown that Introception is a source of nonsensuous, nonconceptual knowledge. We now know that such a form of experience exists, that no predicate strictly applies to it, and the change in base of reference that it produces pervasively alters the significance of all relative knowledge. The noetic character of the "self-flowing thought," the knowledge concerning the negation of all predicates to the state, and the shift in base of reference all qualify as knowledge acquired from this function. Nevertheless, claims that issue forth from its operation do not share the sense of complete assurance that is characteristic of the state itself. Thus the metaphysical statements that Wolff derives from Introception are not the only conceivable formulations.

Finally, as Wolff acknowledges, there is no possible proof (or refutation) of the stronger versions of the noetic thesis solely by using our common sources of knowledge. It calls for a personal verification in the immediacy of consciousness. Whatever insights are Realized through this function are unquestionably authoritative for the mystic personally, but may be shown to have a restricted application if superseded by a more comprehensive Realization. No such authority compels the nonmystic. Even so, the mystic's insights and ideational presentations may provide valuable inspiration and orientation for the nonmystic, not only for understanding and living, but, what is more important, as a catalyst for Realization. These considerations are possible to assess pragmatically. Although there is no possibility of providing coercive proof, and the strict authority of Realization extends only to the individual mystic, it is reasonable to accept Introception as a third cognitive function.

CHAPTER 9

Introceptualism

WOLFF'S PHILOSOPHICAL LEGACY

The published work of Franklin Wolff is becoming regarded as a classic in mystical literature, a unique contribution to modern philosophy, and a source of inspiration to many. The nature and significance of this legacy may be conveyed by sketching the general orientation and essential features of Introceptualism. This will show how it advances a new paradigm for philosophy based upon the role and interpretation of Fundamental Realization. Our discussion of Franklin Wolff and his philosophy has employed a double-edged critical exposition. On the one hand, this not only has clarified the advantages and difficulties of his position, but also it has drawn meaningful comparisons to many established schools of philosophy. On the other hand, the critique has extended to treat these schools, primarily to show where Wolff is able to remedy their deficiencies and limitations.

His formal philosophy is noteworthy for no greater reason than because it is grounded explicitly on his personal realizations. Other things being equal, the more comprehensive and soundly based position is that which takes into account the greater range of immediately experienced indefinables and is formulated by one who is acquainted with them firsthand. This alone is sufficient to justify the inclusion of Introceptualism within the corpus of Western philosophy. Moreover, Wolff's autobiographical reports of his mystical experiences and the process of transformation in consciousness constitute exceptional primary material. Few mystics either are aware of its importance, are willing to share such intimately personal information, or possess sufficient skill to articulate it. Inasmuch as he deliberately makes his descriptions as free from interpretation as possible, when he uses language in a sense that extends beyond literal meaning, we then know that it is due to the transcendent nature of the awareness. His self-reflective psychological account of the realizations, from which his conceptual formulation is derived, is invaluable for both the philosophy and the psychology of religion.

This metapsychological material enables Wolff to draw some basic distinctions and establish several points crucial to an adequate understanding of mysticism. Most centrally, he finds a clear dichotomy between relative and nonrelative consciousness. Ordinary consciousness contrasts diverse objects of awareness within a subject-object structure. Transcendent Consciousness is devoid of multiplicity, either because the field in which objects appear is empty of content or—more profoundly—because the subject-object structure is transcended in a distinctionless unity. Relative consciousness is determinate, inasmuch as conceptual distinctions are able to map a definite manifold, but nonrelative consciousness is a zone of awareness wherein both words and concepts do not, and cannot, strictly apply. Wolff verifies that this essence of Fundamental Realization (that which may be regarded as a common, universal core of mystical experience) is ineffable. However, within its Presence, precipitation of extremely abstract cognitive content within relative consciousness constitutes a zone that he calls "determinate-indeterminate," where language may apply symbolically by using pointer concepts. Tracing the process by which it coalesces from the mystical state, he finds that it arises either spontaneously or as a result of a desire within relative consciousness (in cases where consciousness is bimodal) to grasp the content of such awareness. The explicit distinction between the descriptive and interpretive levels within a mystic's account has hitherto been exceptionally rare in literature available to the West. Yet it is sorely needed for an accurate and comprehensive understanding of the epistemological and metaphysical significance of mystical experience.

The presentation of the evidence from psychic immediacy enables Wolff to ground the two central tenets of his philosophy—namely, that Consciousness has primacy and that mystical experience is a source of knowledge. The foremost feature of his approach is his orientation to consciousness—in particular, Primordial Consciousness. His experientially based discussion of the nature of the self and its relation to objects, and the nature of consciousness, especially Transcendent Consciousness, is a valuable addition to the literature on this topic. In particular, it provides strong confirmation of the nonegological theory of consciousness—that nonrelative consciousness is derived neither from the subject nor the object. Rather, both subject and object depend upon consciousness.

The case for the epistemological—and even methodological—primacy of consciousness is quite plausible, for it may also be argued on more familiar grounds. However, he further wishes to establish the ontological primacy of consciousness, but this remains inconclusive short of personal Introceptive Realization. He asks, "In what degree or sense, if any, is a necessity for thought also a necessity for reality?"[1] but he does not fully answer it. More precisely, it is the referent of Consciousness as Field Consciousness (or Consciousness-without-an-object) that he designates as the most primordial ontological foundation. However, this claim is not amenable to rational demonstration, as he found that Primordial Consciousness transcends all distinction between pairs of opposites—including being/nonbeing. It would therefore also be beyond all relation—including ontological relation! The status of his ontological claim is thus metaphysical in nature and would seem limited by the sort of relativism that he admits in this regard. This would make it symbolic, rather than literal. Still, the use of symbolic language is justified, so long as it is understood as symbolic. Thus the proper interpretation of the ontological primacy of consciousness should emphasize the foundational role of consciousness for anything that appears. Whereas the existence of phenomena (though not their being) depends on consciousness, consciousness (as Consciousness Itself) is self-existent. Also, because nothing can be known apart from consciousness, and the Transcendent ground is known through identity, it cannot be characterized as other than Consciousness. Moreover, consciousness is real, not merely a formal structure. At any rate, Wolff has shown that nothing within the phenomenal realm may be *determined* to have ontological primacy, for the ground that all determination presupposes is consciousness, which is, in itself, nonphenomenal. This establishes its primacy in a crucially pervasive sense.

More convincing is his case for the noetic value of mystical experience. By carefully establishing the noetic thesis in a well-defined, though circumscribed manner, he has shown how mystical experience may be a source of knowledge apart from conception and perception, thereby justifying further metapsychological research. He focuses on the issue of the factual existence and cognitive character of this function, while avoiding ontological presuppositions. As a consequence, one need not subscribe to any specific theory or interpretation to personally validate it as a fact of human experience.

Since this cognitive function inherently transcends both language and concepts, he argues that it only may be expressed symbolically. His aphorisms, derived from Fundamental Realization, will find a unique place in the present store of mystical expression. In addition, as a result of his treatment of the problem of communicating mystical experience, he has revealed a most interesting application pertinent to the philosophy of language.

On the scientific side, he introduces modern mathematical ideas (including a geometrical mandala) as an interpretative, symbolic tool for accessing the mystical. Thus he advances the path of mathematical yoga, which has remained mostly neglected since the time of Pythagoras. Even though Wolff owes a debt to the inspiration of the East and incorporates its spiritual wisdom, he emphasizes that the West must develop a path in harmony with its basic theoretical orientation. He correctly assigns the origin of the Judeo-Christian tradition to the East, albeit the Middle East. Its pervasive influence in the West counts no more against his point than does the observation that, in practice, the unreflective outlook of the typical Westerner is that of rational materialism. Accordingly, bringing to light that advanced mathematics is the way of the indeterminate theoretic continuum, he believes, is a major contribution to the spiritual path indigenous to the West.[2]

Even so, Wolff considers his preeminent legacy to philosophy to be showing how the cognitive function of mystical experience may be a source of metaphysical knowledge. He has established on phenomenological grounds that there is a noetic dimension to mystical experience and that its operation results in an increase in relative knowledge, specifically:

1. the existence of an autonomous mode of thought, apart from any definable content,
2. the existence of a state of consciousness to which only negation of all predicates strictly applies, and
3. a shift in the base of consciousness having a sense of deeper or more profound grounding.

These factors justify the acceptance of Wolff's noetic thesis—mystical experience is a source of knowledge.

However, Wolff acknowledges that the further claim that Introception gives us metaphysical knowledge cannot be demonstrated rationally. It just cannot be proven that the nonphenomenal content of Introception is noumenal—that it can be identified as the *ultimate* reality behind appearances. In popular usage, the term *metaphysics* is ambiguous, in that it may be applied to all but sensory phenomena. Wolff distinguishes among gross phenomena (sense experience), subtle phenomena (psychic awareness of a hidden reality behind gross phenomena), and nonphenomenal awareness of a nonultimate sort.[3] However, he is unable to establish that any of this can be identified, in a positive sense, as noumenal reality—how things ultimately are *in themselves*. Although he personally adopts the view that he has discovered metaphysical knowledge, in his most careful assertions he does no more than maintain the possibility that this nonphenomenal awareness reveals a metaphysical reality—that it "opens the door," as it were. Nevertheless, the possibility of individual Realization makes verification of Introception attainable.

Wolff's version of the mystic's view of reality is that phenomenal objects are real, but not self-existent—that is, phenomena are not inherently substantial. Indeed, they exist only in and for consciousness, which constitutes their substantial ground. This ground is known, by consciousness itself, to transcend the ego, which is itself a phenomenon. In contrast, Pure Consciousness is nonphenomenal and transempirical. Hence, it is not unreasonable to distinguish it from the phenomenal by designating it as *noumenal*.

Wolff guards against metaphysical hypostatization or speculation of any sort, instead proposing a way of understanding mysticism and metaphysics that explicitly avoids dogmatism. First, it is grounded in direct, originary awareness. So it is not merely a product of speculative reasoning, but of an immediately Realized reality. Second, he acknowledges the possibility of diverse Realizations, as well as different expressions for the same Realization. Historically, most Western philosophers have supposed that there is, at most, one correct position concerning ultimate reality and that efforts to construct and establish philosophical systems must strive for demonstration of exclusive validity. Continual failure in practice and the growing awareness of its theoretical impossibility have led to a general skepticism concerning all metaphysics. The metaphysical relativism entailed by the process that Wolff Realized illustrates a third option. He contends that metaphysics grounded on Realization is possible if its expression is not interpreted as a literal description. Rather than continuing the dubious project of trying to discover and formulate a uniquely correct account of ultimate reality, we might instead see our task as involving mutually complementary formulations of an immediate, nonphenomenal (perhaps supraphenomenal, or even noumenal) awareness, each enriching our understanding.

Having been trained in the philosophy of his day, it is not surprising that Wolff initially adopts the Kantian problematic to focus his efforts toward making a meaningful breakthrough to metaphysical knowledge. He even uses the term *Copernican revolution* to characterize his solution to the problem—namely, orienting to Consciousness Itself, rather than either the subject or the object of relative consciousness. However, the radical penetration afforded by Fundamental Realization would ultimately transcend interpretation according to any single conceptual framework. Indeed, not only does he explore the problem of metaphysical knowledge within various conceptual systems, but he also advocates this kind of multifaceted approach. Therefore, it seems odd that he never explicitly questions the adequacy of his own philosophical starting point within the Kantian context, especially considering his avowed metaphysical relativism. He acknowledges that the nature of Realization would imply

1. that any Realization may be superseded by a deeper, more profound Realization, and
2. that there is no uniquely correct formulation for expressing any Fundamental Realization, the root or core of which is intrinsically ineffable.

From his new base, continued reliance upon any single philosophical school, approach, or conceptual system would appear to be insupportable. Introceptualism cannot be contained within Kant's perspective, but constitutes a more comprehensive framework within which critical idealism may be appraised.

Wolff's account also may explain the appeal of idealism and the tenacity with which rationalist philosophers tend to hold their respective conceptual schemes. Independent of content, metaphysical notions grounded in Introception share a sense of unchallengeable authority for whoever Realizes them. If philosophers remain uncritical regarding the nature of the ground, scope of authority, and means of justification for metaphysics, then it would account for the competition between diverse rationalist metaphysical systems. Wolff thus not only would be able to explain the situation that Kant found so embarrassing for philosophy, but also the key to its resolution.

As a counterpoint to metaphysical relativism, Wolff also suggests that whenever two expressions grounded in Fundamental Realization seem incompatible, we should seek an integrating conception. This is actively dynamic, but, if it is to be truly synthetic, the resulting insight and formulation also should be grounded in Realization. In the end, he upholds the legitimacy of both metaphysical pluralism and philosophical synthesis.

The final point deserving attention concerns the necessity of personally experiencing the Introceptive ground from which Wolff's philosophy arises. He insists that it is necessarily unsatisfactory merely to rely upon

> the external study of mysticism by scientific methodology, which is grounded in certain limiting epistemological assumptions. One must personally achieve the inside view of the mystical state, and not be content with conceptual reports supplied by mystics. It is as little possible to derive the state from the conceptual portrayal

> of it as it would be for someone born blind to know the immediate actuality of light from the conceptions related to light.[4]

Perhaps no objective criterion is possible here. Wolff admits that basing his philosophy on an element that is neither available to ordinary consciousness nor discursively derivable from common elements begs the question. Even so, his irrefutable rejoinder is that every diverse, comprehensive world view includes fundamental question-begging presuppositions. In this case, however, the difficulty of attaining mystical experience makes any general or widespread verification of his base exceedingly unlikely. This Thought is autonomous—not under our direction or control—so it is only by deep spiritual introversion that one achieves direct acquaintance with it.

Wolff encourages the reader to verify it personally by means of immediate Realization, but he makes it clear that this cannot be achieved simply by following a formula. Nevertheless, inasmuch as, in the deepest sense, one is already identical with the goal, it is always theoretically possible to Recognize it. Because he is not only a philosopher, but also an Enlightened mystic, his work has value for the mystic and nonmystic alike for developing a fully adequate world view. For the mystic, the greatest value may lie in a more profound and comprehensive conceptual understanding. The nonmystic, however, will more likely appreciate Wolff's practical instruction and guidance for personal attainment. Furthermore, he has imbued his writings, and more noticeably his tapes, with a subtle, yet powerful, sense of the Transcendent ground from which he speaks, and for which the aspirant strives. Consequently, study of his works is a fruitful means of catalyzing the relevant states and experiences.

OROBOROS

Wolff has personally exemplified how mysticism functions as an inexhaustible source of renewal for philosophy and shown the need for philosophy to acknowledge this source. Stephan Tyman gives a succinct account of their interconnection.

> The most germinal forms of insight are mystical, and yet mysticism comes to fruition only by understanding itself philosophi-

> cally, but always in such a way that the philosophical proceeding must accommodate the character of the mystical throughout, by appropriating it to itself. Philosophy conceals the seeds of mysticism, while for its part mysticism flowers into philosophy.[5]

Schools of thought, such as materialism, that eschew this ground give the impression of sterility, as disconnected from real human existence. Other schools (idealism, for example) that clearly manifest this ground may attempt a purely rational justification, either because they fail to grasp its true nature or because they do not know how else to satisfy the requirements of philosophical rigor. In contrast, where expression arises from an acknowledged mystical ground, but remains unreflective and uncritical, as occurs in some forms of religion and spirituality, it falls short of philosophy in the comprehensive sense. Introceptualism authentically strives to be a complete philosophy by acknowledging its mystical roots, encompassing all forms of immediate awareness, and self-critically evaluating the adequacy of its formulation.

Mysticism is intrinsically related to philosophy in its essential sense—that is, as love of wisdom. This involves the contemplation of ultimate questions dealing with knowledge and reality, as well as reflection on our possibilities of being. Mysticism is germane to any approach that is concerned with ways of being human. Wolff found that mystical experience resolves the problem of human existence for the individual who has Realized it and provides an indirect source of wisdom for the nonmystic.

What emerges from the encounter with mysticism in general, and Wolff in particular, is a deep appreciation of the mystery of ultimate reality. From this perspective we must be aware that a statement is true only within its proper zone of application. The mystical intrinsically confronts the limits of whatever framework is used to attempt to understand and evaluate it—and it will not do either to ignore this challenge or to meet it by imposing a Procrustean reductionism within the limitations of an antecedently held outlook or system. Even the law of noncontradiction is found not to apply to That which Transcends our necessarily dualistic structures of interpretation. If there is no ultimate, fixed objective base upon which philosophy may be constructed, then we are thrown back upon our own resources—a mysterious process that involves the endless quest for an ever more profound starting point. Philip Bossert is content to allow that "the understanding that no conceptual system can ever do full justice to the explication of experience should not reduce one to silence and inaction, but rather resolve one to an acceptance of the human condition of being always on the road to understanding and forever in pursuit of truth."[6] This may be symbolized by Oroboros—the serpent swallowing its tail.

At the point where the serpent vanishes, as it were, one *becomes* the Mystery. Wolff invites us to Awaken to it, for he Knows IT to be an infinite source of Wisdom and Value. Then philosophy truly may become a Way of Life. In an unguarded appraisal of the fulfillment of his quest he exclaims: "I succeeded in finding this Goal, and now I KNOW, and can also say to all others: 'IT IS ABSOLUTELY WORTH ANYTHING THAT IT MAY COST, AND IMMEASURABLY MORE.' "[7]

NOTES

CHAPTER 1. A UNIQUE PHILOSOPHER

1. Wolff published his major works and is more popularly known under the name *Franklin Merrell-Wolff*, adopted at the time of his first marriage. However, he authored his academic writing using his original name, *Franklin Fowler Wolff*, to which he later reverted in private life.

2. Because he wishes to provide a fresh understanding, Wolff usually prefers to use the terms *Realization* and *Recognition*, rather than *mysticism* or *mystical experience.* (See Franklin F. Wolff [Franklin Merrell-Wolff], *Experience and Philosophy* (Albany: State University of New York Press, 1994), 377). *Recognition* is essentially synonymous with *Realization*, but it emphasizes the noetic aspect, that is, the Awakening to knowledge one already possesses, but of which one is not yet aware. In contrast to Kant, he also uses *Transcendent* and *Transcendental* interchangeably to characterize any awareness that wholly supersedes the relative structure of ordinary subject-object consciousness. Note that Wolff often capitalizes common terms when used in a mystically Transcendent sense—a practice that the present work follows more sparingly.

3. Franklin F. Wolff, "Religion, Psychology and Philosophy," Tape #23, Side 2, 203–409, 5/31/70. References to Wolff's tapes include the tape number (#), leader color (red [R], green [G] or blue/black [B]), channel recorded (right [R] or left [L]), span on tape counter, date, and location (if other than Lone Pine, California).

4. Franklin F. Wolff, "Is Metaphysical Knowledge Possible?" Tape #39, R/L 825–end, 6/16/75. *Metaphysics* simply means the study of ultimate reality. More completely, "Metaphysics does tend toward the building of systems of ideas; and these ideas either give us some judgment about the nature of reality, or a reason why we must be content with knowing something less than the nature of reality, along with a method for taking hold of whatever can be known" (*Dictionary of Philosophy*, s.v. "metaphysics").

5. Immanuel Kant, *Critique of Pure Reason,* trans. with a preface by Norman Kemp Smith (London: Macmillan, 1929), 268–72.

6. Wolff contrasts consciousness with Consciousness Itself. Consciousness is intrinsically indefinable, yet is easily known by reflecting upon our immediate awareness. Consciousness in the familiar, relative, subject-object sense "is generally viewed as a relationship between a knower and a known and does seem to have a history of arising and disappearing—arising every time we awaken from sleep and disappearing when we return to sleep" (Franklin F. Wolff, "Absolute Consciousness," Part II, Tape #39, R/R 367–785, 9/25/75). By comparison, Consciousness (or Consciousness Itself) refers to a unitary, nonrelative awareness that Transcends dualistic structures.

7. This includes parapsychological phenomena, which, like mystical experience, also appear to transcend space, time, and causality. Cf. H. H. Price, "Some Philosophical Questions About Telepathy and Clairvoyance," *Philosophy* 15 (1940):363–85. Epistemology is the theory of knowledge.

8. Wolff, *Experience and Philosophy*, 319–20; Franklin F. Wolff, "My Philosophy," Part IV, Tape #28, R/R 85–430, 2/14/72; Part VIII, G/L 558–1016, 3/23/72.

9. Id., "Summary of the Five Realizations," Tape #39, G/R 0–391, 7/12/75.

10. A satisfactory preliminary definition of the term *Introception* is "the noetic dimension of mystical experience."

11. Wolff, *Experience and Philosophy,* 422. Provisionally, Transcendent Consciousness is equivalent to nonempirical consciousness (ibid., 425), and Cosmic Consciousness is any Awakening from subject-object consciousness (ibid., 418).

12. Franklin F. Wolff [Franklin Merrell-Wolff], *Transformations in Consciousness,* ed. with a foreword by Ron Leonard (Albany: State University of New York Press, 1995), 174.

13. Wolff never uses this precise formulation. Rather, he expresses his transitional insight as "I am already that which I seek" (Wolff, "Absolute Consciousness," Part II). Even so, the similarities to the Vedāntin inspiration that set its context make the succinct contracted version particularly appropriate.

14. Id., "My Philosophy," Parts IV, VIII.

15. The term *experience* must be used in an extended sense when applied to mystical consciousness, but Wolff prefers to avoid the term whenever possible in this regard. Instead, he introduces the word *imperience* to indicate the immediate nonperceptual, nonconceptual content of nonrelative consciousness. For convenience, we shall retain the more familiar term here, but the reader must remain alert for contexts where the transcendent sense is intended. He also prefers to contrast the term *relative consciousness* with *nonrelative consciousness,* rather than *absolute consciousness,* to avoid implying that there is a final limit to mystical penetration.

16. Wolff, "Realizations."

17. Ibid.

18. Franklin F. Wolff, "The Power of the Will," Tape #34, R/L 0–140, 9/18/73. *Sādhana* is the effort of the aspirant by various means to attain Enlightenment or Liberation.

19. Id., *Experience and Philosophy,* 317.

20. Id., *Transformations in Consciousness,* 149–50.

21. Id., *Experience and Philosophy,* 317. Mystics commonly report that the most profound depths of their experience reveals an unfathomable mystery beyond all capacities of reason. In any case, it is not reasonable to insist that reality ultimately must be entirely, or fundamentally, rational. The alternative need not be viewing this domain as irrational, which would imply that it could be characterized as opposing reason. Where all duality is experientially transcended, no term strictly applies—even the more precise *nonrational.*

22. Id., *Transformations in Consciousness,* Part I.

23. There is a sharp distinction between Wolff's writings before and after his Enlightenment. Prior to 7 August 1936 he had published both *Yoga* and *Re-Embodiment* (Franklin F. Wolff [Yogagñani] (San Fernando: Merrell-Wolff Pub. Co., Printed by Skelton Pub. Co., 1930). The pseudonym *Yogagñani* was bestowed upon him by Swami Hari Rama, a spiritual teacher with whom he at one time had a close association.) His early works, though knowledgeable and erudite, lack the inspiration and sense of authority so obviously manifest subsequent to his breakthrough.

During the following decade Wolff produced his seminal writings: Franklin F. Wolff [Franklin Merrell-Wolff], *Pathways Through to Space* (New York: Richard R. Smith, 1944), his autobiographical account of personal transformation, and his *opus magnum, The Philosophy of Consciousness Without an Object.* The first volume, Franklin F. Wolff [Franklin Merrell-Wolff], *The*

Philosophy of Consciousness Without an Object (New York: Julian Press, 1973), was recently combined with *Pathways Through to Space* and republished as *Experience and Philosophy.* The second volume, Franklin F. Wolff [Franklin Merrell-Wolff], *Introceptualism* (Phoenix: Phoenix Philosophical Press, 1975), was republished recently as *Transformations in Consciousness.* Wolff's sole journal article is "Concept, Percept and Reality" (Franklin F. Wolff, *Philosophical Review* 48 [1939]:398–414).

Following this brief, prolific period, Wolff virtually ceased formal writing, other than articles intended for private circulation among his associates and followers. From 1951 he preferred to record his lectures and thoughts via magnetic tape. All unpublished material, including correspondence, resides in the Wolff Archives, administered by Doroethy Leonard, Phoenix Philosophical Press, P.O. Box 32014, Phoenix, AZ 85064.

24. He calls his philosophy "Introceptualism" to emphasize that it is grounded in Introception.

CHAPTER 2. FRANKLIN WOLFF: LIFE AND INFLUENCES

1. See, for example, Wolff's discussions concerning *Nirvāṇa* in *Experience and Philosophy* (370–71, 402, 421–22) and "Concept, Percept and Reality" (404–14).

2. See Franklin F. Wolff, "Convention: Autobiographical Material," Tape Z_0, B/L 471–end, 7/6/78). His granddaughter Doroethy Leonard is presently completing his detailed biography.

3. Id., *Experience and Philosophy*, 90. In particular, he found no one able to answer his penetrating questions to his satisfaction.

4. Ibid., 252.

5. Franklin F. Wolff, "The Yoga of Mathematics," Tape #37, G/L 365–568, 8/15/74.

6. Id., *Experience and Philosophy*, 90.

7. Ibid.

8. Ibid., 124–26.

9. Ibid., 252–53.

10. Ibid., 90–91.

11. An *āśrama* (ashram) is a place of religious retreat. People in the area refer to this building as the "monastery" or the "stone house."

12. See the videotaped documentaries: "The Philosopher's Stone" (Faustin Bray, 1980), "Franklin Merrell-Wolff: Ashrama and Interview" (Joel Morwood, 1983), and "Ashrama Man" (Mammoth TV, 1983).

13. Paul Deussen, *The System of the Vedānta,* trans. Charles Johnson (Chicago: Open Court Pub. Co., 1912). This is Paul Deussen's philosophical interpretation of the Vedānta based on Śaṃkara's commentaries on the *Brahmasụtras.*

14. *Thao-sophia* [Gk] = divine wisdom. Although our necessarily sparse treatment cannot hope to do justice to the intricacy and complexity of the Theosophical viewpoint, its role in Wolff's development should not be ignored.

15. Wolff, *Experience and Philosophy,* 112–13.

16. Helena Petrovna Blavatsky, *The Secret Doctrine* (New York: Theosophical Society, 1888), vii–viii. Her major writings, which also include *Isis Unveiled,* 2 vols. (New York: J. W. Boulton, 1877), comprise the initial literary base for this movement.

17. Franklin F. Wolff, "Is Theosophy Authentic?" (Phoenix: n.p., 1975), 4. It is not possible to demonstrate that all religion is ultimately rooted in a common source. Even so, the religious processes of synthesis, integration, and unification accord well with the etymology of the terms *religion* (to bind back) and *yoga* (yoke or union). In practice, Theosophy obscures the focus on mystical realization by its preoccupation with paranormal phenomena.

18. Wolff speculates that the reason for this may be that seven is the number of combinations of three elements taken singly, in pairs, and all together (Franklin F. Wolff, "The Tri-kāya," Part I, Tape #31, G/L 0–140, 6/7/71).

19. Id., "Convention: Biographical Material." Wolff advances this general warning against uncritical belief without providing criteria for judging the authenticity of the Theosophical movement as a whole—that is, as springing forth from actual realizations. He defends Blavatsky at length from the charge that her work is fraudulent, but declines to address the more critical problem of determining the truth of the statements found there (Franklin F. Wolff, "Is the Theosophia Authentic?" Tape Z_2, R/L 574–981, 11/13/78).

20. Franklin F. Wolff, "The First Fundamental," Tape Z_4, 0–345, 3/13/79.

21. *Encyclopedia of Philosophy,* s.v. "Pythagoras and Pythagoreanism," by W. K. C. Guthrie.

22. W. K. C. Guthrie, *The History of Greek Philosophy* (Cambridge: University Press, 1962), 1:217.

23. Ibid., 253. As might be expected, no independent corroboration is presently available.

24. Robert S. Brumbaugh, *The Philosophers of Greece* (New York: Thomas Y. Croswell Co., 1964), 42.

25. Ibid.

26. Guthrie, *History*, 258.

27. Ibid., 317.

28. Ibid., 225.

29. Ibid., 213.

30. Id., *Pythagoreanism*, 38.

31. Id., *History*, 259.

32. Id., *Pythagoreanism*, 38.

33. Franklin F. Wolff, *"Pythagoras,"* Tape Z_7, B/R 0–end, 10/24/80.

34. This revolution in mathematical demonstration, which formerly was done empirically (John Mansley Robinson, *An Introduction to Early Greek Philosophy* [Boston: Houghlin-Mifflin, 1968], 67), constitutes a far greater contribution than the Pythagorean theorem, for which he is better known (ibid., 3). Guthrie demurs, claiming that the first Pythagorean we know with confidence to have made a mathematical contribution was Archytas. Furthermore, the equation for the Pythagorean theorem

$$h^2 = a^2 + b^2$$

where *a* and *b* are the legs of a right triangle having *h* as its hypotenuse, was found on a Babylonian tablet dated from the time of Hamurabi (Guthrie, *History*, 117–18). Similarly, Kirk and Raven contend that "there is no reliable evidence whatever concerning the nature of Pythagoras's scientific teaching: any reconstruction must be conjectural" (G. S. Kirk and J. E. Raven, *The Pre-Socratics* [Cambridge: University Press, 1957], 228).

35. Brumbaugh, 33.

36. Robinson, 68.

37. Wolff, "Pythagoras."

38. Ibid.

39. Id., "Yoga of Mathematics."

40. Charles Musès, "Altering States of Consciousness by Mathematics, with Applications to Education," *Journal for the Study of Consciousness* 3, (January–June 1970):43. A personal handwritten note by Musès on Wolff's copy of one of these booklets indicates that they were in correspondence, but there is no evidence that they ever actually met.

41. Ibid., 44.

42. Ibid., 46–47.

43. Ibid., 44.

44. Wolff, "Pythagoras."

45. Ibid.

46. Wolff, "Yoga of Mathematics."

47. Charles Musès, "Working with the Hypernumber Idea," *Consciousness and Reality*, ed. Charles Musès and Arthur M. Young (New York: Avon, 1974), 448.

48. Ibid., 453–54.

49. Id., in Arthur Paul, "The Possible Meaning of Imaginary Numbers," *Consciousness and Reality*, 192n.

50. Ibid.

51. The Pythagoreans were known to worship Apollo, the god who symbolized the Logos (Guthrie, *History*, 205); he was also the god of moderation (id., "Pythagoreanism," 37).

52. Wolff, *Experience and Philosophy*, 86.

53. Id., *Transformations in Consciousness*, 87.

54. Id., *Experience and Philosophy*, 251.

55. Ibid., 419.

56. Rationalism uses pure reason to discover the innate ideas we possess a priori, which are believed to correspond to reality, or from which it may be deduced. Empiricism opposes this view with the belief that our minds are originally empty and passive, so all we can know of reality comes from sense experience.

57. Wolff, *Transformations in Consciousness*, 87.

58. Ibid., 86.

59. Ibid., 137; *Experience and Philosophy*, 317.

60. Id., *Experience and Philosophy*, 317.

61. Id., *Transformations in Consciousness*, 161.

62. Ibid., 137.

63. Id., *Experience and Philosophy*, 45.

64. Ibid., 33. *Manas* may be taken to mean intelligence or the faculty of thinking or reasoning, as well as the sense mind.

65. Ibid., 86.

66. Ibid., 33. For Kant, *apperception* means the implicit unity of self-consciousness transcending the multiplicity of its contents.

67. Ibid., 375.

68. Ibid., 109.

69. Id., *Transformations in Consciousness*, 86.

70. Ibid., 119.

71. Ibid., 107–8.

72. Ibid., 124–25.

73. Ibid., 94–96. Wolff relates this distinction to the difference between *nous* and *logos* in Greek thought, simplifying the essential meaning of each.

74. Ibid., 95.

75. Ibid.

76. Ibid., 5–7.

77. Ibid., 103–5.

78. Id., *Experience and Philosophy*, 14.

79. Ibid., 32.

80. Id., *Transformations in Consciousness*, 84.

81. Swami Nikhilānanda, *The Upanishads*, trans. and ed. with a preface, general introduction, individual introduction, notes, expositions, and commentaries by Śrī Śaṃkarācārya, 4 vols. (New York: Bonanza Books,

1949; repr. ed. London: Allen & Unwin, 1963; abridged ed. New York: Harper & Row, 1963), 22. The title *Śrī* honors one of high spiritual attainment, whereas the suffix *ācārya* designates a spiritual teacher.

82. Eliot Deutsch, *Advaita Vedānta* (Honolulu: East West Center Press, 1969; pb. repr., University Press of Hawaii, 1973), 3.

83. Nikhilānanda, 21.

84. Wolff, *Experience and Philosophy*, 415.

85. Deutsch, *Advaita Vedānta*, 3.

86. Wolff, *Transformations in Consciousness*, 242.

87. Id., *Yoga*, 146.

88. Id., *Transformations in Consciousness*, 251 (originally taken from Śaṃkara's *Ātmanātma Viveka* [*Discrimination of Self and Not-Self*]).

89. Ibid., 242.

90. Nikhilānanda, 25.

91. Ibid., 165. The three ordinary states of consciousness are waking consciousness, dreaming, and dreamless sleep. *Turīya* is the fourth state, which is Pure Consciousness Itself, or Primordial Consciousness.

92. Ibid., 25.

93. Wolff, *Transformations in Consciousness*, 126.

94. Ramlal Singh, "An Advaitic Emendation of Kant: A Study in Comparative Metaphysics," *Indian Philosophical Quarterly* 6 (October 1978): 175–83. He is referring to A. C. Mukerji, *The Nature of the Self*, 2nd ed. (Allahabad: Indian Press, 1943), 367.

95. Wolff, *Transformations in Consciousness*, 243.

96. Ibid.

97. Ramakant Sinari, "The Phenomenological Attitude in the Śaṃkara Vedānta," *Philosophy East and West* 22 (July 1972):281–90.

98. Wolff, *Transformations in Consciousness*, 244.

99. Franklin F. Wolff, "A Primitive View of the World," Tape Z_2, R/R 0–291, 11/13/78.

100. Franklin F. Wolff, "The Sense in Which I Am a Buddhist," Tape #41, R/R 813–1038, 11/8/76.

101. Singh, 181–82.

102. Wolff, *Experience and Philosophy,* 253–54.

103. Ibid., 3. During the preceding three weeks Wolff had been intensely reading and meditating upon *The System of the Vedānta,* for he sensed that Śaṃkara held the vital key to the goal that he sought.

104. Ibid., 254.

105. Ibid., 14.

106. Ibid., 3.

107. Franklin F. Wolff, "Śaṃkara's Cosmology," Tape #41, B/R 468–942, 9/22/76.

108. Ibid.

109. Id., "Buddhist."

110. Id., *Experience and Philosophy,* 298.

111. Id., *Transformations in Consciousness,* 84.

112. Id., "Buddhist."

113. Satprem, *The Adventure of Consciousness* (Pondicherry: Sri Aurobindo Ashram Press, 1968), 171–74.

114. Franklin F. Wolff, "The Yoga of Knowledge," Part I, Tape #26, Side 1, 487–end, 9/10/70. Wolff reveals his synthetic approach to philosophy, especially schools grounded in direct Realization, by mediating between Aurobindo and Śaṃkara ("Aurobindo and Śaṃkara: The Reconciliation of Universal Realism and Universal Illusionism" [Flagstaff: n.p., 1968]; "Further Thoughts on the Relation of Buddhism, Vedānta and Śrī Aurobindo," Part IV, Tape #33, G/R 246–642, 4/14/71).

115. F. S. C. Northrop, *The Meeting of East and West* (New York: Macmillan, 1947).

116. Wolff, "Pythagoras."

117. Id., *Experience and Philosophy,* 229; Franklin F. Wolff, "My Philosophy," Part III, Tape #28, G/R 900–end, 2/14/72. Wolff would caution that one must determine for oneself the means that are appropriate and effective, but advises beginning from a sound ethical base.

118. Ibid., 232.

CHAPTER 3. REALIZATION

1. Wolff, "My Philosophy," Part IV.

2. Ibid., Part VIII.

3. Id., *Experience and Philosophy*, 220. There is something inherently arbitrary about a conceptual system invented apart from experience, as is true of speculative metaphysics. Because correspondence with any experienced reality would be fortuitous in such cases, logical coherence would seem to be the more appropriate criterion for the truth of claims within a speculative system. However, the set of all negations of these propositions would be equally consistent, so the logical compatibility of a set of statements does not, by itself, tell us anything about reality.

4. Id., "My Philosophy," Part IV.

5. Ibid., 258.

6. Id., "Realizations."

7. Id., "My Philosophy," Part IV.

8. Id., *Experience and Philosophy*, 249–50.

9. Ibid., 293–94n. 7.

10. Wolff's first realization occurred around 1922 (ibid., 5, 257).

11. Ibid., 257.

12. Ibid.

13. Ibid., 174.

14. Ibid., 419.

15. Ibid., 416.

16. Id., "Realizations."

17. Id., "My Philosophy," Part IV.

18. Id., "Realizations."

19. Id., *Experience and Philosophy*, 25.

20. Ibid., 291n. 3.

21. Ibid., 258.

22. Ibid., 291n. 3; Id., "My Philosophy," Part IV.

23. Id., *Experience and Philosophy*, 258.

24. Ibid.

25. Ibid., 25.

26. Ibid., 293n. 3.

27. Ibid., 258.

28. Ibid., 26.

29. Ibid., 258.

30. Ibid., 258–59.

31. Ibid., 25.

32. Ibid., 259.

33. Ibid., 291n. 3.

34. Ibid., 25. The Current is experienced as a blissful, psychophysical, directionless flux that pervades one's entire being.

35. Ibid., 26, 259. The catalyst in this case seems to have been the repeated reading of the words of Ramana Maharshi, reported in Paul Brunton, *A Search in Secret India* (New York: Dutton & Co., 1935), cited in Wolff, "My Philosophy," Part IV.

36. Id., *Experience and Philosophy*, 5.

37. Ibid., 26.

38. Ibid., 259.

39. Ibid., 26.

40. Ibid., 259.

41. Ibid.

42. Id., "My Philosophy," Part IV.

43. Id., *Experience and Philosophy*, 5.

44. Ibid., 259.

45. Ibid., 26.

46. Ibid. This was true even though the listener might not understand the concepts that he used, or their connection.

47. Ibid., 260.

48. Franklin F. Wolff, *Mathematics, Philosophy and Yoga*, 59.

49. Id., *Experience and Philosophy*, 261.

50. In conversation, Wolff explained that the significance of an experience only becomes clarified much later.

51. Id., *Mathematics, Philosophy and Yoga*, 59.

52. Id., "My Philosophy," Part V, R/R 445–940, 2/14/72.

53. Id., *Experience and Philosophy*, 4.

54. Ibid., 261–62.

55. Id., *Transformations in Consciousness*, 189.

56. Id., "My Philosophy," Part IV.

57. Ibid.

58. Id., *Experience and Philosophy*, 261.

59. Ibid., 262–63.

60. Ibid., 292–93n. 6.

61. Id., "My Philosophy," Part V.

62. *Book of Golden Precepts*, trans. with annotation by H. P. Blavatsky (Los Angeles: Theosophy Co., 1928), 61.

63. Wolff, *Experience and Philosophy*, 263.

64. Ibid.

65. Id., "My Philosophy," Part VIII.

66. Id., *Experience and Philosophy*, 294n. 9.

67. Ibid.

68. Id., "Absolute Consciousness," Part II.

69. Id., "My Philosophy," Part IV.

70. Id., *Experience and Philosophy*, 263. He suggests that this is the true meaning of *the Void.*

71. Id., "Realizations."

72. Ibid.

73. Id., *Experience and Philosophy*, 263.

74. Id., "My Philosophy," Part VII, G/L 133–558, 2/14/72.

75. Id., *Experience and Philosophy*, 264.

76. Id., "My Philosophy," Part VII.

77. For Wolff, enantiodromia is the psychological law "that any psychical state tends to be transformed into its opposite" (id., *Experience and Philosophy*, 368).

78. Ibid., 264.

79. Ibid., 265.

80. Ibid.

81. Id., "My Philosophy," Part VII, G/L 133–558, 8/6/71.

82. Ibid.

83. Ibid.

84. Id., *Experience and Philosophy*, 265. It is analogous to the way that nuclear fluid (a mass of atoms having no space between their nuclei) may be considered the compacted essence of matter. Although Wolff reports that it made available the entire knowledge he had gained in life, it far transcends the domain of the merely personal.

85. Ibid. Mystics often use the juxtaposition of opposites to indicate the nature of their experiences, which transcends the dualities of concept and language.

86. Id., "My Philosophy," Part VII. This has an analogous significance to the role played by base of reference in mathematics and the shift from the Ptolemaic (geocentric) to the Copernican (heliocentric) base of reference in astronomy.

87. Ibid.

88. Ibid.

89. Id., *Experience and Philosophy*, 272. Here, *experience* must be understood in the narrow, empirical sense. He also found a curious connection with the experienced Transcendent Life Force, which either spawned such concepts or paralleled their birth.

90. Ibid., 273.

91. Id., "My Philosophy," Part VII.

92. Ibid.

93. Wolff's use of the term *God* clearly avoids the popular connotation of a deity having a definable personality and existing separate from the physical universe. He contends that "the real and genuine reference here is to a Power beyond the individual and self-conscious personal self that is realized as operative . . . something quite real though very imperfectly understood by the larger number of mystics" (id., *Experience and Philosophy*, 245). Those such as Wolff, whose intellect gives sufficient control to navigate the Transcendent realm as well as our common empirical domain, may omit the term *God* from their vocabulary.

94. Ibid., 268.

95. Id., "My Philosophy," Part VII.

96. Id., *Experience and Philosophy*, 266.

97. Ibid. Wolff does not clearly distinguish between two separate considerations here. Guilt (or sin) is a moral notion, as well as an affective state. By comparison, karma is an impersonal compensatory law of action to which one is bound equally by good, evil or indifferent actions, the awareness of which may be theoretical rather than affective. Thus Wolff's stipulated rationale for the affective change that he experienced, using a schema involving the transcendence of this law, appears to be an interpretive element.

98. Id., *Experience and Philosophy*, 266.

99. Ibid., 7.

100. Ibid., 267.

101. Ibid., 277–78. Wolff was concerned that the *Nirvāṇic* state might be so attractive that he would permanently lose contact with relative consciousness (and hence all awareness of the world).

102. Ibid., 267.

103. Id., "My Philosophy," Part VII.

104. Id., *Experience and Philosophy*, 21.

105. Ibid., 269.

106. Ibid., 20.

107. Ibid., 268.

108. Ibid., 271.

109. Id., "My Philosophy," Part VII.

110. Id., *Experience and Philosophy*, 271.

111. Ibid., 276.

112. Id., "My Philosophy," Part VIII.

113. Id., *Experience and Philosophy*, 275.

114. Ibid., 274.

115. Ibid., 276.

116. Ibid., 277.

117. Ibid.

118. Ibid.

119. Ibid., 278.

120. Ibid.

121. Ibid., 219.

122. Ibid., 280–81.

123. Ibid., 280.

124. Ibid.

125. Franklin F. Wolff, "On the High Indifference," Tape #39, G/L 357–725, 4/30/75.

126. Id., "My Philosophy," Part XI, Tape #28, R/L 561–1091, 4/17/72.

127. Id., *Experience and Philosophy*, 100.

128. Ibid., 280.

129. Ibid., 100.

130. Id., "My Philosophy," Part XI.

131. Sherifa's records, Wolff Archives.

132. Franklin F. Wolff, "Questing" (Lone Pine: n.p., 1968).

133. Id., "High Indifference."

134. Id., "My Philosophy," Part XI.

135. Id., *Experience and Philosophy*, 100.

136. Ibid., 281.

137. Ibid., 101.

138. Ibid., 281.

139. Ibid., 299n. 24.

140. Ibid., 101.

141. Ibid., 281.

142. Ibid., 102, 281.

143. Ibid., 282.

144. Ibid., 283.

145. Ibid., 103.

146. Ibid., 221.

147. Ibid., 282.

148. Id., "High Indifference."

149. Id., *Experience and Philosophy*, 103.

150. Id., "High Indifference."

151. Id., *Experience and Philosophy*, 281–82.

152. Ibid., 105.

153. Ibid.

154. Id., "My Philosophy," Part VII.

155. Id., *Experience and Philosophy*, 103.

156. Ibid., 283.

157. Ibid.

158. Ibid., 284.

159. Ibid., 106, 288.

160. Ibid., 283.

161. Ibid., 285.

162. Ibid., 286.

163. Ibid., 284. The "sense of objectivity" contrasts markedly to the subjective penetration that characterized his preceding Recognition.

164. Ibid.

165. Ibid.

166. Id., "High Indifference."

167. Id., *Experience and Philosophy*, 286.

168. Ibid.

169. Ibid., 106.

170. Ibid., 287.

171. Ibid., 106.

172. Ibid., 288.

173. Ibid., 106.

174. Ibid., 288.

175. Id., "My Philosophy," Part XI.

176. Id., "High Indifference."

177. Ibid.

178. Ibid.

179. Ibid.

180. Id., "Absolute Consciousness," Part II.

181. Id., *Experience and Philosophy*, 99–100.

182. Ibid., 288.

183. Ibid., 289.

184. Ibid.

185. Ibid.

186. Ibid.

187. Ibid., 290.

188. Ibid.

189. Id., "High Indifference."

190. Id., "Realizations."

191. Ibid.

CHAPTER 4. MYSTICISM AND PHILOSOPHY

1. *Encyclopedia of Philosophy,* s.v. "Mysticism, History of," by Ninian Smart.

2. *Encyclopedia of Philosophy,* s.v. "Mysticism, Nature and Assessment of," by Ronald W. Hepburn.

3. William James, *The Varieties of Religious Experience* (New York: Modern Library, 1902).

4. Walter T. Stace, *Mysticism and Philosophy* (London: Macmillan & Co., 1960).

5. James T. Horne, *Beyond Mysticism* (Waterloo: Wilfrid Laurier Press, 1978).

6. Leon Rosenstein, "Mysticism as Preontology: A Note on the Heideggerian Connection," *Philosophy and Phenomenological Research* 39 (September 1978):63–64.

7. Nils Bjorn Kvastad, "Philosophical Problems of Mysticism," *International Philosophical Quarterly* 13 (1973):192.

8. Stace, 44.

9. Ibid., 46.

10. Ibid., 131–32. Stace hedges by saying that mystics *allege* that it is ineffable, but gives no reason to discount this particular feature of their reports.

11. Ibid., 110.

12. Ibid.

13. Ibid., 79.

14. Ibid., 132–33.

15. Ibid., 125.

16. William Wainwright, *Mysticism* (Madison: University of Wisconsin Press, 1981), 38.

17. This is perhaps the best known example, but by no means is it unique. The Tibetan *dzogchen* tradition has more ancient roots, but all rely upon our inherent ground of Primordial Consciousness.

18. There are stories of Indian yogis who do not return to mundane existence from deep states of meditation, allowing their bodies to die eventually in their caves.

19. Tradition records that the Buddha attained his Enlightenment under the bodhi tree while engaged in the meditative technique of breath awareness.

20. Henri Bergson, *The Two Sources of Morality and Religion*, trans. R. Aundra and C. Cloudesley Brereton with the assistance of W. Horsfall Carter (Garden City, NY: Doubleday, 1954), 226–27. Illustrative examples of cultural prejudice are taken from Christianity because they are most familiar—not because other traditions are immune to this sort of conditioning.

21. R. C. Zaehner, *Mysticism Sacred and Profane* (Oxford: Clarendon Press, 1957).

22. Martin C. D'Arcy, *The Meeting of Love and Knowledge* (London: Allen & Unwin, 1958), 88–89.

23. Wainwright, *Mysticism*, 81–82. He believes that these criteria resemble those that we use to judge whether the claims derived from ordinary experience are veridical (William Wainwright, "Mysticism and Sense Perception," *Religious Studies* 9 [September 1973]:262). Be that as it may, it is ironic that strict application of these standards would justify the rejection of Jesus by the Jews.

24. Steven Katz, ed., *Mysticism and Philosophical Analysis* (New York: Oxford University Press, 1978), 26.

25. Wolff, *Experience and Philosophy*, 407.

26. Horne, 17–18.

27. Franklin F. Wolff, "The Unconscious," Tape #34, R/R 50–322, 12/30/73; also see Franklin F. Wolff, "Further Thoughts on the Relation of Buddhism and Vedānta," Part I, Tape #33, R/L 232–624, 4/14/71.

28. Id., *Experience and Philosophy*, 298n. 21.

29. The mystic uses language in other ways as well, which we shall discuss in the following chapter.

30. Evelyn Underhill, *Mysticism* (New York: Meridian, 1955).

31. William Earle, "Phenomenology of Mysticism," *Monist* 59 (1976): 519–31.

32. Ninian Smart, "The Purification of Consciousness and the Negative Path," *Mysticism and Religious Traditions*, ed. Steven Katz (Oxford: Oxford University Press, 1983), 128n. 1.

33. Wolff, *Experience and Philosophy*, 250.

34. Stace, 134–35. Persuasive as the mystics' general acceptance of the authenticity of each others' accounts may be, this does not and cannot show that their claims are true.

35. *Dictionary of Philosophy and Religion: Eastern and Western Thought,* ed. William L. Reese (New Jersey: Humanities Press, 1980), s.v. "subject," "object."

36. Stace, 147.

37. Ibid.

38. The term *metaphilosophy* strictly refers to that branch of philosophy that inquires into the nature of philosophy itself, without implying that it has access to some privileged viewpoint from which to determine an answer.

39. Franklin F. Wolff, "Religion, Psychology and Philosophy," Tape #23, 203–409, 5/31/70.

40. Id., *Experience and Philosophy,* 319.

41. Ibid., 241.

42. Noteworthy exceptions are gaining credibility in the scientific community. John Lilly's work with dolphins involved intimate interaction, and his exploration of "inner space" was intensely personal (John C. Lilly, *The Center of the Cyclone* [New York: Julian Press, 1972]). Also, the notion of the scientist as participant is replacing the understanding of her role as observer (See Michael Talbot, *Mysticism and the New Physics* [New York; Bantam Books, 1981]).

43. Kenneth Schmitz, "Philosophy of Religion and the Redefinition of Philosophy," *Man and World* 3 (May 1970):63. Reprinted with kind permission from Kluwer Academic Publishers.

44. Ibid., 79.

45. Ibid., 81.

46. Eliot Deutsch, *On Truth* (Honolulu: University Press of Hawaii, 1979), 62.

47. Schmitz, 84.

48. Ibid., 64–65.

49. Wolff, *Experience and Philosophy,* 241.

50. Ian Watson, "The Anti-Wisdom of Modern Philosophy: A Passing Note," *Studies in Comparative Religion* 6 (1972):221–24.

51. Ibid., 222. Watson claims that the resulting neglect of wisdom in Western philosophy must result in humanities subjects losing their viability. As evidence, he cites the fact that there are no departments of philosophy in any of the newer African universities nor in those recently reopened in China. Fortunately, this is balanced by a countertrend in established Western universities, where there is growing interest in mysticism and acceptance of its legitimacy as a subject for research. This is partly due to an increase in the influence of Eastern scholars, but also is the fruit of the seeds sown by James, Wittgenstein, Heidegger, Stace, and others.

52. Nicholas Maxwell, *From Knowledge to Wisdom* (Oxford: Basil Blackwell, 1984).

53. Rosenstein, 57.

54. Ibid., 64.

55. Ibid., 73. We must be careful to avoid unbalancing the philosophy-religion equilibrium in either direction. Because of his prior commitment, Wolff resolved this issue by returning to the world from Fundamental Realization to philosophize *from* this mystical ground.

56. Neal Grossman, "Consciousness Expansion: A New Paradigm for Philosophy," *Metaphilosophy* 5 (October 1974):345. Paradigms are the set of presuppositions that form the context for inquiry. Grossman credits Thomas Kuhn (*The Structure of Scientific Revolutions* [Chicago: University of Chicago Press, 1962]) with the introduction of the notion of a paradigm in a scientific context, and he implies that it may be adapted to philosophy. However, the notion is open to easy misinterpretation. Daniel Goldman Cedarbaum points out that Kuhn used the term in twenty-one different ways ("Paradigms," *Studies in the History of Philosophy of Science* 14 [1983]:174).

57. Grossman, 346–47.

58. Ibid., 345.

59. Ch'ing Yuan, in Alan Watts, *The Way of Zen* (New York: Mentor Books, 1959), 127, quoted in H. Gene Blocker, "The Language of Mysticism," *Monist* 59 (1976):560.

60. Blocker, 561.

61. Louis Nordstrom, "Mysticism without Transcendence: Reflections on Liberation and Emptiness," *Philosophy East and West* 31 (January 1981):95.

62. Ibid.

63. John Visvader, "The Use of Paradox in Uroboric Philosophies," *Philosophy East and West* 28 (October 1978):455.

64. Ibid.

65. Whereas there is a similarity between the radical empiricism of David Hume and that of Buddhism, Wolff contends that the former is oriented to a manifold of experience, the latter to the notion of a continuum—more precisely, a definite aesthetic continuum. In contrast to both, Wolff orients to the indeterminate theoretic continuum (Wolff, "On Paradox").

66. Franklin F. Wolff, "Tantra and Zen," 5 parts, Tape #35, G/R 300–end, Tape #37, G/L 0–364, June–July 1974.

67. Franklin F. Wolff, "On the Limits of Clear Definition: Human Nature and Conceptuality," Tape #38, R/R 321–630, 3/1/75.

68. Wolff, *Experience and Philosophy*, 383–84.

69. Ibid., 359.

70. Ibid., 86–87, 358.

71. Id., "Concept, Percept and Reality," 403.

72. Ibid., 399.

73. Id., *Experience and Philosophy*, 290.

74. The terms *indefinable* and *ineffable* are virtually interchangeable, but Wolff uses the former as a substantive noun in this context. This allows him to treat preconceptual material objectively, even though some of it (consciousness, for example) is not intrinsically an object or objects.

75. Wolff, *Experience and Philosophy*, 290.

76. Ibid., 402.

77. Id., *Transformations in Consciousness*, 12.

78. Id., "Concept, Percept and Reality," 401.

79. Ibid., 400.

80. C. O. Evans, *The Subject of Consciousness* (London: George Allen & Unwin, 1970), 35, citing *The Philosophy of C. D. Broad,* ed. A. Schillp (New York: Tudor Pub. Co., 1959), 814.

81. Wolff, *Experience and Philosophy,* 246.

82. Ibid.

83. Ibid.

84. We are assuming that truth means that which corresponds to reality, not merely that a statement's truth depends solely on logical compatibility with other statements (the coherence theory).

85. Lawrence LeShan cites the rejection of paranormal phenomena and their unsettling implications as a noteworthy phenomenon in need of study (Lawrence LeShan, "On the Non-Acceptance of the Paranormal," *International Journal of Parapsychology* 8 (Summer 1966):367–86; reprinted in Lawrence LeShan, *The Medium, the Mystic, and the Physicist* (New York: Viking Press, 1974), Appendix A, 197–217).

86. Wolff, "Concept, Percept and Reality," 402–3.

87. Id., *Experience and Philosophy,* 348.

88. Id., *Transformations in Consciousness,* 99.

CHAPTER 5. MYSTICAL LANGUAGE

1. Wolff, *Experience and Philosophy,* 194.

2. Id., "The Unconscious."

3. Id., *Experience and Philosophy,* 309–14.

4. Id., *Transformations in Consciousness,* 126–27.

5. A mandala is a somewhat symmetrical design organized around an implied central point, either generated spontaneously by an individual undergoing psychological transformation and integration or intentionally produced as an aid for centering and integrating the self. Primary references dealing with Wolff's mandala are: Franklin F. Wolff, *Mathematics, Philosophy and Yoga*; "On Stupas," Tape #41, B/R 0–348, 6/21/76; "Purpose, Method and Policy of This Work" ("The Transcendental Component"), Tape #41, R/L 0–610, 6/21/76; "My Philosophy," Part V, R/R 430–928, 2/14/72.

6. Id., *Experience and Philosophy,* 359.

7. Leonard Angel, "Reconstructing the Ineffable: The Grammatical Roles of 'God'," *Religious Studies* 14 (December 1987):485–95. In Angel's response to W. P. Alston ("Ineffability," *Philosophical Review* 61 [1956]: 506:22) he concludes "that no first-order predicates apply in a context-free way to God" (495), but that "'ineffable' quite simply may be taken to be a second-order predicate, so that to say that God is ineffable is to say that no first-order predicate applies meaningfully to God" (485).

8. Leonard Angel, *The Silence of the Mystic* (Toronto: Morgan House, 1983), 42. For a more comprehensive phenomenological study of silence, see Bernard Dauenhauer, *Silence: The Phenomenon and its Ontological Significance* (Bloomington: Indiana University Press, 1980), and from a symposium on Dauenhauer's book at the 1982 meeting of the American Academy of Religion in New York.

9. J. Kellenberger, "The Ineffabilities of Mysticism," *American Philosophical Quarterly* 16 (October 1979):309.

10. Ibid.

11. Wolff, *Experience and Philosophy*, 339.

12. Ibid.

13. Ibid., 369.

14. Ibid., 264.

15. Ibid., 359.

16. Ibid., 263.

17. Ibid., 264.

18. Ibid., 280–81.

19. Ibid., 265. It is the nature of discursive language to require an objective multiplicity, independent of its application.

20. Ibid., 369.

21. Ibid.

22. Kellenberger, 309.

23. Stace, 283–84.

24. Ibid., 283.

25. Wolff, *Experience and Philosophy*, 359–60.

26. Ibid., 369. Wolff's cryptic assertion that "only a mystic really understands another mystic" should be qualified to avoid the impression that every mystic *always* adequately understands another mystic. Here understanding refers only to the ground in their common awareness of the wholly ineffable core. Differences in their respective Realizations, psychological types, languages, world views, and so on, may produce genuine misunderstanding concerning precipitated effects within the relative domain.

27. Kvastad, 198–99.

28. Wolff, *Experience and Philosophy*, 369.

29. Arthur C. Danto, "Language and the Tao: Some Reflections on Ineffability," *Journal of Chinese Philosophy* 1 (1973):45–55.

30. Richard H. Jones, "A Philosophical Analysis of Mystical Utterances," *Philosophy East and West* 29 (July 1979):259, reprinted in Richard H. Jones, *Mysticism Examined* (Albany: State University of New York Press, 1993), 101–123. Wittgenstein's version of logical atomism illustrates this approach.

31. Ibid.

32. Ibid., 272. It is more likely that positivists who subscribe to this theory would hold that all claims were meaningless, rather than false.

33. Ibid., 271.

34. Wolff, *Experience and Philosophy*, 23.

35. Jones, 263ff.

36. Ludwig Wittgenstein, *Tractatus Logico-Philosophicus,* including translation by D. F. Pears and B. F. McGuinness, with an introduction by Bertrand Russell (London: Routledge & Kegan Paul, 1961). We shall follow the common practice of using the abbreviation *Tractatus* and refer to the aphorisms parenthetically by number. The development of Wittgenstein's later philosophy will not concern us here. He abandoned logical atomism, in which language is thought to function as a mirror of the world. Yet he never repudiated the basic theme of the *Tractatus,* which is a demonstration of how to *show* what cannot be *said.*

37. Jerome Bickenbach, "The Status of the Propositions in the *Tractatus,*" *Dialogue* 13 (1974):765–66. These fail to picture the world.

38. Ibid., 766.

39. Ibid., 770–71.

40. K. T. Fann, *Wittgenstein's Conception of Philosophy* (Berkeley: University of California Press, 1969), 26–27.

41. Ignace Verhack, "An Uncommon Reading of the *Tractatus*," *International Philosophical Quarterly* 18 (1978):438.

42. Ibid.

43. Ibid.

44. Wolff, *Experience and Philosophy*, 299n. 23.

45. Jones, 263, citing Śaṃkara's *Brahmasūtra Bhāṣya* III.2.17.

46. Wolff, *Experience and Philosophy*, 397.

47. Jones, citing *Bṛhadāraṇyaka Upaniṣad Bhāṣya* II.3.6.

48. Ibid., 264, citing *Sutta Nīpata* 1075, 1076: *Saṃyutta Nikāya* IV. 373–402.

49. Ibid., citing Plotinus, *Enneads* VI.9.3.

50. Ibid., citing *The Mystical Theology*, chapter 5.

51. Stace, 353–57.

52. Ibid., 257–60.

53. Ibid., 260–62.

54. Ibid., 262–65.

55. Jones, 265, citing Paul Henle, "Mysticism and Semantics," *Philosophy and Phenomenological Research* 9 (1949):416–22; cf. Galen K. Pletcher, "Mysticism, Contradiction, and Ineffability," *American Philosophical Quarterly* 10 (1973):201–11.

56. Stace, 305.

57. Wolff, *Experience and Philosophy*, 286.

58. Ibid., 281.

59. Wolff sees their significance as a matter of objective/subjective emphasis respectively (Franklin F. Wolff, "On Paradox," Tape #33, G/L 924–end; R/L 0–230, Phoenix, Ariz., 3/22/71).

60. Id., *Experience and Philosophy*, 384.

61. Jones, 268–69. Laurence C. Wu elaborates the mystics' common use of light and mirror as mystical symbols ("Light and Mirror: Two Mystic Metaphors of Mind," *Philosophical Forum* 14 (1974):145–60).

62. *Dictionary of Philosophy and Religion*, s.v. "sign," "symbol"; *Encyclopedia of Philosophy*, s.v. "symbol."

63. Icons usually are restricted to visual representations in two or three dimensions, but logically we may extend this function to other senses. For example, in the "Grand Canyon Suite," there is a clear musical representation of hoofbeats.

64. Haig Khatchadourian, "Symbols and Metaphors," *Southern Journal of Philosophy* 6 (Fall 1968):181–82.

65. *Dictionary of Philosophy and Religion*, s.v. "symbol."

66. Erich Fromm, *The Forgotten Language* (London: n.p., 1952), in J. E. Circlot, *A Dictionary of Symbols*, trans. Jack Sage, with a foreword by Herbert Read (New York: Dorset Press, 1991), xxx.

67. Wolff, *Experience and Philosophy*, 245.

68. Stephen W. Hawking, *A Brief History of Time*, with a foreword by Carl Sagan (New York: Bantam Books, 1988), 99, reprinted as "Black Holes Ain't So Black," in *The World Treasury of Physics, Astronomy and Mathematics*, ed. Timothy Ferris, with a foreword by Clifton Fadiman (Boston: Little, Brown & Co., 1991), 226. Note that a black hole is radically different from a neutron star, in which matter is incredibly condensed, but whose properties are definable and understandable according to scientific theory.

69. This is a consequence of the theory, which holds that both the surface area and mass of the collapsed star shrink to zero.

70. Roger Penrose, *Cosmology Now*, Copyright © 1974 by BBC Publications, reprinted as "Black Holes," in *The World Treasury of Physics, Astronomy and Mathematics*, ed. Timothy Ferris, with a foreword by Clifton Fadiman (Boston: Little, Brown & Co., 1991), 216.

71. John Archibald Wheeler, *Albert Einstein: A Biographical Memoir*, Copyright © National Academy Press, 1980, reprinted as "Albert Einstein," *The World Treasury of Physics, Astronomy and Mathematics*, ed. Timothy Ferris, with a foreword by Clifton Fadiman (Boston: Little, Brown & Co., 1991), 572.

72. John Tierney, *A Passion to Know*, ed. Allen Hammond, Copyright © American Association for the Advancement of Science, 1984, reprinted as "Quest for Order," in *The World Treasury of Physics, Astronomy and Mathe-*

matics, ed. Timothy Ferris, with a foreword by Clifton Fadiman (Boston: Little, Brown & Co., 1991), 607.

73. The term *hypernumber* is preferable to *imaginary,* for the latter suggests that it might be grasped in an image of some sort, or that it is unreal and illigitimate—and neither connotation applies here. Equations involving electricity involve *i,* and other hypernumbers are essential for the development of quantum theory.

74. Wolff, *Mathematics, Philosophy and Yoga.* We may believe that we are able to conceive ∞ only if we confuse it with a number that is incredibly large, but finite. A brief mental exercise should dispel this illusion. A googol is defined as the numeral *1* followed by one hundred zeros, and a googolplex is the numeral *1* followed by a googol of zeros. There would not be enough space in the known physical universe to write the zeros unless we shrank them to about the size of atoms. Let us imagine that a computer that is capable of 1 trillion calculations per second has been counting at the rate of a googolplex every 1 trillionth of a second since the beginning of the universe (estimated at 12–13 billion years ago). What *proportion* of infinity would it have counted? Because the number computed, say x, would still be finite, and the proportion would be x/∞, the result would be infinitesimal—that is, virtually indistinguishable from zero.

75. Foreword to *Dictionary of Symbols,* by J. E. Circlot (New York: Dorset Press, 1991), x.

76. Mircea Eliade, *Images et Symboles* (Paris: n.p., 1952), in *Dictionary of Symbols,* xiv.

77. Circlot, *Dictionary of Symbols,* xxx.

78. Carl G. Jung, *Psychological Types,* trans. by Godwin Baynes (New York: Harcourt, Brace & Co., 1933), 295. Jung's definition of archetypes in terms of primordial images may be too narrow because it restricts symbolic representation to the visual.

79. Circlot, *Dictionary of Symbols,* xxxv.

80. Carl G. Jung, *On Psychic Energy,* in *Dictionary of Symbols,* xxxv.

81. Circlot, *Dictionary of Symbols,* xxxi.

82. Marius Schneider, *El origen musical de los animales-simbolos en la mitalogia y la escultura antiguas* (Barcelona: n.p., 1946) in *Dictionary of Symbols,* xxix.

83. Circlot, *Dictionary of Symbols,* xxxi.

84. René Guénon, *Aperçu sur l'Initiation* (Paris: n.p., 1929), in *Dictionary of Symbols*, xxxi.

85. Ibid. The term *supernatural* is unfortunate, for it suggests superstition and dogmatism, but the symbolic function does not, in itself, imply this attitude.

86. Circlot, *Dictionary of Symbols*, xxxvii.

87. Ibid., xxxiii. Common points of correspondence may be found between a plant or animal, a shape, a color, a feeling or emotion, and so on.

88. Marius Schneider, *La danza de espadas y ta tarantela* (Barcelona: n.p., 1948), in *Dictionary of Symbols*, xxxiii.

89. Circlot, *Dictionary of Symbols*, xxxvii.

90. Mircea Eliade, *Tratado de historia de las religiones* (Madrid: n.p., 1954), in *A Dictionary of Symbols*, xxxi–xxxii.

91. The issue of metaphorical meaning is the focus of the response by David Novitz ("Another Look at Metaphorical Meaning," *Philosophia* 15 [December 1985]:325–38) to Donald Davidson ("What Metaphors Mean," in *On Metaphor*, ed. Sheldon Sacks [Chicago: University of Chicago Press, 1979]). Novitz rejects Davidson's attempt to reduce metaphorical meaning to a strictly literal interpretation, employing Davidson's own semantic theory to demonstrate a nonliteral meaning beyond a metaphor's usual cognitive and affective functions.

92. *Encyclopedia of Philosophy*, s.v. "metaphor," by Monroe C. Beardsley.

93. Joseph Campbell, *The Power of Myth*, with Bill Moyers, ed., Betty Sue Flowers (New York: Doubleday, 1988), 31.

94. *Encyclopedia of Philosophy*, s.v. "metaphor," by Monroe C. Beardsley.

95. Douglas Berggren, "The Use and Abuse of Metaphor," *Review of Metaphysics*, v. 16 (1962–1963), 237–58, cited in *Encyclopedia of Philosophy*, s.v. "metaphor."

96. Ted Peters, "The Problem of Symbolic Reference," *Thomist* 44 (January 1980):72.

97. Ibid., 73.

98. Ibid., 74.

99. Circlot, *Dictionary of Symbols*, xlix–l.

100. Ibid., l.

101. Donald R. Burrill, "The Meaning of Religious Symbols: Paul Tillich and His Critics," *Personalist* (Summer 1973):274. The formulation of the problem in terms of "words," without reference to images, prejudices the issue somewhat, insofar as symbols may be either linguistic or nonlinguistic, and are usually understood as the latter.

102. Paul Tillich, *Dynamics of Faith* (New York: Harper & Row, 1957), 41–43.

103. Ibid., 43. For a modern study of the unconscious, see Carl G. Jung and others, eds., *Man and His Symbols* (London: Aldus Books, 1964). The development of Wolff's mandala exemplifies this process.

104. Ibid., 44.

105. Ibid., 47.

106. Ibid.

107. Ibid., 48–54.

108. Tillich's dualistic interpretation of the symbol's function of relating a person to the ultimate leads him to reject mysticism, which transcends the dualistic conception of both in an awareness of identity. However, we might easily hold a nondualistic interpretation without rejecting his general account of symbols.

109. Wolff, *Experience and Philosophy*, 195.

110. Ibid., 317.

111. Ibid., 233.

112. Ibid., 405.

113. Ibid., 378.

114. Ibid., 393.

115. Ibid., 397.

116. Khatchadourian, 189.

117. Wolff, *Experience and Philosophy*, 315.

118. For convenience Wolff usually abbreviates the full representation of the term *Consciousness-without-an-object* and *without-a-subject.*

119. This echoes Nagarjuna's technique of fourfold negation, which is a way of showing that ultimate reality cannot be captured within any scheme of logical classification.

120. Jones gives Eckhart's closing to a sermon as evidence of the degree of importance he felt it had: "If no one had come to listen, I should have had to preach it to the offering box" (Jones, 256, citing Raymond B. Blakney, trans., *Meister Eckhart* [New York: Harper & Row, 1941], 266).

121. Carl A. Keller, "Mystical Literature," *Mysticism and Philosophical Analysis*, 79. The category "reports on visions" would be inaccurate, according to Stace, for mystical experiences are not the same as visionary experiences, and he goes so far as to exclude visions from a proper definition of mystical experiences (47–51). Wolff's accounts of his mystical experiences also clearly show that they are quite other than visions.

122. Wolff, *Experience and Philosophy*, 127.

123. Bray.

124. Wolff, *Experience and Philosophy*, x.

125. Ibid., 249–50.

126. The term *phenomenographical* (along with *phenomenography*) is Richard Schacht's suggestion for distinguishing "the careful description—simply as such—of particular phenomena of various sorts, exactly as they are immediately encountered or experienced," from "phenomenology proper . . . the attempt to *go beyond* such description in some way or other, in order to ascertain the *logos* of the 'phenomena' immediately encountered or experienced" ("Husserlian and Heideggerian Phenomenology," *Philosophical Studies* 23 [1972]:313).

127. Keller, 87–89.

128. Jones, 272. Ch'an is the Buddhist school in China that became Zen in Japan.

129. Keller, 94.

130. Wolff, *Experience and Philosophy*, xi.

131. Ibid., 18n.

132. Satprem, 209. Wolff's sparing use of allegory (for instance, "The Supreme Adventure" [Wolff, *Experience and Philosophy*, 213–18]) also employs poetic form, and usually deals with processes on the Path.

133. Ibid., 268.

134. Original haiku by Ron Leonard.

135. R. H. Blyth, *A History of Haiku*, 2 vols. (Japan: Hokuseido Press, 1964), 2:363.

136. Ibid.

137. Keller, 80.

138. Wolff, *Experience and Philosophy*, 308.

139. Id., "My Philosophy," Part XII, R/L 1091–1382, 5/18/72.

140. Id., *Experience and Philosophy*, 309.

141. Id., "My Philosophy," Part XII.

142. Id., *Experience and Philosophy*, 315.

143. Ibid., 354.

144. Ibid., 315.

145. Ibid.

146. Ibid., 307.

147. Ibid., 286.

148. Ibid., 354–55.

149. Ibid., 310.

150. Ibid., 405.

151. Ibid., 314, 405–8.

152. Ibid., 309, 356–60.

153. Ibid., 314.

154. Id., "Mathematics."

155. Id., *Mathematics, Philosophy and Yoga*, 46–47.

156. Ibid., 49–51. This is particularly applicable to his initial report concerning the High Indifference (Id., *Experience and Philosophy*, 99–100).

157. *Dictionary of Symbols*, s.v. "mandala."

158. Ibid.

159. Wolff rotated the axes $\pi/4$ radians (45°) from its original position, but in the final form, neither axes nor asymptotes are shown. It is not feasible here to elaborate the wealth of detail involved in the developmental process or the numerical relationships and their symbolic significance.

160. *Dictionary of Symbols*, s.v. "mandala."

161. Wolff, *Mathematics, Philosophy and Yoga*, 59–69.

162. *Dictionary of Symbols*, s.v. "squaring the circle." This represents the esoteric significance of the ancient exoteric geometric problem.

163. Wolff, *Mathematics, Philosophy and Yoga*, 37.

164. Id., "My Philosophy," Part V.

165. Ibid.

CHAPTER 6. TRANSCENDENCE OF THE SELF

1. Franklin F. Wolff, "Three Fundamentals of the Philosophy," Part I, Tape #34, R/L 141–534, 11/5/73.

2. Id., *Experience and Philosophy*, 328.

3. Ibid., 3. Of course, we should not interpret "derived from" causally in this context.

4. These three aspects of grounding refer to knowing, procedures for acquiring or determining, and orders of being, respectively. Ontology is the branch of metaphysics concerned with the study of being.

5. When capitalized, the term *Self* refers to self-awareness experienced or posited as universal, rather than individual.

6. Wolff, *Experience and Philosophy*, 373–74; cf. 320.

7. René Descartes, *The Meditations*, trans. John Veitch (Open Court: La Salle, 1962).

8. Wolff, *Experience and Philosophy*, 255.

9. Ibid., 320.

10. *Dictionary of Philosophy*, s.v., "egocentric predicament."

11. Aron Gurwitsch, *The Field of Consciousness* (Pittsburgh: Duquesne University Press, 1964), 4.

12. Frederick Kersten, "The Originality of Gurwitsch's Theory of Intentionality," *Research in Phenomenology* 5 (1975):19–27.

13. Quentin Lauer, trans. with an introduction to *Phenomenology and the Crisis in Philosophy*, by Edmund Husserl (New York: Harper & Row, 1965).

14. Gurwitsch, *Field*, 157.

15. Ibid.

16. Ibid., 161.

17. Ibid., 162.

18. Ibid., 163.

19. Lauer, 11.

20. Gurwitsch, *Field*, 158.

21. Richard Schmitt, *Encyclopedia of Philosophy*, s.v. "phenomenology."

22. Verier Smitheram, "The Criteria of Objectivity: Physical Science and the Challenge of Phenomenology," *International Studies in Philosophy* 16 (1984):65–79.

23. Gurwitsch, *Field*, 158. Various phenomenologists see their primary tasks differently (such as Heidegger, who focuses on the inquiry into Being), but description of the structures of phenomena is a common unifying theme.

24. Ibid., 166.

25. Ibid., 159.

26. Wolff, *Experience and Philosophy*, 361.

27. Gurwitsch, *Field*, 166.

28. Lauer, 60.

29. Bishop George Berkeley's subjective idealism follows from his basic principle that reality consists solely in percepts and minds (mental substance) that are aware of them.

30. Lauer, 11.

31. Gurwitsch, *Field*, 164. Heidegger believes that we must do phenomenology beginning with prereflective (originary) data—not reduced data.

His approach is existential, and his overriding goal is the practice of what he terms *fundamental ontology*—the quest for Being.

32. Ibid., 165.

33. Ibid., 165–66.

34. Ibid., 167.

35. Ibid.

36. Ibid., 168.

37. Ibid., 381.

38. Ibid., 382.

39. Martin Heidegger, *Being and Time*, trans. J. M. MacQuarrie and E. Robinson (Oxford: Basil Blackwell, 1967); originally *Sein und Zeit* (Tübingen: Max Niemeyer, 1967).

40. Marion Tapper, "The Priority of Being or Consciousness for Phenomenology: Heidegger and Husserl," *Metaphilosophy* 17 (April/July 1986): 157. Husserl, in response, equates Heidegger's program of fundamental ontology to "philosophical anthropology" (J. C. Morrison, "Husserl and Heidegger: The Parting of the Ways," in F. Ellison, ed., *Heidegger's Existential Analytic* [New York: The Hague, 1978]).

41. Tapper, 157.

42. Ibid., 154.

43. Ibid., 157.

44. William Vallicella, "Kant, Heidegger and the Problem of the Thing in Itself," *International Philosophical Quarterly* 89 (March 1983):35, referring to *Sein und Zeit*, 152.

45. Ibid., referring to *Sein und Zeit*, 152.

46. Edward Farley, "Phenomenological Theology and the Problem of Metaphysics," *Man and World* 12 (1979):506.

47. Richard Holmes, "Is Transcendental Phenomenology Committed to Idealism?" *Monist* 59 (1975):98.

48. Wolff, *Experience and Philosophy*, 285–86.

49. Husserl explains this method in *Experience and Judgment* (Evanston: Northwestern Press, 1973), 374–75.

50. Norman Melchert, "Mystical Experience and Ontological Claims," *Philosophy and Phenomenological Research* 37 (July 1977):448.

51. Like phenomenology, phenomenalism (such as that of Hume) holds that we can know nothing behind phenomena, or the way the world appears. However, in contrast to phenomenology, it upholds the logical consequences of a strict application of empiricist principles, so it tends to reduce the study of phenomena to empiricist psychology. Hence it leads to unmitigated skepticism concerning scientific as well as metaphysical knowledge.

52. *Dictionary of Philosophy and Religion,* s.v. "consciousness."

53. Wolff, *Transformations in Consciousness,* 79.

54. Franklin F. Wolff, "Consciousness and Reality," Tape #35, G/L 31–300, 1/19/74. This is consistent with Deutsch's interpretation of Advaita Vedānta.

55. Id., *Transformations in Consciousness,* 147.

56. *Dictionary of Philosophy,* 15th ed., s.v. "consciousness." Wolff is familiar with Ladd's definition, which also appears in Baldwin's *Dictionary of Philosophy and Psychology,* a source Wolff often quotes (See Wolff, *Transformations in Consciousness,* 79–80).

57. Franklin F. Wolff, "Consciousness Is Not Subject to the Principle of Dualism," Tape #33, R/R 616–1016, 5/21/71.

58. Ibid.

59. C. O. Evans, 46–47.

60. Ibid., 48.

61. Wolff, "Dualism."

62. Ibid.

63. Id., *Experience and Philosophy,* 418.

64. Ibid., 424.

65. Ibid., 418.

66. Ibid.

67. Ibid., 419.

68. Ibid., 523.

69. Ibid., 425.

70. Ibid., 418.

71. Richard Maurice Bucke, *Cosmic Consciousness* (Philadelphia: Innes & Sons, 1901); reprint (New York: E. P. Dutton & Co., 1923), 3. Bucke also regards it as a new, thus far extremely rare, faculty of consciousness.

72. Wolff, *Experience and Philosophy*, 425.

73. Ibid., 327.

74. Ibid., 285.

75. Ibid., 350.

76. Ibid., 362.

77. Id., "Absolute Consciousness."

78. Id., *Experience and Philosophy*, 320–21.

79. Id., "Dualism."

80. Id., "Unconscious."

81. Id., *Experience and Philosophy*, 285.

82. Pierre Teilhard do Chardin, *The Phenomenon of Man*, trans. Bernard Wall, with an introduction by Julian Huxley (New York: Harper & Row, 1959); Śrī Aurobindo Ghose, *The Life Divine* (New York: Greystone Press, 1949).

83. Wolff, "Unconscious."

84. Id., *Experience and Philosophy*, 285.

85. Id., "Unconscious."

86. C. O. Evans, 53, citing Alan R. White, *Attention* (Oxford: Basil Blackwell, 1964).

87. Ibid., 48–49. See James Mill, *Analysis of the Phenomena of the Human Mind* (London: Longmans, Green, Reader & Dyer, 1869).

88. C. O. Evans, chapters 4 and 5, 104–81.

89. Ibid., 145.

90. Gurwitsch, *Field*, 4.

91. C. O. Evans, 145.

92. Ibid., 149. Gilbert Ryle discovered by introspection that the 'I' systematically eludes objectification (*The Concept of Mind* [London: Hutchinson & Co., 1949], 198).

93. Ibid., 19–38.

94. Ibid., 11.

95. Ibid., 21.

96. Ibid. A central example is Peter F. Strawson, *Individuals* (London: Methuen, 1959).

97. Ibid., 23.

98. Ibid., 24.

99. Ibid., 25.

100. Ibid.

101. Ibid.

102. Ibid., 29. Wolff uses *substance* to refer only to Consciousness-without-an-object, as the underlying reality of all that appears to relative consciousness. However, because its nature is nondualistic, no attribute strictly applies—and even in conjunction with its opposite, predication of an attribute is not strictly accurate. He wishes to oppose phenomenalism, but he seems unaware of certain unwanted connotations associated with a substantialist terminology.

103. Ibid.

104. Ibid.

105. Thomas Busch, "Consciousness and Transcendental Philosophy: A Response to Professor Tibbitts," *Philosophy Today* 14 (Winter 1970): 299–300.

106. Ibid., 300.

107. Wolff, *Experience and Philosophy*, 320.

108. Ibid., 320–21.

109. Ibid., 177.

110. C. O. Evans, 37.

111. Wolff, *Experience and Philosophy*, 336.

112. Id., *Transformations in Consciousness*, 13.

113. Thomas Nagel, "Physicalism," *Philosophical Review* 74 (July 1965); reprinted with a postscript in *Modern Materialism: Readings on Mind-Body Identity*, ed. John O'Connor (New York: Harcourt, Brace and World, 1969). References are to the O'Connor volume.

114. Thomas Nagel, "What Is It Like to Be a Bat?" *Philosophical Review* 83 (October 1974):442.

115. Andrew Ward believes that he has shown that the materialists' "best hypothesis argument" is circular ("Materialism and the Unity of Consciousness," *Analysis* 40 [June 1980]:444).

116. J. B. Watson, *Behaviorism*, 3d ed. (Chicago: University of Chicago Press, 1930), v.

117. C. Stephen Evans, "Reductionism as Absentmindedness: Existentialism and Phenomenology as Strategies for Defending Personhood," *Man and World* 14 (1981):177–78.

118. Wolff, *Transformations in Consciousness*, 28.

119. Ryle, 58.

120. Ludwig Wittgenstein, *Philosophical Investigations*, trans. G. E. M. Anscombe (Oxford: Basil Blackwell, 1968), 580. Numbers refer to the section, not the page.

121. Ibid., 304.

122. Ibid., 308.

123. Mark L. Conkling, "Ryle's Mistake about Consciousness," *Philosophy Today* (Winter 1977):376–88.

124. Ryle, 58.

125. Bryan Magee, "Conversations with Gilbert Ryle," *Modern British Philosophy* (New York: St. Martin's Press, 1971), 108.

126. Conkling, 376.

127. Ibid.

128. Ibid., 382–84. Conkling's phrasing is misleading. The relation of intentionality lies within relative consciousness and is directed toward the object experienced. Close analysis reveals that the person, the objective complex of states, qualities, and dispositions (which is radically other than the pure self) lies at the object side of the subject-object distinction and is

known through an act of reflection. Furthermore, mysticism shows that there are other modes of consciousness that are not intentional.

129. Ibid., 387.

130. Wittgenstein, *Philosophical Investigations*, 304.

131. Alan Paskow, "A Phenomenological View of the Beetle in the Box," *New Scholasticism* 48 (Summer 1974):279.

132. Edward Sankowski faults Anthony Kenny's *Wittgenstein* (Cambridge, Mass.: Harvard University Press, 1973) for misinterpreting Wittgenstein with respect to the possibility of this sort of self-knowledge ("Wittgenstein on Self-Knowledge," *Mind* 87 [April 1978], 87).

133. Paskow, 278.

134. Ibid., 304.

135. Wolff, *Experience and Philosophy*, 321.

136. Ibid., 329. Objective knowledge is restricted to relative consciousness. Introception derives from a state that transcends and is discontinuous from the subject-object structure, so it would differ radically from objective or propositional knowledge.

137. Ibid., 321.

138. Ibid., 367.

139. Id., *Transformations in Consciousness*, 145. The empirical approach to psychology has virtually ignored Kant (or given his philosophy a neo-empiricist interpretation).

140. Id., *Experience and Philosophy*, 329.

141. Id., *Transformations in Consciousness*, 184.

142. Ibid., 98–99.

143. Ibid., 28.

144. Id., *Experience and Philosophy*, 362–63.

145. Id., *Transformations in Consciousness*, 82, quoting Aurobindo, *Life Divine*, 643.

146. Id., *Experience and Philosophy*, 341.

147. Id, *Transformations in Consciousness*, 184. (See also "Unconscious.")

148. Id., "Absolute Consciousness," Part II.

149. Id., "Unconscious."

150. Id., *Experience and Philosophy*, 24.

151. Ibid., 25.

152. Ibid., 71.

153. Ibid., 23.

CHAPTER 7. PRIMACY OF CONSCIOUSNESS

1. Wolff, *Experience and Philosophy*, 328.

2. Ibid., 320–21.

3. Ibid., 393.

4. William Fowkes, "The Concept of the Self in Husserl and Beyond," *Philosophy Today* 24 (Spring 1980):44–45. Fowkes acknowledges the gross inaccuracy of the term *entity*, but is at a loss to find a better one.

5. Ibid., 45.

6. William Earle, *Objectivity* (New York: Noonday Press, 1955; reprint, Chicago: Quadrangle Books), 48.

7. Ibid., 49.

8. Ibid.

9. Ibid., 48.

10. Ibid., 50. The self is characterized more properly as a mystery than an entity and as a subject rather than an object.

11. Wolff, *Experience and Philosophy*, 362.

12. Thomas Natsoulas, "The Unity of Consciousness," *Behaviorism* 7 (Fall 1979):48–49.

13. Ibid.

14. Aron Gurwitsch, "Die mitmenschlichen Begegnungen in der Milieuwelt" ◊7 (n.p., 1931), quoted in Alexandre Métraux, "Aron Gurwitsch's Non-Egological Conception of Consciousness," *Research in Phenomenology* 5 (1975):46. Perhaps making love would be the best example of a "shared-and-reciprocal" experience, but our normal social life reveals a plethora of less dramatic cases.

15. Métraux, 47–48. (27) Cf. Aron Gurwitsch, "A Non-Egological Conception of Consciousness," *Philosophy and Phenomenological Research* 1 (September 1940/June 1941); reprinted in Gurwitsch, *Studies in Phenomenology and Psychology* (Evanston: 1966), 290 and n8. (28) Cf. Ibid., 292: " 'As long as we do not adopt the attitude of reflection, the ego does not appear. On the level of non-reflection, there is no ego at all. A conscious act, inasmuch as it is free from reflection, does not deal with the ego and is not related to it in any way whatever. This holds good from the psychological standpoint as well as from that of transcendental phenomenology.' " (29) "This, too, is the reason why the ego is included in social themes and, furthermore, in their thematic evolution."

16. Gurwitsch, "A Non-Egological Conception of Consciousness," 299, cited in Métraux, 49. The parallel with Sartre's analysis of consciousness is striking, though Métraux can find no evidence that they did not develop their insights independently.

17. Métraux, 47.

18. Edward Conze, *Buddhism: Its Essence and Development* (New York: Harper & Row, 1951; Harper Torchbooks ed., 1965), 19.

19. P. T. Raju, *The Philosophical Traditions of India* (London: George Allen & Unwin, 1971), 120.

20. Surendranath Dasgupta, *A History of Indian Philosophy*, 5 vols. (Cambridge: Cambridge University Press, 1922), I:93–98.

21. Conze, 107–8; cf. Natsoulas, 48.

22. Wolff, *Experience and Philosophy*, 416. Since this only reflects the interpretation of the translators, its significance is unknown.

23. Id., *Transformations in Consciousness*, 254.

24. Ibid.

25. Raju, 119.

26. Wolff, *Experience and Philosophy*, 220–21.

27. Ibid., 412n. 1. Wolff's affinity for Yogācāra Buddhism—the school most compatible with *Advaita Vedānta*—is evident here, for it is the only form of Buddhism for which this analysis would be valid.

28. Jean-Paul Sartre, *The Transcendence of the Ego*, trans. Forrest Williams and Robert Kirkpatrick (New York: Noonday Press, 1957).

29. Wolff, *Experience and Philosophy*, 347.

30. Ibid.

31. Ibid., 360.

32. Ibid., 365–66.

33. Ibid., 365.

34. Ibid., 342.

35. Ibid., 178. This approach is somewhat *Vedāntin.*

36. Ibid., 342; cf. 178.

37. Ibid. 341–42.

38. Sartre, 98.

39. Ibid., 52.

40. Ibid., 97.

41. Ibid., 31, 59–60.

42. Wolff, "Absolute Consciousness."

43. Sartre, 31.

44. Ibid., 60.

45. Ibid., 74.

46. Ibid., 54. This is Edmund Husserl's view in *Ideas,* trans. by W. R. Boyce Gibson (New York: Collier Books, 1971), according to Phyllis Sutton Morris, "Sartre on the Transcendence of the Ego," *Philosophy and Phenomenological Research* 46 (December 1985):191. On this account, Husserl's earlier view (*Logical Investigations,* trans. by J. N. Findlay [New York: Humanities Press, 1970]) is nonegological, but he finally came to hold an egological position.

47. Wolff, *Experience and Philosophy,* 366.

48. Sartre, 75–76.

49. Ibid., 88–89.

50. Ibid., 80–81.

51. Ibid., 100.

52. Ibid., 101.

53. Ibid., 102.

54. Fowkes, 47.

55. Ibid., 48, 51.

56. Ibid., 48.

57. Ibid., 51.

58. Charles E. Scott, "Self-Consciousness without an Ego," *Man and World* 4 (1971):194–95. Reprinted with kind permission from Kluwer Academic Publishers. Although Scott no longer personally holds this position, the original viewpoint is plausible and needs to be considered.

59. Ibid., 194, citing Dieter Henrich, "Self-Consciousness: A Critical Introduction to Its Theory," *Man and World* 4 (Fall 1971):3–28.

60. Ibid., 193.

61. Earle, "Mysticism," 520–21.

62. Ibid., 520.

63. Ibid.

64. Melchert, 448.

65. Earle, "Mysticism," 521.

66. Ibid., 522.

67. Ibid., 523–24.

68. Ibid., 524. Earle seems to adopt a Heraclitean notion of time.

69. Ibid., 524–25.

70. Ibid., 527–28.

71. Wolff, *Experience and Philosophy*, 413n. 3.

72. Earle, "Mysticism," 526.

73. Ibid. The terms *God, Absolute Reality,* and *Absolute Being* are not indisputably equivalent.

74. Wolff, *Experience and Philosophy*, 286.

75. Stace, 272.

76. Earle, "Mysticism," 526.

77. Ibid., 526–27.

78. Ibid., 527–28.

79. Ibid., 527.

80. Ibid., 529.

81. Ibid.

82. Ibid.

83. Franklin F. Wolff, "The Derivation of Consciousness," Tape #36, G/L 0–200, 4/28/74.

84. Id., *Experience and Philosophy,* 320–21.

85. Ibid., 219.

86. Id., "Dualism."

87. Id., *Experience and Philosophy,* 406.

88. Ibid., 321.

89. Ibid., 356.

90. Ibid. Wolff's philosophy lends no support to theism.

91. Ibid., 285–86.

92. Ibid., 356.

93. Ibid.

94. Ibid., 370.

95. Id., "Absolute Consciousness," Part II; "My Philosophy," Part XII.

96. Id., *Experience and Philosophy,* 378.

97. Ibid., 350.

98. Id., "Absolute Consciousness," Part II.

99. Id., *Experience and Philosophy,* 314, 408.

100. Ibid., 409.

101. Ibid., 409–11.

102. Charles Hartshorne, "Panpsychism: Mind as Sole Reality," *Ultimate Reality and Meaning* 1 (1978):117. There are numerous versions of panpsychism (see *Dictionary of Philosophy and Religion,* s.v. "panpsychism"), but Hartshorne's has the advantage that it is contemporary and cogently argued. We present it here in simplified form for the sake of emphasizing the essential features that are relevant to our discussion.

103. Hartshorne, 119.

104. Ibid., 120.

105. Wolff, "Absolute Consciousness."

106. Raju, 125.

107. Wolff, "Buddhist."

108. Ibid.

109. Raju, 125.

110. Ibid., 126–27.

111. Wolff, *Experience and Philosophy*, 357.

112. Ibid., 405–8.

113. Ibid., 411.

114. Ibid., 408.

CHAPTER 8. THE NOETIC THESIS

1. The analysis of knowledge as justified true belief needs further qualification, for if there are different types of truth, then there may be different corresponding types of knowledge. Furthermore, Margery Naylor points out that the Gettier problem (testing the adequacty of this definition) depends on the definition of the term *justified* ("Epistemic Justification," *American Philosophical Quarterly* 25 [January 1988]:49–58). Also, there are significant logical, epistemological, and psychological differences between knowing and believing.

2. Wolff, *Experience and Philosophy*, 414n. 5.

3. James, 371–72.

4. Wolff, *Experience and Philosophy*, xi–xii.

5. The original manuscript.

6. Wolff, *Experience and Philosophy*, xii.

7. Id., *Transformations in Consciousness*, 299.

8. Franklin F. Wolff, "Perception, Conception and Introception," Part I, Tape #20, Side 2, 268–881, 2/2/70.

9. Id., *Transformations in Consciousness*, 144.

10. Franklin F. Wolff, "An Abstract of the Philosophy," Part XIII ("Communication of the Introceptual"), Tape #38, G/L 466–1017, 4/7/75.

11. *Dictionary of Philosophy*, s.v. "noetic."

12. Wolff, *Transformations in Consciousness*, 278.

13. Id., *Experience and Philosophy*, 6.

14. Ibid., 374.

15. George A. Coe, "The Sources of Mystical Revelation," *Hibbert Jr.* 6 (1907):367, quoted in James Leuba, *The Psychology of Religious Mysticism* (London: Routledge & Kegan Paul, 1925), quoted in Franklin F. Wolff (*Transformations in Consciousness*, 239).

16. Wolff, *Transformations in Consciousness*, 239–40.

17. Id., "My Philosophy," Part VII, Tape #28, G/L 135–582, 9/6/71.

18. Ibid.

19. Id., *Experience and Philosophy*, 108–9.

20. Id., *Transformations in Consciousness*, 248.

21. Ibid.

22. Ibid., 248–49.

23. Ibid., 282.

24. Ibid.

25. Ibid., 277. Because Wolff sees the possibility of applying mathematics to metaphysics, he desires to fuse the autonomous thought that is the source of the former with the directed thought of the latter ("Directed/Autonomous Consciousness," Tape #44, G/R 918–83, 6/12/77).

26. Ibid., 276–77. The degree of profundity felt at the time of formulation is no guarantee that one will give the same appraisal later.

27. Ibid., 277.

28. Id., *Experience and Philosophy*, 343–44.

29. Ibid., 344.

30. Ibid.

31. Stace, 131.

32. Wolff, *Experience and Philosophy*, 343.

33. Ibid., 372.

34. Ibid.

35. Id., *Transformations in Consciousness*, 280.

36. Ibid., 282.

37. Ibid., 280.

38. Ibid., 282.

39. Ibid., 280–81.

40. Ibid., 281.

41. Ibid.

42. Ibid.

43. Ibid., 281–82.

44. Id., *Experience and Philosophy*, 196.

45. Ibid., 197.

46. Id., *Transformations in Consciousness*, 144.

47. Id., "Perception, Conception and Introception," Part I.

48. Id., *Transformations in Consciousness*, 166.

49. Ibid., 104. Wolff equates *Introception* to the Buddhist *dhyana*, or meditation.

50. Id., *Experience and Philosophy*, 9.

51. Ibid., 21.

52. Ibid., 138.

53. Ibid., 11.

54. Ibid.

55. Ibid., 11–12.

56. Id., "My Philosophy," Part VIII.

57. Id., *Transformations in Consciousness*, 147. It is strongly suggested that the reader compare the two versions explicitly. Their juxtaposition serves as a parallax view that reveals nuances of meaning that might be missed if only one were used.

58. Id., "Unconscious."

59. Id., *Experience and Philosophy*, 21.

60. Id., *Transformations in Consciousness*, 104.

61. David Hume, *A Treatise of Human Nature*, ed. L. A. Selby-Biggs (Oxford: Clarendon Press, 1888), 252.

62. Wolff, *Transformations in Consciousness*, 106.

63. Id., *Experience and Philosophy*, 250.

64. Mael Melvin, "Introduction to *Introceptualism*," ii.

65. Wolff, *Transformations in Consciousness*, 208.

66. Id., *Experience and Philosophy*, 346.

67. Id., *Transformations in Consciousness*, 111–12.

68. Ibid., 132; cf. *Experience and Philosophy*, 285.

69. Franklin F. Wolff, "The Methodology of the Empirical Sciences and Mathematics," Tape #35, G/L 635–1164, R/L 637–end, G/R 0–299, 2–4/74.

70. *Encyclopedia of Philosophy*, s.v. "Schopenhauer, Arthur," by Patrick Gardiner.

71. Wolff, *Transformations in Consciousness*, 164.

72. Ibid.

73. Ibid., 163. Wolff discusses intuition in some detail in Franklin F. Wolff, "Concerning Intuition" (San Fernando: n.p., 1939).

74. Id., "Concept, Percept and Reality," 402–3.

75. Id., *Experience and Philosophy*, 250.

76. Kant supplied the necessary distinction with the notion of the transcendental ego, albeit with the additional erroneous assumption that it could only be known inferentially by human consciousness. For a penetrating discussion of the difference between the transcendental and empirical ego, see A. J. Mandt, "The Inconceivability of Kant's Transcendental Subject: An Impasse in Kant's Metaphysics," *International Philosophical Quarterly* 23 (March 1983):13–33. Mandt depicts Kant's transcendental ego as "a self-subsisting thing viewed as primordial being" (ibid., 31), but because it is unconditioned, it is unintelligible (that is, beyond discursive thought).

77. Wolff, *Experience and Philosophy*, 305–6.

78. Ibid., 272. The hyphenation of *Knowledge-through-Identity*, introduced in the present work, is a modification Wolff likely would approve. It has the effect of orienting to the state as the *source* of the knowledge, rather than something *about which* we gain knowledge—a subtle but crucial distinction.

79. Ibid., 110. See also "Concerning Intuition."

80. Wolff, *Experience and Philosophy*, 65.

81. Id., *Transformations in Consciousness*, 196.

82. Ibid., 426.

83. *Dictionary of Philosophy*, s.v., "*vidyā*."

84. Wolff, *Experience and Philosophy*, 354–55.

85. Richard Alpert (pseud. Baba Ram Dass), "Here We All Are" (Las Crucis, New Mexico: Lama Foundation, c. 1971).

86. Wolff, *Experience and Philosophy*, 355.

87. Ibid., 268; "My Philosophy," Part IV.

88. Id., *Experience and Philosophy*, 272.

89. Id., *Transformations in Consciousness*, 132–33.

90. Id., *Experience and Philosophy*, 273.

91. Ibid., 272–73. Wolff believes that Spinoza, Plotinus, and Śaṃkara exemplify this type of mystical unfoldment. However, if this is true of Spinoza, who is generally known as a rationalist, it would be a case of unacknowledged mysticism.

92. Ibid., 308.

93. Id., *Transformations in Consciousness*, 277.

94. Id., *Experience and Philosophy*, 263.

95. Ibid., 195.

96. Ibid., 211.

97. Ibid., 308.

98. Ibid., 309.

99. Ibid., 306–7.

100. Ibid., 309–14. Comparison with the treatment of Wolff's aphorisms in chapter 5 is recommended.

101. Id., *Transformations in Consciousness*, 126–27.

102. Ibid., 126.

103. Ibid.

104. Ibid., 127.

105. Ibid.

106. Id., *Experience and Philosophy*, 309–10.

107. Id., "My Philosophy," Part XII.

108. Ibid.

109. Id., *Experience and Philosophy*, 310.

110. Ibid., 357.

111. Id., "My Philosophy," Part XII. Wolff possibly has in mind imaginary numbers derived from taking the square root of negative numbers, as well as the mathematics of the transfinite.

112. Id., *Experience and Philosophy*, 85.

113. Franklin F. Wolff, "Epistemology and Realization," Tape #14, Side 1, 2/19/69.

114. Id., *Experience and Philosophy*, xi.

115. Kenneth Dorter, "First Philosophy: Metaphysics or Epistemology?" *Dialogue* 11 (March 1972):3.

116. See W. J. Kilgore, "Is Metaphysics Outmoded?" *Southwestern Journal of Philosophy* (Fall 1972):109–16. We need not evaluate the degree of Kant's success in establishing upon this foundation the conditions for an adequate metaphysics.

117. Dorter, 1.

118. Ibid., 22.

119. Henry E. Allison, "Things in Themselves, Noumena, and the Transcendental Object," *Dialectica* 32 (1978):56.

120. Ibid., 49. Allison claims that his study owes much to the work of Gerold Praus, *Kant und das Problem der Dinge an sich* (Bonn: Bouvier, 1974). We find a similar approach that introduces the distinction between ontology and epistemology in Rolf Meerbote's "The Unknowability of Things

in Themselves," *Proceedings of the Third International Kant Congress,* ed. Lewis White Beck and D. Reidel (Dordrecht: Reidel, 1972):414–23.

121. Nicholas Rescher, "On the Status of 'Things-in-Themselves' in Kant," *Revue Internationale de Philosophie* 35 (Jan./Feb. 1981):356.

122. Ibid., 351. This notion is the result of Kant's search for a satisfactory answer to Hume's skeptical phenomenalism.

123. Wolff, *Transformations in Consciousness,* 89.

124. Rescher, 350.

125. Allison, 53.

126. Kant, *Critique of Pure Reason,* trans. Smith, 270 (A254).

127. Id., trans. with an Introduction by J. M. D. Meikeljohn, and a Special Introduction by Brandt V. B. Dixon, rev. ed. (New York: P. F. Collier & Son, 1900), 164. This shows that he affirms this point in both editions.

128. Id., trans. Smith, 270 (A254).

129. Id., trans. Meikeljohn, 164.

130. Ibid., 165.

131. Id., trans. Smith, 270 (B309).

132. Ibid.

133. Wolff, *Experience and Philosophy,* 411, quoting Immanuel Kant, *Critique of Pure Reason,* trans. with a Preface by F. Max Müller, with a Historical Introduction by Ludwig Noiré (London: Macmillan & Co., 1881), 219 (italics Wolff's).

134. Ibid., 373; *Transformations in Consciousness,* 109.

135. Id., *Experience and Philosophy,* 374.

136. Ibid., 317.

137. Ibid., 243. Wolff notes several designations for this phase of consciousness in the West: *Cosmic Consciousness, Mystical Insight, Transhumanism,* etc. In the East, he contends, it is known as *samādhi, dhyāna, prajñā,* etc. The term *satori* would now also be familiar. He coins the terms *Introception* and *Knowledge-through-Identity* as more philosophically oriented and semantically precise, emphasizing the noetic aspect of the experiential referent of these terms. A common referent neither excludes, nor is ex-

cluded by, the richness of meaning each of these terms has within its own unique context.

138. Id., *Transformations in Consciousness*, 277.

139. Franklin F. Wolff, "Cognition as Unconditioned by Perspective," Tape #40, G/L 699–1035, 2/4/76.

140. Singh, 175–83.

141. Ibid., 176.

142. Ibid.

143. Ibid., 177.

144. We should keep in mind that Kant viewed God, as well as the noumenon, as purely of significance for thought, not as something real that could be known.

145. Singh, 178–79.

146. Ibid., 180.

147. Ibid.

148. Ibid., 181. See Mukerji, *Self*, 167.

149. Ibid., 182.

150. Wolff, *Transformations in Consciousness*, 134–35.

151. Ibid., 169.

152. Ibid., 247–48.

153. Ibid., 170.

154. Ibid.

155. Ibid., 171.

156. Ibid., 134–35.

157. Meister Eckhart, cited by Stace, 63, quoting Rudolf Otto, *Mysticism East and West* (New York: Macmillan, 1932), 61.

158. Jacob Boehme, cited by Stace, 69, quoting H. H. Brinton, *The Mystic Will* (New York: Macmillan, 1930) (italics Stace's).

159. Stace, 71–72.

160. Ibid., 71.

161. Wolff, *Transformations in Consciousness,* 175.

162. Id., "My Philosophy," Part VII.

163. Ibid.

164. Ibid., Part IV.

165. Id., "Abstract," Part VII. This would also account somewhat for the absolutist tone of some mystics who remain unaware of the possibility that their respective Realizations might be superseded.

166. Ibid.

167. Id., *Transformations in Consciousness,* 197–98.

168. Ibid., 177.

169. Ibid., 133; cf. Wolff, "Abstract," Part VII ("On Certainty"), Tape #37, R/R 0–376, 1/1/75. Our present focus is Wolff's account of the transcriptive process whereby Introceptive thought is transformed by "precipitating" into relative consciousness.

170. Id., *Experience and Philosophy,* 39.

171. Ibid., 99.

172. Id., *Transformations in Consciousness,* 197–98.

173. Id., *Experience and Philosophy,* 71.

174. Ibid., 40.

175. Id., *Transformations in Consciousness,* 144. No doubt, other sorts of treatment by mystics who lack this background are legitimate, and nonmystics, though handicapped by lack of firsthand acquaintance with the material, may nonetheless provide useful commentary.

176. Id., "My Philosophy," Part IV. Wolff explicitly concurs with Aurobindo here.

177. Ibid., Part VII, Tape #28, G/L 135–582.

178. Ibid.

179. Franklin F. Wolff, "On Certain Knowledge," Tape #44, G/R 994–1325, 7/12/77.

180. Id., "My Philosophy," Part VII.

181. Id., *Experience and Philosophy,* 243.

182. Ibid., 374.

183. Id., *Transformations in Consciousness,* 290–91.

184. Id., *Experience and Philosophy,* 361.

185. Id., *Transformations in Consciousness,* 290–91.

186. Ibid., 291.

CHAPTER 9. INTROCEPTUALISM

1. Franklin F. Wolff, "Fundamental Epistemological Question," Tape #30, G/R 90–375, 3/22/73.

2. Id., "My Philosophy," Part III, G/R 900–end, 2/14/72. Although not all who are influenced by Wolff have a theoretical orientation, several who do (Imants Barušs, Thomas McFarlane, Joseph Rowe, Robert Briggs, etc.) have verified its effectiveness and contributed to its theoretical elaboration.

3. Franklin F. Wolff, "A Mystical View of the World" (San Fernando: n.p., 1937).

4. Id., *Transformations in Consciousness,* 272.

5. Stephan Tyman, "Mysticism and Gnosticism in Heidegger," *Philosophy Today* 28 (Winter 1984):363.

6. Philip J. Bossert, "Paradox and Enlightenment in Zen Dialogue and Phenomenological Description," *Journal of Chinese Philosophy* 3 (June 1976):276.

7. Wolff, *Experience and Philosophy,* 117.

SELECTED SOURCES

WORKS BY FRANKLIN F. WOLFF

Books and Articles

Wolff, Franklin F. [Franklin Merrell-Wolff]. "Concept, Percept and Reality." *Philosophical Review* 48 (1939):398–414.

———. "Concerning Intuition." San Fernando: n.p., April 1939.

———. *Experience and Philosophy* (Containing his *Pathways Through to Space* and *The Philosophy of Consciousness without an Object*). Albany: State University of New York Press, 1994.

———. *Introceptualism: The Philosophy of Consciousness without an Object*—Part II. Phoenix: Phoenix Philosophical Press, 1975.

———. "Is Theosophy Authentic?" Phoenix: n.p., 1975.

———. *Mathematics, Philosophy and Yoga.* Edited and Illustrated with a Foreword by Ron Leonard and a Preface by Doroethy Leonard. Phoenix: Phoenix Philosophical Press, 1995.

———. "A Mystical View of the World." San Fernando: n.p., 1937.

———. *Pathways Through to Space: A Personal Record of Transformation in Consciousness.* New York: Richard Smith, 1942.

———. *The Philosophy of Consciousness without an Object: Reflections on the Nature of Transcendental Consciousness.* New York: Julian Press, 1973.

———. "Questing." Lone Pine: n.p., 1968.

———. [Yogagñani]. *Re-Embodiment.* San Fernando: Merrell-Wolff Pub. Co. Printed by Skelton Publishing Co., 1930.

———. *Transformations in Consciousness* (Containing his *Introceptualism*). Edited with a Foreword by Ron Leonard. Albany: State University of New York Press, 1995.

———. [Yogagñani]. *Yoga.* San Fernando: Merrell-Wolff Pub. Co. Printed by Skelton Publishing Co., 1930.

Lectures and Discourses

———. "Absolute Consciousness." 2 parts. Lone Pine. 12, 25 September 1975. Tape #39: R/R 0–785.

———. "An Abstract of the Philosophy." 14 parts. Lone Pine. August 1974–April 1975. Tapes #37–#39.

———. "Aurobindo and Śaṃkara: The Reconciliation of Universal Realism with Universal Illusionism." Flagstaff, AZ. Spring 1968.

———. "Cognition as Unconditioned by Perspective." Lone Pine. 4 February 1976. Tape #40: G/L 699–1035.

———. "Consciousness and Reality." Lone Pine. 19 January 1974. Tape #35: G/L 30–300.

———. "Consciousness Is Not Subject to the Principle of Dualism." Lone Pine. 21 May 1971. Tape #33: R/R 618–1016.

———. "Convention: Autobiographical Material." Lone Pine. 6 July 1978. Tape Z_0: B/L 478–end.

———. "The Derivation of Consciousness." Lone Pine. 28 April 1974. Tape #36: G/L 0–200.

———. "Directed/Autonomous Consciousness." Lone Pine. 12 June 1977. Tape #44: G/R 918–983.

———. "Epistemology and Realization." Lone Pine. 19 February 1969. Tape #14: Side 1.

———. "The First Fundamental." Lone Pine. 13 March 1979. Tape Z_4: R/R 0–345.

———. "Fundamental Epistemological Question." Lone Pine. 22 March 1973. Tape #30: G/R 90–175.

———. "Further Thoughts on the Relation of Buddhism, Vedānta and Aurobindo." Lone Pine. 14 April 1971. Tape #33: R/L 232–624.

———. "Induction Tape." Phoenix. 24 January 1970. Tape #20: Side 1, 0–587.

———. "Is Metaphysical Knowledge Possible?" Lone Pine. 16 June 1975. Tape #39: R/L 825–1385.

———. "Is the Theosophia Authentic?" Lone Pine. 13 November 1978. Tape Z_2: R/L 574–981.

———. "Mathematics, Philosophy and Yoga." 6 parts. Phoenix. November 1966. Tapes #5–#10.

———. "The Methodology of the Empirical Sciences and Mathematics." Lone Pine. February–April 1974. Tape #35: G/L 635–1164; R/L 637–end; G/R 0–299.

———. "My Philosophy." 12 parts. Lone Pine. September 1971–May 1972. Tape #28.

———. "On Certain Knowledge." Lone Pine. 12 July 1977. Tape #44: G/R 994–1325.

———. "On the High Indifference." Lone Pine. 30 April 1975. Tape #39: G/L 357–725.

———. "On the Limits of Clear Definition: Human Nature and Conceptuality." Lone Pine. 1 March 1975. Tape #38: R/R 321–630.

———. "On Paradox." Lone Pine. 22 March 1971. Tape #33: G/L 924–end; R/L 0–230.

———. "On Stupas." Lone Pine. 12 June 1976. Tape #41: B/R 0–348.

———. "Perception, Conception and Introception." 2 parts. Lone Pine. 2 February–1 March 1970. Tape #20, Side 2: 268–end; Tape #21, Side 1: 0–220.

———. "The Power of the Will." Lone Pine. 18 September 1973. Tape #34: R/R 0–140.

———. "A Primitive View of the World." Lone Pine. 13 November 1978. Tape Z_2: R/R 0–291.

———. "Purpose, Method and Policy of This Work." Lone Pine. 21 June 1976. Tape #41: R/L 0–610.

———. "Religion, Psychology and Philosophy." Lone Pine. 31 May 1970. Tape #23: Side 2, 203–409.

———. "Śaṃkara's Cosmology." Lone Pine. 22 September 1976. Tape #41: B/R 468–942.

———. "The Sense in Which I Am a Buddhist." Phoenix. 6 November 1976. Tape #41: R/R 813–1038.

———. "Summary of the Five Realizations." Lone Pine. 12 July 1975. Tape #39: G/R 0–391.

———. "Tantra and Zen." 5 parts. Lone Pine. June–July 1974. Tape #35: G/R 300–end; Tape #37: G/L 0–364.

———. "Three Fundamentals of the Philosophy." Phoenix. 5 November 1973. Tape #34: R/L 141–534.

———. "The Trikāya." 4 parts. Lone Pine. 7 June 1971. Tape #31: G/L 0–1208.

———. "The Unconscious." Phoenix. 30 December 1973. Tape #34: R/R 50–322.

———. "The Yoga of Knowledge." Lone Pine. 10 September 1970. Tape #26: Side 1, 487–end; Side 2, 0–541.

———. "The Yoga of Mathematics." Lone Pine. 15 August 1974. Tape #37: G/L 364–567.

Videotaped Interviews with Franklin Wolff

Bray, Faustin. "The Philosopher's Stone." Lone Pine. 1980.

Mammoth TV. "Ashrama Man." Lone Pine. 1983.

Morwood, Joel. "Franklin Merrell-Wolff: Ashrama and Interview." Lone Pine. 1983.

SECONDARY WORKS

Allison, Henry E. "Things in Themselves, Noumena and the Transcendental Object." *Dialectica* 32 (1978):41–76.

Alpert, Richard [pseud. Baba Ram Dass]. "Here We All Are." Lecture. University of British Columbia, Vancouver, Canada. Las Crucis, NM: Lama Foundation, c. 1971.

Angel, Leonard. "Reconstructing the Ineffable: The Grammatical Roles of 'God'." *Religious Studies* 14 (December 1978):485–95.

———. *The Silence of the Mystic.* Toronto: Morgan House, 1983.

Berggren, Douglas. "The Use and Abuse of Metaphor." *Review of Metaphysics* 16 (1962–63):237–58.

Bergson, Henri. *Two Sources of Morality and Religion.* Translated by R. Ashley Audra and Cloudesley Brereton with the assistance of W. Horsfall Carter. Garden City, NY: Doubleday & Co., 1954.

Bickenbach, Jerome. "The Status of the Propositions in the *Tractatus*." *Dialogue* 13 (December 1974):763–72.

Blakney, Raymond B. *Meister Eckhart.* New York: Harper & Row, 1941. Quoted in Raymond Hubert Jones. "A Philosophical Analysis of Mystical Utterances." *Philosophy East and West* 29 (July 1979):256.

Blavatsky, Helena P. *Isis Unveiled.* 2 vols. New York: J. W. Boulton, 1877.

———. *The Secret Doctrine.* New York: Theosophical Society, 1888.

———, ed. *The Voice of the Silence.* In *Book of Golden Precepts.* Translated with Annotation by H. P. Blavatsky. Los Angeles: Theosophy Co., 1928. Quoted in Franklin F. Wolff. "My Philosophy," Part V. Lone Pine. 14 February 1972. Tape #28: R/R 430–928.

Blocker, H. Gene. "The Language of Mysticism." *Monist* 59 (1976):551–62.

Blyth, R. H. *A History of Haiku.* 2 vols. Japan: Hokuseido Press, 1964.

Bossert, Philip J. "Paradox and Enlightenment in Zen Dialogue and Phenomenological Description." *Journal of Chinese Philosophy* 3 (1976): 269–80.

Brumbaugh, Robert S. *The Philosophers of Greece.* New York: Thomas Y. Croswell, 1964.

Brunton, Paul. *A Search in Secret India.* New York: E. P. Dutton & Co., 1935. Quoted in Franklin F. Wolff. "My Philosophy," Part IV. Lone Pine. 14 February 1972. Tape #28: R/R 85–430.

Bucke, Richard Maurice. *Cosmic Consciousness.* Philadelphia: Innes & Sons, 1901; reprint, New York: E. P. Dutton & Co., 1923.

Burrill, Donald R. "The Meaning of Religious Symbols: Paul Tillich and His Critics." *Personalist* 54 (Summer 1973):274–83.

Busch, Thomas. "Consciousness and Transcendental Philosophy: A Response to Professor Tibbitts." *Philosophy Today* 14 (Winter 1970): 299–304.

Campbell, Joseph. *The Power of Myth.* With Bill Moyers. Edited by Betty Sue Flowers. New York: Doubleday, 1988.

Cedarbaum, Daniel Goldman. "Paradigms." *Studies in History and Philosophy of Science* 14 (1983):173–213.

Circlot, J. E. *A Dictionary of Symbols.* Translated by Jack Sage with a Preface by Herbert Read. New York: Dorset Press, 1991.

Coe, George. "The Sources of Mystical Revelation." *Hibbert Jr.* 6 (1907):357–72. Quoted in James Leuba. *The Psychology of Religious Mysticism.* London: Routledge & Kegan Paul, 1925.

Conkling, Mark L. "Ryle's Mistake about Consciousness." *Philosophy Today* (Winter 1977):376–88.

Conze, Edward. *Buddhism.* Preface by Arthur Waley. Oxford: Bruno Cassirer, 1941; reprint, New York: Harper & Row, 1965.

Danto, Arthur C. "Language and the Tao: Some Reflections on Ineffability." *Journal of Chinese Philosophy* 1 (December 1973):45–55.

D'Arcy, Martin. *The Meeting of Love and Knowledge.* London: George Allen & Unwin, 1958.

Dasgupta, Surendranath. *A History of Indian Philosophy.* 5 vols. Cambridge: University Press, 1922.

Dauenhauer, Bernard. *Silence: The Phenomenon and Its Ontological Significance.* Bloomington: Indiana University Press, 1980. See also "Soundings of Silence." *Philosophy Today* 28 (Summer 1983):358–71. Symposium papers from American Academy of Religion in New York, 1984.

Davidson, Donald. "What Metaphors Mean." In *On Metaphor,* ed. Sheldon Sacks, 29–45. Chicago: University of Chicago Press, 1979.

Descartes, René. *Meditations.* Translated by John Veitch. La Salle: Open Court, 1962.

Deussen, Paul. *The System of the Vedānta.* Translated with a Preface by Charles Johnson. Chicago: Open Court Pub. Co., 1912; reprint, New York: Dover Pub., 1973.

Deutsch, Elliot. *Advaita Vedānta.* Honolulu: East West Center Press, 1969.

———. *On Truth: An Ontological Theory.* Honolulu: University Press of Hawaii, 1979.

Dictionary of Philosophy. Edited by Dagobert D. Runes. 15th ed. Ames, Iowa: Littlefield, Adams, 1956.

Dictionary of Philosophy and Psychology. Edited by James Mark Baldwin. 3 vols. New York: Macmillan, 1925.

Dictionary of Philosophy and Religion: Eastern and Western Thought. Edited by William L. Reese. New Jersey: Humanities Press, 1980.

Dorter, Kenneth. "First Philosophy: Metaphysics or Epistemology?" *Dialogue* 11 (March 1972):1–22.

Earle, William. *Objectivity.* New York: Noonday Press, 1955; reprint, Chicago: Quadrangle Books, 1968.

———. "Phenomenology of Mysticism." *Monist* 59 (October 1976): 519–31.

Eliade, Mircea. *Images et Symboles.* Paris: n.p., 1952.

———. *Tratado de historia de las religiones.* Madrid: n.p., 1954.

Encyclopedia of Philosophy. S.v. "Metaphor," by Monroe C. Beardsley.

———. S.v. "Mysticism, History of," by Ninian Smart.

———. S.v. "Mysticism, Nature and Assessment of," by Ronald W. Hepburn.

———. S.v. "Phenomenology," by Richard Schmitt.

———. S.v. "Pythagoras and Pythagoreanism," by W. K. C. Guthrie.

———. S.v. "Schopenhauer, Arthur," by Patrick Gardiner.

———. S.v. "Sign and Symbol," by William P. Alston.

Evans, C. O. *The Subject of Consciousness.* London: George Allen & Unwin, 1970.

Evans, C. Stephen. "Reductionism as Absentmindedness: Existentialism and Phenomenology as Strategies for Defending Personhood." *Man and World* 14 (1981):177–78.

Fann, K. T. *Wittgenstein's Conception of Philosophy.* Berkeley: University of California Press, 1969.

Farley, Edward. "Phenomenological Theology and the Problem of Metaphysics." *Man and World* 12 (1979):498–508.

Ferris, Timothy, ed. *Physics, Astronomy, and Mathematics.* With a Foreword by Clifton Fadiman, General Editor. Boston: Little, Brown & Co., 1991.

Fowkes, William. "The Concept of the Self in Husserl and Beyond." *Philosophy Today* 24 (Spring 1980):44–52.

Fromme, Erich. *The Forgotten Language.* London: n.p., 1952.

Ghose, Śrī Aurobindo. *The Life Divine.* New York: Greystone Press, 1949.

Grossman, Neal. "Consciousness Expansion: A New Paradigm for Philosophy." *Metaphilosophy* 5 (October 1974):340–47.

Guénon, René. *Aperçu sur l'Initiation.* Paris: n.p., 1929.

Gurwitsch, Aron. "Die mitmenschlichen Begegnungen in der Milieuwelt." N.p., 1931. Quoted in Alexandre Métraux. "Aron Gurwitsch's Non-Egological Conception of Consciousness." *Research in Phenomenology* 5 (1979):46.

———. *The Field of Consciousness.* Pittsburgh: Duquesne University Press, 1964.

———. "A Non-Egological Conception of Consciousness." *Philosophy and Phenomenological Research* 1 (September 1940–June 1941). Reprinted in Gurwitsch. *Studies in Phenomenology and Psychology.* Evanston: Northwestern Press, 1966, 287–300. Quoted in Alexandre Métraux. "Aron Gurwitsch's Non-Egological Conception of Consciousness." *Research in Phenomenology* 5 (1979):43.

———. *Studies in Phenomenology and Psychology.* Evanston: Northwestern Press, 1966.

Guthrie, W. K. C. *The History of Greek Philosophy.* Cambridge: Cambridge University Press, 1962.

Hartshorne, Charles. "Panpsychism: Mind as Sole Reality." *Ultimate Reality and Meaning* 1 (1978):115–29.

Hawking, Stephen. *A Brief History of Time.* With a Foreword by Carl Sagan. New York: Bantam Books, 1988.

Heidegger, Martin. *Being and Time.* Translated by J. MacQuarrie and E. Robinson. Oxford: Basil Blackwell, 1967; originally *Sein und Zeit.* Tübingen: Max Niemeyer, 1967.

Henle, Paul. "Mysticism and Semantics." *Philosophy and Phenomenological Research* 9 (1949):416–22. Quoted in Richard Hubert Jones. "A Philosophical Analysis of Mystical Utterances." *Philosophy East and West* 29 (July 1979):265.

Henrich, Dieter. "Self-Consciousness: A Critical Introduction to Its Theory." *Man and World* 4 (Fall 1971):3–28. Quoted in Charles E. Scott. "Self-Consciousness without an Ego." *Man and World* 4 (1971): 194–95.

Holmes, Richard. "Is Transcendental Phenomenology Committed to Idealism?" *Monist* 59 (1975):98–114.

Horne, James. *Beyond Mysticism.* Waterloo: Wilfrid Laurier Press, 1979.

Hume, David. *A Treatise of Human Nature.* Edited by L. A. Selby-Biggs. Oxford: Clarendon Press, 1788.

Husserl, Edmund. *Experience and Judgment.* Revised and edited by Ludwig Landgrebe. Translated by James S. Churchill and Karl Ameriks, with an Introduction by James S. Churchill and an Afterword by Lothar Eley. Evanston: Northwestern Press, 1973.

———. *Ideas.* Translated by W. R. Boyce Gibson. New York: Collier Books, 1962.

———. *Logical Investigations.* Translated by J. N. Findlay. 2 vols. New York: Humanities Press, 1970.

James, William. *The Varieties of Religious Experience.* New York: Modern Library, 1902.

Jones, Richard Hubert. "A Philosophical Analysis of Mystical Utterances." *Philosophy East and West* 29 (July 1979):255–74.

Jung, Carl G., and others, eds. *Man and His Symbols.* London: Aldus Books, 1964.

———. *Psychological Types.* Translated by Godwin Baynes. New York: Harcourt, Brace & Co., 1933.

Kant, Immanuel. *The Critique of Pure Reason.* Translated with an Introduction by J. M. D. Meikeljohn and a Special Introduction by Brandt V. B. Dixon. Rev. ed. New York: P. F. Collier & Son, 1900; Translated with a Preface by F. Max Müller and an Historical Introduction by Ludwig Noiré. London: Macmillan & Co., 1881; Translated with a Preface by Norman Kemp Smith. London: Macmillan & Co., 1929.

Katz, Steven, ed. *Mysticism and Philosophical Analysis.* New York: Oxford University Press, 1978.

———, ed. *Mysticism and Religious Traditions.* Oxford: Oxford University Press, 1983.

Kellenberger, J. "The Ineffabilities of Mysticism." *American Philosophical Quarterly* 16 (October 1979):307–15.

Keller, Carl A. "Mystical Literature." In *Mysticism and Philosophical Analysis,* ed. Steven Katz, 75–100. New York: Oxford University Press, 1978.

Kersten, Frederick. "The Originality of Gurwitsch's Theory of Intentionality." *Research in Phenomenology* 5 (1975):19–27.

Khatchadourian, Haig. "Symbols and Metaphors." *Southern Journal of Philosophy* 6 (Fall 1968):181–90.

Kilgore, W. J. "Is Metaphysics Outmoded?" *Southwestern Journal of Philosophy* 3 (Fall 1972):109–16.

Kirk, G. S., and J. E. Raven. *The Pre-Socratics.* Cambridge: Cambridge University Press, 1957.

Kuhn, Thomas. *The Structure of Scientific Revolutions.* Chicago: University of Chicago Press, 1962. Quoted in Neal Grossman. "Consciousness Expansion: A New Paradigm for Philosophy." *Metaphilosophy* 5 (1974):345.

Kvastad, Nils Bjorn. "Philosophical Problems of Mysticism." *International Philosophical Quarterly* 13 (June 1973):191–207.

Lauer, Quentin. Translation with Introduction to *Phenomenology and the Crisis in Philosophy,* by Edmund Husserl. New York: Harper & Row, 1965.

LeShan, Lawrence. "On the Non-Acceptance of the Paranormal." *International Journal of Parapsychology* 8 (Summer 1966):367–86.

Leuba, James. *The Psychology of Religious Mysticism.* Rev. ed. London: Routledge & Kegan Paul, 1929.

Lilly, John C. *The Center of the Cyclone.* New York: Julian Press, 1972.

Maddox, Randy L. "Hermeneutic Circle—Vicious or Victorious." *Philosophy Today* 26 (Spring 1983):66–76.

Magee, Brian. "Conversations with Gilbert Ryle." *Modern British Philosophy.* New York: St. Martin's Press, 1971.

Mandt, A. J. "The Inconceivability of Kant's Transcendental Subject: An Impasse in Kant's Metaphysics." *International Philosophical Quarterly* 23 (March 1983):13–33.

Maxwell, Nicholas. *From Knowledge to Wisdom.* Oxford: Basil Blackwell, 1984.

Meerbote, Rolf. "The Unknowability of Things in Themselves." In *Proceedings of the Third International Kant Congress,* ed. Lewis White Beck and D. Reidel, 414–23. Dordrecht: Reidel, 1972.

Melchert, Norman. "Mystical Experience and Ontological Claims." *Philosophy and Phenomenological Research* 37 (June 1977):445–63.

Métraux, Alexandre. "Aron Gurwitsch's Non-Egological Conception of Consciousness." *Research in Phenomenology* 5 (1979):43–50.

Mill, James. *Analysis of the Phenomena of the Human Mind.* London: Longmans, Green, Reader & Dyer, 1869.

Morris, Phyllis Sutton. "Sartre on the Transcendence of the Ego." *Philosophy and Phenomenological Research* 46 (December 1985):179–98.

Morrison, J. C. "Husserl and Heidegger: The Parting of the Ways." In *Heidegger's Existential Analytic,* ed. F. Elliston. New York: The Hague, 1978.

Mukerji, A. C. *The Nature of Self.* 2d ed. Allahabad: Indian Press, 1943. Quoted in Ramlal Singh. "An Advaitic Emendation of Kant." *Indian Philosophical Quarterly* 6 (October 1978):181.

Musès, Charles. "Altering States of Consciousness by Mathematics, with Applications to Education." *Journal for the Study of Consciousness* 3 (January–June 1970):43–50.

———. "The Exploration of Consciousness." In *Consciousness and Reality,* ed. Charles Musès and Arthur M. Young, 102–31. New York: Avon, 1974.

———. "Working with the Hypernumber Idea." In *Consciousness and Reality,* ed. Charles Musès and Arthur M. Young, 448–69. New York: Avon, 1974.

Musès, Charles, and Arthur M. Young, eds. *Consciousness and Reality.* New York: Avon, 1974.

Nagel, Thomas. "Physicalism." *Philosophical Review* 74 (July 1965):339–56. Reprinted with a Postscript in *Modern Materialism: Readings on Mind-Body Identity,* ed. John O'Connor. New York: Harcourt Brace & World, 1969.

———. "What Is It Like to Be a Bat?" *Philosophical Review* 83 (October 1974):435–50.

Natsoulas, Thomas. "The Unity of Consciousness." *Behaviorism* 7 (Fall 1979):45–63.

Naylor, Margery Bedford. "Epistemic Justification." *American Philosophical Quarterly* 25 (January 1988):49–58.

Nikhilānanda, Swami, ed. *The Upanishads.* Translated with a Preface, General Introduction, and Individual Introductions by Swami Nikhilānanda. Notes, Expositions, and Commentaries by Śrī Śaṃkarācārya. 4 vols. New York: Bonanza Books, 1949; reprint, London: George Allen & Unwin, 1963; abridged reprint, New York: Harper & Row, 1963.

Nordstrom, Louis. "Mysticism without Transcendence: Reflections on Liberation and Emptiness." *Philosophy East and West* 31 (January 1981): 89–95.

Northrop, F. S. C. *The Meeting of East and West.* New York: Macmillan, 1947.

Novitz, David. "Another Look at Metaphorical Meaning." *Philosophia* 15 (December 1985):325–38.

Paskow, Alan. "A Phenomenological View of the Beetle in the Box." *New Scholasticism* 48 (Summer 1974):277–304.

Paul, Arthur. "The Possible Meaning of Imaginary Numbers." In *Consciousness and Reality,* ed. Charles Musès and Arthur M. Young, 192n. New York: Avon, 1974.

Penrose, Roger. *Cosmology Now.* N.p.: BBC Publications, 1974.

Peters, Ted. "The Problem of Symbolic Reference." *Thomist* 44 (January 1980):72–93.

Pletcher, Galen K. "Mysticism, Contradiction and Ineffability." *American Philosophical Quarterly* (1973): 201–11. Quoted in Richard Hubert Jones. "A Philosophical Analysis of Mystical Utterances." *Philosophy East and West* 29 (July 1979):265.

Plotinus. *Enneads.*

Praus, Gerold. *Kant und das Problem der Dinge an sich.* Bonn: Bouvier, 1974.

Price, H. H. "Some Philosophical Questions about Telepathy and Clairvoyance." *Philosophy* 15 (1940):363–85.

Rajchman, John, and Cornell West, eds. *Post-Analytic Philosophy.* New York: Columbia University Press, 1985.

Raju, P. T. *The Philosophical Traditions of India.* London: George Allen & Unwin, 1971.

Rescher, Nicholas. "On the Status of 'Things-in-themselves' in Kant." *Revue Internationale de Philosophie* 35 (January/February 1981):346–57; also *Synthese* 47 (May 1981):289–99.

Robinson, John Mansley. *An Introduction to Early Greek Philosophy.* Boston: Houghlin Mifflin, 1968.

Rosenstein, Leon. "Mysticism as Preontology: A Note on the Heideggerian Connection." *Philosophy and Phenomenological Research* 39 (September 1978):57–73.

Ryle, Gilbert. *The Concept of Mind.* London: Hutchinson & Co., 1949.

Sankowski, Edward. "Wittgenstein on Self-Knowledge." *Mind* 87 (April 1978):256–61.

Sartre, Jean-Paul. *The Transcendence of the Ego.* Translated by Forrest Williams and Robert Kirkpatrick. New York: Noonday Press, 1957.

Satprem. *The Adventure of Consciousness.* Pondicherry: Sri Aurobindo Ashram Press, 1968.

Schacht, Richard. "Husserlian and Heideggerian Phenomenology." *Philosophical Studies* 23 (1972):293–314.

Schillp, A., ed. *The Philosophy of C. D. Broad.* New York: Tudor Pub. Co., 1959, 814. Quoted in C. O. Evans. *The Subject of Consciousness,* 35. London: George Allen & Unwin, 1970.

Schmitz, Kenneth. "Philosophy of Religion and the Redefinition of Philosophy." *Man and World* 3 (May 1970):54–82.

Schneider, Marius. *El origen musical de los animales—simbolos en la mitalogia y la escultura antiguas.* Barcelona: n.p., 1946.

———. *La danza de espadas y ta tarantela.* Barcelona: n.p., 1948.

Scott, Charles E. "Self-Consciousness without an Ego." *Man and World* 4 (1971):193–201.

Sinari, Ramakant. "The Phenomenological Attitude in the Śaṃkara Vedānta." *Philosophy East and West* 22 (July 1972):281–90.

Singh, Ramlal. "An Advaitic Emendation of Kant: A Study in Comparative Metaphysics." *Indian Philosophical Quarterly* 6 (October 1978):175–83.

Smart, Ninian. "The Purification of Consciousness and the Negative Path." In *Mysticism and Religious Traditions,* ed. Steven Katz, 117–29. Oxford: Oxford University Press, 1983.

———. "Understanding Religious Experience." In *Mysticism and Philosophical Analysis,* ed. Steven Katz, 10–21. New York: Oxford University Press, 1978.

Smitheram, Verier. "The Criteria of Objectivity: Physical Science and the Challenge of Phenomenology." *International Studies in Philosophy* 16 (1984):65–79.

Stace, Walter T. *Mysticism and Philosophy*. London: Macmillan, 1960.

Strawson, Peter F. *Individuals*. London: Methuen, 1959.

Suzuki, D. T. *Selected Writings of D. T. Suzuki*. Edited by William Barratt. New York: Doubleday & Co., n.d.

Talbot, Michael. *Mysticism and the New Physics*. New York: Bantam Books, 1981.

Tapper, Marion. "The Priority of Being or Consciousness for Phenomenology: Heidegger and Husserl." *Metaphilosophy* 17 (April/July):153–61.

Teilhard de Chardin, Pierre. *The Phenomenon of Man*. Translated by Bernard Wall, with an Introduction by Julian Huxley. New York: Harper & Row, 1959.

Tierney, John. *A Passion to Know*. Edited by Allen Hammond. N.p.: American Association for the Advancement of Science, 1984.

Tillich, Paul. *Dynamics of Faith*. New York: Harper & Row, 1957.

Tyman, Stephen. "Mysticism and Gnosticism in Heidegger." *Philosophy Today* 28 (Winter 1984):358–71.

Underhill, Evelyn. *Mysticism*. New York: Meridian, 1955.

Vallicella, William. "Kant, Heidegger and the Problem of the Thing in Itself." *International Philosophical Quarterly* 23 (March 1983):35–43.

Verhack, Ignace. "An Uncommon Reading of the *Tractatus*." *International Philosophical Quarterly* 18 (December 1978):433–44.

Visvader, John. "The Use of Paradox in Uroboric Philosophies." *Philosophy East and West* 28 (October 1978):455–67.

Wainwright, William. *Mysticism*. Madison: University of Wisconsin Press, 1981.

———. "Mysticism and Sense Perception." *Religious Studies* 9 (September 1973):257–78.

Ward, Andrew. "Materialism and the Unity of Consciousness." *Analysis* 40 (June 1980):144–46.

Watson, Ian. "The Anti-Wisdom of Modern Philosophy: A Passing Note." *Studies in Comparative Religion* 6 (1972):221–24.

Watson, J. B. *Behaviorism.* 3d ed. Chicago: University of Chicago Press, 1930.

Watts, Alan. *The Way of Zen.* New York: Mentor, 1959. Quoted in H. Gene Blocker. "The Language of Mysticism." *Monist* 59 (1976):560.

Wheeler, John Archibald. *Albert Einstein: A Biographical Memoir.* N.p.: National Academy Press, 1980.

White, Alan R. *Attention.* Oxford: Basil Blackwell, 1964.

Wittgenstein, Ludwig. *Philosophical Investigations.* Translated by G. E. M. Anscombe. Oxford: Basil Blackwell, 1968.

———. *Tractatus Logico-Philosophicus.* Translated by D. F. Pears and B. F. McGuinness, with an Introduction by Bertrand Russell. London: Routledge & Kegan Paul, 1961.

Wu, Laurence C. "Light and Mirror: Two Mystic Metaphors of Mind." *Philosophical Forum* 14 (1974):145–60.

Zaehner, Richard C. *Mysticism Sacred and Profane.* Oxford: Clarendon Press, 1957.

INDEX